Listening to the Sirens

The publisher gratefully acknowledges the generous contribution to this book provided by the Hull Memorial Publication Fund of Cornell University.

Listening to the Sirens

Musical Technologies of Queer Identity
from Homer to *Hedwig*

Judith A. Peraino

UNIVERSITY OF CALIFORNIA PRESS

Berkeley   Los Angeles   London

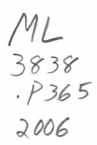
The following excerpts are used by permission of Oxford University Press: John Hilton, "Here Is an Old Ground," and Henry Purcell, "Jack, Thou'rt a Toper" and "A Farewell to Wives," from *The Catch Book*, ed. Paul Hillier. © Oxford University Press, 1987. All rights reserved.

University of California Press
Berkeley and Los Angeles, California

University of California Press, Ltd.
London, England

Library of Congress Cataloging-in-Publication Data

Peraino, Judith Ann.
   Listening to the sirens : musical technologies of queer identity from Homer to Hedwig / Judith A. Peraino.
       p.   cm.
   Includes bibliographical references and index.
   ISBN 0–520–21587–7 (cloth : alk. paper)
   1. Gender identity in music.   2. Homosexuality and music.
3. Music and literature.   4. Music—History and criticism.   I. Title.

ML3838.P365   2005
780'.86'64—dc22   2005006234

Manufactured in the United States of America

14   13   12   11   10   09   08   07   06   05
10   9   8   7   6   5   4   3   2   1

This book is printed on Natures Book, which contains 50% post-consumer waste and meets the minimum requirements of ANSI/NISO Z39.48–1992 (R 1997) (*Permanence of Paper*).

For my parents
and
in memory of Philip Brett

CONTENTS

ILLUSTRATIONS

ACKNOWLEDGMENTS

Coming to the end of six years of writing this book, I feel like Dorothy at the end of *The Wizard of Oz*. She wakes from her deep, queer slumber and slowly recognizes in the faces gathered around her bed those who had helped her on her arduous but magical odyssey home. "You were there . . . and you . . . and you."

I have many teachers, colleagues, friends, and family to recognize for their assistance along the road of my own queer odyssey, of which this book is the result. They all contributed to the book in fundamental ways. I take full responsibility, however, for any wayward interpretations and errant judgments in the text.

I must first acknowledge my profound gratitude to Philip Brett (1937–2002), who did not live to see the completion of this project—a project that began in a seminar he conducted at the University of California, Berkeley, in the spring of 1990. Called "Sexual Identities and Music," it was the first course of its kind in the country. Philip inaugurated gay and lesbian studies in musicology in 1976, with a public presentation on how Benjamin Britten's gay identity affected the musical composition of his opera *Peter Grimes* (this study was published in *Musical Times* in 1977). But it took more than fifteen years for the revolutionary implications of Philip's work on Britten to make their impact in musicology. The 1993 collection *Musicology and Difference* (edited by Ruth A. Solie) contained four essays on music and queer sexual identities, including another of Philip's on Britten; in 1994 *Queering the Pitch,* which he coedited with Elizabeth Wood and Gary C. Thomas, became the first collection of essays devoted solely to the topic. That volume includes his now classic essay "Musicality, Essentialism, and the Closet," which set the highest standard of critical thinking and graceful writing about music and queer identity.

As a teacher and friend, Philip was a model of courage, elegance, perseverance, and generosity. This book could not have been written without his example and his early guidance.

In that 1990 seminar, my fellow students and I understood that we were participating in a historic moment for musicology—the hammering out of new questions, new vocabularies, and new ways of listening. I was forever changed by the freedom of thought and energetic exchanges that characterized the seminar. I owe much to the incredible intellects and abiding friendships of my Berkeley peers from that class: Kristi Brown-Montesano, Ruth Charloff, Robert Fink, Alan Lewis, Alan Mason, Mitchell Morris, Gregory Salmon (1961–1991), and Luisa Vilar-Payá. I owe a special thanks to Mitchell Morris, whom I consulted on numerous occasions over the years while writing this book, for reading a draft of the book, and for his encouragement, wit, and encyclopedic mind.

The pioneering essays of Susan McClary constituted some of our principal reading in 1990. At that time they were hard to find, if they were published at all, and we circulated them through third- and fourth-generation photocopies. Her application of feminist theory to music of all types—from Monteverdi to Madonna—ushered in what came to be called "new musicology." Under this rubric, inquiries into music and sexual identity found a place within the discipline. My debt to her work is significant. I also wish to acknowledge here the influence of Suzanne Cusick's exquisite writing on lesbian perspectives and historical women in music.

Susan McClary, Byron Adams, and Robert Walser read my manuscript for the University of California Press. I feel extremely fortunate to have had feedback from some of the most creative minds in the field. Their suggestions improved the manuscript immensely.

I cannot adequately express my gratitude to Richard Crocker, who advised my 1995 Ph.D. thesis on medieval song, and who returned in a similar capacity with inexhaustible enthusiasm for this project. By the time I had a complete draft to show around in the summer of 2002, Philip Brett had become quite ill with cancer. Richard promptly and generously volunteered to read the entire manuscript. And read he did—several times! Over the next two years Richard shepherded my manuscript through a rigorous revision, sharpening my thoughts with conceptual challenges and improving my prose with sentence-by-sentence edits and suggestions. I have long admired his clear, elegant writing and his imaginative approach to music history. I hope that I have proven to be a good student.

The shape and contents of this book first took the form of a course called "Music and Queer Identity," which I designed for the Gay and Lesbian Studies Department at City College of San Francisco in 1996, and which I also taught at Cornell University. I am indebted to Jonathan D. Katz (now at Yale University) for his enthusiastic response to my course proposal, and for his tireless effort seeing this course through the bureaucratic thicket of City College. I am also grateful to Madeline Morton-Mueller of the Department of Music for her assistance in this as well. In many respects I received a true education in music and queer identity from the students at City College and Cornell. Their keen observations and openness consistently astonished me. Numerous ideas developed within these pages first emerged in those weekly conversations about music and queer life.

I could not have written this book without the tremendous resources offered by Cornell University, the most important of which come in human form. My colleagues in the Department of Music have given me unreserved support in my queer career path. I am particularly grateful to James Webster, whose deep critical reading of portions of the book resulted in significant improvements. I am greatly indebted to my colleague and friend Anna Marie Smith of the Government Department for her encouragement and theoretical expertise. She generously tutored me in Foucault, Butler, Althusser, and Nietzsche, among others. Many times she listened to half-formed ideas and saw their larger implications, then directed me to references that would become integral to the project. She also made invaluable detailed comments on drafts of several chapters. I would also like to thank Kate Morris, a Mellon postdoctoral fellow in the Department of Art History in 2003/4, for her reading of several chapters, and for her many dinners and good company during that long, snowy winter.

The extraordinary Cornell University Library, especially their extensive microfilm collection and the Human Sexuality Collection in the Carl A. Kroch Library of Rare and Manuscript Collections, allowed me to sift through a wide range of material, from seventeenth-century song booklets to obscure 1960s gay ephemera, without leaving Ithaca. I especially want to acknowledge Brenda Marston, the archivist for the Human Sexuality Collection. Chuck Raniewicz of the Cornell Music Library cheerfully and expertly came to my aid in digital technology emergencies. The publication of this book has been generously supported by grants from the Department of Music and the Hull Memorial Publication Fund of Cornell University, and the Gustave Reese Publication Endowment Fund of the American Musicological Society.

Chapters 1 and 5 and portions of the introduction were previously published as "Listening to the Sirens: Music as Queer Ethical Practice," in *GLQ: A Journal of Lesbian and Gay Studies*. I must thank the editors, Carolyn Dinshaw and David Halperin, and the anonymous reviewer for their substantive suggestions. I also thank Lynne Withey at the University of California Press, who had faith that my sketchy book proposal had the makings of a valuable study, and Mary Francis, Lynn Meinhardt, Sharron Wood, and others who saw the production of this book through to completion.

Many friends in Chicago, Berkeley, Ithaca, and elsewhere have contributed to this book through their companionship and numerous conversations in loud bars, by e-mail, over dinner, and on long walks: Jim Armstrong, Jim Bailey, Barb Blom, Susana Darwin, Nadine Hubbs, Edith Juarez, Doug Miller and the staff at the Common Ground, Linda Nicholson, Deb Rivera, Tracy Sabo, Penny VanSchoick, Ellie Wallace, Paula White, and Gwen Wilkinson.

My parents, Nancy and Carl Peraino, deserve much credit for this book. They have sustained me in innumerable ways through the course of my career, and their work with Parents, Families and Friends of Lesbians and Gays (PFLAG) in the suburbs of Chicago has been a true source of inspiration for me.

Finally, to my partner Carmen Enid Martínez: simply, thank you.

Introduction

Sailing home from war, Odysseus decides to make a brief detour in order to listen to a song sung by creatures called Sirens. Legend tells that listening to this song has dire consequences; it draws the listener to a rocky shore and certain death. But Odysseus plugs the ears of his crew with wax and has himself bound to the mast so that he alone can listen. With his cunning plan, he manages to hear the song and escape its consequences.

Or does he?

This ancient Greek story about the warrior Odysseus, as recounted in Homer's *Odyssey* (ca. 700 B.C.E.), has been used through the ages as a starting point for artistic, religious, and philosophical contemplation.[1] In *Dialectic of Enlightenment* (1947), Max Horkheimer and Theodor Adorno place the Siren episode from the *Odyssey* at the center of their Marxist critique of the ideological and subjugating tendencies of Enlightenment thinking. They characterize Odysseus as a "prototype of the bourgeois individual," his crew as "proletarians," and their encounter with the Sirens as a critical moment in which the rational cunning of the individual conquers the mythical powers of the Sirens' song.[2] Odysseus becomes enlightened by listening to it, for he is made to struggle with, and overcome, a self-destructive desire to return to the past. But his crew hear nothing; they are left out of enlightenment. For these authors, the separate experiences of Odysseus and his crew signify, on one level, the exploitation of a labor force for the gain of an individual from the ruling class; on another level, Odysseus's experience itself signifies the triumphant yet impoverishing separation of rationalistic thought from physical practice. The Siren episode is thus the "presentient allegory of the dialectic of enlightenment," in which intellectual progress is remote from participation in labor.[3]

Adorno and Horkheimer see in this story other costs and rifts besides this social one, namely, the domination of nature, the rift between mind and body, and the distance imposed between subject and object through abstraction. All these result in a disenchantment of music, a disenchantment that compromises the freedom that is the goal of enlightenment ideology: the Sirens' "temptation is neutralized and becomes a mere object of contemplation—becomes art. The prisoner is present at a concert, an inactive eavesdropper like later concertgoers, and his spirited call for liberation fades like applause." Horkheimer and Adorno go on to lament, "since Odysseus' successful-unsuccessful encounter with the Sirens all songs have been affected, and Western music as a whole suffers from the contradiction of song in civilization—song which nevertheless proclaims the emotional power of all art music."[4]

The contradiction that the Sirens' song *qua* music poses for these authors, and one Adorno addresses specifically in his many writings, is its ability to inspire both resistance and complacency—to instigate defiance yet perpetuate domination. The high value placed on reason since the Enlightenment has relegated music to an inferior status, as a merely pleasurable pastime. Yet, for Adorno, "art music" still harbors the mythic lure of the Sirens' song, which holds the key to resisting enlightenment as ideology. Adorno famously championed high modernist music and eschewed popular music, arguing that difficult music requires intellectual work by the listener, and that the effort of that work brings the estrangement between music and its auditor that is needed to counter complacency and alienation from ideological superstructures. In this view, popular music, by contrast, requires little intellectual work and thus lulls the listener into mechanistic conformity of taste and thought while promising pseudo-individuality.[5] The contradiction in Adorno's thought is that he, too, forgets the crew; he can only imagine such ideological resistance coming from an enlightened Odysseus, who has struggled with music.

But the Sirens' song can be considered music that has mass appeal; after all, anyone who hears it becomes its captive. Odysseus simply found a technique for listening to this popular song, with its inherent difficulties. The Sirens' song, then, has the power to call each and every listener to a critical focus on the past and future self, on the self in relation to society, to ideology. Its mythical power was far from neutralized with Odysseus's survival. Indeed, his survival has made us all wonder about what he heard.

. . .

In another story of Sirens, but one not usually recognized as such, Louis Althusser made a now famous conceptualization of how omnipresent ideology "recruits" individuals and transforms them into "subjects," individuals who have a sense of autonomous agency and coherent selfhood. Althusser used a metaphor to describe the mechanism of transformation—and it is

important that the metaphor was a sonic one. He wrote of the action of calling into subjectivity as one of "hailing," or "interpellation," and to illustrate
he imagined the ordinary event of a policeman's hailing—"Hey, you there!"
Althusser writes, "the hailed individual will turn round. By this mere one-
hundred-and-eighty-degree physical conversion, he becomes a *subject*. Why?
Because he has recognized that the hail was 'really' addressed to him, and
that 'it was *really him* who was hailed' (and not someone else)."[6] Deep in the
background of Althusser's notion of interpellation as an irresistible calling
into subjectivity lies the song of the Sirens. For Althusser, the alluring sound
was not musical, but rather the phonetic materiality of language, which he
believed had a structuring force on individual unconscious thoughts as well
as on social relations.[7] The paradox of what Althusser meant by "subjectivity" is that we think we are free agents when we are really not. The terms of
our subjectivity (he says) have been predetermined by social structures and
institutions such as the capitalist market, the education system, family, culture, religion, laws, and gender. Subjectivity as a sense of autonomy is thus
an imaginary effect of these "ideological apparatuses," all of which, according to Althusser, feed into the power of the ruling class and the state. His critics have noted, however, that these apparatuses and even the nature of ide-
ologies do not simply foreclose struggle, debate, and resistance, but rather
must somehow allow for such actions, as his own writing attests.[8] Indeed,
Althusser missed a critical moment in his story of hailing: the moment of
questioning "Is it me?" may yield "yes" or "no."[9]

This book, too, begins with Odysseus and the Sirens. But rather than trying to read the song of the Sirens (either what they sang or what people have
said about it), I am here suggesting what the song's function might be—to
invite an imagining of what things would be like if they were different. The
fact that the Sirens are reported in myth as singing suggests that the imagining works best in musical form. For Adorno, music provokes individuals to
question their subjectivity, their social identity in relation to ideological
superstructures; in this view, music can lead to the question that Althusser
did not think could be asked: "Is it me?" And further: "What am I?"

Odysseus had a technique for asking these questions; one could even say
it was a musical technique. It involved careful preparation with his crew, and
a surefire means of disciplining himself as he listened to the Sirens sing. A
"technique" is commonly understood to mean a set of repeatable, practical
skills or methods employed for a certain end. Though Odysseus used his
technique for listening only once, it became a conceptual, if not also a practical, model for subsequent approaches to such songs, as Adorno's comment
about concert audiences suggests. Musicians are often said to have technique—skills acquired through many years of practice, of disciplining muscles and breath. Those with good technique have developed efficient ways
to play passages that are physically challenging. They also learn to listen care-

fully to themselves, other musicians, the audience; composers learn to hear music that is not yet sounding.

Michel Foucault has written abundantly on disciplinary techniques that impact our sense of self. These techniques are practiced on all levels, by governments, institutions, and social groups that wish to discipline individuals, as well as by individuals who wish to discipline themselves. In many cases, as Foucault's work reveals, it is not possible to distinguish between these levels in tracing the cause and effect of certain practices or techniques. In his studies of the higher-level disciplinary techniques (those of governments, institutions, academic *disciplines*), Foucault, influenced by Althusser among others, often used the term "discourse" or "discursive practice," suggesting a linguistic analogy: if (social) language can be understood to structure (individual) thought, then other social practices can be understood as having a similar structuring effect; they are also "discursive." When, later in his career, Foucault turned to a consideration of lower-level disciplinary techniques (those of the individual), he began to favor the term "techniques," and also "technologies."

The musical techniques that concern this study involve not only the composition and delivery of musical notes, but also the "techniques" that, according to Foucault, create human subjectivity and identity. He writes, "my objective for more than twenty-five years has been to sketch out a history of the different ways in our culture that humans develop knowledge about themselves: economics, biology, psychiatry, medicine, and penology. The main point is not to accept this knowledge at face value but to analyze these so-called sciences as very specific 'truth games' related to specific techniques that human beings use to understand themselves." "Technology" is commonly understood to mean the science of machines, or, more specifically, the systematic study and application of empirical knowledge to practical, mechanical purposes. Foucault uses "technology" in a similar way, to indicate larger systems of techniques that can be analyzed and studied. He goes on to list four types:

> (1) technologies of production, which permit us to produce, transform, or manipulate things; (2) technologies of sign systems, which permit us to use signs, meanings, symbols, or signification; (3) technologies of power, which determine the conduct of individuals and submit them to certain ends or domination, an objectivizing of the subject; (4) technologies of the self, which permit individuals to effect by their own means, or with the help of others, a certain number of operations on their own bodies and souls, thoughts, conduct, and way of being, so as to transform themselves in order to attain a certain state of happiness, purity, wisdom, perfection, or immortality.[10]

Although Foucault set out these categories, or technologies, as discrete domains of inquiry, he acknowledged that they are fundamentally intertwined in their operations.

This book presents a series of case studies, using Foucault's four technologies as a framework for examining how music functions as a technique in the conceptualization, configuration, and representation of queer subjectivity and identity. Foucault's notion of technologies offers us sets of questions and analytical tools for approaching music, and the focus on music helps us better understand Foucault, by illustrating the interrelatedness of his four technologies with musical descriptions for each. But these musical descriptions also call attention to the inadequacy of Foucault's technological metaphor for subjectivity, for music frequently serves as a site or an action of resistance—the queer technique that unsettles the technology.

Following Adorno, I examine how musical technologies invite individuals to question their subjectivity and social identity; more specifically, I examine how music can lead to questioning the ideological superstructure of "compulsory heterosexuality." This means the organization of social identities into the two "opposite" genders of male and female, the assumption that natural sexual desire requires a man and a woman, and the determination of other non-procreative sexual practices as illegitimate.[11] In exploring the ways in which music functions in this questioning process, I use the word "queer" as a sexually freighted synonym for "questioning."

The etymology of "queer" is uncertain. One source suggests its origin in the early English *cwer* (meaning "crooked, not straight").[12] Another possible origin is the Indo-European root *twerkw*, which yielded the Latin *torquere* (to twist) and the German *quer* (transverse). The word first appears, however, in early sixteenth-century Scottish sources as an adjectival form of "query," from the Latin *quaerere* (to seek, to question).[13] The question associated with "queer" became one of sexuality and gender in the late nineteenth and early twentieth centuries: the word peppers novels that probe homosexuality such as Henry James's *The Turn of the Screw* (1898) and Radcliffe Hall's *The Well of Loneliness* (1928), and it was used to describe non-normative sexual behavior in at least one sociological study from 1922. At about this time, "queer" also became a term of self-identification within some homosexual subcultures, as well as a term of derision used by the mainstream.[14]

In the early 1990s, the word "queer" emerged as a term of resistance to the 1970s identity labels "gay" and "lesbian"; these identities were rooted to a large extent in gender separatism and in a naturalized hetero/homosexual binary.[15] "Queer," according to David Halperin, describes a subject position "at odds with the normal, the legitimate, the dominant . . . an identity without an essence . . . a positionality that is not restricted to lesbians and gay men but is in fact available to anyone who is or who feels marginalized because of her or his sexual practice."[16] In Eve Kosofsky Sedgwick's words, it is "the open mesh of possibilities, gaps, overlaps, dissonances and resonances, lapses and excesses of meaning when the constituent elements of anyone's gender, of anyone's sexuality aren't made (or *can't be* made) to signify monolithically."[17] Queer theory, then, questions given concepts of identity based on same-sex desire alone, expanding the scope to include intersections of gender and sexuality with race, class, ethnicity, and nationhood. I use "queer" in a similar way, to refer to an unsteady state of questioning one's sexual identity; this state of questioning implies that there might not be a conclusion, but also that "identity" might not be restricted to "sexuality."

Same-sex desire and gender inversion, however, continue to have a centripetal force in queer theory. As a term of relation, "queer" describes not a simple binary opposition to normative heterosexuality, nor simply a position outside and in dialectic with the status quo; rather, "queer" can describe a threat, the sexual ignition of cultural phobias. These phobias, primarily about gender confusion and the displacement of the patriarchal heterosexual family, become anxieties about the integrity of the self, subjectivity, and social identity. Individuals who live openly as gays and lesbians, or who live outside or between the binary male/female, constitute the main queer threat igniting such phobias, and thus are themselves threatened with the greatest material and political consequences.[18]

But if "queer" describes a resistance to rigid categories of sexual identity such as straight/gay, male/female, married/single, can one speak of a "queer identity"? Philosopher Linda Martín Alcoff distinguishes between "identity" and "subjectivity" as, respectively, "the sense one has of oneself as seen by others and of one's own self-perception, or between one's third-person and first-person selves."[19] For psychoanalytic theorists, identity is a psychosocial formation through which subjectivity is focused and articulated: social and antisocial tendencies, mediated through the body and psychic processes such as identification and sublimation, yield "the Self that identifies itself" as an object of contemplation both internally and externally.[20] For Foucault, identity is the regulated disposition of subjectivity: it involves the internalization of normalizing and disciplinary social structures, mechanisms, and practices—or, to use Foucault's linguistic metaphor, "discourses."

Some feminist and queer theorists have attempted to reconcile the microscopic explanations of psychoanalysis with the macroscopic explanations of poststructuralism in order to rethink identity as potentially resistant to pressure, or even exerting its own pressure. Biddy Martin has called for queer theory to consider the complexity in our conception of the psyche and the body, of identity and social networks, as well as of the relations between these. She argues that gender and sexual identity, even "played straight," should not be understood as immobile "effects of internalized norms" but rather as encompassing "the agency of a never static givenness" that interacts with "what it encounters, internally and in the world thought to be outside itself."[21] Judith Butler has similarly attempted to reconcile Freud and Foucault, saying: "the psyche, which includes the unconscious, is very different from the subject: the psyche is precisely what exceeds the imprisoning effects of the discursive demand to inhabit a coherent identity, to become a coherent subject." As an example, Butler refers to Althusser's famous scene of hailing and describes the possibility of "misrecognition," in which the production of the subject can fail:

> The one who is hailed may fail to hear, misread the call, turn the other way, answer to another name, insist on not being addressed in that way. . . . To be hailed as a "woman" or "Jew" or "queer" or "Black" or "Chicana" may be heard or interpreted as an affirmation or an insult, depending on the context in which the hailing occurs (where context is the effective historicity and spatiality of the sign). If that name is called, there is more often than not some hesitation about whether or how to respond, for what is at stake is whether the temporary totalization . . . of identity performed by that particular hailing is politically strategic or regressive, or, if paralyzing and regressive, also enabling in some way.[22]

Thus, queer identity could be both recognized and elected by the individual, or it could be the subtle effect of misrecognizing or questioning some other hailing, throwing a wrench into the discursive production of subjectivity.

The root of Butler's loosening of "subjectivation" is a questioning of theories, such as those of Jacques Lacan, that see language as the principal force that structures the unconscious; she wonders "whether the effects of the psyche can be said to be exhausted in what can be signified or whether there is not . . . a domain of the psyche which contests legibility."[23] Music is notoriously resistant to legibility; and although cultural, feminist, and queer theorists within musicology have worked hard to reveal the signatures of subjectivity and ideology in musical sounds, it is arguably music's resistance to legibility that allows for the use of music as a strategy for negotiating queer identity within dominant heterosexual culture.

As a discursive practice, music is double-tongued, participating in both the normalizing and *ab*normalizing of the subject, as Philip Brett's groundbreaking article "Musicality, Essentialism, and the Closet" describes. Similarly, Suzanne Cusick, in another pioneering article, explores how music allows for a rethinking of sexual pleasure as nongenital and thus outside the phallic economy of power.[24] She thus conceives of a listener's nonpatriarchal and nonphallic relationship "with" music as analogous to lesbian relationships. Hence music can facilitate—indeed, hail—the lesbian subject.

As these and other scholars have shown, music demarcates a space and time wherein gender and sexuality lose clear definition.[25] In my opinion, that is part of music's enduring appeal, and part of its cultural work. Western culture has long used music to explore, celebrate, manage, and police aspects of gender and sexuality that are irreducible to verbal description and visual representation, as evidenced in the anxiety and ambivalence that frequently condense around music and musicians. The association of music with queer sexualities is, as I will argue in chapter 1, at least as old as the Homeric Sirens, and continues today with Marilyn Manson, *Hedwig and the Angry Inch,* and the increasing numbers of out gay-, lesbian-, and queer-identified musicians.

The association is perhaps most easily explored in the writings of Western thinkers who use music as an idea, building a centuries-long tradition of mythic, theological, and philosophical discourse. How the realm of ideas affects music as a practice, with its three distinct branches of activity—composition, performance, reception—poses the greatest challenge for the musicologist. The field of ethnomusicology holds as a central tenet that music has meaning only as part of a large cultural matrix; "the music itself" is always a partial or problematic concept. In other words, "the music itself" cannot be divorced from the history of ideas that supports its practice; the ideas set up the conditions under which those practices become and remain meaningful. Indeed, the fact that no music survives for the Sirens' song, or appears with Augustine's references to psalms and hymns, should not deter us from imagining these as types of musical texts.

This book covers diverse styles of music under the rubrics of Foucault's four technologies, in order to show the persistent yet varied use of music throughout history as a technique for negotiating queer identity in the face of normalizing social pressures. The first two chapters concern technologies of the self, and address how music has been considered a practice of desire as well as discipline. Chapter 1, "Songs of the Sirens," presents a historical overview from ancient Greece to the late twelfth century, tracing the idea of music as an extension of desire, indulgent and excessive. This chapter culminates with two examples of musical practice, one in the chants of Hildegard of Bingen, and another in the chansons of Arnaut Daniel. Chapter 2, "A Music of One's Own," focuses on music as discipline, as an ascetic and confessional self-practice, using Peter Ilich Tchaikovsky's Sixth Symphony and Benjamin Britten's opera *Billy Budd* and canticle *Abraham and Isaac* as case studies.

Chapter 3, "Queer Ears and Icons," turns to technologies of sign systems; it considers the different ways in which three musical "gay icons"—Judy Garland, Melissa Etheridge, and Madonna—represent queer identity within mainstream culture. Chapter 4, "Homomusical Communities," looks at recordings of "women's music" and disco from the 1970s as technologies of production that contributed to the formation of separate gay and lesbian identities, and new active modes of sexual identity politics.

Finally, chapter 5, "Flights of Fancy," traces the deployment of music in technologies of power, technologies that Foucault argues became specifically centered on categorizing and controlling sexuality after the seventeenth century. This chapter examines a wide array of music—seventeenth-century English catches, a Roman cantata by George Frideric Handel, rock songs performed by Queen, Marilyn Manson, and within the plays-turned-movie-musicals *Rocky Horror Picture Show* and *Hedwig and the Angry Inch*—finding ways in which music has made a space for self-conscious self-transformations that interrupt masculinity and its patriarchal regulation of sexuality.

1

Songs of the Sirens

desire

The history of Western thought about music has been, in part, a history of ambivalence and anxiety. Since before Homer, musical creatures, musical gods and demigods, musical humans, and music-addled or -inspired listeners have given evidence of a moral dilemma. Music presents an occasion of conflict between discipline and desire that seems not only irreconcilable but also inexplicable. A musician may discipline voice, fingers, breath, and mind in order to attain control over them in musical performance, but the performance itself may evoke undisciplined, frenzied emotions in those who hear it. Through the medium of a musical performance, then, a discipline "of the self on the self"[1] potentially results in excessive desire. This desire may not have a definite object, may not, in fact, be a desire *for* anything; but rather, it may be a desire to do something other than what you were just doing, or simply to question what you are doing.

Musical activity can be at once ascetic and hedonistic: formed by supervision and regulation of the senses, it can overpower them, flooding the listening self and sweeping it away. And, ultimately, reflection on the activity of the musical performer must allow for the performer's own rapturous response to the music, just as the response of the listener may assume the posture of a disciplined activity. So performers and listeners both confront the same musical constitutions of discipline and desire within their own selves. Negotiation of conflict between individual and society, between desires and moral codes, seems as fraught here as with sexual activity. Hence the ambivalence—and the anxiety.

In his last two volumes of *The History of Sexuality*, and in other scattered late essays, Foucault began to put together what he called the "genealogy of desire as an ethical problem," and to formulate his own notion of ethics.[2] From the formulation of problematic desire, he argued, arose the institution of ascetic practices, or what Foucault variously called "practices of the self" or "technologies of the self." This refers to an individual's "techniques" or practices of body, thought, and behavior "in order to attain a certain state of happiness, purity, wisdom, perfection, or immortality."[3] Such technologies take into account positive or negative feedback issuing from the moral codes (i.e., socially acceptable ranges of conduct) produced within a given culture.[4] For Foucault, the goal was aesthetic—life as a work of art;[5] the practice was ethics—life as a discipline of desire, including the desire to be complacent or acquiescent. In this way, Foucault maintained his long-held view of subjectivity as fundamentally mutable, formulated by institutionalized domination, while newly recognizing the possibilities for individual resistance arising from internal processes that strive toward "the artistic creation of the self."[6]

Foucault stated, "it is not enough to say that the subject is constituted in a symbolic system . . . [the subject] is constituted in real practices—historically analyzable practices. There is a technology of the constitution of the self which cuts across symbolic systems while using them."[7] It is Foucault's integration of ethics and aesthetics that holds promise for an account of music as a self-practice that cuts across yet engages symbolic systems, and instigates ethical questions of individual conduct vis-à-vis discipline and desire within or against in-place social and symbolic structures.

The vectors of discipline and desire, operating within the space of musical and sexual relationships, must be tracked within the awareness of an individual. This chapter explores the reports of a number of tracks left in myths, philosophy, and song from Mediterranean antiquity to the European Middle Ages. Some of these individuals, such as Plato and Augustine, left views that were unconventional in their own time, but which became foundational to later philosophical thought. Others, such as Sappho, Hildegard of Bingen, and Arnaut Daniel, recorded their individual poetic and musical ruminations that reflect sensibilities shared among their peers and companions. A wide variety of interactions between discipline and desire, involving infinitely nuanced versions of each, can be read in the accounts of Greek myths.[8] These can seem to hide a compelling truth, a reason for human behavior other than those motivations we might readily provide. Myths, whether about heroes or gods, are usually contemplations about individuals and their very human motivations, or they focus on one individual's behavior in social relationships.[9] So while philosophy can assert generalities about human behavior, about what might be true of music, sex, discipline, desire for all individuals, myth, like poetry, can record what was the case for one individual, and potentially for others.

More specifically, this chapter considers the hedonistic side of music, notions and practices of music that concern shaping the self through excessive desire. Chapter 2 will explore the ascetic side, the discipline. Indeed, the high tension between these two facets of music is perfectly represented in the image of Odysseus strapped to the mast of his ship in order to listen to the Sirens' song.

MUSICAL SELF-QUESTIONING

Homer's *Odyssey* (ca. 700 B.C.E.) transmits an archetypal story of music, sexual seduction, and questioning in the episode of the Sirens from book 12. This is the first written account of the Sirens. It does not describe their visual appearance, but Homeric vase and tomb decorations persistently depict them as half human (most often female) and half bird (see figure 1).[10] Sirens also appear in a variety of contexts in both pre- and post-Homeric art—as evil omens, as emissaries from the divine world, and in association with a number of deities such as Artemis, Athena, and Dionysus. During the sixth century B.C.E. the Sirens even became a symbol for a blessed afterlife.[11] Homeric Sirens, however, sing so beautifully that those who hear them become entranced, irrationally and hopelessly drawn to their deaths on the rocky shore. Odysseus, making a long, much-interrupted journey home to Ithaca from the Trojan War, is forewarned of the Sirens by the sorceress Kirke, who mentions how he alone might listen to their song while still avoiding its threat to his reunion with wife and child:

> The Sirens you will come to first, who charm *(thelgousin)* all men—anyone who comes to them. Anyone who approaches in ignorance and hears the Sirens' voice, for him his wife and infant children do not stand at his side or take delight in him on his return home: no, the Sirens charm *(thelgousin)* him with their clear-sounding *(ligurēi)* song *(aoidēi)* as they sit in their meadow with a huge pile of bones round them from decaying men whose skins wither round them. Press on past them, and smear your comrades' ears with honey-sweet wax *(meliēdea)* after kneading it so that none of the others hears them. Hear them yourself if you want: let them tie you up hand and foot in the fast ship, upright in the mast-socket, and let ropes *(peirat)* be fastened [on you] from [the mast] itself, so that you can hear and enjoy *(terpomenos)* the voice of the Siren pair. If you beg your comrades, and order them to release you, they are to tie you up then with even more bonds *(desmoisi)*. (12.39–54)[12]

The *Odyssey* is filled with significant names and wordplay. The name of Kirke, who held Odysseus and his men captive for a year, stems from *kirkos,* a bird of prey such as a hawk or falcon, and also connotes a limit, as in our related word "circle."[13] So, too, the name of the Sirens *(Seirēnes)* may derive from *seirē,* meaning rope or cord, though the word for rope in this episode is consistently *peirat,* derived from *peirar,* meaning "end," "limit," or "boundary." Thus the Siren story is filled with a variety of words *(Seirēnes, peirat, desmoisi)* alluding to or describing bondage and containment.[14] Yet these are paired with words that connote sexual pleasure and magical enchantment. The verb *terpō* describes pleasure and enjoyment associated with listening to bardic song as well as sexual activity. Even the meadow from which the Sirens sing has erotic associations in Greek poetry, as does the word *thelgousin* (from the verb *thelgō*, meaning to touch with magic power), which Kirke uses to describe the beguiling effects of the Sirens' song, and which also describes the effects of Kirke's potions.[15]

The *Odyssey* includes a total of four renditions of the Siren story, each rehearsing and refining the scene of bondage. In the second, Odysseus passes the message on to his crew, turning Kirke's flirtatious suggestion into a compelling proposition:

> She instructed me alone to listen to their voice: but tie me in harsh bonds so that I stay fast where I am, upright in the mast-socket, and let ropes be fastened from [the mast] itself. If I beg you and order you to release me, you are then to load me down with more bonds. (12.158–64)

In the third, Odysseus begins to describe the moment of the performance, so to speak, when his crew makes ready for the encounter:

> They bound me in the ship, hands and feet together, upright in the mast-socket, and fastened ropes from [the mast] itself. Sitting down themselves they struck the grey sea with their oars. When we were as far away as a man's voice carries when he shouts, lightly pursuing [our course], the swiftly-bounding ship did not go unnoticed by them as it sped close, and they furnished their clear-sounding song *(ligurēn aoidēn)*. (12.178–83)

In the fourth account, Odysseus tells of straining against the bonds as he listens to the Sirens, and the application of more ropes by his crew:

> So they [the Sirens] spoke, projecting their fair voices, and my heart wanted to listen. I ordered my comrades to release me, frowning at them with my eyebrows, but they fell to and rowed on. At once Perimedes and Eurylochos got up and tied me with more bonds *(desmoisi)* and weighed me down more. (12.192–97)

Pietro Pucci has observed that throughout the *Odyssey*, Odysseus suffers from "a sort of self-destructive nostalgia" for his past warrior identity, which he must shed in order to return to domestic life.[16] The Sirens sing of Odysseus's famed heroism in the Trojan War, as recounted in the *Iliad*, reproducing the diction and rhetoric of that earlier epic and claiming the power to bestow knowledge and pleasure, like the epic Muses:

> Come hither, Odysseus of many stories, great glory of the Achaeans. Stop your ship, listen to our voices. Never has any man passed by in his black *(melainēi)* ship without hearing the honey-sweet *(meligērun)* voice from our lips *(stomatōn)*, but he has taken his pleasure *(terpsamenos)* and has gone on with greater wis-

dom. For we know all the pains Argives and Trojans suffered in the wide land
of Troy because of the gods' will, and we know whatever happens on the boun-
tiful earth. (12.184–91)[17]

The Sirens dress forgetfulness in the guise of past and future knowledge,
enticing Odysseus to wallow in a nostalgia for adventure that threatens his
spiritual odyssey. Such pining for the past appears elsewhere in the *Odyssey*,
when the minstrel Demodokos, at the request of an unrecognized Odysseus,
sings of the hero's conquering of Troy. Odysseus becomes an engrossed listener of his own story to the point that he empathizes with his past victims,
for Homer describes him weeping as if a woman grieving for her husband
killed in war (8.523).[18] Odysseus's song-sparked lamentation occurs after the
Siren episode in the chronology of events, but prior to it in the circuitous
narrative of the epic, for Odysseus narrates his encounter with the Sirens in
his own recital of his wanderings since the *Iliad*. Thus the Sirens' song is both
the first and last singing of Iliadic stories in the *Odyssey*, and this epic-scale
temporal knot is tightened in the entwining of past and future in the words
of their song.[19]

The lure of the deceptive Sirens points a finger at all "tellers of tales,"
Homer included, and implicates the audience in their own desires to suspend time with bardic songs. Odysseus, himself a cunning storyteller, perhaps listens to the Sirens as an apprentice or thief,[20] his apparent victorious
emergence representing a self-reflexive moment celebrating the skill of en-
thralling listeners through words and music. Unlike Achilles in the *Iliad*,
however, Odysseus does not sing, and his "triumph" over the Sirens is also a
milestone in the story of his resocialization back into the domestic sphere; it
is a step forward in the reconciliation of the individual and his social and
domestic responsibilities. But in spite of the enchantment that betrays a
"readiness to leave the wandering of the *Odyssey* in favor of the splendid toils
of the *Iliad*,"[21] Homer forces his subject to stay on course, binding him to the
mast of the ship, hence to the agenda of the present epic.

But what of that tightly trussed body? The metanarratives of heroic transcendence or authorial self-reflection do not account for the attention paid
to the scene of the hero's bondage and his utter failure of mind in the presence of this music. Indeed, figure 1 shows a fourth-century B.C.E. burlesque
of this scene in which Odysseus is made to look markedly *unheroic*. In the standard depictions, Odysseus is bound back to mast, bravely facing the Sirens;
here, in contrast, he is bound front to mast, feet dangling below the heads of
his crew, who look at him and the Sirens in bewilderment. Their gaze marks
both Odysseus and the Sirens as queer for the viewer of the illustration.[22] In
the context of the performed epic, the audience, along with the crew, sails
past the meadow of the Sirens without stress or restraint, knowing only that

they have not really heard the Sirens' song. They may notice the euphony of *melainēi* (black) and *meligērun* (honey-sweet) in the Sirens' song, which recalls the honey-sweet wax *(meliēdea)* that protects the crew of the ship from its effects—that *melos* (melody) implied in all three words but never actually described except for the phrase *ligurēn aoidēn,* clear-sounding or shrill song.[23] It is this clear and penetrating melody, issuing paradoxically from the viscous voices of the Sirens, that enchants Odysseus, while the audience's ears remain forever protected by temporal distance, just as the crew's are by the filter of *meliēdea.*

The Sirens' song is fundamentally a song of seduction that nets the audience and Odysseus in rumor, for it is Kirke who begins the seduction in her foretelling of the aural encounter, describing the song's enchanting, paralyzing effect. Furthermore, in the musical image of the honey-sweet voices offering pleasure in the singing of epic tales, the Sirens' song mixes the lure of nostalgia with that of sexuality. Elsewhere in the *Odyssey,* sexually assertive women, such as Kalypso and Kirke, threaten Odysseus's physical and spiritual return home; the Sirens' seduction has the same sexual tone, even though its expression is purely aural.[24] Kirke, who enters the narrative singing and weaving (10.210–23), initiates the Sirens' song through the power of suggestion, inviting Odysseus to continue his experience of her undomesticated eroticism and her song (of weaving) as it is extended in the Sirens. Odysseus's cunning here is not his own; rather, by subjecting himself to the Sirens' peculiarly disembodied sexual attraction, he seems to serve Kirke's purpose—perhaps even her continued pleasure.

To the masculine-gendered rational mind, sexually assertive women can represent the irrational, corporeal, emotional—and can represent these as threats. But not to Odysseus: hearing the song, he is taken by it, body, mind, and soul. The point of the story is to tell of Odysseus's desire to experience aural-eros, and to depict his mental and physical strain against his bonds. For the Homeric audience, *erōs* signified an acute desire akin to hunger and thirst principally stimulated by visual beauty.[25] The *erōs* provoked by the Sirens is thus something quite unusual: Odysseus's desire stems solely from hearing, specifically hearing a song about himself. The audience then envisions his *erōs*—his musical autoeroticism—through the descriptions of his bondage, which strikingly positions Odysseus as a tortured slave rather than a heroic leader. Page duBois argues that the ancient Greek practice of torturing slaves reflected and reinforced "the dominant notion . . . that truth was an inaccessible, buried secret." Torture guaranteed the emergence of truth from a body that by nature could not access the truth through reason (as could a free citizen). She also notes that in the *Odyssey,* quests for truth were frequently associated with female-gendered images of interiority, such as Odysseus's journey to the underworld (a space deep within the female-gendered Earth), where he gains important knowledge from his dead

Figure 1. Odysseus and the Sirens, attributed to Python Painter, ca. 330 B.C.E. Greek red-figure bell krater from Paestum, Italy. Antikensammlung, Staatliche Museen zu Berlin. Photo: Bildarchiv Preussischer Kulturbesitz / Art Resource, NY.

mother. Women's and slaves' bodies were analogous in that they both could signify the containment of truth and its potential revelation.[26] In this sense, it might be said that Odysseus becomes both slave and woman, forced by bondage on an inward search for the truth that his body encases—a truth that is, paradoxically, not sustainable. The ropes that bind him mark the meeting of two seemingly opposed forces, the psychosexual reach of the Sirens' song and the psychosocial magnet of homeland and family.

The Sirens' song exposes the porous nature of mind, body, and humanly determined boundaries, calling into question the desire to remain bound by these. Odysseus knows beforehand the dangers of listening: these include the rupture of social order, as when a crew must tie the captain to the mast and not heed his orders; also the contamination of identity, as when his motives are indistinguishable from Kirke's; and still further, the threat of regression in his own awareness, when the boundary between knowing and forgetting collapses in listening to the Sirens' song. Odysseus knows all this; he knows also that the Sirens have no knowledge of any value to offer a listener doomed ahead of time to death on the rocks.

The Siren episode, I propose, is not a story of genius, craftiness, transcendence, or authorial self-reflection. Rather, it is a story of how Odysseus, while assuming he can control his transgression, gives in to a sexualized self-curiosity and, importantly, a desire to become otherwise, to question and to be questionable, to risk self-obliteration in music. This is a desire to become queer to oneself.

Indeed, it would be a special kind of curiosity that drove a man to such risks. In the second volume of his *History of Sexuality,* Michel Foucault links curiosity to existential and ontological concerns. He describes his own swerve off the original course of his investigation as motivated by "the only kind of curiosity, in any case, that is worth acting upon with a degree of obstinacy: not the curiosity that seeks to assimilate what it is proper for one to know, but that which enables one to get free of oneself . . . knowing if one can think differently than one thinks . . . is absolutely necessary if one is to go on looking and reflecting at all."[27] If we apply this notion of curiosity— "to get free of oneself"—to the Siren episode, then Odysseus achieves this "getting free" by subjugating his will to Kirke's design and to the bonds that discipline as well as indulge his desire.[28] In this case bondage allows, or even constitutes, freedom; and that is only one of the paradoxical aspects of the Siren episode, particularly when considered together with subsequent events in the *Odyssey.*

Odysseus's conduct, even though antiheroic, in the end distinguishes him from the crew (who cannot hear the song), as well as from those who previously perished in hearing it. Also paradoxical is that his successful transit past the Sirens is followed by a string of encounters with disastrous results, eventually wiping out his entire crew and leading to his own sexual enslavement by the nymph Kalypso. Odysseus is bound again, this time in an unnatural union of human and divine, until Zeus himself intercedes.

In light of these latter events, the Siren episode does seem an odd triumph: a relatively harmless encounter with queer sexual desire. It is harmless because it is solitary, policeable, musical. It is not, however, without effect, for it infuses Odysseus with a surge of desire to continue listening; this desire energizes him to struggle against his bonds, those of crew as well as of family. As readers we follow the gradual release of that energy until it drives him to Kalypso. And ultimately Odysseus, the only one to hear the Sirens' song, is the only one left to be heard, and to be heard about; he alone survives in song. We can note that a woman told him how.

DIVINE MUSIC

To face the music of the Sirens is to engage with a monstrous queer desire, a desire that can disenfranchise and destroy, but also energize and sustain. Later interpretations, as well as Christian allegory, of the Sirens emphasize the "rite of passage" aspects of this episode: the gaining of secret knowledge, or the testing of faith against seductions of paganism or the flesh.[29] I will return to these aspects later in this chapter, but here I want to linger on the persistent association in ancient Greek culture of music with sexuality—and not just incidentally, but rather as an operative factor in the vital dynamic represented by particular gods.[30] What follows is a brief survey of some key players; musical-sexual gods who were central to the religious life of ancient Greece, and who remained important archetypes for philosophers, writers, and artists far into the modern era. These gods present a nexus from which we can learn more, for the music involved in the diverse sexual contexts of their myths and rituals was performed (by the gods and their celebrants)—not just contemplated. And instruments figure here in primary ways. Thus music itself can be said to be an instrument—of Dionysian catharsis, of Apollonian control, of sexual Pan(ic).

Music was central in the myths, plays, and cultic rituals devoted to the Olympïan gods Dionysus and Apollo. In Friedrich Nietzsche's early philosophical work these two gods were represented as opposing forces in Greek culture—as if in some kind of Hegelian dialectic.[31] Nowadays scholars tend to see polarity expressed within a single god, and they are inclined to view mythology as manifesting diverse human responses, in which sexual responses, also diverse in nature, are prominent.

Both the name of Dionysus and his associated song type *(dithyramb)* begin with the syllable "di," meaning two, which may refer to Dionysus's paternity *(dios,* "of god," "of Zeus"), as well as his double birth. Dionysus was the son of Zeus and the mortal Semele, but Dionysus's mother died before his birth. Zeus then took Dionysus within his own body until Dionysus emerged in a "second birth" from Zeus's thigh.[32] By his first birth Dionysus could be considered a man, by his second same-sex birth, a god. *Dios,* then, refers to his maternity as well as his paternity. The poet of the *Iliad* knew him as a Greek god, but by the fifth century B.C.E. he was clearly marked as a foreigner, said to come from Asia Minor in the region of Phrygia (now northern Turkey). His alleged foreignness metaphorically described and explained the strangeness of behavior demonstrated by his worshipers.[33] Dionysus represents what we might call the melodramatic forces of nature, the polarities of epiphany and deception, ecstasy and horror, death and rebirth and—above all—liberation.[34]

To his followers he revealed himself most clearly, and paradoxically, in the delirious abandon kindled by wine. Despite his same-sex second birth, Dionysus was closely associated with women in myth and ritual, believed to have been raised by nymphs and always accompanied by the maenads, a group of frenzied women celebrants often depicted dancing wildly to the accompaniment of *aulos* and tambourine. Male worshipers and even the god himself take part in his rituals as transvestites: they donned the long flowing robes of women, with turbans or ivy garlands, or sometimes satyr costumes. Playwrights and artists often depict Dionysus himself as womanly, with long curls, soft plumpness, and a fair complexion.[35]

Dance and song constitute the central and most essential component of Dionysian rituals. The dancing was accompanied by the *aulos,* a pair of reed pipes, said to have come from Phrygia, that became one of the two most important instrumental resources of ancient Greek music (the other being the kithara, together with its smaller, specifically Greek, form, the lyre). Dionysian song was represented by *dithyrambs,* a large-scale song type performed by about fifty men and boys and accompanied by an *aulos.*[36] Pottery art shows the maenads dancing to these songs, with heads and arms raised and bodies twisted as they move forward.[37] Such dancing worshipers may or may not enter an altered state of consciousness, but when they do, they become momentarily liberated from social norms of duty and behavior. Savagery, specifically the tearing and eating of raw flesh *(sparagmos),* and sexual licentiousness, commonly represented by satyrs, haunt every Dionysian ritual, just as destruction haunts the very principle of liberation. The success of the ritual in liberating women, powerless and housebound by marriage or slavery, is obvious. Men who participated through ritual transvestism thereby took on the mantle of passive sexuality, believed to be a characteristic of women and antithetical to adult male citizens.[38] Transgressions of gender seemed to flirt with the chaos of savagery and orgy. The god himself, however, is often depicted as unperturbed and unaroused, modeling the very civic order and discipline his rituals unravel.[39]

Stepping into a Dionysian dance, then, meant stepping into a high sexual tension; yet the ritual itself circumscribed the transgression and liberation.

Just as the Sirens' song offered Odysseus an opportunity for controlled transgression, Dionysian ritual dance and song resulted in eventual pacification, for the men as well as the women, and this in turn reinstated the civic ideals of unity and tranquility.[40] By another apparent paradox, in the Hellenistic period (fourth to first century B.C.E.) the musical performers of Dionysian ritual became professionalized. These musicians, known as *technitai Dionusou*—artists of Dionysus—enjoyed a position of privilege in civic life and duties.[41]

Apollo represented the driving force behind the arts, especially music and poetry. One theory connects his name with the words *apeilē* (a promise) and *apellai* (to hold an assembly). Thus he presides over all types of speech (including song and poetry) and all types of public spoken performances.[42] Literally and figuratively the "youngest" of the Olympian gods, he was the last to enter the Greek cultural record, possibly through the Dorians on Crete, who represented him as an idealized perpetual ephebe—an adolescent boy on the brink of adulthood. In addition to music and fine arts, Apollo governed both the natural dynamics of sheep and wolves as well as plagues and healing, and the human dynamic of archery and hunting in association with his twin sister, Artemis. On a more metaphysical level, he was associated with order and prophecy, symbolized by the sun and light. He is, in sum, a god of revelation and initiation whose means vary from abduction and infection (sheep/wolves, archery/hunt, plagues) to inspiration (music, poetry) to education and restoration (poetry, prophecy, healing).[43]

As the ephebe, Apollo represents the initiate who enters adult male citizenship through pedagogical and sexual rites of passage. In early Hellenic Dorian practices (eighth to sixth century B.C.E.) an adult male symbolically abducted the initiate, who became an apprentice in hunting and fighting, as well as an *erōmenos* (passive lover). The role of passive lover remained a common one in the education of young male citizens through the time of Plato and Aristotle.[44] But as a god, Apollo necessarily functions as the teacher, the adult male citizen and *erastēs* (active lover). Thus Apollo paradoxically embodies both adult and ephebe, initiator and initiate, teacher and student, lover and beloved.

There were ecstatic rituals associated with Apollo's cults, notably the assembly of naked ephebes of the Gymnopaidiai in Sparta (a Dorian city), where singing and dancing were a part of endurance tests in their rites of passage.[45] But he revealed himself mostly through prophetic oracles (famously at Delphi and Delos) and lyric poetry; Apollo's service as inspiration and educator came together in music and its words. His instrument was the lyre (hence the term "lyric"), though it was invented by the trickster Hermes.[46] As the most popular and esteemed Greek polystringed instrument, the lyre was plucked or strummed, providing a musical double to Apollo's other principal attribute, the bow. Both bow and lyre project Apollo into the world in complementary ways, through arrows and songs.[47] The kind of poem most closely associated with Apollo was the *paean,* which originally included the hail *Ie Paean* (Hail, Healer). Apollo was also closely associated with a song type called *nomos.* The word means "law," possibly indicating the role of law (of some unspecified kind), or custom and convention, in the generation and evaluation of music. Possibly related is Apollo's epithet *Nomimos,* "the Law giver."[48]

Unlike music in Dionysian rituals, which facilitated and circumscribed transgression, Apollo's music brings calm to the passions of animals, humans, and gods, as Pindar (518–ca. 438 B.C.E.) writes in his first Pythian ode:

> O golden Lyre, possession of Apollo and the violet-haired
> Muses that speaks on their behalf, to whom the dance step harkens . . .
> and whose signal the singers obey . . .
> you even quench the warlike thunderbolt
> of ever-flowing fire; and as the eagle sleeps
>   on Zeus's scepter, his swift wings
>   relaxed and folded on each side . . .
> . . . Indeed, even strong Ares, abandoning the rough
> violence of spear points, cheers his heart
> in utter quiet, while your shafts enchant the minds of other gods as well.[49]

For Pindar, then, the lyre is an instrument of civic order, the bow that sends forth sweet songs. As the voice of Apollo and the Muses, it brings peace to the Olympic gods and, by extension, to mortal society. Such music is an agent of control, of initiation into citizenship—the instrument of an *erastēs* that pacifies (literally making passive) both men and other gods, turning them into *erōmenoi.* Here we see again music making for a graceful transition from one inner state to another: for just as Odysseus willingly converted from hero to slave in order to listen to the Sirens' song, so do the most virile and warlike gods, Zeus and Ares, become receptive and submissive partners to the ephebe's lyric shafts.

Liberation into orgy, seduction into serenity—these would seem to provide ample scope for music's transgressive power. But the figure of Pan, perhaps more than any other, manifests the queer sexual potency of music. A lusty and rustic half-goat, half-man who terrified humans and entertained the gods, Pan originated in Arcadia, the mountainous region of central Peloponnesus (that is to say, he was not Olympian, and not Asian, and certainly not urban). Though a minor deity in myths, his cult spread into Athens by 490 B.C.E., and he seems to have been much worshiped, judging by the many dedications to him in the medieval collection of ancient epigrams known as *The Greek Anthology.* As a patron of herds and herders (being himself both human shepherd and animal flock), he looked after the propagation of life, hence his generalized sexuality, for Pan coupled with animals, men and women, and nymphs. But he represents all that is repellent to humankind, the ugly animal (nature) from which civilized people flee (*panic* being the sudden fright Pan causes—with unidentifiable noises and echoes—in humans who enter his wild woods). The Athenians called upon Pan during wartime, asking him to cause disorder in the ranks of the enemy.

As a god, Pan represents indiscriminate desire and indiscriminate fear, both present in the images and myths of his numerous attempts at rape. But he is also the god who causes joyful abandon and who entertains with leaping dances. By the fifth century B.C.E. the name Pan was poetically associated with the word *pān*, meaning "all" in Greek, though the more likely etymology is from words sharing the Indo-European root **pa-* (watch, protect, feed), and referring to *pa*storal activities and identities.[50]

Pan's most frequently cited family history reads like a nineteenth-century Gothic account of sexual psychopathology. According to Athenian tradition, he was the son of the immortal Hermes and the mortal Penelope or the nymph Dryope. After his birth, Pan's mother fled from her monstrous infant in disgust, and this maternal rejection seemingly left him doomed to violent, restless, and often frustrated desire. Many myths relate Pan's predestined attraction to nymphs—the virgin companions of Artemis—who always reject him, as his mother had done. In one such case, the nymph Syrinx escaped Pan's grasp with the aid of the Earth goddess, who turns her into marsh reeds. These Pan cut, violently. The breath from Pan's woeful sighing caused the reeds to vibrate and sing. In this way Pan achieved a manner of sexual union with Syrinx, and the resulting musical instrument—the syrinx or panpipe—became his regular attribute, a proxy for sexual fulfillment.

Pan's music was comparable to that of the Sirens: it evoked uncontrollable desire for contact outside duly constituted relationships. Ironically, as a symbol of frustrated and sublimated premarital desire, his music became associated with some prenuptial rites of passage for young women.[51]

In his overt eroticism, Pan was closely associated with Dionysus, who was thought to have a special fondness for the goat-god. This is evident from Pan's appearance—as a clear visual echo—in the image of the satyrs who dance around Dionysus; and the punishing Dionysian frenzy clearly resembled panic. Pan is also associated with Orpheus; they share prophetic powers and their music can enchant all of nature.[52] In this regard, and as a musician god of shepherds and flocks, Pan comes close to Apollo as well. Their legendary musical contest, in which Pan was judged the winner by Midas, suggests that the music of this wild and unruly creature can exert greater powers of attraction and persuasion than the music of even "the most Greek" of the Greek gods. Although without the clear civic function attached to the music of Dionysus and Apollo, Pan's music nonetheless offers a lesson: one cannot enter his undomesticated realm and expect to remain undefiled.[53]

. . .

A survey of queer musical figures of ancient Greece should include the two famous musicians Orpheus and Sappho. Both are examples of an early mapping of same-sex eroticism onto a musician's identity. They, like Dionysus, Apollo, and Pan, appear throughout the centuries in discussions of music and musicians, as well as transgressive sexuality.

Orpheus is traditionally considered the son of Apollo and the muse Kalliope, though he seems to have originated in association with the Thracian Dionysian god Oeagrus around the sixth century B.C.E.[54] His powers, like those of Apollo, resided in his singing and lyre playing, which enchanted nature and could sway the hearts of gods. One myth from late antiquity even has Orpheus outsinging the Sirens, protecting the Argonauts with his own musical charm.[55] Though not considered a god, Orpheus had magical and healing powers. He was a shaman figure who became the center of ascetic vegetarian cults that sprang up in the fifth century B.C.E. as tempered versions of Dionysus cults.

The two most stable stories of Orpheus are his descent to Hades to resurrect his wife (ending in failure), and his death at the hands of Thracian (also called Ciconian) women. Both have a fourth-century B.C.E. witness in Plato's *Symposium* (179d), though Plato had a low opinion of Orpheus, calling him a mere kithara player, a lukewarm lover, and lacking in courage. Thus, in Greco-Roman culture, Orpheus was an ambivalent figure, for alongside stories of his musical charms there was a long-standing tradition associating him with pederasty and misogyny.

These diverse Orphic myths and traditions come together in Ovid's *Metamorphoses* (ca. 8 C.E.). Unified by an overarching theme of metamorphosis ("forms changed to other bodies"), Ovid's compendium of myths told in verse became, along with Virgil's *Aeneid* (ca. 20 B.C.E.), one of the most important sources of Greco-Roman mythology for writers in late antiquity all the way down to modern times. Ovid's immediate source for the Orpheus story is Virgil's *Georgics* 4. Virgil only hinted at the pederastic and misogynistic Orpheus, preferring to cast the singer as noble and tragic, whereas Ovid, satirizing Virgil, called attention to exactly those less noble characteristics that Virgil suppressed.[56] At the beginning of book 10, Ovid tells how Eurydice, the new bride of Orpheus, was bitten by a serpent and fell dead, sinking to Hades; and how a grieving and lovesick Orpheus enchanted all the souls of the dead and the king and queen of Hades, Pluto and Proserpina. Taken by Orpheus's musical supplication, Pluto grants Eurydice a second chance at life on the condition that Orpheus not turn to look at her until they were securely out of Hades. Orpheus does look back at Eurydice, however, causing her to die a second time. The burden of transformation in this episode seems to belong to Eurydice (from life to death to life to death), but Ovid ends the story with Orpheus's own metamorphosis—an erotic one: "And now because it had ended sadly for him, or because he had vowed to be faithful, Orpheus fled the love of females. Yet many women longed for unions with the bard, and many grieved when he rejected them. He even taught the men of Thrace to turn their desire to tender males and so to pluck the first blossoms boys offer in that brief springtime before they become young men" (10.79–85).[57]

This Orphic legend had had a long history by the time of Ovid's recording. In the third century B.C.E., the poet Phanokles wrote about Orpheus's love of boys, noting also his introduction of pederasty to Thrace. Orpheus as the point of origin for homosexual pederasty was a theme that circulated well into the early modern era, competing with Christian allegories of Orpheus as Christ or Adam.[58] Albrecht Dürer's famous print "The Death of Orpheus" (1494), for example, labels Orpheus "the first pederast" (*Orpheus der erst puseran*).[59] These words are inscribed on a scroll woven into the leaves of a tree, which serves as a natural witness to Orpheus's death at the hands of frenzied Thracian women.

Ovid links this martyrdom to Orpheus's spurning of women. After the second death of his bride, we might expect Orpheus to sing laments about his loss, but in Ovid's account he sings songs about pederastic gods and immoral women, gathering an attentive audience of animals, trees, and rocks. Book 11 begins with the scene of this concert disrupted by the violence of the Ciconian women, who throw spears and stones at the musician's mouth—the source of his power and his misogyny. But as each object is hurled toward him, "it was overcome by the sweet harmony of his voice and lyre and came to rest at his feet like a suppliant seeking forgiveness for such a mad attack." Here, in contrast to the penetrating effects of the Sirens' song on Odysseus's body, music protects Orpheus's body from the women's missiles. This inversion of the power of music—to protect rather than to pierce—highlights Orpheus's musical mastery and magic. The women, who in some traditions are identified as maenads, then find a new tactic: fighting Apollonian music with that of Dionysus.[60] Ovid writes, "all the angry weapons would have been soothed by Orpheus' singing if the shouting, if the shrill cry of Phrygian flutes with flared bells, if the rattle of drums, the clapping of hands, the wailing, and the howling had not drowned out the sound of his lyre. But finally the stones no longer heard the poet as he sang, and they grew red with his blood" (11.15–19).[61] Ovid's black humor is in evidence here as music itself becomes metamorphic, changing from shield to spear; the Dionysian cacophony renders Apollonian song impotent, leaving Orpheus's body vulnerable. The women tear him to pieces as if in the throes of a Dionysian *sparagmos,* scattering his limbs in the rivers.[62] His still-singing head and sounding lyre floated on the Hebrus to the sea, and finally washed up on the shores of Lesbos, an island off the Asiatic coast. This legend, too, has Phanokles as an early witness. He tells how the head and lyre were entombed on Lesbos, and how "after this, the island had both songs and the lovely art of harping, and of all islands it is the most tuneful."[63]

Lesbos was indeed an appropriate destination for the singing voice of Orpheus; the island had been the home of many well-known and innovative lyric poets since the seventh century B.C.E. Of these, the female poet Sappho (fl. ca. 600 B.C.E.) has gained broad and lasting notoriety while her fellow male Lesbian poets have faded into the past. Sappho does not mention Orpheus by name, whose legends did not become widely known until a century or two later.[64] Yet Sappho's lyrics, intimate, emotional, and distinctively homoerotic, have given her the status of Orpheus among scholars of classical poetry, and particularly among her present-day lesbian readership.[65]

Only one complete poem and nearly two hundred fragments of Sappho's lyrics survive—an extant oeuvre filled with more tantalizing and mystifying gaps than clarifying words. Yet these fragments, culled from ancient papyri, potsherds, and quotations by later writers, present a compellingly subjective female voice. Translators and literary scholars often treat the fragments as coherent, interpretable statements, and the verbal lacunae, though an accident of history, as itself an inscription of the poet's amorous yearning.[66]

A woman of high social standing, Sappho composed songs that focused on emotional and erotic bonds among women. Male authority figures are notably few in her lyrics. She herself became a figure of authority: Plato has Socrates mention her as a source for wisdom about love in *Phaedrus* (235c), and classical writers proclaimed her the tenth Muse, and one of the nine great Greek lyric poets.[67] As a woman, Sappho could not participate in the symposia (gatherings of male intellectuals), which provided an important occasion for the composition and performance of much lyric poetry of the time. She nevertheless seems to have been the center of a circle of adult women companions and *parthenoi*, young unmarried girls perhaps associated with her as pupils and performers of her choral songs.[68] These songs fall into a number of types: *epithalamia* (wedding songs), hymns or prayers to certain deities (especially Aphrodite), songs about members of her family, a possible epic, and songs about *parthenoi*. Some of these fragments are satirical in tone; some are erotic love songs, and were recognized as such by classical writers.[69]

There is much debate about whether Sappho was a practicing lesbian (as currently defined), and whether such a practice might have been a parallel to institutionalized male pederasty.[70] Comedies from the fourth century B.C.E. portray her as a woman of riddles or a somewhat lusty heterosexual; a late papyrus fragment, probably recording material from the third or second century B.C.E., reports the rumor that she was called a *gunaikerastria* (a female *erastēs* of women).[71] Ovid used the by-then solid reputation of Sappho as a lover of women to parody her legendary heterosexual love for Phaon.[72]

Sappho was, of course, a Lesbian, and this "ethnic" identity—Asian as opposed to Attic—factors strongly in her lyrics, which are filled with references to deities, cities, personages, garments, and perfumes from her island and lands to the East.[73] The short fragment 106 evinces a particular pride in Lesbian musicality:

> . . . superior, just as when a Lesbian
> singer [outdoes] foreign ones . . .

Another fragment (176), consisting entirely of three words, *barbitos, barōmos, barmos,* offers a brief glimpse into what seems to be a poetic meditation on the low-pitched, long-armed lyre native to Lesbos.[74] The *barbitos* was supposedly invented by the seventh-century Lesbian musician Terpander, who, like Orpheus, charmed men through his music.[75] Sappho is herself depicted playing the *barbitos* on a red-figure wine vessel of the fifth century B.C.E.,[76] and her association with sounding music was later affirmed in the pseudo-Plutarchian *De Musica* (ca. 100), which ascribes to her the invention of the emotional Mixolydian mode.[77]

Sappho's gendered, musical, and Lesbian (i.e., Asian) identity can be read in the homoerotic fragment 22. Here Sappho appeals to another woman, Abanthis, for a song about a third woman, Gongula, whom Abanthis once desired. Sappho's song about the desire of another singer culminates in the appearance of Aphrodite, the goddess of sexual love. Originally a Phoenician deity, Aphrodite entered the Greek pantheon via Cypress; Sappho frequently identifies her simply as "the Cyprian."[78]

> . . . I bid you sing
> of Gongula, Abanthis, taking up . . .
> [your] harp, while once again desire (or longing *[pothos]*) flutters about you,
> the lovely one. For the
> drapery of her clothing set your heart aflutter as you
> looked, and I take delight.
> For the holy Cyprian herself
> once blamed me . . .
>
> As I pray . . .
> this word . . .
> I wish . . . [79]

On one level the topic of this song is Abanthis's past desire for Gongula, here explicitly instigated by vision, specifically by a revealing dress. Yet on another level this song is about the desire for song, Sappho's desire to hear Abanthis sing of that past erotic moment, and to see Abanthis's desire reanimated by song. Music serves as the erotic conduit between Sappho and Abanthis. This link, however, seems less about Sappho's sexual desire, triangulated and voyeuristic, than an amplification and perhaps a celebration of an active, erotic female subjectivity—a queer subjectivity, to be sure, within the phallocentric culture of archaic Greek society (and for historians of sexuality, who tend to focus on men in classical Athens).[80]

Eva Stehle speculates that this song was not sung by Sappho to Abanthis but rather given to Abanthis to sing. Thus Sappho's authorial command to sing, which ignites Abanthis's desire, functions much like a bard's petition to the Muse or Pindar's invocation of Apollo, conjuring a mythic authorization for speech.[81] Perhaps this is why Aphrodite enters the poem with a reproof, for it is she who customarily sets desire to fluttering.[82] And it seems Sappho answers the goddess with a continued assertion of her subjectivity: "I pray . . . I wish." Elsewhere, as many scholars have noted, Sappho uses her subjective, incantatory voice to revise the masculine poetics of Homeric epics. In fragment 16 she champions the lyric beauty of "what one loves" over the epic beauty of an army of horsemen, infantry, and ships. Sappho reinterprets the story of Helen of Troy as a prelude to a poetic rumination about her absent beloved Anaktoria. Helen is cast as a hero, a subject rather than object of desire who rightly chose to leave her husband and family (in Sparta) and follow her lover to Troy (thus sparking the Trojan War).[83] Here, too, we may glimpse some of Sappho's Lesbian identity, for Troy was an Asiatic city, favored by Aphrodite in the war. Challenging the authority of Homeric (read also: Greek) bards, Sappho claims, "It is completely easy to make this intelligible to everyone" (ll. 5–6) . . . "[the Cyprian] led her away" (ll. 11–12). Sappho's musical powers of persuasion are not to be disputed, for she has the advantage, in her mythic tale, of being a woman; she is part of an infantry that includes her circle of adult women and *parthenoi* as well as the most desirable Helen, all led by the most powerful Cyprian goddess.

MUSIC EDUCATION

The Greek word *mousikē* could refer to any activity inspired by the Muses; the art of song was referred to more directly by *melos*. Song, dance, poetry, drama, even literature and philosophy, can all be said to be under the protection of the Muses.[84] Any kind of performance, if properly crafted by *technē* (skill, art, craft), and if graciously inspired by the Muse(s), can be music. According to Hesiod, in his *Hymn to the Muses* (possibly written soon after the *Odyssey*), the Muses came from an incestuous union of Zeus and his sister Mnemosyne (Memory). In association with Memory, and later Apollo, the Muses supplied the bards with historical knowledge and the ability to sing it; as children of Zeus they enjoyed authority for their inspiration.

In pre- and post-Homeric epic poetry it was customary to begin with an appeal to one or more Muses, who were understood to be the originating impulse.[85] Thus in his *Theogony*, Hesiod tells how the Muses "breathed into me their divine voice, so that I might tell of things to come and things past, and ordered me to sing."[86] Hesiod, who was perhaps the first to describe multiple Muses, links *mousikē* with *erōs* through epithets, sensual metaphors, and suggestive names such as Erato, "the Passionate."[87] The Muses' performance, then, is sexually charged; and when, as a female voice, it is infused into the poet's male body, it can be regarded as transgendered. In this way the poet becomes a musical instrument that, like the song of the Sirens, incites a passionate desire to listen. Indeed, the poet of the *Odyssey* implicates them with the Sirens, whose song refers to the Muse-inspired *Iliad*, which, in its new Odyssean context, leads to destruction.[88] With similar sinister implications, the Muses tell Hesiod this: "We know how to say many lies similar [or identical] to true things, but if we want, we know how to sing the truth."[89] Here Hesiod, in describing the terrific power of the Muses, seems also to be attacking the veracity of epic poets, or heroes, such as Odysseus, who, like the Sirens, deliberately tell falsehoods. In any case, there is a problem: how can we know whether it is Sirens or Muses we hear?[90]

Not trusting the epic poets or their Muses to have useful knowledge, or to be willing to share it, Plato (427–347 B.C.E.) worked hard to find a place for music in the worldview that he constructed according to the dictates of reason. Plato was, it seems, deeply affected by a revolution in musical style that occurred in the decades around 400 B.C.E. in Athens, when a barrage of radical novelties exploded on the scene, to the despair of conservative tastes. This revolution seems to have been part of a broad cultural and social-political dislocation of the aristocracy (of which Plato was a member). The expansion of public festivals and theater in fifth-century-B.C.E. Athens brought with it a decline in the influence and prestige of aristocratic patrons. Because of this expansion, musicians—especially *aulos* players, who did not specialize in any one genre and so experimented by mixing musical idioms—could significantly improve their financial and social status. The rise of *aulos* players also had a deleterious impact on the social importance of "string instruments" (lyre and kithara), which had long been associated with the education of the elite.[91] Plato's two largest works, the *Republic* (ca. 380 B.C.E.) and *Laws* (published posthumously), take up the issue of music's role in education; in both works, education (for a meritorious few) is assigned a major role in the maintenance of a healthy state.[92]

The importance of music in this program is expressed directly by the "Athenian," the principal interlocutor in *Laws*. At one point in *Laws*, the Athenian relates a story of civic degradation as a function of gradual musical corruption and a pandemonium of musical mixing.

Later as time went on, composers arose who started to set a fashion of breaking the rules and offending good taste. They did have a natural artistic talent,
but they were ignorant of the correct and legitimate standards laid down by the
Muse. Gripped by a frenzied and excessive lust for pleasure, they jumbled
together laments and hymns, mixed paeans and dithyrambs, and imitated the
pipe (aulos) tunes on the lyre. The result was a total confusion of styles. Unin-
tentionally, in their idiotic way, they misrepresented their art, claiming that in
music there are no standards of right and wrong at all, but that the most "correct" criterion is the pleasure of a man who enjoyed the performance, whether
he is a good man or not. (700d–e)[93]

The new music, Plato worries, betrays a new confusion of "pleasure" with
"goodness," and it opens up the possibility that a good man might enjoy bad
music, and thus fall prey to bad reason. Plato goes on to trace a spiral of
decay from innovations in music to a general unraveling of social order. He
writes, "This freedom will then take other forms. First people grow unwilling
to submit to the authorities, then they refuse to obey the admonitions of their
fathers and mothers and elders. As they hurtle along towards the end of this
primrose path, they try to escape the authority of laws; and the very end of
the road comes when they cease to care about oaths and promises and religion in general" (701b–c). For Plato, it is the transgressive mixture of styles
and genres (laments with hymns and Apollonian paeans with Dionysian
dithyrambs), along with other mixtures, such as feminine melody joined to a
verse composed for men, virtuosic displays joined to uncouth themes, that
initiate a tumble down the slippery slope of freedom and liberty, leading to
the abandonment of social boundaries and responsibility (quite like the
experience of Odysseus listening to the Sirens' song).[94] The Athenian's complaint bears witness to innovative musical practices of Plato's day, and his
conservative stance makes sense in light of Plato's investment in music as a
primary regulator of human intellectual but also physical life. For Plato,
music provides a model that the soul imitates, and this in turn provides a
foundation for educating the young, as he says here in Laws:

The soul of the child has to be prevented from getting into the habit of feeling
pleasure and pain in ways not sanctioned by the law and those who have been
persuaded to obey it; he should follow in their footsteps and find pleasure and
pain in the same things as the old. This is why we have what we call songs, which
are really "charms" for the soul. These are in fact deadly serious devices for producing this concord we are talking about. (659d–e)

So singing and playing could be for good or for bad. Plato's discussion of
music attempts to enlist music as a force for good while avoiding its possible
bad effects. His problem in this attempt was to demonstrate how to distinguish good music from bad reason. He tried to do this by aligning the idea
of music with other ideas he claimed to be rational—the structure of the

macrocosm and the microcosm, the universe, and the soul. He did all this as his solution to the pressing problem of deteriorating social order. Lawrence Hatab explains that the "Greek philosophical development of rational abstraction from the lived world" undertaken in the fifth century B.C.E. by Plato and others sought to reform "the contentious plurality of sensuous experience and existential concerns" that was conveyed in myths and epic poetry and which was also recorded in the terms that described the new music—*polychordia, polyharmonia, polyeidia, polyphōnia.*[95] Whereas myths and epics celebrated both human and divine worlds as pluralistic, dynamic, and unpredictable, Plato attempted to abstract and systematize concepts in order to create a universal monism.

Plato focused on the idea of "harmony" as the most decisive factor in the constitution of the macrocosm as well as microcosm. The word itself had an everyday meaning, referring to a joint in carpentry, a fitting together—without gaps—of two pieces of wood. In the plural, "harmonies" *(harmoniē)* appears in the *Iliad* and the *Odyssey* as a concept that denotes the process and result of uniting diverse and even opposing elements.[96] This concept was also personified in the figure of Harmonia, who was, according to the most popular legend, the daughter of Aries (the god of war) and Aphrodite (the goddess of sensual love). As her parentage discloses, she symbolized a unity of opposites, opposites that kept the universe as much in flux as in accord.[97] At some point, probably during the seventh century B.C.E., harmony as a word and idea came to be applied to music. How this happened is not clear, but the result was that by Plato's time the idea of harmony was accepted as a given in music, as it had already been in other contexts, and it was applied to music in several specific ways. Plato refers to all these applications, and—for the sake of solving the problem of good and bad music—depends on all their meanings.

In one simple application in (or before) the fifth century, *harmonia* designates the various tunings in common use for the kithara or lyre. In a second application, related to scales, a structure of pitches identified by ratios of string lengths, 6:8:12, for instance e-B-E (descending) was labeled by Archytas, last of the fifth-century-B.C.E. neo-Pythagoreans, as "the subcontrary mean, which they call harmonic"; it was in opposition to the "arithmetic mean" 6:9:12, for instance e-A-E. In a third application, the two means, harmonic and arithmetic, were combined, 6:8:9:12, for instance e-B-A-E, to form a rational framework for all Greek scales. This third application, called Pythagorean harmony, has been understood as a harmony in the sense of an interlocking join, in which two fifths, e-A and B-E—formed by the consecutive fourths e-B and A-E—overlap in the tone B-A.[98]

Plato, much influenced by neo-Pythagoreans such as Archytas, undertook to describe the creation of the universe in a famous passage of the *Timaeus.*[99] Not trusting the traditional creation myths of poets, Plato made up his own—

one that later was easily assimilated to Christian doctrine. In creating the world soul, the demiurge (Plato's mythical cosmic agent) combined sameness, difference, and an intermediate form he called "Being" to make the stuff of the cosmos. This demiurge sliced the cosmic stuff to form two axes, one laid out in the numbers 1, 2, 4, 8 (powers of 2, describing octaves in musical terms), the other 1, 3, 9, 27 (powers of 3, describing twelfths). The space between the numbers of each axes was "filled" (or divided) with Pythagorean harmony, that is, the combination of arithmetic and harmonic means that results in the ratios 2:3 (perfect fifth), 3:4 (perfect fourth), and 8:9 (whole tone). Finally he filled in each fourth (there are two in each Pythagorean harmony) with two whole tones each 8:9, along with the necessary remainder 243:256 (the semitone), to form the standard diatonic tetrachord [TTs].[100] The result is two cosmic strips each having the sequence of intervals of a diatonic scale. Having exhausted the mixture through this apportioning, the demiurge then performs various operations on this newly ordered stuff of the world soul (splitting, crossing, bending, splitting again, and spinning) that result in the orbits of the seven planets, the ratios of each corresponding to a tone within a seven-tone diatonic scale and their rates of speed corresponding to their position and tuning within tetrachords.[101] This, then, is the harmony of the spheres, the structure of the universe according to the kinds of mathematical relationships that the neo-Pythagoreans called "harmony."

Plato's purpose, clearly, is to find harmony existing in cosmic reality in a form that can be taken as a model for harmony within an individual soul. Thereby he can get from what *is* to what *ought to be*—for no reasonable person can deny that relationships within the soul ought to be similar to what they really, ideally, are. In the following passage from later in the *Timaeus,* Plato gets easily to the function of music in the proper relationship of the cosmos and the soul.

> All such composition as lends itself to making audible musical sound is given [by the gods] in order to express harmony, and so serves this purpose well. And harmony, whose movements are akin to the orbits within our souls, is a gift of the Muses, if our dealings with them are guided by understanding, not for irrational pleasure, for which people nowadays seem to make use of it, but to serve as an ally in the fight to bring order to any orbit in our souls that has become unharmonized, and make it concordant with itself. (47d)[102]

In *Phaedo,* Socrates disabuses his interlocutors of the popular idea that the "harmony" of the soul is an attunement of the body, arguing that the soul, rather than vibrating in accordance with the physical instrument of the body, "[rules] over all the elements of which one says it is composed, opposing nearly all of them throughout life, directing their ways, inflicting harsh and painful punishments on them . . . holding converse with desires and passions and fears as if it were one thing talking to a different one" (94d).[103] In light of this discussion in *Phaedo*, the quote from *Timaeus* (47d) suggests that the music taken in by the physical senses recalibrates the harmony of the soul through a metaphysical mimesis that tunes the soul to the cosmic scale (rather than to the physical body) so that the soul can supervise the physical body and the body's instincts in an ideal, essentially ascetic self-practice. Here we can glimpse the crisis that surfaces in the *Republic* and *Laws* concerning performed music, for if heard music recalibrates the soul, and the soul in turn controls human behavior, then musicians potentially have tremendous powers of persuasion over citizens. Hence, to the problem of telling good music from bad is added the question of who gets to tell.

The locus of these problems then becomes education. According to a passage from *Laws* (795d) regarding the education of children, "formal lessons will fall into two categories, physical training for the body, and cultural [musical] education to perfect the personality." In book 3 of the earlier *Republic*, Plato took pains to outline a program for the body and one for the psychic state, which in Plato's thought is so closely associated with music. Plato warns that "those who devote themselves exclusively to physical training turn out to be more savage than they should, while those who devote themselves to music and poetry turn out to be softer than is good for them" (410d).[104] But "music," or better "harmony," also describes the ideal mixture of these opposing disciplines: "The person who achieves the finest blend of music and physical training and impresses it on his soul in the most measured way is the one we'd most correctly call completely harmonious and trained in music, much more so than the one who merely harmonizes the strings of his instrument" (412a). Here Plato tries to foist off the problem of telling good music from bad onto a distinction between a performer and a philosopher, between practice and theory—an easier distinction to maintain and demonstrate. Plato can argue that mimetic relationships between music and the soul do not result from the activities of the quotidian musician just because he can harmoniously tune the strings of his instrument; rather, the true musician is one who achieves harmonious balance and, above all, moderation in the practice of the self.

Nonetheless, in the third book of the *Republic*, Plato does review current musical styles at the level of *technē*, musical craft. Through the narrator Socrates, Plato lays out a program to purge the overly luxurious city of the materials of sounding music that might have a deleterious effect on the balance of the young guardians. First he considers the melodic styles, dismissing the "mixo-Lydian" and "syntono-Lydian," which correspond to poetic lamentations (rejected earlier), and those Lydian and Ionian modes that accompany symposia filled with drinking, idleness, and "softness" (398d–e). Socrates, who professes not to know anything about the technical aspects of tunings and styles, declares he will permit only those modes that convey "the tone and rhythm of a courageous person" (that is, Dorian style) and men engaged "in peaceful, unforced, voluntary action" (Phrygian style). Similarly, only those rhythmic meters commonly used in poetry illustrating courage or a balanced disposition will be admissible (398a–400e).

Socrates then considers instruments, proposing to purge all those that are "poly-stringed" *(polychorda)* and "panharmonic" *(panharmonia)* (399d), and he lists a couple of these. He proclaims that the *aulos* (associated with Dionysus, and the new music of the day) is the most "poly-stringed" instrument of all, which the other "panharmonics" *(panharmonia)* imitate. Socrates finds the lyre and kithara (associated with Apollo, and the elite Athenian old guard) most acceptable for the city, and allows the syrinx for use by shepherds in the country—far from the city. The syrinx, however, as Pan's instrument, can rightly be called *"panharmonic."* But Plato here is referring to the musical innovations of *aulos* players that he feels are creating social and political havoc in Athens (namely, a democracy); and he might be implying that Dionysus and Pan have had a hand in this. Socrates notes, "we certainly aren't doing anything new in preferring Apollo and his instruments to Marsyas and his" (399e).[105] Plato's reference to the satyr Marsyas and not specifically to the deity Pan effects an important rhetorical move. Marsyas, as a mortal figure (and the first *aulos* player), audaciously challenged divine order and rule by daring to compete with Apollo in musical performance. Unlike Pan, he lost the competition, and as punishment Apollo flayed him alive. Marsyas's transgressive musical effrontery is, by virtue of the double meaning of *nomos,* also a transgression of the law.[106]

Later in the *Republic,* Socrates summarizes this association of music and law in his admonishment against musical innovations: "the guardians must beware of changing to a new form of music, since it threatens the whole system. The *tropoi* of music are never changed without change in the most important of a city's laws *(nomōn)*" (424c).[107] *Tropos* can either mean "mode" generically as "way," "manner," or "winding path"; or specifically a musical mode as a pitch scale, also called *tonos* and *harmonia.*[108] Thus Plato alludes to both performance practice and pitch content in his reference to music. Even though in this case the meaning of *nomōn* is clearly "laws" and not "songs," the dual meaning of *tropoi* nevertheless brings about a semantic slippage of "law" into "song" such that the "paths" or "practices" of music directly correlate with the "paths" or "practices" of the law.

In *Laws (Nomoi),* Plato fully exploits the double entendre of *nomos,* writing, "Let's assume we've agreed on the paradox: our odes *(odas)* have turned into laws *(nomoi)* [799e]. . . . However that may be, let's adopt this as our agreed policy: no one shall sing a note, or perform any dance-movement, other than those in the canon of public songs, sacred music, and the general body of chorus performances of the young—any more than he would violate any other 'nome' or law" (799e–800a).[109]

If both meanings of *nomoi*—songs and laws—are themselves in harmony, then the result is beneficial for the individual and, importantly, the state; if not, sounding *nomos* can adversely affect individuals and turn them against civic *nomos,* thus unleashing a disastrous and transgressive liberty. Plato acknowledges that music made by humans, even with the inspiration of the Muses, can produce bad psychic states. So the individual soul cannot be trusted to come into a harmonious relationship with the order of the macrocosm and microcosm of its own accord; nor are laws developed by reason sufficient to produce harmony in these relationships. Laws, once determined, have to be fostered through education, in order for tradition (conservatism as embodied in the elite) to be inculcated in the young.[110]

The more emphasis is placed upon conserving tradition, educating the young in order to maintain social order, the more problematic becomes the role of music, the more uncertain the role of reason in finding and producing the harmonious relationships presumed immanent in the macrocosm and microcosm. In the passage from *Timaeus* already quoted (47d–e), Plato said that harmony comes from the Muses, but can produce disorder unless used according to reason. Harmony, then, is not good in itself, but its goodness depends upon human behavior, our individual "fight to bring order to any orbit in our souls that has become unharmonized." The harmony that is experienced in music, and possibly understood there with the help of reason, is not exactly the same, nor automatically the same, as that harmony that is necessary for the well-being of the soul, and of the state.

Plato's attempt in *Timaeus* to deduce what *ought to be* harmony in the soul from what *is* harmony in the cosmos started out as an exercise in reason, but resorted finally to myth—his myth of creation. Elsewhere he seems to abandon the idea of a macro-micro mimesis, and rather puts his trusts in moderation, a simple discipline of desire. In a number of his dialogues, Plato contemplated and worried over the control of *erōs* within the traditional Athenian relation of teacher and pupil in the modality of *erastēs-erōmenos.*[111] For example, in the *Republic,* Plato says, "The right kind of love is by nature the love of order and beauty that has been moderated by education in music and poetry . . . [S]exual pleasure mustn't come into it. . . . [I]f a lover can persuade a boy to let him, then he may kiss him, be with him, and touch him, as a father would a son, for the sake of what is fine and beautiful" (403a–b). Music, here, is the agent of discipline and a guide to the fine and beautiful. In the *Symposium,* Plato offers a more comical critique of immoderate love, also involving music, but in a different way. At this drinking party, the guests entertain one another with their theories of love. Immediately after a lengthy, abstract disquisition by Socrates on love as desire for an unattainable ideal beauty and good, and its pursuit through philosophy, the renowned politician and general Alcibiades, here drunk and lovesick, bursts into the room. He recounts how in his youth Socrates displayed his own immoderate *erōs* by seducing him and other young men through philosophy. Curiously enough, Plato gives Alcibiades the last word on love in the *Symposium,* as Alcibiades proceeds to compare Socrates to famously suspect mythological musicians—the Sirens and, importantly, the satyr Marsyas.

> You are quite an aulos player, aren't you? In fact, you're much more marvelous than Marsyas, who needed instruments to cast his spells on people. . . . The only difference between you and Marsyas is that you need no instruments; you do exactly what he does, but with words alone. . . . [L]et anyone—man, woman, or child—listen to you or even to a poor account of what you say—and we are all transported, completely possessed. . . . [T]he moment he starts to speak, I am beside myself: my heart starts leaping in my chest, the tears come streaming down my face, even the frenzied Corybantes[112] seem sane to me. . . . [T]hat is exactly how this Marsyas here at my side makes me feel all the time . . . he always traps me, you see, and makes me admit that my political career is a waste of time, while all that matters is just what I most neglect: my personal shortcomings, which cry out for the closest attention. So I just refuse to listen to him; I stop my ears and tear myself away from him, for, like the Sirens, he could make me stay by his side till I die. (215b–216b)[113]

Alcibiades goes on to describe his efforts to woo Socrates "as if *I* were his lover and he my young prey" (217c). This transposition of the active and passive roles, along with the distraction away from civic responsibility, is analogous to the effect of the Sirens' song on Odysseus in relation to his crew and his family, and lays out material consequences for immoderate "musicality."

One wonders what kind of ethics Plato would have us learn from this vignette. Alcibiades, a charismatic and power-hungry member of the aristocracy who would eventually betray Athens, represents the failure of philosophy to educate precisely the sort of young man Plato envisions elsewhere as future leaders. But Socrates, too, seems tainted as the co-player in a "platonic" but nonetheless erotic relationship that reverses roles, thereby transgressing social order and endangering a young politician's career. In sum, platonic love, so disciplined by music (that is, philosophy), is a sexual tease.[114] The Muses and the Sirens are one and the same. This, then, is the queer result of the Socratic method: a music that heightens desire through philosophical discipline and calls into question prior determinations of self and identity.

From our vantage point in modern civilization, where music education is considered more of a luxury than a necessity in elementary school, it may be hard to comprehend Plato's passionate stance on musical practice; however, Plato's concept of music as a possible threat to education and the state resound in panic-ridden criticisms of popular music by conservative academics such as the classicist Allan Bloom (whose debt to Plato is self-conscious), and, as will be discussed in further detail in chapter 5, by members of the U.S. Senate in the 1997 hearing entitled *Music Violence: How Does*

It Affect Our Children. As with Plato, musicians—especially the figures of Mick Jagger (in Bloom) and Marilyn Manson (in the Senate hearing)—are targeted for their breach of gender and sexual categories and their excessive moral "liberty," which threaten the rupture of civic order. Bloom writes, "[Mick Jagger] played the possessed lower-class demon and teen-aged *satyr* up until he was forty, with one eye on the mobs of children of both sexes . . . [I]n his act he was male and female, heterosexual and homosexual . . . he was beyond the law, moral and political, and thumbed his nose at it" (emphasis added).[115] For Bloom, the music of this rock and roll satyr is exactly that *panharmonia* that offers too many scales for the young soul to emulate, which leads to a premature liberty of "sexual desire undeveloped and untutored." This "ruins the imagination of young people and makes it very difficult for them to have a passionate relationship to the art and thought that are the substance of liberal education."[116] Consequently, the expenditure of sexual passion for the satyr's music represents a costly configuration of one's soul, an excessive musical self-practice that exhausts the very stuff our being.

QUESTIONING CHANT

The Sirens, along with other mythic figures from classical antiquity, emerged anew as the first administrators of the burgeoning Christian religion struggled to define their religious practices and rituals against those of various pagan and Jewish cults. Clement of Alexandria (ca.150–ca. 215) turned the Odyssean episode into Christian allegory in which the Sirens' song represented the lure of pagan myths, distracting the hearts and minds of people from God; the mast represented Christ, to whom the pious should bind themselves.[117]

As with Plato, instead of romping around in the realm of myth, as gods and goddesses or legendary musicians, the forces of sex and music were now observed, in the light of an intensified inner awareness, to act within the self. For Christians of the first and second centuries, as Peter Brown notes, belief in the Resurrection suspended "the inflexible laws of the normal," the cycle of life and death that necessitated procreative sex; and this, in turn, opened the way for extreme forms of sexual prohibition and the renunciation of marriage, "providing the Christian Church with a distinctive code of behavior" in comparison to pagans and Jews.[118] In this context, then, Christianity presented a queer identity, one more concerned with the forms and meanings of sexual desire itself than with its procreative function.

During late antiquity and the Middle Ages, in ideas of Christian devotion and love, as in the medieval secular cult of love, there can be found some of the most forthright and vivid descriptions of music as being close to sexual feeling and activity, perverse or illegitimate, as well as forms of sexuality able to constitute a new identity. Early Church Fathers brought a broad, strong condemnation against performance with musical instruments and dance such as might be associated with Apollonian or Dionysian rituals.[119] Arnobius, a writer in the fourth century, offers a typical invective against what he regarded as the moral decadence (including homoeroticism) of instrumental music and dance.

> Was it for this that he sent souls, that as members of a holy and dignified race they practice here the arts of music and piping, that in blowing on the tibia they puff out their cheeks, that they lead obscene songs . . . under the influence of which a multitude of other lascivious souls abandon themselves to bizarre movements of the body, dancing and singing, forming rings of dancers, and ultimately raising their buttocks and hips to sway with the rippling motion of their loins? Was it for this that he sent souls, that in men they become male prostitutes, and in women harlots . . . ?[120]

On the other hand, some Christian writers found resources in music, especially in the words of the Psalms of David, useful not only for Christian worship but also actually to combat the idolatrous or lascivious effects they perceived in pagan music. In describing the good effects flowing from "spiritual psalms," John Chrysostom (ca. 347–407) seems to reference Orpheus's use of song as a musical shield against the Ciconian women. Here the psalms participate in a song war over the soul:

> Since this sort of pleasure is natural to our souls, and lest the demons introduce licentious songs and upset everything, God erected the barrier of the psalms, so that they would be a matter of both pleasure and profit. For from strange songs, harm and destruction enter in along with many a dread thing, since what is wanton and contrary to the law in these songs settles in the various parts of the soul, rendering it weak and soft. But from the spiritual psalms can come considerable pleasure, much that is useful, much that is holy, and the foundation of all philosophy, as these texts cleanse the soul and the Holy Spirit flies swiftly to the soul who sings such songs.[121]

Clement of Alexandria thoroughly appropriated and Christianized Plato's conception of a macrocosm constituted in accord with music and an analogous order in the microcosm. Clement (who likened Christ to the mast in the Siren episode) conceived of man as an instrument created in the image of the Lord, and the New Song as Christ, the Word of God, who tunes mankind, through salvation, to the divinely harmonious instrument that is God, just as Plato understood *harmonia* to be expressed in both the human and celestial levels of creation.[122] For Plato, of course, this attunement required a rigorous self-discipline—a careful negotiation and balance of the duality of *nomos*—and so, too, for the Christian faithful.

After two centuries (100–300) of free creativity in Christian worship and song, the fourth century brought a heightened degree of regulation, administered by a new power structure, best illustrated by the career of St. Ambrose (ca. 339–97), who was first a Roman governor, and later the bishop of Milan. With a zeal for legislation, what Ambrose and other church officials found in need of regulating was the fact that singing for public worship was done by individuals who might thereby experience or occasion private pleasure, or engage in public exhibitionism. And it was here, in the performance of individuals, that was observed the sexuality of which Clement and Arnobius, along with many others, had complained.[123]

The most eloquent and passionate account of this conflict of discipline and desire in music appears in the *Confessions* of Augustine. The *Confessions,* written between 397 and 401, recounts his tortuous path to conversion and baptism in 387 and his subsequent moral questioning of all sensual stimuli, even his fantasies, as a means of testing the purity of his intentions and discerning his internal, spiritual well-being. Near the time of his conversion, which he equates with the moment he renounces sex, Augustine fantasizes that his many sexual partners call to him, "plucking at my garment of flesh." But "the austere beauty of Continence" counsels him to "'stop your ears against your unclean members, that they may be mortified. They tell you of delights, but not of such as the law of the Lord your God tells.'" The Kirke and the Siren reference is close to the surface here. Augustine, like Odysseus, feels the erotic pull of his past life and the desire to question himself. "This was the controversy raging in my heart," he writes, "a controversy about myself against myself" (8.11).[124]

It is Augustine's writing on music that demonstrates the shift from an external space of myth to an internalized space of moral scrutiny, such that performing and listening always require surveillance. For Augustine, all music prompts an incessant questioning of desire and motive. While the mind wants to go toward the spirit and away from the flesh, the body is subject to appetites that disrupt an ideal, prelapsarian unity of body and soul. Such divisive desires were clearly signaled for Augustine by the involuntary erection.[125] The problem of the involuntary erection haunts much of Augustine's writings, both explicitly and implicitly, yielding a phallocentric discourse of asceticism and morality that, ironically, placed sexuality as central to the formation of subjectivity.

In book 14 of *The City of God* (ca. 413), Augustine presented his influential interpretation of the Fall of Adam and Eve (Genesis 3) as caused by the corruption of the human will by pride. As punishment, God bound man more closely to himself by binding his spirit to the flesh, which "by its disobedience [testifies] against the disobedience of man." After eating the fruit forbidden them, Adam and Eve suddenly know "their members warring against their will . . . a shameless novelty which made nakedness indecent."[126] Involuntary sexuality is not the original sin but the original punishment. Furthermore, it is reproduced in every generation and in all forms of wanted and unwanted physical arousal. Only through rigorous self-examination and the renunciation of all sexual practices and sensual appetites can one achieve a purity of intention and continence.[127]

In the view of Foucault, this created a new interior terrain for the practice of piety. The spiritual struggle consisted primarily of "turning our eyes continuously downward or inward in order to decipher, among the movements of the soul, which ones come from the libido."[128] Fredric Jameson has similarly argued that from this "space of a new inwardness," predicated upon "a new entity called sexuality," emerged another new concept—the Self—which linked sexuality and truth by way of subjectivity and asceticism.[129]

In Augustine's *Confessions,* music—specifically the music he hears in church—is a means of exploring that "space of new inwardness" where sexuality and piety paradoxically competed with and complemented each other in the formation of individual identity. Augustine has a strong emotional reaction to the songs he hears in church, which he describes: "I wept at the beauty of Your hymns and canticles, and was powerfully moved at the sweet sound of Your Church's singing. Those sounds flowed into my ears, and the truth streamed into my heart so that my feeling of devotion overflowed, and the tears ran from my eyes, and I was happy in them" (9.6). Yet he distrusts his response to it, as if it were lascivious pagan music. In the following passage we encounter another allusion to the Sirens in his rich description of being entangled *(implicaverant)* and yoked or subjugated *(subjugaverant)* by song.

> The pleasures of the ear did indeed entangle and yoke me more tenaciously, but You have set me free. Now when I hear those sounds *[sonis],* in which Your words breathe life, sung with sweet and skillful *[artificiosa]* voice, I do, I admit, find a certain satisfaction in them, yet not such as to hold me fast *[haeream],* for I can depart when I will. . . . I observe that all the varying emotions of my spirit have modes proper to them in voice and song, whereby, by some secret affinity, they are made more alive. It is not good that the mind should be enervated by this bodily pleasure. But it often deceives me *[fallit]* . . . [and] having been admitted to aid the reason, strives to run before and take the lead. (10.33)

The value of the Psalms of David is that they control the words, which otherwise let in false, dangerous doctrine. But when sung, they might still let in danger with the melody. And the psalm texts sung by the congregants cannot be expected to fill the needs of the entire service. St. Ambrose, in devising new forms of musical participation for the congregants, found one solution in *responsorium psalmi,* whereby the people repeat a short part of the psalm sung by the lector. Another solution, also attributed to Ambrose, was singing antiphonally (alternating phrases between two groups), especially using jubilation, the short wordless responses (oo's and ah's), which was a traditional practice of the people's musical performance.[130] But the oo's and ah's, not subject to verbal control, tap into purely musical individual feeling with all its dangers—something later chant reformists will recognize in melismatic chant performance. The following account from Augustine is usually taken by musicologists to refer to Ambrose's use of antiphonal singing.

> It was only a little while before that the church of Milan had begun to practice this kind of consolation and exhortation *[genus hoc consolationis et exhortationis]*, to the great joy of the brethren singing together with heart and voice *[fratrum concinentium vocibus et cordibus]*. . . . It was at this time that the practice was instituted of singing hymns and psalms after the manner of the Eastern churches. . . . The custom has been retained from that day to this, and has been imitated by many, indeed in almost all congregations throughout the world. (9.7)

Augustine's rhetoric—the *genus hoc consolationis et exhortationis* and the *fratrum concinentium*—also points to the musical practice of singing songs *quasi una voce*, many bodies coming together as one voice, producing one sound, and becoming one body (the Church). This musical doctrine, which resulted in what we call chant, is the best solution to the dangers of song, for the words are completely controlled—not necessarily by being from the psalms, but by preventing individuality.[131]

We can get a sense of Augustine's views on singing *quasi una voce* and *canticum novum* from a sermon he probably delivered in 403, shortly after completing his *Confessions,* for the Feast of Saint Cyprian the Martyr, that glosses Psalm 33 (32 in the Vulgate). In one passage Augustine seems to make another allusion to *una voce* congregational singing: "To such [upright believers] as these the psalm speaks in the following verses, inviting them to *confess to the Lord on the lyre, and sing psalms to him with the ten-stringed psaltery.* This is what we were singing just now, giving expression with voices in unison [or agreement; *ore consono*] to what was in our hearts, and as we did so this is what we were teaching."[132] Despite the scriptural references to instruments, Augustine quickly points out that the command to play the "lyre" should not be understood literally, writing, "None of you must think that we are meant to turn to the musical instruments of the theatre. All of us have within ourselves the means of doing what we are bidden."[133] Thus the pious Christian has internalized the pagan lyre, and the unison voice of the congregation is the lyric confession to God.[134]

Later in his sermon, Augustine engages in Plato-like maneuvering between two meanings of "song": the theological meaning of the "New Song" and the mystical yet practical meaning of singing to God.

> *Sing him a new song.* Strip off your oldness, you know a new song. A new person, a New Covenant, a new song. People stuck in the old life have no business with this new song; only they can learn it who are new persons. . . . *Sing him a new*

song, sing skillfully to him. Each one of us is anxious to know how to sing to God. Sing to him, yes, but not out of tune. We don't want to grate on his ears. . . . Which of us, then would volunteer to sing skillfully to God, who so shrewdly judges the singer . . . ? Do not worry, for he provides you with a technique for singing. Do not go seeking lyrics, as though you could spell out in words anything that will give God pleasure. Sing to him *in jubilation.*[135]

By "jubilation" he refers to the singing associated with rustic people and peasant workers. He writes, "think of people who sing at harvest time or in the vineyard, or any work that goes with a swing, when they begin to exalt in their joy in words of songs, but after a while they seem to be so full of gladness that they find words no longer adequate." As this and other idealized descriptions indicate, *jubilatio* for Augustine carries the valence of a naturalistic but nonetheless communal expression, one pure in intention and uncluttered by problematic words (he does not mean to implicate the psalms, but rather other types of lyrics).[136] Jubilation is an earthy "shout of joy" from the heart of clergy and commoners alike, "bringing forth what defies speech," namely, joy in God.[137]

This and other passages on wordless jubilation in his glosses of the psalms seem, on the surface, to contradict his perseveration in *Confessions* 10:33 about the sensual pleasures of music.[138] But the issue is still one of intention—especially the intention of a listener (not a performer, as it is with discussions of jubilation), even when listening to the Psalms of David in church. What does an individual response to music mean for measuring one's spiritual well-being? Augustine ponders and rejects radical solutions for both his own individual bodily freedom, and for the collective body of the Church:

Yet there are times when through too great a fear of this temptation, I err in the direction of overseverity—even to the point sometimes of wishing that the melody of all the sweet songs with which David's Psalter is commonly sung should be banished not only from my own ears, but the Church's as well. . . . Yet when I remember the tears I shed, moved by the songs of the Church in the early days of my new faith: and again when I see that I am moved not by the singing but by the things that are sung—when they are sung with a clear voice and most accordant [unified, orderly] rhythm *[cum liquida voce et convenientissima modulatione cantantur]*—I recognize once more the usefulness of this practice. Thus I fluctuate between the peril of indulgence and the profit I have found.[139]

This passage might seem to depend upon the notion, previously only implied in ancient discourse, that sounding music potentially creates a split between mind and body such that music's sensual gratification has the power to lead the mind astray from the words that engage the mind in piety. But *Confessions* 10:33 contains one remarkably specific description of musical performance—*"cum liquida voce et convenientissima modulatione cantan-*

tur"—which I believe is key. Many translations of this passage interpret *convenientissima* in a generic manner, to mean "appropriate" or "suitable";[140] however, the more apt meaning of the adjective *conveniens* is "agreeing" or "accordant" (from the verb *convenire*, "to come together," "unite"). Similarly, *modulatione* has also been translated generically as "melody" or "music," but it bears the connotation of the rhythmic aspect of performance rather than melodic—and Augustine's early treatise on rhythm, *De musica*, uses the word in this way.[141] We can read the passage as describing a performance that has a superlative quality of "coming together" or, as I have translated, "most accordant rhythm." This rhythmic description, together with the qualifying phrase *"liquida voce"* (*liquida* applied to the voice has the connotation of "clarity"), suggests the unison singing of the schola or congregation. Thus for the listener, as well as the performer, singing *quasi una voce* provides a solution to the problem of bodily engagement with music, one that aligns melody and words, and hence body and soul.

But Augustine's peace of mind can be attained only through a joining of the individual to the collective that ensures a pious reception of the music. At the heart of Augustine's concern, I believe, is not so much a split between mind and body as the splitting off of the individual body from the body of the Church through the distraction of self-gratification, which finds its strongest expression in *concupiscentia carnis* (lust of the flesh), but also, to a lesser extent, in the indulgence of other organs, such as the ears, eyes, and mouth (lust being generalized to all such pleasures). This stance is not inconsistent with his later idealizations of natural wordless jubilation, for jubilation describes a purity of motivation and intention, a divinely inspired spontaneous and unmediated sounding off that cannot be traced in the listener, but which can be encouraged by singing chant.

Regulating words and the singing of them *quasi una voce* does not solve the problem of inner conflict. Questions remain. Augustine remarkably ends his interrogation of aural pleasure in *Confessions* with an anguished cry over his experience of indecision regarding the pros and cons of hearing sacred songs. In desperation, it seems, he turns toward the collective as well as toward the divine, writing "Weep with me and weep for me, all you who feel within yourselves that goodness from which good actions come. Those of you who have no such feeling will not be moved by what I am saying. But do Thou, O Lord my God, hear me and look upon me and see me and pity me and heal me, Thou in whose eyes I have become a question to myself; and that is my infirmity" (10.33).[142] Here, as in the *Odyssey* and the writings of Plato, we find sounding music instigating a questioning of the self and a partitioning off of the individual from the social. From this incessant questioning is born a subjectivity that walks a fine line between ascetic and excessive self-practice, between a moral goodness and an infirmity of the soul.

In the second and third volumes of *The History of Sexuality,* Foucault traces three historical technologies of the self, each of which called for a different calculus of intellectual, physical, relational, and solitary ascetic practices. These technologies can be summarized as the Platonic "care of the self" for political ends, the Stoic "administration of the self," for aesthetic ends, and the Augustinian "hermeneutics of the self" for juridical ends.[143] Foucault explains that the "care of the self" described a finite period of learning for young men, especially those who had political aspirations but gaps in their education. Pedagogy was an occasion for sexual involvement between teacher and student; thus the young subject was not only subordinate, but essentially a receptacle, both intellectually and physically. The "care of the self," however, was the transition from youth to adulthood, from subordination to domination, the moment of potential, when the youth might also resist sexual advances as a display of self-mastery. The Stoic era shifted the telos of the earlier technology from politics to personal aesthetics, an art of life, of self-fashioning. One didn't simply take care of the gaps, rather one constantly practiced a type of self-creation. As his *Confessions* bear witness, Augustine inherited from the Stoic philosophers a confidence in the powers of human reason and will, after proper education and training, to make correct judgments between good and evil, and to order our desires accordingly. Marcia L. Colish has investigated how Augustine mitigated Stoic rationalism with a Christianized Neoplatonic transcendentalism in the notion that man's apprehension and practice of virtue depends upon his relationship to God, from whom springs all goodness. For Augustine, the application of judgment to the interior terrain of the self ultimately served to help one know and love God better, and to create a sustained contact with God through a united practice of mind and body.[144]

Though musical worship served as a technology of the self that united mind and body and directed both toward God, Augustine considered it a crutch that could potentially isolate the individual from the community of the faithful. For Hildegard of Bingen, as we shall see, musical worship was not simply a means to an end, but the end itself—not only the practice of unity, but the practice of an impossible subjectivity. Technologies of the self are really only available to those individuals who have sovereignty over themselves, namely adult free males—not slaves, not youths, not women—though not being a sovereign citizen within the power structure does not necessarily give one freedom from its laws. So applying this concept to Hildegard of Bingen and her nuns will have its gaps. But gaps are precisely the issue.

THE SINGING SELF

Much is known about the life of Hildegard of Bingen (1098–1179) from her many extant letters and writings and a biography written in the thirteenth century by two monks. Born to noble parents, she experienced visions in early childhood. At the age of eight she was committed by her parents to the monastery at Disibodenberg, where she learned Latin and read both sacred scriptures and the writings of the Church Fathers, including Augustine. In 1136, at age thirty-eight, Hildegard was elected *magistra* of the convent associated with the monastery, and five years later she began to record her visions, auditions, and revelations, after receiving a divine commission. Hildegard wrote on a wide array of subjects, leaving a substantial body of work: six major works, including creative, scientific, and contemplative writings; six minor works, such as biblical commentaries and accounts of saints' lives; and seventy-seven musical compositions. She also wrote letters to many important religious figures throughout Europe, and went on preaching tours. In 1147 Hildegard's mystical gifts were endorsed by the pope. Taking advantage of her growing fame as a healer and oracle, and running counter to the trends of monastic reform, which sought to dismantle independent convents, Hildegard and her nuns broke away from the monastery at Disibodenberg; together with her nuns she formed their own convent at Rupertsberg.[145] Her theological and devotional writings, as well as her image-rich gynocentric lyrics (which some observers regard as renegade, or homo-erotic),[146] can be understood as her own remarkable creative response to these cultural circumstances—circumstances that placed music, sexuality, and women in an ambiguous and ambivalent relationship to Christian mores.

Even though Augustine was most concerned with Adam's involuntary erection as the mark of original sin, it is Eve, the instigator of the Fall, who came to represent rampant sexuality and the corrupting body. Women, as well as men, could of course be assumed to experience involuntary arousal, but women's arousal could not be visually located. Nonetheless, "woman" was understood as sexuality incarnate; and furthermore, all sources of sensory pleasures, such as music, poetry, visual arts, and even food, came to be gendered as feminine.[147]

As the ultimate symbol of sanctified inwardness, the Virgin Mary not only redeemed (virgin) women from the curse of Eve, she also placed them beyond the physical, in the realm of the pure idea. But in this realm the relationship to the idea of sexuality was still strong. R. Howard Bloch notes that "in the patristic totalizing scheme of desire, there can be no difference between the state of desiring and of being desired": to look at, to speak of, to think about a virgin was to defile her.[148] Thus a true virgin must remain a signifier without a signified, an ideal, absolute virginity without an empirical referent. The Virgin, then, also connotes that internal, subjective space born of self-examination in light of sexuality. Indeed, how do we express the inexpressible, or show that which cannot be revealed, except through its seeming opposite, recognizing, in effect, the contamination of terms in a binary opposition? Thus sexuality points to virginity, and virginity, then, must also point to sexuality.

Hildegard's music and poetry frequently articulate this peculiar situation of virginity as sexuality by envisioning the interior space of the Virgin Mary's womb as materially and spiritually potent. In *O quam preciosa,* a responsory for the Blessed Virgin, Hildegard dwells on impregnation and birth, and the particular paradox of the initial bypassing of and then ultimate passing through the female genitalia.

> Verse 1 (solo):
> O quam preciosa est virginitas virginis huius,
> que clausam portam habet:
> et cuius viscera sancta divinitas calore suo infudit,
> ita quod flos in ea crevit.
>
> Respond (chorus):
> Et Filius Dei per secreta ipsius quasi aurora exivit.
>
> Verse 2 (solo):
> Unde dulce germen, quod Filius ipsius est,
> per clausuram ventris eius paradisum aperuit.
>
> Respond (chorus):
> Et Filius Dei per secreta ipsius quasi aurora exivit.
>
> (Oh how precious is the virginity of this virgin,
> who has a closed gate:
> and whose womb Holy Divinity suffused with his warmth
> so that a flower grew in her.
> And the Son of God through her secret passage came forth like the dawn.
> Hence the tender shoot, which is her Son,
> opened paradise through the enclosure of her womb.
> And the Son of God through her secret passage came forth like the dawn.)[149]

The poem describes the birth of Christ in terms of the Virgin's own series of erotic experiences: the initial security of her vaginal state (the "closed gate"); the divine insemination ("suffused with his warmth"); the expansion of her womb and the engorging of her genitals ("a flower grew in her"); the opening of her vagina and the orgasmic salvational ejaculation ("the Son of God came forth like the dawn through her secret passage"); and finally an ongoing pleasure in a type of reverse penetration from the inside out: Christ, the tender shoot, emerges from the Virgin's enclosed womb to penetrate the world and open paradise. One can, of course, read this poem with a purely patriarchal program; God the Father and Christ the Son—as alpha and omega—are initially and ultimately responsible for virginal/vaginal ecstasy and worldly salvation.[150] Hildegard, however, seems to make the actions of the divine Father and Son contingent upon the condition of Mary's vagina—her closed gate, her secret passage, the enclosure of her womb from which a shoot emerges. She clearly links expansiveness and growth (flowers, shoots, dawn) to the womb's initially sequestered state.

In a number of her writings Hildegard uses a second image—the image of music and musical instruments—to convey the sexual potency of Mary's womb. One striking example places the description in the mouth of the Virgin Mary herself: "O most beloved Son, to whom I gave birth in the womb by the force of the revolving wheel of the holy Godhead which created me and formed all my members and set up in my womb every kind of musical instrument in all the flowers of the modes."[151] The Virgin's womb is the location where music and sexuality are equated: to be a virgin is to be in a heightened state both sexually and musically, one term pointing to the other. To imagine music in the virginal womb is, then, to posit a specifically female embodiment of that conceptual space in which Augustine wrestled with the ethics of sexual and sensual appetites. In contrast to the Psalms of David, which inspired and provoked Augustine, Hildegard refers to a specifically female music through which the self reaches toward the divine. And if we imagine performing this music?

Many scholars have noted that Hildegard's chants are distinctive for their excessive style, filled with frequent dramatic leaps, long melismas, and ranges that often span more than two octaves. A few musicologists have counterbalanced such emphasis on Hildegard's idiosyncrasy by placing her choice of chant genres and melodic style into their musical and liturgical contexts.[152] Although chants for the Mass were fixed long before the twelfth century, antiphons and responsories for the Divine Office (the weekly cycle of daily psalm recitations practiced by all monastic communities) were frequently customized or newly written to fit the needs of a particular community. Hildegard wrote mostly for the Divine Office in the grand, expansive style characteristic of eleventh-century responsories and antiphons, especially the Marion antiphons, which she occasionally used as models.[153]

Responsories like *O quam preciosa*, sung at Matins, functioned as moments of communal musical meditation after a reading from the Scriptures, a saint's biography, or patristic literature. For Hildegard, who likely sang the solo intonation for her chants,[154] these musical moments signified the pinnacle of devotion, when the Holy Spirit inhabits the body and exposes the divine to the faithful. In accord with Augustine's Christianized Stoical ethics, and against the mysticism of her contemporary Bernard of Clairvaux, Hildegard believed that humans had the rational capacity to know God, and, as Constant Mews notes, she emphasized "the importance of correct living" rather than "grace conferred through the sacraments."[155] But for Hildegard, this knowledge was achieved fundamentally through a musical practice of piety:

And so the words symbolize the body, and the jubilant music indicates the spirit; and the celestial harmony shows the Divinity. . . . And as the power of God is everywhere and encompasses all things . . . so, too, the human intellect has great power to resound in living voices, and arouse sluggish souls to vigilance by song.

. . . And you also, O human, with your poor and frail little nature, can hear in the song the ardor of virginal modesty embraced by the blossoming branch; and the acuity of the living lights, which shine in the heavenly city; and the profound utterances of the apostles . . . and the procession of virgins, blooming in the verdancy of Heaven.[156]

Thus music arouses the soul for the purpose of knowing (through hearing) various mysteries of faith (note that virgins in bloom begin and end this list); furthermore, music can also be said to be incarnational, having the power to incarnate—in this case giving a "living voice" to the Holy Spirit. We saw in *O quam preciosa* that the Virgin Mary experienced a suffusion of "warmth so that a flower grew in her." The feast of the Annunciation, based on Luke 1:26–38, celebrates the insemination of Mary by the Holy Spirit. Medieval art depicts this event as simultaneous to the hail of the angel Gabriel: "Ave (Maria) gratia plena Dominus tecum" ("Hail you [Mary] who are full of grace, the Lord is with you" [Luke 1:28]). The Holy Spirit was typically represented as rays of heavenly light shining upon Mary, and also as a dove hovering over Mary's head or singing into her ear.[157] This latter motif is a redundant image that doubles Gabriel's already potent vocality.

Writing about the Annunciation, Hildegard describes how "the power of the Most High overshadowed her [Mary], for he so caressed her in his warmth that . . . he utterly cleansed her from all the heat of sin."[158] Elsewhere she directly relates warmth to sexual arousal in women, writing, "For if she did not have the fluid of fertility with heat, she would remain fruitless like dry ground. . . . [T]his fluid of fertility is not always inflamed into the ardor of desire in a woman, unless she has previously been touched by a man and so knows the passion of the ardor of desire; for desire in her is not as strong and burning as in a man" (*Scivias*, 2.3.22). Barbara Newman notes that for Hildegard, the heat of the Annunciation paradoxically cools and purifies the original sin of the Virgin's own conception. Newman writes "there is an unlike likeness between the fallen intercourse, with its ardor and moisture, and virginal union with the Spirit."[159] But just as important as the infusion of the Holy Spirit's cooling warmth is Mary's own utterance, "Ecce ancilla Domini fiat mihi secundum verbum tuum" (Behold I am the handmaid of the Lord; let it be done to me according to his word" [Luke 1.38]). One German depiction of the Annunciation from around 1290 shows the verbal exchange of Gabriel and Mary in scrolls; Gabriel's words fall to the ground while Mary's words float above her as if to represent their holiness. Only a dove intrudes

Example 1. Hildegard of Bingen, respond from *O quam preciosa* (ca. 1160), transcribed from the Riesencodex (Wiesbaden, Hessische Landsbibliothek, Hs. 2, f. 468).

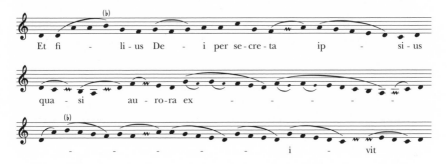

upon them, singing to Mary's inclined head.[160] Hildegard compares Mary's response to Gabriel with the creational utterances of God in Genesis: "Through the Word all creatures . . . came into being; and the same Word was incarnate of the Virgin Mary as in the twinkling of an eye, when she said with humility, 'Behold the handmaid of the Lord.' "[161]

Thus, according to Hildegard, music arouses the ardor of the soul and incarnates the Holy Spirit, just as masculine "heat" provides the warmth that arouses women's desire in the service of reproduction. So, too, the Holy Spirit filled the Virgin Mary with warmth through her ear with the Word, and Mary responded with her own words, thus begetting Jesus Christ, the Word Incarnate. The nuns through their singing become themselves like the Virgin Mary, suffused with the warmth of the Holy Spirit that comes to them through music, and they respond in kind, participating in an incarnational sonic loop, from voice to ear to voice. Though the Incarnation through Mary corrected the sins of Eve, singing was for Hildegard's nuns as much self-incarnation as *imitatio Mariae*.[162] For one "hears in the song the ardor of virginal modesty embraced by the blossoming branch . . . and the procession of virgins, blooming in the verdancy of Heaven."

The choral respond of *O quam preciosa* (example 1) offered one such embracing musical "blossoming branch" that allowed Hildegard's "procession of virgins" to perform and experience the incarnational "ardor of virginal modesty." Hardly a modest melody, this chant displays compositional procedures that, although not without precedent in the chant repertory, were used particularly frequently and effectively by Hildegard.[163] That musical language was characterized by a tight control of the final note over the organization of the other pitches, producing a goal-oriented melodic style that contrasted with the meandering, esoteric style of older chants.

We can divide this respond into two roughly equal halves. The first half consists of eight words, from *Et* to *aurora,* set in a modestly ornamented style in which each word is given a group of notes, up to a maximum of six. The second half, however, is a melisma, consisting of a single word—the verb *exivit*—extended through roughly ten note-groups, some as long as nine notes. The entire range of the chant (not shown in the example) spans a thirteenth (an octave plus a sixth, from a to f²). The leap of a fifth, from d to a¹, and the use of a¹ as a hovering point suggest that the chant is in the first ("authentic") melodic mode using the central modal octave d¹–d². But the respond explores the pitch-space of the tenth from a to c², which surrounds the d¹ final. This distribution of notes, with the final embedded in the middle of the range, is a feature of the second ("plagal") mode.[164] So Hildegard, in effect, pulls the low blossoming branch of the first mode into a space more characteristic of the second mode. Lowering the branch briefly at first, Hildegard just touches the low a in the first half; then she repeats and decorates the low a at the cadence point midway through the melisma.

The melisma is divided into two parts: after the midpoint cadence on the final (see the end of the second line of music), the melodic phrase that opened the respond, setting the words "Et Filius Dei," returns in decorated form to complete the melisma. This serves as a melodic reference point that sets up the rest of the melisma as a type of regeneration. Just before the change of syllables that will complete the action of the text ("[he] came forth"), Hildegard musically elaborates the vertical downward expansion as nearly every note-group falls dramatically.[165] The melisma ends with a remarkable series of three runs, incremental branchings down the scale of a stepwise descending figure: first the top note moves, then the bottom note, ending in a final flourish or "dawn" of a doubly ornamented and encircled final.

Hildegard's melisma over *exivit* is not only a musical meditation on the dawnlike emergence of Christ from the enclosed and secreted Virgin womb, but a manifestation of this process in space and time through a slow "birthing" and flowering of the final. The nuns, themselves in a state of ornate enclosure, singing in unison, musically aroused to spiritual ardor, perform through chant their impossible but sanctioned sexuality.

We can well imagine that the homosocial communal performance of these chants, which described, celebrated, and enacted a type of exclusive female sexuality, unleashed erotic energy among the participants.[166] Was their experience homoerotic, or autoerotic? Both erotic potentials were certainly available, but I believe these categories are inadequate for describing the complex sexual and self-reflexive religious fervor unique to these virgin nuns and inflamed by music. Music, as formulated by Hildegard, was not just a diffuse sexual practice of virginity (the "*ardor* of virginal modesty"), it was, more importantly, an ethical ontology—a technology of the self that produced, through musical "ardor," virginal *modesty.* It was through Mary's performance of virginal modesty, signaled by her utterance "Behold the hand-maid of the Lord," that she participated in the Incarnation. Although vir-ginity—however sexualized—was a female subject position authorized by patriarchal discourse, Hildegard's music and musical theology gave her nuns a means of verbal and material negotiation within the abstracting ten-dencies of that discourse.[167] With Mary's utterance, in addition to Christ's birth, as the model act, Hildegard's songs provided a solution to the onto-logical crisis of her nuns' impossible, gaping identity. For Hildegard and her monastic charges, singing cooled and disciplined virginal ardor as it sub-stantiated (and instantiated) virginal modesty, filling their ears and their wombs, and transforming them from aesthetic signifiers to ethical subjects.

Another virginal icon, in addition to Mary, figures prominently in Hilde-gard's oeuvre. She is Saint Ursula, a Christian princess from the British Isles who led a troupe of virgin handmaidens (anywhere from five to eleven thousand, depending on the source) on a pilgrimage to Rome. They were all slaughtered by Attila the Hun because Ursula refused to become his concubine. Ursula was of local importance in Disibodenberg, but no doubt Hildegard felt an affinity with this particular saint as a strong woman, convinced by faith to become a leader of many young virgin women. *O Ecclesia,* one of her most impressive sequences dedicated to Saint Ursula, contains a remarkably dense networking of individual and collective identity, and it illustrates the central position of com-munity in Hildegard's musical theology. The first stanza presents a mystical per-sonification of the church, Ecclesia, whose body parts are described in the boldly erotic and geographic language found in the Song of Songs.

O Ecclesia,
oculi tui similes saphiro sunt,
et aures tue monti Bethel,
et nasus tuus est sicut mons mirre et thuris,
et os tuum quasi sonus aquarum multarum.

(O Church your eyes are like sapphire, and your ears like Mount Bethel, and your nose is like a mountain of myrrh and incense, and your mouth is like the sound of many waters.)

Compare this with the Song of Songs 7:4:

Your neck is like a tower of ivory
Your eyes are like the pools in Heshbon,
        by the gate of Bath-rabbim:
Your nose is like the tower of Lebanon,
        that looks toward Damascus.[168]

The Song of Songs is a dialogue between two lovers, which theologians, beginning with Origen (ca. 185–254), understood as an allegory for the Church and Christ, united as bride and bridegroom in a mystical marriage.[169]

Stanza three of Hildegard's chant continues to reference the Song of Songs through this allegorical tradition, and also mingles the voice of Ursula, an individual, with the corporate identity of Ecclesia as the Bride of Christ.

> In multo desiderio desideravi ad te venire
> et in celestibus nuptiis tecum sedere,
> per alienam viam ad te currens
> velut nubes que in purissimo aere
> currit similis saphiro.

> (In great yearning, I have yearned to come to you and at the heavenly wedding feast sit with you, running to you by a strange path, like a cloud that in the purest air, runs like sapphire.)

The recurring simile of sapphires, in stanza one for the eyes of Ecclesia (the Bride) and in stanza three for Ursula's path to God, links these two female figures through a shared lexicon. Ursula's path, however, is "strange." *Alienam* carries a range of valences, from "foreign" and "hostile" to "incongruent" and "insane"; its meaning becomes clear with the following stanzas.

The sequence continues with a description of Ursula being ostracized by a crowd of people who began to "mock her in great symphony until the fiery burden fell upon her" (*ceperunt ludere cum illa in magna symphonia, usque dum ignea sarcina*, stanza 5). This image recalls the mocking of Christ as he carried the cross, which literarily unites the bodies of Ursula and Christ. Hildegard thus depicts Ursula as the pious individual choosing a path to God that alienates her from the social collective. Yet this hostile social body is no match for the collective body of Ecclesia and the martyred virgins, whose sacrifice represents the consummation of the mystical wedding and a triumph over the *magna symphonia*. The heavenly host responds to her martyrdom with their own song (stanzas 9–10):

> Wach! rubicundus sanguis innocentis agni
> in desponsatione sua effusus est.

> Hoc audiant omnes celi
> et in summa symphonia laudent Agnum Dei,
> quia guttur serpentis antiqui in istis margaritis
> materie Verbi Dei suffocatum est.

> (Ach! the scarlet blood of the innocent lamb is poured out in her betrothal. Let all the heavens hear this and in supreme symphony praise the Lamb of God, because the throat of the ancient serpent in these pearls from the matter of the Word of God is strangled.)

Though the hostile strains of the earthly *symphonia* are great, they are not robust with the Word of God, which has given matter and heft—indeed, has incarnated—the virgin martyrs (symbolized as a string of "pearls") whose sacrifice redeemed the sin of Eve (symbolized by the ancient serpent) and inspired the *summa symphonia* of the heavenly host.

Hildegard did compose modest melismas over the words *summa symphonia*, but she reserved her musical peaks, reaching a tenth above the a final, for phrases that link the bodies and fates of Ursula and Ecclesia: "and your mouth like the sound of many waters" (stanza 1); "like a cloud that in the purest air, runs like sapphire" (stanza 3); and, "until the burden of flame fell upon her" (stanza 6).[170] These points of *summa symphonia* in the unison singing of her nuns physically realize the allegorically mingled identity of Ursula and Ecclesia.

The tale of Ursula might also be considered an allegory for Hildegard and her nuns, and how virginal sexuality becomes an ethical actuality. As Christians, Hildegard and her nuns were subjects in a state of patriarchal domination by husbands, priests, and bishops. As monastics, they were a step removed from husbands and bishops. In her break with the monks of Disibodenberg and through her musical theology, Hildegard, like Ursula, led her nuns to further material and ideological independence from patriarchal structures.[171]

ROMANTIC LOVE AND MUSICAL SELF-INVENTION

Julia Kristeva notes that the musical dialogue of the Song of Songs occurs between a female lover, whose voice dominates, and her absent beloved male object, identified as Solomon. Both lover and beloved conjure up each other through erotic fantasies and metaphors linked to flora, fauna, and geography, in which, Kristeva finds parallel functions of incantation and incarnation:

> Because of its corporeal and sexual thematics ("My Beloved thrust his hand / through the hole in the door; / I trembled to the core of my being"— 5:4), indissolubly linked with the dominant theme of absence, yearning to merge, and idealization of the lovers, sensuality in the Song of Songs leads directly to the problematics of incarnation. The loved one is not there, but I experience his body; in a state of amorous incantation I unite with him, sensually *and* ideally.[172]

Through self-incantation, then, the female lover can conjure up the male beloved so vividly that he seems to stand incarnate before her. This metaphorical reading is analogous to the familiar Christian allegorical one: the woman's love and desire for Solomon becomes man's love and desire for a distant God. The idea springs easily from the metaphorical language of the Song of Songs; as Kristeva puts it, "how can it indeed be avoided, if I love God, if the loved one is, beyond Solomon's body, God himself?"[173]

The distant beloved became a central element in the troubadour love lyrics and the cult of love that emerged in southern France in the first quarter of the twelfth century, and later spread northward. These medieval songs about "courtly love," as the phenomenon was labeled in the late nineteenth century, concerned a stereotypic scenario from which many variations sprang. The troubadour, a young man of the court, socially and perhaps geographically remote from the object of his sexual desire, proclaims his love and devotion despite the numerous obstacles that make consummation unattainable. The obstacles are frequently identified as rival courtiers who act as scandalmongers or false flatterers, as well as the beloved's own neglect or haughtiness. The love is clandestine, for the union of lover and beloved imagined in these love lyrics is fundamentally outside marriage, and hence illegitimate. It is this illegitimacy that paradoxically renders the love of the troubadour as *fin'amor*, a love made chaste, pure, and "noble" through the threat of social censure. And it is the lover's *fin'amor* that provides him, in fantasy, with class mobility, which elevates his social standing among his rivals.

The encoding of feudal concerns in the love relationship is further supported by language describing various qualities of "courtliness" *(cortezia)*, attributed to the woman, the poet, or the poem itself. These qualities include generosity *(largueza)*, worth *(pretz)*, excellence *(proeza)*, moderation or self-restraint *(mesura)*, and youthful potential *(joven)*, as well as the imagined erotic fulfillment of desire *(joi)*. The songs also use metaphors that equate the act of singing *(cantar)* with loving *(amar)* and composing *(trobar)*, recalling the incarnational language (better, self-incarnational language) of the Song of Songs. To be a troubadour, in these songs, is to compose words and melodies that incarnate the beloved in song, seeming to bring the beloved vividly before him (and us); but then the troubadour also brings himself— as troubadour lover—before us in the same song. For example, one song by Bernart de Ventadorn (fl. 1145–75) begins:

Chantars no pot gaire valer	Singing can hardly be of worth
si d'ins dal cor no mou lo chans,	if the song does not come from within the heart,
ni chans no pot dal cor mover	nor can song come from the heart
si no·i es fin'amors coraus.	unless there be noble love in it.
Per so es mos chantars cabaus,	Hence is my singing supreme,
qu'en joi d'amor ai et enten	for in love's joy I hold and direct
la boch'e·ls olhs e·l cor e·l sen.	my mouth, my eyes, my heart, my feeling.

Bernart directly relates the value of the song to the sincerity and noble quality of the troubadour's love, the love that in turn controls his creative faculties (mouth to sing, eyes to gaze on the beloved, heart as the organ of feeling), all of which somatically express his "joy of love" *(joi d'amor)*. Thus both love and the troubadour become incarnated through the song.

The female beloved in these poems often does not appear until a later stanza; in Bernart's poem she finally arrives in stanza six (of seven).[174]

Mout ai be mes mo bon esper	Right well have I placed my good hope
cant cela·m mostra bels semblans	when she shows me her fair face
qu'eu plus dezir e volh vezer;	whom I most desire and long to see;
francha, doussa, fin'e leiaus,	pure, gentle, noble and loyal,
en cui los reis serïa saus,	in whom the king would be saved,
bel'e conhd'ab cors covinen,	lovely and graceful, with pleasing body,
m'a faih ric ome de nïen.	she has made me a rich man from nothing.[175]

Here, poetic incarnation and feudal language combine to conjure a beloved of such purity and nobility that she, like the Blessed Virgin Mary, subordinates kings (which, in turn, leads to their spiritual salvation). The last line, however, reveals the denouement of this stanza: the beloved as an object of such supreme value elevates the troubadour-lover to the level of a rich man, on a poetic par with a king.

In singing his song of passionate devotion, the troubadour is not only ideally incarnate, but really so, physically present to an all-male audience of rival courtiers, noble patrons, and perhaps even the legitimate spouse of his beloved. Given that the female beloved, on the other hand, is never really present, this suggests that the clandestine heterosexual intrigue is a facade, an image. In such a reading the erotic unattainability of the beloved can be understood as an allegory, one running exactly parallel to the medieval reading of the Song of Songs, in which the soul desires union with the male figurehead of Christ (and ultimately God). Guided by this parallel, we can see the troubadour's "lady" as a figure for the real object of desire, really incarnate before the singer: the feudal lord.[176]

The love songs of the troubadours reveal a "traffic in women" between men, but of a particularly abstract kind. Kinship ties are created through the giving of women as gifts in marriage; feudal ties are created through the conduit of the desired lady, with whom marriage is expressly forbidden.[177] In the feudal context, as Simon Gaunt points out, "composing and performing *cansos* takes place within the hierarchical social world of the court, a space riven with rivalries between men and governed by rituals designed to differentiate men within a carefully gradated hierarchy." He goes on to note that in the shortened stanzas that end most troubadour songs, called *tornadas* in Occitan (and *envois* in Old French), "the fiction of a man addressing a woman in the troubadour lyric is frequently belied by signs that the real *destinataires* of the songs were other men."[178] The *tornadas* are lines of direct address, either to the intended recipient of the song or to an intermediary who will take the song to the intended party. But it is noteworthy that they also call attention to the song itself as a vehicle for the troubadour's identity. *Chantars no pot gaire valer* ends with two *tornadas:*

Lo vers es fis en naturaus,	The poem is true and perfect,
e bos celui que be l'enten,	and good for him who understands it well,
e melher es, qui·l joi aten.	and better for him who awaits joy.
Bernartz de Ventador l'enten,	Bernart de Ventadorn understands it,
e·l di e·l fai, e·l joi n'aten.	and says it, and composes it, and awaits joy from it.[179]

The first *tornada* implies a male audience with its promotion of the song as a sort of litmus test for discerning courtly men: the song is good for those who understand it superficially, but better for those who understand the *joi*— the imagined fulfillment of desire—that the song expresses. The second *tornada* functions as the troubadour's signature as well as his self-incarnation through the song. The final line *(e·l di e·l fai, e·l joi n'aten)* harks back to the final line of the first stanza *(la boch'e·ls olhs e·l cor e·l sen),* which described love's power to animate his body and heart, making his singing supreme. In the last lines of the entire lyric we hear how Bernart himself—not *fin'amor*— animates the song, making love supreme by the *joi* that the song will deliver. Thus the *joi* for which the other men wait is the *joi* generated by Bernart's song. In actual experience, transport of music might be hard to distinguish from transport of sex, or music from romantic love.

Among the troubadours of the late twelfth century, Arnaut Daniel (fl. 1175–1200) was singled out for his poetic craft and craftiness, and honored by later generations of poets such as Dante, Petrarch, Tasso, and Ezra Pound. In Dante's *De vulgari eloquentia* (1303–5), a treatise on poetic composition, Arnaut is named as one of the finest vernacular poets on the theme of love (2.2.8). Dante also pays a special tribute to Arnaut in the *Purgatorio* (after 1307), which will be discussed below. According to his *vida,* Arnaut came from Ribeirac in the Limousin region (southwestern France) and was a member of the nobility (probably lesser nobility) who "had learned letters well." His reputation as an educated man is borne out in an existing miniature that depicts him in clerical garb. His *vida* also states that "he delighted in composing in *caras rimas* (difficult rhymes), which is why his songs are not easy to listen to or learn" *(e deleitet se en trobar et en caras rimas, per que las soas chanssos non son leus ad entendre ni ad aprendre).*[180] A satirical poem written by the Monk of Montaudon (ca. 1190) echoes this sentiment:

There are seven with Arnaut Daniel
Who in all his life did not sing well,
Only foolish words that nobody understands;
Since he chased the rabbit with an ox

And swam against the swelling tide,
His singing isn't worth a hawthorn pip.[181]

In these verses, the monk cleverly integrates Arnaut's own most famous and enigmatic signature *tornada* from *En cest sonet coind'e leri,* also quoted in his *vida:*

Ieu si Arnatuz, q'amas l'aura,	I am Arnaut, who hoards the wind
e chatz la lebre ab lo bou,	and chases the rabbit with the ox
e nadi contra suberna.	and swims against the swelling tide.[182]

As these contemporaneous anecdotes demonstrate, Arnaut gained a reputation as an obscurantist and an innovator within the style known as *trobar clus* (closed or "hermetic" composition); sometimes he blended this style with the *trobar plan* or *leu* (plain, polished, or simple composition) most often associated with Bernart de Ventadorn.[183] *Trobar clus* was characterized by recondite vocabulary, rare rhyming sounds, complex rhyming schemes, word echoes that locked stanzas into a particular order, esoteric metaphors, and convoluted word games. *Trobar leu,* by contrast, described a relatively accessible, uncomplicated style—though, as we saw with Bernart's *Chantars no pot gaire valer* above, one that plays its own games of meaning.

Arnaut Daniel's song *Chansson do·il mot son plan e prim,* one of the two songs that survive with music, offers a perfect example of his learned *trobar clus* style.[184] This song features a series of rhymes (aaabbcddc) that seems as though it ought to be predictable but, unaccountably, is not; it also features a pattern of irregular line lengths (88444 6'4 4 6'), a word echo between the last sentence of the stanza and the first sentence of the following stanza *(coblas capfinidas),* and difficult rhyming sounds that change their pattern every two stanzas (*coblas doublas* with the exception of the c rhyme) but utilize the same sounds in every stanza *(coblas unissonans).* In short, this poem is a tour de force of poetic skill. Table 1 illustrates the cycling through of rhyme sounds in the six stanzas and *tornada.*

About one hundred years separate the presumed dates of composition for Arnaut's songs and the dates of the written sources for them, which makes it impossible to identify the melody as the troubadour's own creation; this is especially so if the melody has only one manuscript witness, as is the present case. The poetic theme of composing and singing as an ideal means of expressing desire had little to do with the practicalities of medieval secular musical life. The mutable relationship between words and music in the written documents renders more tenuous the relationship between creator and creation—a weak link often addressed in the signature *tornadas* and perhaps in the very idea and practice of *trobar clus* itself.[185]

The surviving melody for *Chansson do·il mot son plan e prim* (example 2)

TABLE 1. Rhyme sounds in *Chansson do·il mot son plan e prim*

Line	Stanzas			Tornada
	I/II	III/IV	V/VI	
1	a	b	d	c
2	a	b	d	b
3	a	b	d	b
4	b	d	a	c
5	b	d	a	
6	c	c	c	
7	d	a	b	
8	d	a	b	
9	c	c	c	

seems itself to be somewhat hermetic. It has A as the central organizing pitch and final, but the pitches that close lines within the stanzas seem to bear no particular relationship to the pattern of rhymes. There is no schematic repetition of phrases, with the possible exception of the strong resemblance between the second and last phrases; but even this association is thrown off by a B-flat in the penultimate line, which shifts the tonal orientation. The melody does, however, produce its own "reading" of the poem. The tonal momentum and undulating melodic profile of the first two phrases suggest performing enjambment through lines three and four, and five and six. This often makes rhetorical sense, but it obscures the rhyme scheme and syllable count, running over the second "b" rhyme and rendering the third line ending an orphan in each stanza (thus aabcddc). Of course, the embedded "b" rhyme does receive a strong sonic boost as it falls on the organizing pitch A, and the movement of that third-line orphan rhyme to the pride of place at the beginning of subsequent stanzas could itself seem a clever play with rhyme sounds that motivates a musical realization.

The poem features an intense contemplation of the "stuff" of songs and the craftsmanship of composition.

I.

Chansson do·il mot son plan e prim	A song in which the words are plain (smooth, clear) and prime (fine, elegant)
farai puois que botono·ill vim,	I'll make since the twigs are now in bud,
e l'aussor cim	and the highest tops
son de color	are in color

Example 2. Arnaut Daniel, *Chanzon do·l moz son plan e prim* (ca. 1200), transcribed from troubadour manuscript G (Milan, Biblioteca Ambrosiana, R 71 Superiore, 73v).

de mainta flor,	with many a flower,
e verdeia la fuoilla,	and the leaves are green,
e·il can e·il braill	and the songs and the cries
son a l'ombraill	of the birds
dels auzels per la *broilla*	are heard in the shadows through the *groves.*

II.

Pelz *bruoills* aug lo chan e·l refrim   Through the *groves* I hear the song
                                            and the refrain

e, per so que no·m fassa crim,	and, so that nobody may reproach me,
obre e lim	I work and I file
motz de valor	words of great value
ab art d'Amor	with the artistry of Love,
don non ai cor qe·m tuoilla;	from which I have a heart that will never waver;
que si be·is [be·m] faill,	for if Love fails me
la sec a traill	I still follow on her trail,
on plus vas mi s'orguoilla.	even where she shows me greater pride.

The first stanza joins the theme of composition with another common theme, spring, in which the fruition of nature signifies the potential fruition of love. Arnaut directly links his song making to the season; his craftsmanship with words emerges as if part of the flowering and singing of nature. Stanza two continues this vital linkage of song and nature, but now the song and refrain are *of nature,* the raw materials from which he fashions through the "art of Love" *(art d'Amor)* "words of great value." Love, however, acts as a muse who can abandon the poet and thus diminish the value of his artistry. A subtle paradox is at work: love as craft shapes the song from love in nature (springtime), but the quality of the poet's song also provides a measure of the poet's unwavering heart, his devotion to love, which is conflated with his constant pursuit of art. Thus greater artifice demonstrates greater sincerity.

Arnaut addresses this paradox in the following two stanzas, in which he distinguishes his song from those of prideful "jabberers" *(janglor)*.

III.

Petit val orguoills d'amador	Of little value is the *pride* of any lover
que leu trabucha son siegnor	that easily lays low its lord
del luoc aussor	from the highest place
jus el terraill	down to the ground
per tal trebaill	through such suffering
que de joi lo despuoilla;	that it will strip him of all joy; ·
dreitz es lagrim	it's right that he should cry
et arda et rim	and burn and crack [rhyme]
qi'n contra Amor janguoilla.	who contrary to love *jabbers.*

IV.

Ges per janglor no·m vir aillor,	Never as a *jabberer* do I turn aside,
bona dompna, ves cui ador;	good lady, whom I adore;
mas per paor	but through fear
del devinaill,	of others' divining [or: of gossip],
don jois trassaill,	from which joy is quaking,

fatz semblan qu no·us vuoilla;	I give the appearance of not wanting you;
c'anc no·ns gauzim	for we never enjoyed ourselves
de lor noirim;	with their patronage [or: nourishment];
mal m'es que lor acuoilla.	it is painful for me to welcome them.

These two stanzas tangle the pairing of artifice and sincerity with another pair, appearances and linguistic deception. In stanza three Arnaut indicates that pride and insincere poetry will rob the poet of *joi* and reduce his poetry to jabbering, which he indicates through a clever pun using the two meanings of the word *rimar*, to burn or crack, as well as to rhyme. Thus we can read the last three lines of stanza three as mocking poets who artificially exaggerate their feelings, who "cry and burn and rhyme" and whose rhymes "crack" and "jabber." Yet in stanza four, Arnaut presses poetic artifice into the service of stealth and deception, which protects the *joi* of the lovers. Just as the troubadour carefully sculpts his song out of natural material into *art d'Amor*, so must he likewise fashion his natural adoration (*ardor*, as opposed to the *arda* of the jabberers) into a social semblance of its opposite: sincerity thus is equated with deception. The feudal concern voiced in the last three lines causes the *bona dompna* and the carefully wrought *chansson* to converge, for the livelihood of the troubadour, which compromises both his *art d'Amor* and his *joi d'Amor*, ultimately depends upon the male social networks of the court.

Despite the critique of prideful lovers in stanza three and the concern for appearances in stanza four, the final two stanzas and the *tornada* of this song turn the courtly values of *mesura* and *pretz*—of (sexual) restraint and worth—on their heads with boldly explicit language and metaphors.

V.

Si be·m vau per tot a es[t] daill,	Although I move through all in this fashion [or: as a scythe]
mos pessamens lai vos assaill;	my thought leaps out to you over there;
q'ieu chant e vaill	for I sing and I am strong
pel joi qe·ns fim	because of the joy we had
lai on partim;	over there where we parted;
mout sovens l'uoills mi muoilla	very often my eyes grow wet
d'ira e de plor	with anger and with tears
e de doussor,	and with tenderness,
car per joi ai qe·m duoilla.	for through joy I have what may grieve me.

VI.

Er ai fam d'amor, don badaill,	Now I hunger for love, for which I gape,

e non sec mesura ni taill:	and I don't follow moderation or curtailing:
sols m'o egaill!	if only I may be equal to it [or: if love pays me equally for it]!
C'anc non auzim	For we have never heard
del temps Caym	since the time of Cain
amador meins acuoilla	of a lover who would less welcome
cor trichador	a trickster or deceptive heart;
ni bauzador;	
per que mos jois *capduoilla!*	so that my joy is ever *mounting!*

Tornada

Bella, qui qe·is destuoilla,	Beautiful, whoever else may turn aside,
Arnautz dreich cor	Arnaut runs straight ahead
lai o·us honor,	over there to honor you
car vostre pretz *capduoilla!*	for your value is ever *mounting!*

Although the meaning of the first line of stanza five is disputed, we can understand in any case a shift from a theme of deception to one of radical disclosure about a past moment of *joi* fulfilled; a sexual union between lover and beloved that fortifies the troubadour and keeps him singing. Yet his display of emotion (anger, tears, tenderness) and the typical antithesis of joy and grief in the last line seem to parallel the weeping, burning, and cracking/rhyming of the prideful jabberers in stanza three. Stanza six continues with more radical disclosures, including the rejection of *mesura,* and the prideful boasting of the lover who does not "welcome" *(acuoilla)* trickery or deception, just as he felt pain to welcome the gossipers (see stanza 4). And it is this portrait of the poet himself as the *amador,* utterly deserving (either as *egaill* or of *egaill*) of love, that yields what certainly seems a sexual innuendo in the line "*mos jois capduoilla*" (my joy is ever mounting). This line is echoed in the *tornada* in reference to the addressee, Bella, about whom he writes "*vostre pretz capduoilla*" (your value is ever mounting).[186] The twin events of *capduoilla* provide the poetic refrain that links lover and beloved in a sexualized economy of feudal relationships: the mounting joy of the troubadour, whose somatic expression of *joi* and *pretz* is the song, in turn elevates the *pretz* of his beloved, which will reflect back onto him. In this way, the beloved and the song serve identical functions: Bella could be the lady or the *chansson.*

The *tornada* makes another important comparison, however, between "those who turn away" *(destuoilla,* also "deviate" or "detour") and "Arnaut who runs straight" *(dreich).*[187] R. Howard Bloch notes that grammarians and rhetoricians from late antiquity to the thirteenth century made distinctions between plain or simple discourse and ornate or figurative discourse that involved metaphor and the use of tropes, and that some writers imagined this dichotomy in linear terms. He writes that John of Salisbury, in his *Metalogicon* (1159), "associates grammar with a highway or straight path"; "errors of speech are the equivalent of 'forsaking the proper thoroughfare.'" Bloch further explains that "among the rhetoricians and grammarians of the thirteenth century, it is impossible to separate the *ornatus difficilis* from the general technique of amplification by periphrase. . . . [E]laborate poetic ornament is thus equated not with 'straight writing' (orthography) but with 'circular writing' (circumspection)."[188] Arnaut constructs a final deception that in fact leads us back to the beginning of the lyric, and thus secures a metaphorical reading of the Bella of the *tornada* as the song itself. For Arnaut's verbal path is far from "straight," and those who "deviate" from Bella are those who would not create an *art d'Amor* that would honor and increase his or her worth. In other words, the only straight path for a true poet is a circuitous one; the only way to make a song *"plan e prim"* (clear and fine) is to make it *"clus."*

Bloch describes the *trobar clus* as "a discourse which seems not only to refuse any representational function but to revel in such a refusal . . . as its name implies, closed upon itself, self-referential, disruptive of linguistic integrity." He goes on to argue that this signifies something tantamount to "a fornication with language that stretches meaning to its limits, and sometimes beyond."[189] The conceptual link between poetry and sexual perversity lies close to the surface in Allan of Lille's famous diatribe against sodomy, *De planctu naturae* (ca. 1160–70). Allan likens sodomy to grammatical "vice" *(vitium)*, the improper use of words paralleling the improper use of bodies.[190] The figurative language in the *trobar clus* forms the linguistic equivalent of infidelity—or, worse, sodomy, for the hermeticism of *trobar clus* can be considered nonprocreative. It results in bastard meanings, deviant linguistic offspring that cause a detour or a break in the connection of word and thing—in other words, jabbering.[191] Indeed, the intense circular fetishizing of the song and its figurative language in Arnaut's *Chansson do·il mot son plan e prim* finds an analog in the circular recycling of the rhyme sounds—the incessant "musical" repetitions that show off the skill of the poet but also threaten to outperform verbal semantics by sheer sensory overload, and to reduce his poetry to *janguoillan*.

Nowhere is such a virtuosic display of poetic music more in evidence than in Arnaut's famous sestina *Lo ferm voler q'el cor m'intra*, a poem that Dante emulated with his early sestina *Al poco giorno e al gran cerchio d'ombra*. The literature on Arnaut's sestina is ample, so I will only mention a few important details here. In this poem, probably the first of its kind, Arnaut not only recycled and systematically shuffled the same rhyme sounds for every stanza, but he also used the same six rhyme words, thus creating a narrower circulation of sound while at the same time forcing a broader network of meanings for each word. All six words together present a potent mixture of religious, familial, and sexual innuendo:

1. *arma* (soul, spirit, to arm)
2. *cambra* (chamber, vagina)
3. *intra* (to enter, to penetrate)
4. *oncle* (uncle)
5. *ongla* (fingernail)
6. *verga* (virgin, rod, branch, scepter, penis).

The gist of the poem is that the poet's carnal secular love supersedes love of family, social governance, and even religion. The *tornada* presents a particularly dense constellation of meanings, as laid out by James J. Wilhelm:

Arnautz tramet sa chansson d'ongla e d'oncle,

Arnaut sends his song of the nail and uncle,

a grat de lieis que de sa verg'a [verga] l'arma

for the pleasure [with the thanks] of her who,

1. arms him with her rod (wand, scepter);
2. has the soul (spirit) of her scepter;
3. has the soul (spirit) of his rod (penis),

son Desirat, cui pretz en cambra intra.

his Desired One, whose value (worth) enters into the chamber.[192]

Here, perhaps, we approach a sodomitical statement encoded in Arnaut's poetic language; the use of masculine *senhals* (code names) such as *Desirat* is not uncommon in reference to a lady, but, as we have seen, neither is the address of other men. In the haze of overdetermined meanings, along with the compression of the rhyme words into pairs, we glean that the spirit and weaponry *(arma, verga)* of the "song of uncle and nail" *(ongla, oncle)* is phallic penetration *(cambra, intra)*. But we might very well ask, "Who is fucking whom?" All three options for interpreting the middle line indicate that the troubadour gains the phallus—the power to penetrate and its concomitant social value—from the lady, whether she arms him with it, or has a soul that reflects it. The *Desirat* clearly refers to the penetrating object, though the poetic sleight of hand that substitutes the abstract *pretz* for the robust *verga* cleverly muddies the carnality of the image with courtly jargon. One manuscript version, however, adds another twist in the already winding path of this *tornada*. Troubadour manuscript H (Rome, Biblioteca Vaticana 3207), dating from the last quarter of the thirteenth century, not only contains a quasi-critical edition of Arnaut's lyrics, but also contains a marginal gloss beside *Desirat* that lists the name of another troubadour, Bertra[n] d[e] Born, and the note: "with whom he shared the name Deszirat" *(ab cui se clamaua deszirat).*[193]

In the examples treated above, we can observe the circulation of desire that flows from the troubadour through the conduit of the lady and song (or the lady as a cipher for the song) to his male patron or, especially in the case of the *trobar clus,* his rival troubadours. The homoerotic implications of similar triangles have been examined most prominently by Eve Kosofsky Sedgwick in poetry and prose from William Shakespeare to Walt Whitman.[194] Sedgwick hypothesizes a continuum between "homosocial" relations—the tight social bonds between persons of the same sex—and homosexual relations. The significance of this continuum "between men" within patriarchal power structures lies in the potential infusion of homosocial bonds with erotic energy, drawing those relations into the "orbit of desire." This erotic energy jeopardizes the very masculinity that such bonds enshrine, and ultimately reveals heterosexual "normativity" to be inherently unstable.[195]

Some twelfth-century observers of court culture seemed to recognize this instability, criticizing rivalrous courtiers and slothful nobility as effeminate and perverse, concerned more with fashion and pleasure than chivalrous behavior. Orderic Vitalis, writing in 1142, attacked the fashions and customs of French courts: "Effeminates set the fashion in many parts of the world: foul catamites, doomed to eternal fire, unrestrainedly pursued their revels and shamelessly gave themselves up to the filth of sodomy."[196] In the Middle Ages, unlike today, the charge of effeminacy often sprung from the observation of a knight or courtier having *too much* interest in women, and not enough interest in manly pursuits—a medieval dissociation of gender identification and sexual preference. But Orderic, through words such as "catamite" and "sodomy," seems to suggest that an excessive interest in women could also lead to perverse sexual practices; men who behave like women at court could also behave like women during sex.

Dante, an ambivalent participant in later court culture, describes two classes of sodomites in his *Divine Comedy*—those in Hell for violence against God and nature (*Inferno* 15 and 16), and those in Purgatory for excessive lust (*Purgatorio* 26). Both classes include poets and men of letters whom Dante esteems.[197] Arnaut Daniel is given particular honor in *Purgatorio* 26. Here Dante introduces him through the mouth of the Italian poet Guido Guinizzelli as the "better craftsman of the mother tongue, verses of love and tales of romance, he surpassed them all" (*miglior fabbro del parlar materno, versi d'amore e prose di romanzi, soverchiò tutti,* 26.117–19).[198] Later, in a dramatic display of homage, Dante has Arnaut speak seven lines in Occitan, thus allowing the troubadour's mother tongue to interrupt that of Dante. But the most intriguing aspect about this moment of textual penetration stems from its context: Dante has placed Arnaut not only among the lustful in Purgatory, but more specifically among the hermaphrodites.

In the Middle Ages, the concept of hermaphroditism implied a biological mixing of genders or a transgression of gender roles, exemplified by the passive partner in a male homosexual union.[199] Dante, however, seems to associate such a transgression of gender not with those he calls hermaphrodites, but with another group who cry out "Soddoma" in self-reproof (26:79–80). "Sodomy" referred to many things in the pre- and early modern periods, extending from anal intercourse between two men to any nonprocreative sexual act; in addition, it was a term of condemnation for all manner of dissidence and difference in religious practice, ethnicity, region of origin, and language.[200] In the *Purgatorio* 26, the poet Guido Guinizzelli explains the meaning of "Soddoma" to Dante by pointing to another group of sinners and referring to a story of Julius Caesar having acted as the passive partner in a homosexual love affair with King Nicomedes of Bythinia.[201]

La gent che non vien con noi, offese	The people who do not come with us offended
di ciò per che già Cesar, trïunfando,	in that for which Caesar, in his triumph,
"Regina" contra sé chiamar s'intese.	once heard "Queen" cried out against him. (26.76–78)

By way of contrast, he proclaims, "Our sin was hermaphrodite" *(Nostro peccato fu ermafrodito)*, and he goes on to associate this with "following (sexual) appetites like beasts" (*seguendo come bestie l'appetito,* 26.82 and 94). Joseph Pequigney interprets the use of "hermaphrodite" here to mean "heterosexual" and the sodomitical crime to be unrestrained indulgence of sexual desire. John Boswell, however, argues that both heterosexual and homosexual interpretations of "hermaphrodite" were probably in play. He writes, "it almost seems a wry joke, inviting readers to rethink what is 'natural' and what 'unnatural.'"[202]

Thus Arnaut Daniel appears as a genius of poetry and a hermaphrodite of either possible stripe. In terms of Dante's own poem, however, the penetration of Arnaut's *lingua franca* into Dante's *parlar materno* flips the respective position of the two poets, aligning Dante himself with those who cry "Soddoma." Furthermore, in the same way that in the Song of Songs the female lover conjures up her male beloved through his own imploring language (e.g., "My beloved spake, and said unto me, 'Rise up, my love, my fair one, and come away,'" 2.10), Dante conjures up Arnaut through Arnaut's own poetic language. Arnaut's reported speech exactly replicates the fundamentally self-incarnational property of troubadour song:

Ieu sui Arnaut, que plor e vau cantan;	I am Arnaut, who weep and sing as I go
consiros vei la passada folor,	contritely I see my past folly
e vei jausen lo joi qu'esper, denan.	and joyously I see before me the joy that I await. (26:142–44)

Even in purgatory Arnaut sings of a hoped-for *joi,* the troubadours' dream of sexual union. Here it is brought into the orbit of religious fervor and devotion; Arnaut's *art d'Amor* seems purified of its original sexuality. Yet Dante allows that this art was also the self-practice that earned him a place among hermaphrodites. Arnaut's lustful singing remains definitive of his identity, an identity that calls into question Dante's own.

2

A Music of One's Own
discipline

Foucault called attention to the paradox that behavioral restriction can produce intellectual expansion; in other words, asceticism and prohibition can
yield "self-knowledge." The point of intersection of these seemingly per-
pendicular vectors is confession, which can be regarded as an evacuation of
self (a bearing of witness against oneself as a purification of the psyche)
simultaneously with an articulation of self (a fundamentally egocentric
expression).[1]

In this chapter I explore how the notion of confession applies to music,
that is, how music can function as disclosure and as discipline. My primary
focus will be on the post-Freudian cultural climate, in which Christian confession was secularized through psychoanalysis. At nearly the same point in
time in the late nineteenth century, the medical category of the "homosexual" emerged. Two composers, Peter Ilich Tchaikovsky and Benjamin Britten, will provide case studies for the role of musical disclosure and discipline
in the modern homosexual subject. The finale of Tchaikovsky's Sixth Symphony offers an exemplar of presumed sexual sublimation and confession,
while Britten's compositions *Billy Budd* and *Abraham and Isaac* together disclose a methodical exploration of the ethics and erotics of self-discipline.

FROM CONFESSION TO THE COUCH

In the writings of Augustine, knowledge of the "truth of God" can only be
achieved through a process of thorough self-examination that leads to self-
regulation of sexuality. But equally important to sexual discipline in the production of truth and subjectivity is the discipline of disclosure. For Augustine, *confessio* was a particularly potent discipline of disclosure that combined
an account of one's life with a meditation on God. Though addressed to

God, who presumably does not need a verbal text to "read" Augustine, Augustine wrote his *Confessions* as a disciplinary practice in "reading" himself, and to provide a text of authentic Christian subjectivity for others to read.[2]

More than thirteen centuries later, the philosopher, critic, and composer Jean-Jacques Rousseau responded to Augustine by writing his own *Confessions* (completed in 1770), in which he reveals "a man in all the truth of nature."[3] Like Augustine, Rousseau turns inward to give an account of his most personal thoughts and feelings; unlike Augustine, Rousseau's focus is the truth of human nature, its sources of goodness and wickedness, and not the truth of God's nature. And it is not God to whom Rousseau primarily confesses, but to the public, specifically a public who may side against him in the quarrels with his attackers.

Though sexuality is not the touchstone for Rousseau's subjectivity, as it is for Augustine, it is nevertheless the launching pad for his enterprise to articulate the self. Early in book 1, Rousseau confesses his bizarre sexual taste, which developed in his childhood: to be dominated and spanked by an "imperious mistress." This embarrassing revelation functions as the prerequisite for continuing the truthful account of his life. He writes, "I have made the first and most painful step in the obscure and miry labyrinth of my confessions. . . . From now on I am sure of myself, after what I have just dared to say nothing can stop me any more."[4] Once Rousseau has enacted the self-discipline of confessing his desire to be disciplined by a woman, the floodgates are effectively opened for the flow of his truthful words. Indeed, it is the very shamefulness of his sexual taste that guarantees the veracity of its account, and the veracity of what follows.

Music in Rousseau's *Confessions,* as with Augustine, appears as a provocateur of sorts. In book 8, Rousseau undergoes an intellectual conversion that parallels Augustine's spiritual one (also in book 8). But the centerpiece of this important book is his detailed narration of the events surrounding the composition and performance of his 1752 opera, aptly named *The Village Soothsayer (Le Devin du village)*. The reception of his opera leads him to experience the heights of ecstasy and public fashion. Describing the passionate reactions of the women at the premiere, Rousseau confesses, "I soon abandoned myself fully and without distraction to the pleasure of savoring my glory. Nevertheless, I am sure that at this moment the pleasure of sex entered into it much more than an author's vanity."[5] Later, however, Rousseau cites the opera's success as the instigation of his fall from favor with his circle of friends. He writes, "it was the germ of the secret jealousies that burst out only a long time afterward."[6] He goes on to interpret their jealousy as envy of his ability to write music, claiming, "I believe that my so-called friends would have pardoned me for writing Books, and excellent books, because that glory was not foreign to them; but that they could not forgive me for having written an Opera nor for the brilliant success that work had, because none of them was in a condition to forge ahead in the same career nor to aspire to the same honors."[7] As with Augustine, music drives a wedge between Rousseau and his immediate society, not because music leads Rousseau deeper into private pleasures, but because his musicality marks him, gives him a language of expression that can touch the public in a way his friends cannot. Music—here, importantly, his musical "soothsaying"— leads to the exposure of hidden passions, his own and those of his former friends. These are the confession of the psychic world.

The interplay of sex, disclosure, and truth reemerged with new rationalization and vigor in the late nineteenth and early twentieth centuries. Foucault marked 1870 as the year medical literature gave birth to the homosexual as a distinct type of person, who was only one among many newly identified sexual deviants catalogued in an emerging *scientia sexualis*.[8] Psychoanalysis became the new secular form of the "confession," an account of one's life combined not with a religious pursuit of God, but with a scientific pursuit of the human subject, of the truth of consciousness.[9] Foucault writes, "Combining confession with examination, the personal history with the deployment of a set of decipherable signs and symptoms; the interrogation, the exacting questionnaire and hypnosis, with the recollection of memories and free association: all were ways of reinscribing the procedure of confession in a field of scientifically acceptable observations."[10]

The production of truth through religious confession depends upon the selective disclosure of silent thoughts and memories: the speaker is the subject and the knower, while the listener/confessor assumes a silent but authoritative role, certifying the sounding document. The scientifically reinscribed confession depends not only on disclosure, but, more importantly, on a second operation of exposure by the listener who processes and translates the sounding document. Subject and knowledge here become disengaged; the listener is the primary knower and producer of truth.

This shift has implications for music as a disclosure of marked sexuality, specifically the "burden of proof" of musical meaning shifts from the composer-confessor to the listener-interpreter. This issue will be considered in chapter 3. Here I want to focus on the ways in which music functioned in the discourse of sexual psychopathology and how that discourse aligns music with queer subjectivity and its confession. We saw in chapter 1 that for Augustine music occasioned the confession and self-interrogation of sensual pleasures, which then served the formation of subjectivity. In late nineteenth-century and early twentieth-century medical literature, music becomes itself a mode of confession, evidence corroborating homosexuality.

THE PSYCHOLOGY OF THE MUSICALLY INCLINED

Sexological interest in music literally began with "a whistle and a song." Karl Heinrich Ulrichs, a homosexual lawyer and early advocate for the rights of homosexuals (whom Ulrichs called Urnings after a passage on Urania in Plato's *Symposium*), wrote in 1864, "I have found several Urnings [homosexuals] who could not whistle. . . . Even I cannot do it. [Heterosexual] men are always able to do it. Some Urnings are able to whistle." But he also admits, "I have taken pleasure all along, only I cannot tell you how much, singing in falsetto. . . . For me, singing in a manly tone lacks the pleasure of falsetto, although I first sang second bass in the choir. The preference for womanly falsetto, as far as I know, never occurs in men. On the contrary they object to it."[11] Some years later Ulrichs wrote of more Urnings who could not whistle, and he quoted one at length:

> Until the age of 18 I had a very beautiful mezzo-soprano voice and often used to like to sing. The change occurred . . . and my singing voice disappeared. Yet, I have often sung since then "in falsetto," which had formerly been difficult for me. Practice with it was completely successful. The only thing I cannot do is to give a hardy whistle. Only real men can do that. This piercing whistle, however, jars so much on my ears that I sometimes call out on the street, "Oh, my nerves!"[12]

Magnus Hirschfeld (1914) and Havelock Ellis (1915), perhaps taking their lead from Ulrichs, likewise document the relative inability of male "sexual inverts" to whistle.[13] But Ulrichs's particular contrasting of a desire for a falsetto singing voice with a lack of, and retreat from, a "hardy" whistle invites commentary since both sounds are musical and penetrating to the ear. We have here a clear case of gendered sound: the whistle represents an inborn masculine skill ("some of the women inverts can whistle admirably," Ellis notes) connoting less the rendering of a tune than a shrill sonic summons or command (incidentally, Althusser allowed that a whistle could serve as a "hail"), while the control of vocal tessitura in talking or singing represents an acquired craft of expression, a feminine artifice. Albert Moll (1891) dismissed the idea that Uranists cannot whistle, but noted that "while in certain Uranists the voice spontaneously assumes feminine characteristics, others expend much energy acquiring them . . . due to the existence of a sort of instinctive impulse which urges them to effeminacy, insofar as the voice is concerned, as well as other peculiarities of the feminine character."[14]

These texts presume cross-gender attributes and identification in association with homosexuality. They also frequently mix and match theories of nature and nurture to account for the cause of homosexuality and other sexual perversities. Most German sexologists since Ulrichs have built upon his understanding that Urnings are born with a strong component of the opposite sex, thus recognizing two classes of people: those whose sexual instincts correspond to their sexual organs, producing a desire for the opposite sex, and those whose sexual instincts do not, producing an "inversion" of sexual desire, or a desire for the same sex.[15] This was a congenital model and stood in opposition to earlier views of variant sexualities as acquired vices. Some sexologists, however, shaded this congenital model with the rhetoric of neurosis, malady, or perversion of an originally normal disposition (Westphal in 1870 and Krafft-Ebing from 1886 to 1903), citing a genetic predisposition to psychological pathology as the root of homosexual behavior. Others (Moll in 1891, Carpenter in 1896, Ellis and Symonds in 1896, and Hirschfeld in 1914) extended Ulrichs's ideas, arguing that a biological scrambling of gender leads to homosexuality, thus separating "inverted" sexual behavior from disease and psychosis.

Despite the disagreement over the roots of homosexuality in psychopathology or inverted bio-gendered inclinations, the prominent sexologists of this era regarded musical aptitude as organic to sexual inversion. Below are excerpts concerning music from five well-known sexological texts:

1. Krafft-Ebing (1886–1903): "In the majority of cases, psychical anomalies (brilliant endowment in art, especially music, poetry, etc., by the side of bad intellectual powers or original eccentricity) are present, which may extend to pronounced conditions of mental degeneration (imbecility, moral insanity)."[16]

2. Moll (1891): "Uranists often distinguish themselves by their passion for music and the other arts. Coffignon has already cited this love for music as one of the peculiarities of the Uranists' Character."[17]

3. Carpenter (1894–1907): "As to music, this is certainly the art which in its subtlety and tenderness—and perhaps in a certain inclination to *indulge* in emotion—lies nearest to the Urning nature. There are few in fact of this nature who have not some gift in the direction of music—though, unless we cite Tschaikowsky, it does not appear that any thorough-going Uranian has attained to the highest eminence in this art" (emphasis in the original).[18]

4. Symonds (1896): "They [musicians and artists, in whom sexual inversion prevails beyond the average] are conditioned by their aesthetical faculty, and encouraged by the circumstances of their life to feel and express the whole gamut of emotional experience. . . . Some persons are certainly made [sexually] abnormal by nature, others, of this sympathetic artistic temperament, may become so through their sympathies plus their conditions of life."[19]

5. Ellis (1915): "As regards music, my cases reveal the aptitude which has been remarked by others as peculiarly common among inverts. It has been extravagantly said that all musicians are inverts; it is certain that various famous musicians, among the dead and the living, have been homosexual. . . . [Oppenheim] remarks that the musical disposition is marked by great emotional instability, and this instability is a disposition to nervousness. . . . The musician has not been rendered nervous by the music, but he owes his nervousness (as also, it may be added, his disposition to homosexuality) to the same disposition to which he owes his musical aptitude. Moreover, the musician is frequently one-sided in his gifts, and the possession of a single hypertrophied aptitude is itself closely related to the neuropathic and psychopathic diathesis."[20]

Carpenter, who like Ulrichs was homosexual, links musical aptitude to the Urning's indulgence of emotion, and he betrays a certain discomfort by half-heartedly nominating Tchaikovsky as the only instance of musical eminence. Indeed, Carpenter's comments echo criticisms of Tchaikovsky's music as overly sentimental or barbarically indulgent and thus of lesser greatness.[21] Symonds hypothesizes that an aesthetic faculty, such as musical aptitude, is a natural condition that possibly leads to *acquired* homosexuality, comparable to Krafft-Ebing's notion of music as a psychical anomaly that exposes the possibility of other psychotic predispositions leading to homosexuality. Ellis, too, seems to figure the "musical disposition"—a "single hypertrophied aptitude"—as more of a pathology than sexual inversion itself. It is in this passage that Ellis comes closest to Krafft-Ebing when he baldly states that musicality and homosexuality derive from the same disposition.

For these authors, many of whom are sympathetic to homosexuals, the issue seems to be not how homosexuality taints music, but rather how musicality, as the primary natural abnormality, taints homosexuality, bringing it closer to choice, or vice. One key to positioning music in this manner can be found in Havelock Ellis's writing on the sense of hearing in the "sexual selection" process. Following the arguments of various researchers, Ellis maps out a theory of music as rooted in the rhythms of muscular behavior; thus music, as a "developed form" of rhythm, clearly stimulates involuntary muscle activity. Yet he finds that for most men neither the specific qualities of the female voice nor music results in a sexual response that might drive selection.[22] Women, however, show "an actual or latent susceptibility to the sexual significance of the male voice, a susceptibility which, under the conditions of human civilization, may be transferred to music generally." Ellis describes this sexual response as "slight but definite" in normal women, and goes on to cite an extreme case in which the "neuropathic" married female subject "does not understand why intercourse never affords what she knows she wants. But the hearing of beautiful music, or at times the excitement of her own singing, will sometimes cause intense orgasm."[23] In light of these remarks, the pathology of the musical homosexual male is thus twofold: not only is he further feminized by his sexual responsiveness to music, but, ironically, because of this added degree of effeminacy, he possesses a musical skill that could arouse women's sexual response.

Two other prominent sexologists deserve particular attention for their opposing formulations of the musical-homosexual subject. Magnus Hirschfeld included in his 1914 study *Die Homosexualität des Mannes und des Weibes* the most sustained discussion of the relationship between music and homosexuality, while Sigmund Freud, in all his writings from 1891 to 1939, mentions music hardly at all, relegating it to an unmarked sublimation of the libido.

Hirschfeld, himself a homosexual, went into the greatest detail about composers and performers, and especially the typical aesthetic choices of homosexuals. Like Carpenter, he first notes that there are few great homosexual composers, just as there are few great women composers, although he concedes that this historical fact may be changing, as Tchaikovsky and some living composers prove.[24] But he goes on to remark that great composers often have an admixture *(Einschlag)* of feminine and masculine characters, writing, "Particularly in recent times, without being directly homosexual, composers with feminine traits are found much more frequently. In this case, for example, we could name Robert Schumann, the romanticist, who felt he had two natures, that of the strong Florestan and that of the gentle Eusebius. Richard Wagner also belongs here, likewise Peter Cornelius, being under the spell of Richard Wagner's personality. He is supposed to have been bisexual."[25] Hirschfeld here draws upon a common Romantic view that the male genius is fundamentally androgynous, a combination of the innate sensitivity, intuition, and emotion of women with the virile capacities of men.[26]

Though homosexuals are less likely to be found among creative geniuses, they are abundant among the ranks of practicing musicians and virtuosic performers. As an example, Hirschfeld cites the "homosexuality or bisexuality" of Paganini. And because homosexuals frequently have very flexible voices *(eine große Modulationsfähigkeit der Stimme),* they tend to be tenors.[27]

Hirschfeld offers both social and biological reasons for the connection between homosexuals and music. First he quotes a homosexual musician who states that middle-class society's fear of difference drives homosexuals to be artists and musicians; he then argues that homosexuals are attracted to music because of their "emotional constitutions" *(seelische Konstitution),* their imagination and senses *(Sinne)* being particularly sparked by music. "But in most cases," he writes, "they take music only as an element of mood, as pure, sensual impression. . . . For that reason, naturally, it is the romantic, more colorful, more sensual music, the modern music with a 'literary' feature, which attracts homosexuals, while they remain more indifferent toward the classical and older music, which demands more intellectual participation."[28] He goes on to explain in great detail this homosexual musical taste. Homosexuals, he alleges, love a "mixed style" *(Stilvermengung)* such as program music and operas—especially the music dramas of Wagner and his successors—but not classical opera, which they find "unnatural" in its unchanging formal patterns. Indeed, Mitchell Morris has documented a veritable subculture of homosexual devotees of Wagner in fin-de-siècle Germany.[29] Hirschfeld then launches into a long, convoluted sentence fragment that betrays his own devotion to the composer, and hence his own homosexual sensibility:

> These music-dramas, which—considered as purely poetic achievements—can hardly fulfill the requirements of poetical technique without music, which are nonetheless not just pure music; this drama of feelings which produces its intensification less by dramatic and logical construction than by piling up feelings of ecstasy, this pessimistic, martyrlike, pathetic mood, this music which, illustrating and painting the background for the text, is, as it were, only a part of the "total work of art," but is nonetheless its primary means of stimulation, often in parts only an intensification of the stage action, then delighting the ears of the hearers again by means of a well-known "leitmotive" now and then.[30]

Hirschfeld's text itself seems illuminated by the "spark" of "imagination and senses" that he earlier identified as a fundamental link between homosexuals and music. He suddenly becomes a musicologist, explaining how to hear the music, how words and music operate together, paraphrasing Wagner's ideology of the *Gesamtkunstwerk*. At one point, in evaluating the homosexual composer Franz von Holstein, he even quotes from the music historian Karl Storck to corroborate his opinions. Although Hirschfeld does not use any rhetoric of pathology, he does insist that while homosexuals have imagination, ideas, and flashes of creativity *(Einfälle)*, they generally lack the manly craft, energy, and activity to produce great music. He writes, "There are artists who come to their profession out of a superabundance of life, and those who come to it out of refinement, out of over-cultivation. To the latter belong the homosexuals."[31]

Hirschfeld's discussion of music emphasizes in a number of ways, including by means of his self-exposing digression, that homosexuals *have good ears.* They are good interpreters of music, either with their bodies as players, or with their minds as listeners. On one hand, this puts the homosexual subject in a position of mediator between a composer and an audience presumed to be of "normal" sexuality; on the other hand, the homosexual subject can be construed as the ultimate audience, the perfect overly cultivated receptor for the superfluidity of music. Although this sexualized formulation of musical roles implies a clearly dichotomous gendering (masculine composer, feminine listener/performer), Hirschfeld complicates that association by asserting the bi-genderedness of great composers, effectively detaching gender from sexual roles.

Hirschfeld's idea of the bi-gendered composer gave music an aspect of "bio-availability" for the homosexual, that is, it established a biological basis for the close connection between music and homosexuals. He qualifies his comments, however, by specifying that his comments only apply to music and composers of "recent times." Indeed, Hirschfeld is careful to limit his analysis of the homosexuality or mixed gender of composers, and even the affectivity of music, to current or near-current examples. Thus it seems that Hirschfeld has in mind the birth of the modern musical-homosexual, as if such a complex were not possible before the late nineteenth century, before program music, Wagnerian opera, or composers of mixed gender such as Robert Schumann.

Vern Bullough writes, "Three men dominated sexology during the early years of the twentieth century: Magnus Hirschfeld (1868–1935), Havelock Ellis (1859–1939) and Sigmund Freud (1856–1939). Hirschfeld and Ellis could be called empirical data gatherers, while Freud was a system maker who, on the basis of his system, developed a new therapy for those afflicted with sexual and other problems."[32] Freud's comprehensive system follows the path of innate polymorphously perverse sexual drives through a dramatic psychosexual process of socialization within the family, to ideal substitution and sublimation or dysfunctional neurosis, phobia, or regression. For Ellis and Hirschfeld, music and musicality potentially disclose the (mis)direction of an individual's sexuality; for Freud, music told of nothing in particular—or at least nothing he could understand. In "The Moses of Michelangelo" (1914), Freud describes his bewilderment over music, claiming, "with music, I am almost incapable of obtaining any pleasure. Some rationalistic, or perhaps analytic, turn of mind in me rebels against being moved by a thing without knowing why I am thus affected and what it is that affects me."[33] It is strange that this powerful thinker, who did not shy away from applying his psychoanalytic theories to the visual and literary arts, religion, kinship structures, and all of civilization, should fall silent about music. Freud admits this silence is due to his own lack of engagement; he is not affected by music and therefore cannot access its psychoanalytic (and thus psychosexual) significance.

Freud's comments about music in his case studies tend to be inconsequential, although two remarks stand out. In a footnote from his "Analysis of a Phobia in a Five-Year-Old Boy" (1909), Freud interprets musical practice as evidence for the sublimation of a repressed sexual desire for the mother. He writes, "Hans's father even observed that simultaneously with this repression a certain amount of sublimation set in. From the time of the beginning of his anxiety Hans began to show an increased interest in music and to develop his inherited musical gift."[34] Here music, for which Hans has a genetic predisposition, serves as a more appropriate outlet for Hans's repression than his pathological phobia of horses. The juxtaposition of musicality and phobia, however, links the two as qualitatively equal behavioral repositories for repressed sexual energy.

Freud's introductory lecture on the psychoanalysis of dreams (1915–16), offers a second confession of his own ignorance of music:

> Tunes that come into one's head without warning turn out to be determined by and to belong to a train of thought which has a right to occupy one's mind though without one's being aware of its activity. It is easy to show then that the relation to the tune is based on its text or its origin. But I must be careful not to extend this assertion to really musical people, of whom, as it happens, I have had no experience. It may be that for such people the musical content of the tune is what decides its emergence. The earlier case is certainly the commoner one.[35]

Freud goes on to describe how one of his patients was "persecuted" by Paris's song in Offenbach's *La belle Hélène*. It was revealed through analysis that the song was appropriate to the young man's interest in two women, one named Helen and the other Ida (the name of the mountain where Paris had been a shepherd). Thus the song disclosed the patient's psychosexual tumult before therapeutic confession. Freud implies, however, that music offers such an entrée into the psyche only for the patient who is not a musician. For the "really musical" patient, the meaning of music resides in something ineffable, resistant to interpretation—the "musical content of the tune." Freud's disinclination to theorize about the content of music, or musicality, beyond interpreting both as evidence of sublimation casts "the really musical" as themselves somewhat opaque to analysis. The "really musical" are more puzzling and more outside Freud's system than homosexuals, neurotics, and even the insane.

Despite Freud's relative silence on music, music and musicians became an occasional topic of inquiry for later Freudian researchers. In 1960, Michael A. Wallach and Carol Greenberg published a study of how music might function as "symbolic sexual arousal." Wallach and Greenberg start with Freud's premise that "art in general can serve as a way of sublimating sexual energy, thereby channeling it away from its more customary social expression." They go on to say that "music, in these terms, could function as an indirect, compensatory means of expressing sexual arousal."[36] Using only female subjects (undergraduates from Simmons College), who, on the basis of an earlier study, were believed to be more open to symbolic sexual arousal by music than men, Wallach and Greenberg collected stories written in response to several examples of jazz. The reason they chose jazz is not discussed, though by 1960 jazz had a long history of being associated with overt sexuality, motivated in part by its association with African-Americans, who were stereotyped in mainstream culture as sexually promiscuous and even predatory. Rock and roll, more blatantly sexual than jazz, was perhaps still too linked with the subculture of working-class youth. Wallach and Greenberg assessed the sexual symbolic content of the women's stories according to schemata drawn from Freud's interpretation of dreams. They then correlated these analyses with surveys that assessed each subject in terms of social introversion/extroversion and levels of anxiety. They conclude that

> (a) One function of listening to music is to permit the symbolic expression of sexual impulses. (b) The strongest impetus toward such expression arises for persons who claim to be socially introverted, but whose attitude of introversion does not constitute a successful defense as indicated by the presence of a high level of anxiety. Since the need for others remains and yet its direct sexual expression has been prohibited, the only open path is that of fantasy displacement.

Furthermore, they justified women's greater response in terms of cultural pressure, claiming, "The stricter societal prohibitions against girls for direct sexual expression should lead to a stronger need in the case of unmarried women than men for displacement arousal in response to music."[37]

In a Freudian scheme, psychosocial conditions such as prohibition, anxiety, and introversion fortify the psychosexual function of music. The confession of this particular form of sexual displacement is accessible only through translation from music into an apparently more quantifiable symbol system—words. Words then form sexual metaphors, such as descriptions of repetitive rhythmic motions of the body and images of penetration (i.e., "the forceful pushing through a resistant medium"), which can be analyzed for their psychosexual symbolism. The application of such phallocentric verbal symbols to data from women is true to form for Freudian psychological models, and begs questions of appropriateness. Nevertheless, Freudian psychoanalysis understands any heightened response to music as a sublimation of repressed sexual arousal, most clearly discernable in women, given their particular social oppression. This analysis easily extends to people with abnormal sexualities. Although restricted to women, the Wallach and Greenberg study formalized the popular association of social condition, personality type, and musical affinity—an association that appears in numerous early psychological portraits of the homosexual composer Peter Ilich Tchaikovsky.

TCHAIKOVSKY'S MUSICAL CONFESSION

If you like Romanticism, if your heart beats in tune to Rousseau, Heine, Chopin, Dickens, Tennyson, Kipling—if you do not feel uncomfortable at the display of the true heart upon the sleeve, if your own heart renews its strength through tears and confession rather than through reticence and swift constriction—then you love Tchaikowsky!

Catherine Drinker Bowen (1937)

Tchaikovsky may well be the most famous homosexual in the history of Western art music. Themes of confession and psychosexual pathology permeate his biographies and the critical responses to his music (especially his symphonies) published soon after his death, both of which stem from several interpretive frameworks. One is German Romantic literature, against which late nineteenth-century symphonies were evaluated. The character-study novel, or *Bildungsroman*, such as Goethe's *Wilhelm Meisters Lehrjahre* (1796), focuses on the psychological growth and spiritual progress of a single protagonist. The notion of a protagonist's development was then applied to the German symphony; the play of themes and harmonies over the course of a single movement could be understood to represent low-level psychic processes, while the higher-level shifts from movement to movement could be understood to represent significant events or eras in a life.

Another framework—also a theme within German Romantic writing but arguably started by Rousseau—was the identification of the artist with the protagonist of the story or, in the case of the symphony, with the psychic processes that were exposed in music. Richard Taruskin explains that "the discourse of 'self-discovery' . . . celebrated the idiosyncratically personal and the artist's unique subjectivity, presupposing a producer-oriented musical ecosystem that quickly coalesced into a cult around the heroic personality of Beethoven the great symphonist."[38] Interpretations of the symphony from Beethoven up to the present day often show a tension between Germanic Romantic ideals of heroic individual expression and Franco-Italian ideals of beauty and enjoyment. Symphonies of the latter stripe were often judged as pandering to public tastes, and thus decried as vulgar, superficial, and even effeminate in their sentimentality.[39]

Tchaikovsky was resolutely anti-Beethoven and anti-Wagner; he preferred instead a Mozartean aesthetic that placed beauty, pleasure, and an affirmation of aristocracy above what Taruskin describes as "the kind of politics we have been conditioned by the artistic discourse of late, late romanticism to regard as politics, namely the politics of alienation, contention, and resistance."[40] He goes on to argue that the narrative macrostructures used to interpret nineteenth-century German symphonies are misapplied to Tchaikovsky's symphonies. And indeed, during Tchaikovsky's lifetime, German, British, and American reviewers sometimes criticized his symphonies as vulgar, barbaric, and incoherent, full of trivialities, musical padding, and sheer noise. These charges were frequently paired with remarks about his Russian ethnicity. One American reviewer wrote, "The Finale of the Fourth Symphony of Tchaikovsky pained me by its vulgarity. . . . Nothing can redeem the lack of nobleness, the barbarous side by which, according to ethnographs and diplomats, even the most polished Russian at times betrays himself."[41]

A third framework of medical and psychoanalytic discourse led Tchaikovsky commentators to posthumous diagnoses of psychosexual pathology. In her examination of Herman Melville's 1891 *Billy Budd* (a thinly veiled story of homosexual desire and dread), Eve Sedgwick observes that "the death of the text's homosexual [Claggart] marks . . . not a terminus but an initiation for the text, as well, into the narrative circulation of male desire."[42] Similarly, in the course of the reception of Tchaikovsky's music, his death initiated a public discourse of confession *about homosexuality,* pinpointing his last three symphonies as musical expositions of a pathological mind.[43]

The peak of Tchaikovsky's career coincided with the heyday of German sexology and French hypnotherapy for neuropathologies, both of which were to influence Freud. In 1893, the year of Tchaikovsky's death, Freud began presenting his work on hysteria: Freud focused on psychological rather than physiological explanations for this disorder, expanding what was once considered an effect of the womb beyond the physiology of gender; this marked the start of psychoanalysis. Two years later, in 1895, Europe would experience a wave of homosexual panic in the wake of Oscar Wilde's highly public trials and conviction for "committing acts of gross indecency with other male persons." Both psychoanalysis and Wilde's trials reinvigorated the (homo)sexuality of confession, as well as the perceived confessionality of art.

Rumors about Tchaikovsky's own homosexual inclinations had circulated during his lifetime; they were aggravated by his periodic misanthropy as well as a short, stressful marriage in 1876–77. But the composer apparently suffered few social consequences. For most of his professional life, and especially near the time of his death, Tchaikovsky moved in the upper echelons of European society and the Russian aristocracy, many members of which were themselves homosexual, and the rest quite willing to turn a blind eye.[44]

Nevertheless, Tchaikovsky's unsettling death from cholera (then a curable disease associated with the poor) was eventually read in light of the tragic *Adagio lamentoso* finale of his Sixth Symphony, thus giving rise to rumors of suicide. At some point shortly after Oscar Wilde's infamous trials, the theory of Tchaikovsky's alleged suicide became connected to his sexual pathology, which involved, it was said, his despair over a love for his nephew, Vladimir (Bob) Davidov, to whom his last symphony was dedicated—or perhaps some other youthful object fit for a parallel with the case of Wilde.[45] As early as 1899, the American James Huneker described Tchaikovsky's music as "truly

pathological" and full of "the most alarming confessions." Tchaikovsky himself was "out of joint with his surroundings; women delighted him not, and
so he solaced himself with herculean labors—labors that made him the most
interesting, but not the greatest composer of his day."[46] Huneker implied
that Tchaikovsky's pathological distaste for women could be heard in his
musical confession, and that his compositions might be more comparable to
a tabloid newspaper than an edifying novel.

I have already noted that Tchaikovsky's name appears in Edward Carpenter's 1907 discussion of music and sexual inversion. Prior to this, Modest
Tchaikovsky wrote a three-volume biography of his famous brother (published in Russian between 1900 and 1902, and excerpted for publication in
English in 1905).[47] Modest carefully avoided mention of his brother's homosexual activity; he did, however, publish a letter from Tchaikovsky to his
nephew Bob that seemed to confirm the notion that the Sixth Symphony was
a confession—of suicide, homosexuality, or both.

> I must tell you how happy I am about my work . . . the idea came to me for a
> new Symphony. This time with a programme; but a programme of a kind
> which remains an enigma to all—let them guess it who can. . . . This pro-
> gramme is penetrated by subjective sentiment. During my journey, while com-
> posing it in my mind, I frequently shed tears. . . . There will be much that is
> novel as regards form in this work. For instance, the Finale will not be a great
> Allegro, but an Adagio of considerable dimensions.[48]

The playfully cryptic hint at a secret autobiographical program for his new
composition illustrates the intersection of verbal prohibition and a compul-
sion to tell that produces truth. A musical revelation, over which he sheds
tears (of penitence for Augustine, of catharsis for Freud), is also a work that
makes him happy and productive; the confession here is a musical production that sounds the truth.

Later Tchaikovsky biographers, critics, and would-be psychoanalysts
seized upon the rhetoric of secrecy as substantiating evidence for musical disclosure, a paradox that bears witness to the emergence of what Sedgwick
calls the "epistemology of the closet." She points out how many oppositional
binaries—knowledge/ignorance, initiation/innocence, secrecy/disclosure,
private/public, illness/health—become saturated with implications of the
homosexual/heterosexual binary.[49] Knowledge of homosexuality is corroborated by secrecy, its publicity commissioned by privacy. Not until the 1937
biography *"Beloved Friend": The Story of Tchaikowsky and Nadejda von Meck*, by
Catherine Drinker Bowen and Barbara von Meck, was there public docu-
mentation of Tchaikovsky's homosexuality; the book contained uncensored
excerpts from Tchaikovsky's correspondence, which had been published in
Russia between 1934 and 1936 but had later been suppressed. Tchaikovsky's
homosexuality is characterized by the authors as his "dark secret" and "his

affliction—for he considered it so."[50] Moreover, they characterize his nephew Bob as trifling with his uncle's affections.[51] Though "pathetic" in his unrequited homosexual love, Tchaikovsky appears in the eyes of these authors the more noble figure for his sincerity and abjection.

With these bald biographical disclosures, readers "learned too much" about those facts of Tchaikovsky's life that were unutterable. If the sincerity, or truth, of his homosexuality was measured by the prohibition against its disclosure, then its disclosure seemed to highlight the deception or deflection of this truth. Writers in the 1940s, especially British and American critics, exploited this surplus of knowledge in order to solidify the association of homosexuality with subterfuge and sickness.[52] This association is made explicit in the 1945 comment by Edward Lockspeiser, "his neurotic character, of which he was perfectly aware, not only forbade an intimacy with women but drove him into homosexuality with all its *attendant* complications of furtiveness, deception and guilt" (emphasis added).[53] According to Lockspeiser, Tchaikovsky's homosexuality prescribed deception, yet his music failed him in this. "Beginning with the Fourth Symphony and *Eugene Onegin*," Lockspeiser writes, "Tchaïkovsky's music now reflects all the indulgent yearning and the garish exteriorisation of a composer who can never refrain from wearing his heart on his sleeve." Later on Lockspeiser adds, "his is not the 'art of concealing art'; it is music to gorge on, shameless in its sensuousness and splendour."[54]

The contradiction at the heart of much of Tchaikovsky's posthumous reception, fed by the epistemology of the closet, is that Tchaikovsky as homosexual necessarily deceives, yet as composer he obviously confesses. Here we can glean the influence of psychoanalysis, for according to its discourse, the condition of neurosis, and specifically hysteria, occurs from self-deception joined to a confessional symptom. Thus Lockspeiser concludes, "And it was no accident that such music was conceived by a warped neurotic, shy and tortured."[55]

Charges of hysterical display became commonplace in British and American evaluations of Tchaikovsky's music at the same point in time that the rhetoric of psychopathology and neurosis entered his character portraits.[56] By the 1940s, psychologists and musicologists alike understood Tchaikovsky's music, and especially the Sixth Symphony, as not only a clear confession of his homosexuality, but also a musical proof of psychoanalytic theories of displaced libido due to erotic inhibition. In 1941, psychologist Paul C. Squires wrote, "Tschaikowsky's music is the very essence of subjectivity; it is concentrated upon the microcosm—if that is what we care to call the Self. No other music, not even Schumann's, excels his in respect to the quality that may best be called *psychologic*. It is unsurpassed in the portrayal of the sinister mysteries of Mind" (emphasis in the original).[57] In his curiously teasing psychological sketch, Squires attributes to Tchaikovsky nearly every kind of psychological malady, including neurosis, hallucinations, depression, mania, psychopathy, split personality, temporary insanity, hysteria, hystero-epilepsy, and phobia. Squires cites two primary causes: Tchaikovsky's "intensely labile racial combinations" of "Slavic and Romance bloods" and his "psychosexual variations," the specifics of which Squires withholds from the reader until the midpoint of his essay, when he finally "outs" with it: "Let us anticipate: Tschaikowsky was a homosexual. This was his tragic 'secret.'"[58]

Twenty years later psychiatrist James A. Brussel, relying heavily on *"Beloved Friend,"* argued that Tchaikovsky suffered from an unresolved Oedipus complex caused by the death of his mother when he was fourteen years old, and that he displaced his mother-love onto two people who together represent a fractured resolution to the Oedipal drama. His relationship to his longtime patroness Nadejda Philaretovna von Meck was characterized by Brussel as "his surrogate for married life," and his "close companionship" with his homosexual brother Modest as "the actual substitute for heterosexuality."[59] That Modest, in his own biography of the composer, reports having given the name *"Pathétique"* to his brother's last symphony offers Brussel sufficient testimony of their psychosexual intimacy. He writes, "Only Modeste knew his brother well enough to peer into the depths of his mind and so enable the younger man to furnish the title for the *Sixth Symphony.* From a strictly analytic point of view, proof of actual physical contact—something that could not possibly be unearthed—is not required to establish the claim of incestuous homosexuality."[60] For Brussel, only the younger Modest, a psychosexual intimate, could fully understand the disclosure of the Sixth Symphony and translate this into a single word.

Even Tchaikovsky's early apologists seem caught between rejecting and accepting the psychoanalytic terms of the argument. In the same volume as Lockspeiser, Martin Cooper wrote with remarkable insight into the play of nationalism in the reception of Tchaikovsky's music, noting the clash of Romantic and Enlightenment aesthetics. He also employed the modish rhetoric of psychopathology.

> German music, in which the element of struggle, brooding, pain and effort generally predominates, is automatically considered to be in a higher category than the spontaneous affirmation, the immediate unpondered emotion or the delight in sonorous beauty for its own sake, which characterise the best of non-German music. . . . [Tchaikovsky's critics] merely feel that what is essentially simple and immediate in its appeal *must* be blameworthy, however successful it is in actual practice. And no one can question the effectiveness of Tchaïkovsky's style. His saving grace is, of course, his absolute emotional sincerity. You may dislike his emotional world—the panting, palpitating phrases, the strident colours, the sobs and the short bursts of hysterical defiance, but you can never for one moment doubt that this was Tchaïkovsky's inmost self.[61]

Here Cooper deftly performs an interpretive sleight of hand whereby nationalistically motivated, pejorative summations of Tchaikovsky's music as vulgar, sentimental, and superficial become indispensable attributes of a psychological profile (bursts of hysterical defiance, absolute emotion, and inmost self). The medicalizing and pathologizing of creative activities colluded with the Romantic cult of the heroic individual to turn Tchaikovsky the vulgar sensationalist into a composer who bravely plumbed psychopathological depths.

If we could place Tchaikovsky's *Symphonie Pathétique* on the analyst's couch, what would it tell us? Tchaikovsky predicted that it would in fact say very little to its first hearers. In a letter to his nephew, in which he compared an imagined audience reaction with his own, he wrote, "to me, it will seem quite natural, and not in the least astonishing, if this Symphony meets with abuse, or scant appreciation at first. I certainly regard it as quite the best—and especially the 'most sincere'—of all my works."[62] Tchaikovsky here does not imply that the audience will abuse the work because of its sincerity; rather, he seems to be pointing out the gulf between composer and audience, indicating that this piece, which has the most meaning for him, is bound to have less for the general public.

And indeed, the symphony's first performance met with mixed reviews, a testimony to its opacity rather than its clarity.[63] Particularly problematic for the audience then, as now, was the passionate *Adagio lamentoso* finale, for this was Tchaikovsky's conscious diversion from a symphonic norm. The Germanic—or, at any rate, post-Beethoven—understanding of the symphony involved a quasi-narrative progression from initial strife to final victory and redemption, celebrated in a high-energy triumphal ending. Ending with a lament flew in the face of this understanding.

Tchaikovsky's bold concluding lament was, for his confused public, eventually explicated by his death shortly after that first performance. Timothy L. Jackson has recently speculated that the public's reappraisal of this symphony depended upon the rumors of suicide, and an understanding of the music as, in Jackson's words, "self-indictment (i.e., as his own pronouncement through his music that the 'right' and 'proper' solution to his 'homosexual problem' was suicide)." He goes on to say that "only then could the *Pathétique* become morally acceptable."[64] Provided with the gloss on the finale of suicide, the public received the symphony as an undisputed masterpiece, and the finale as the eerie foretelling of his own death—or, in more sensational terms, the composition of his own requiem preceding his suicide.

Such a change of the public's heart, however, certainly does not need the "redemption by suicide" subplot, for, as Alexander Poznansky has documented, Tchaikovsky, then at the height of his career, was himself enthusiastically received by the audience, even if the symphony was less so.[65] The unexpected death of a beloved national figure predictably sparked both increased devotion and morbid curiosity.

According to evidence largely brought to light by Poznansky, Tchaikovsky seemed at ease with his sexual proclivities.[66] He wrote in one letter to his brother that "only now, especially after the story of my marriage, have I finally begun to understand that there is nothing more fruitless than not wanting to be that which I am by nature."[67] Despite this evidence, Jackson and other scholars have held fast to the idea that the *Adagio lamentoso* confesses Tchaikovsky's guilt and abjection regarding his sexual proclivities. Jackson argues that, "the biographer of a composer cannot rely exclusively upon the literary evidence of letters and diaries (as Poznansky has done). . . . As a non-verbal medium, music provides an ideal vehicle for expressing ideas, anxieties and emotions that *must never* be articulated in words" (emphasis added).[68]

Here, Jackson's 1990s argument echoes those of writers of the 1940s such as Lockspeiser and Squires. They articulate the epistemology of the closet, whereby homosexuality equals verbal prohibition and secrecy but also equals knowledge, that "thing" which is known but forbidden expression. So, according to the epistemology of the closet, Tchaikovsky's homosexuality (that is, knowledge) "must never be articulated in words," but, according to psychoanalysis, it must nevertheless be confessed. Music is that confession: understanding Tchaikovsky's music, then, means knowing his sexuality.

Given, however, that Tchaikovsky's letters attest that he could in fact articulate in words some of his anxieties and ideas about his homosexuality, what was it that he did not say in words that he did express in the finale of the Sixth Symphony? What did he confess? Jackson believes he confessed his deep abiding guilt and pessimism about his sexuality, especially his incestuous and pedophilic relationship with his nephew.[69] Jackson further argues that certain musical allusions served as ciphers for Tchaikovsky's homosexuality. These include allusions to Wagner's *Tristan und Isolde*, with its story of incurable love, and to Bizet's *Carmen*, with its themes of exoticism and gambling (with Fate). He adds to these melodic motives that he believes signify crucifixion. For Jackson, the secret program for the symphony is a progression not from strife to redemption but rather from sexual "disease" to punitive death. The final *Adagio lamentoso*, then, would present a "revocation" of the erotic play and bravado of the first three movements, and expectations for a redemptive finale would be replaced by a guilt-ridden requiem for "*unredeemed* homosexuals" (emphasis in the original), the (self-) crucified composer and his beloved.[70] Yet the "thing" that must never be talked about is not the depravity of homosexuality, but rather its very practice. One confesses "I have done X," not "I feel guilty." Thus the lamentation of the finale does not make sense *as a confession*, not even according to Jackson's argument, for he believes that Tchaikovsky admitted his practice as well as his guilt of homo-sexuality by way of suicide, and it was this confession (not one heard in the finale) that made the symphony "morally acceptable" to the public. So if we want to pursue the question of confession encoded in this movement, we should ask what does Tchaikovsky do in this finale that might signify a practice? And what might that practice be that was so very personal and perhaps unspeakable for Tchaikovsky?

The strings open this movement with two striking "wails" of lamentation, expressed as descending parallel-seventh chords, primarily in second inversion, and a "sob" figure of a dotted eighth plus sixteenth-note group. The harmony is lush, the texture dense. A sustained, spare octave F♯ in the flute and bassoon holds the listener in suspense as the strings take a breath for a second cry. This is what the audience hears, but turning to the score, we *see* something that we may not hear. Four angular lines move through dramatic leaps of thirds, fourths, fifths, sixths, and even sevenths, their notes interlocking to produce the rich, dense harmony (example 3). Somber, funereal music follows (mm. 5–8), but it quickly builds up to an emotional fortissimo outburst, only to collapse into languid, descending lines (mm. 9–18). A seven-note chordal anacrusis in measure 19, also written as interlocking angular parts, leads to another statement of the opening wail (mm. 20–23).

A second lyrical theme in D major, by way of contrast, presents a clear octave string texture in which two descending, diatonic four-note phrases (mm. 38–42) are followed by ascending three-note cells (mm. 43–46). As the music becomes progressively louder, the ascending cells become more chromatic (mm. 50–54) and the syncopated accompaniment in triplet eighths gradually permeates the woodwinds, while the principal string melody devolves into a cascading torrent of ever-quickening C-major scales (mm. 71–81) that end in a sudden deafening silence (m. 81).

The silence is broken by a return to the anacrusis and opening wail (mm. 82–86), but now Tchaikovsky "unlocks" the string parts so that the notes as written conform to what is heard, the angular lines having disappeared from view; and thus it remains in subsequent appearances.[71] If there is a moment of confession in the *Adagio lamentoso,* it is a confession to the performer and music reader (not necessarily the listener), and it is not with the initial "eye music" but rather with this ironed-out return.

The opening "eye music" has attracted numerous metaphorical interpretations. David Brown describes the theme as Fate having "initially disguised its optical identity," only to later reveal itself; other writers believe this play of secrecy and disclosure is Death—or Tchaikovsky's death—revealing itself in the course of time.[72] Jackson, in 1995, thought the musical subject to be "torn apart" by the lamentable condition; in 1999, he saw the opening moment as lovers "interlocked in their crucifixion."[73] But disclosure with the return of the strings' lament does not reveal anything the audience or even

Example 3. Peter Ilich Tchaikovsky, Symphony no. 6 in B minor (*Symphonie Pathétique;* 1893), Adagio lamentoso, mm. 1–21.

(continued)

Example 3 *(continued)*

the performers do not already know through their ears, whether it be Fate or Death. And why reconstitute a rent musical subject near the end of the lament? Is this a disentangling of the lovers as they are taken down off their enmeshed crosses? Such literal explanations actually work against the psychological lore that surrounds this movement, suggesting not disclosure but rather dissociation and further sublimation into elaborate but silent madrigalisms.

Richard Taruskin believes that Tchaikovsky's aesthetic was geared to his public.[74] Rather than invoking the interpretive paradigms of individual narrative for Tchaikovsky's symphonies, Taruskin proposes that we should adapt the ideas of metonymy and topos from Wye Jamison Allanbrook's studies of Mozart's rhythmic gestures and their basis in class-encoded social dances. Application to Tchaikovsky is appropriate for two primary reasons: he idolized Mozart, and he, like Mozart, wrote with the aristocracy in mind; that is, he was concerned to please with beauty, convention, and public meaning, and he was invested in class-based social cohesion. Just as Allanbrook traced an undercurrent of musical-social commentary in the dance-based rhythms of Mozart's arias, so Taruskin finds dance-derived topoi and rhythmic gestures operating in Tchaikovsky's operas. He summarizes, "when dance functions as social indicator, as it does so emphatically in *Eugene Onegin,* it is not merely denotative but also connotative, symbolizing not only social milieus but also mores and their *attendant* constraints. . . . It is an attempt, as Allanbrook put it of the Mozartean method, 'to move an audience through representations of its own humanity.' In Chaikovsky's time such a method was known as realism" (emphasis added).[75]

Taruskin reverses the discourse from private homosexuality and its attendant furtiveness to public environments and their attendant constraints. Thus the haunting imperial polonaise rhythms in the Fate melody that opens Symphony no. 4 (written soon after Tchaikovsky fled his marriage) could denote an indifferent force that applies indiscriminately to everyone, or it might suggest the internalized social pressure to marry, an attendant constraint that was especially fateful for Tchaikovsky.[76]

By 1893, the genre of the symphony was itself subject to constraints, heavily burdened with the tasks of both personal expression and transcendent greatness. The Russian title of the symphony, *Pateticheskaya Simfoniya,* seemingly splits the difference, connoting not so much a symphony of suffering (as *pathétique* suggests) as a symphony of passion.[77] In this context, Tchaikovsky's *Adagio lamentoso* offers to the symphony audience the lament, a topos not derived from social dances, but one with powerful social meaning nonetheless.

The lament has a long history in musical traditions both folk and elite, and in both the lament is fundamentally vocal and specifically gendered: women sing laments as a particularly intense emotional display. Ritual lamenting is especially common throughout Eastern Europe and Slavic regions, where it marks important rites of passage, notably marriages and funerals. In these contexts, professional lamenters (called in Russia *plachei, plakal'shitsy,* or *voplennitsy,* literally, "the weepers") function as mediators between the worlds of the living and the dead, communicating with dead ancestors during weddings, or during funerals guiding the soul toward its new dwelling.[78]

One history of Russian folkloric music observes that the melodies of such folk laments [*plach* or *prichet*] are usually based on short "characteristic motives" spanning a third or a fourth, repeated in the fashion of concentrated outburst.[79] Tchaikovsky's *Adagio lamentoso* does not seem to be a folkloric lament melody, for its harmonic and melodic language fits squarely into the late nineteenth-century Western European idiom. Tchaikovsky does, however, employ a characteristic descending motivic cell (mm. 1–2), which sounds twice for the opening phrase. Toward the end of the movement (mm. 127–34) we hear this cell in four concentrated and dramatic outbursts. But just as important as this musical reference to the Slavic lamenting tradition is the function of the lament as a mediation between two worlds. This notion will provide a useful tool for interpreting the two orchestrations of the lament motive itself. Before launching into that discussion, however, I first want to place the finale in the larger context of Western European and Russian art music.

In the early history of opera, the lament was at the apex of affective musical writing and formal developments. As Ellen Rosand notes, "it came to opera as an entity in its own right, with distinct definition and a generic integrity of its own, first purely literary, then musical as well."[80] In the sixteenth century, laments sometimes offered an occasion for eye music, such as the use of black notation where white notation would be the norm.[81] The monodic textures and descending tetrachord ostinato accompaniments of seventeenth-century laments allowed for abundant exploration of vocal effects and musical stylizations of natural crying. Icons of crying included such gestures as melodically leaping sighs, fragmented sobbing phrases, and irregular line lengths that indicated unpredictable passions.[82]

Funereal orchestral movements and independent pieces appeared in the mid-nineteenth century with the advent of character pieces and symphonic poems. Some better-known examples are Beethoven's *Marcia funebre* movement in his Third Symphony ("Eroica"), Hector Berlioz's *Symphonie Funèbre et Triomphale* (op. 15) and *Marche Funèbre* (op. 18, no. 3), and Franz Liszt's *Tasso: Lamento e Trionfo* (Symphonic Poem no. 2). None of these is as vocally iconic as Tchaikovsky's finale. Beethoven and Berlioz used the march as a topos; Liszt's lyrical theme at the *adagio mesto* (mm. 62–88) presents a long-winded folkloric melody, referring to gypsy music with augmented seconds. Perhaps the lament that Tchaikovsky would have been most receptive to is the one near the end of Glinka's opera *Ivan Susanin* (A Life for the Tsar) (1836), a story about the patriotic self-sacrifice of the peasant Susanin for Tsar Michail Fyodorovich Romanov. The epilogue to act 4 encapsulates the dramatic tension between public and private spheres typical of Russian opera. The private grief of three characters—Antonida (Susanin's daughter), her betrothed, Sobinin, and Susanin's ward Vanya—over the death of the hero Susanin is musically juxtaposed to the sounds of a public choral hymn celebrating the new tsar. At the end of Vanya's number "Ne ke moej on grudi" (Not on my breast), in which she recounts to a group of soldiers Susanin's last moments, she gives out a long modal melisma, a stylized wail representing a folkloric funereal lament, which here mediates between public and private realms.

Returning to Tchaikovsky's *Adagio lamentoso*, the music presents two different versions of its lament theme—one "queer" and the other "straight"—which nonetheless sound identical. The motion is from needless complexity to simplification—from fracture to coherence—but most importantly from private to public identification. Like the end of Glinka's opera, Tchaikovsky's symphonic lament combines the folkloric function of mediation with the operatic knot of private/public. Without the dramaturgy of opera, however, such a knot must be manifested in instrumental performance. The two versions of the lament theme provide just such a performative manifestation, each producing a subtly different experience for both the audience and the performers. In the nineteenth-century seating arrangement of the orchestra, first and second violins were separated, seated on either side of the conductor, which would have enhanced the stereophonic sound effect of the opening interlocked orchestration. Thus the audience may have noticed an indescribable change in the iron-out return of the theme. This subtle change for the audience, operating on the level of their subconscious, may also have been enhanced by the different physical experience of the performers. Wide leaps are more effortful than a simple step-wise passage. The effect would be a shift from less control to more control, and, in an inverse relation, from more tension to less tension. Tchaikovsky may have ensured a type of "method acting" for the performers of his psychological realism—a thorough realism taken to the level of praxis and the realm of the private.[83] Indeed, the psychoanalytic charges of musical "hysteria" may not be too far-fetched a description for the fractured melodic lines of the opening theme, especially in light of its coherent and "public" return. The initial string statement appears as lamenting women, with "icons of crying" encoded in a schizophrenic rift between vocality and aurality. After the relative calm and consolidation of voices in the D-major theme, the rift vanishes; private complexities disappear, exposed as inconsequential to the lament's (and the lamenters') public function.

The nuance of transgendered vocality in Tchaikovsky's *Adagio lamentoso* brings us back to the possibility of subjectivity and disclosure. As we have seen in the contemporaneous literature of sexology, gender mediated common conceptions of homosexuality: a third mixed gender, gender inversion, a feminine soul imprisoned in a masculine body—such were the transgendered images through which same-sex desire could be articulated. This mingling of gender and sexuality also appears in Tchaikovsky's own letters, in which he used feminine pronouns or feminine name forms to refer to other male homosexuals, as was common in such circles in the nineteenth century.[84] Furthermore, Tchaikovsky's epistolary relationship with his benefactress Nadejda von Meck—an intense fourteen-year intellectual, emotional, and financial entanglement—afforded him some manner of sympathizing or identifying with a female subject position. It was also, perhaps, his most cherished intimacy. Von Meck abruptly terminated her financial support and their correspondence at the end of 1890, two years before Tchaikovsky began, with difficulty, sketches for a sixth symphony. The end of that relationship affected him deeply. During 1891, Tchaikovsky, who no longer needed her money, tried in vain to continue their correspondence. Of his grief over the loss of his "beloved friend," he wrote, "I could not conceive of change in anyone so *half-divine*. I would sooner have believed that the earth could fail beneath me than that our relations could suffer change. . . . [A]ll my ideas of human nature, all my faith in the best of mankind, have been turned upside down. My peace is broken, and the share of happiness fate has allotted me is embittered and spoilt."[85] Tchaikovsky never recovered from this grief. Modest describes how his brother, in his delirium on the last day of his life, "continually repeated the name of Nadezhda von Meck, reproaching her angrily."[86]

Though the entire *Symphonie Pathétique* was dedicated to Vladimir Davidov, it is probable that for the *Adagio lamentoso* Tchaikovsky drew upon his profound sorrow over the recent death of his intimate relationship with Nadejda von Meck. His choice of the lament, with its gender associations, as the topos to end his "symphony of emotions" is surely significant; he gives to feminine grief (perhaps his own) heroic treatment in the position and form of a finale. Like the traditional laments of women, his can also be understood as mediating between the dead past and the living present, and between subjective and social reality. The queer and straight orchestrations of the wails illustrate two sides of lamenting: one is a physically wrenching private act, the other a sentimental public ritual. Taken together, the two orchestrations suggest the disclosure of something unspeakable about the practice of a man lamenting as if he were a woman and about the practice of a symphony finale singing a lament as if it were a triumph.

BENJAMIN BRITTEN AND THE USE OF MUSIC

A diary entry of Benjamin Britten, dated Sunday, February 7, 1932:

> Rather late breakfast. Go to church at St. Jude's with Beth at 11.0. In afternoon Mr. & Mrs. Bridge take me to Albert Hall to Berlin Phil. Orch. (Furtwängler). Hackneyed Programme. Haydn London Symp; Wagner, Siegfried Id. [Idyll] & Flying Dutchman ov.; Tschaikovsky's Pathetic Symp. F's readings were exaggerated & sentimentalised (esp. so in last item—no wonder a member of the audience was sick!!) The orch. is a magnificent body, tho' slightly off colour to-

day (e.g. wind intonation, 1st clar. & 1st Horn). Strings are marvellous. Timpanist great. Marvellous ensemble & discipline.

Go to tea with Barbara (also Beth) at her flat.

Back, walking, by supper.[87]

The activities that frame Britten's day involve physical and spiritual health—eating, exercise, and church. Britten seems to chide himself for a "rather late breakfast" but is back home early "by supper." The main portion of the entry concerns Britten's musical activity for the day—a disappointingly decadent concert with Tchaikovsky's "Pathetic" Symphony as its climax. Britten remarks that the excessiveness of the Tchaikovsky even provoked sickness. This comment is in line with the many English critics who linked Tchaikovsky's Sixth Symphony with disease, though here Britten seems to blame Furtwängler rather than Tchaikovsky. Nevertheless, Britten can admire the *disciplined* body that provokes the noxious sentiment.

Britten and Tchaikovsky were both avid diarists and letter writers, recording the details of their actions and thoughts for their own reflection as well as for self-disclosure to intimates. Foucault writes about a similar "administration of self" that took place in the Hellenistic and Roman periods; he links this practice to the ideals of asceticism and self-mastery, which had developed from earlier ethical dilemmas concerning sex.[88]

In *The Use of Pleasure,* Foucault investigates the emergence of sexual behavior as a moral issue in ancient Greek and Roman thought. The chief ethical dilemma concerned love between a free man and a free male youth, and the ensuing problem of reconciling the youth's consent to be the passive partner in a sexual relationship with an appreciation for the youth's virility and future status as a free man.[89] This predicament arises out of two perceived isomorphisms: one between the subject and object of desire, and the other between social roles and sexual roles. The elder man admires the youth not just for his beauty, but also for the youth's potential to become an *active* member of society like the elder man himself. Thus the youth's acquiescence in the sex act compromises the isomorphic nature of the desire. To remain true to his potential, the youth has to resist his elder male suitors as a display of self-mastery until a lover comes along who can offer services, commitments, gifts, and education in return for the youth's giving—but, importantly, not receiving—of sexual pleasure. Foucault describes this negotiation and stylization of desire between men and boys as an "erotics": a careful—even artful—use of pleasure that functioned as admirable self-discipline.[90]

Foucault goes on to argue that this problematic desire led Plato and others to elaborate a philosophy of asceticism that renounced physical pleasure for a spiritual pursuit of friendship. Later, in the first-century *Dialogue on Love,* Plutarch applied the discourses of both erotics and spirituality associated with the love of boys to the conjugal union of men and women. By conceiving of an erotics that did not depend upon the isomorphism of subject and object, Plutarch radically polarized the choice of object according to gender, for only in heterosexual marriage can one have honorable passivity and reciprocation.[91]

. . .

"Plutarch—the Greeks and the Romans—their troubles and ours are the same" (act 2, scene 1). So sings Captain Vere in Benjamin Britten's 1951 opera *Billy Budd,* based on the posthumously published novella by Herman Melville.[92] Of the few clearly identifiable gay composers working prior to the gay liberation movements of the 1970s, Benjamin Britten stands out as one whose compositions now seem transparent in their homoerotic content.[93] The rest of this chapter examines Benjamin Britten's use of music as a stylized exploration and regulation of his own attraction to male youths—an attraction he apparently never acted on, though one that haunts his operas and other vocal compositions.[94] His choices of opera libretti cluster around the theme of an older man's passionate feelings for an adolescent boy. These include *Peter Grimes* (1945), *Billy Budd* (1951; revised 1961), *The Turn of the Screw* (1954), and *Death in Venice* (1973). To this list should be added Britten's second canticle, *Abraham and Isaac,* which was written in 1952, immediately after the first version of *Billy Budd,* for the canticle shares a direct thematic connection with that opera. Together the opera and canticle present a sustained musical contemplation about the love between men and boys in terms that resemble Foucault's thinking about the Hellenic problem of desire. More specifically, Britten uses music to valorize the discipline of consent, and to recuperate the erotic pleasure of passivity.

Melville's story of interpersonal strife between the naval officer Claggart and the new recruit Billy Budd, which ends in the death of both men, is set in 1797, at a time of widespread panic in the British navy, shortly after recent infamous mutinies. Mutiny, however, is not the "trouble" to which Captain Vere refers in his remark about Greeks and Romans. The setting for the entire operatic drama, which lacks Melville's historicizing tangents, is the ship, a confined homosocial world of unsavory men seething with sexual frustration.[95] Britten and his librettists E. M. Forster and Eric Crozier brilliantly portray this sexual frustration in the first scene of act 3, in which the British sailors are unable to penetrate the French ship with their cannon shot. Vere's remark about the Greeks and Romans itself comes on the heels of Claggart's scheming for mischief against Billy. Earlier, however, Claggart had described Billy with seeming affection as a "Handsome Sailor"—a moniker that subsequently issues from the mouth of every sailor in the opera. In Melville's story, after Claggart's ambivalence about Billy is exposed, the narrator (who is identified as an "insider")[96] embarks on a lengthy and labyrinthine disquisition in an attempt to describe the quality of Claggart's menace. Turning to "a list of definitions included in the authentic translation of Plato," the narrator hits upon one that fits—"a depravity according to nature" (325).

As Eve Sedgwick notes, this passage thrusts the story into the semantic field of "nature and the *contra naturam*" associated for centuries with "protoforms of the struggles around homosexual definition."[97] For Melville, however, this depravity of nature is not exactly same-sex desire, but rather the misuse of reason "as ambidexter implement for effecting the irrational" (326) as a means of foreclosing interpretation and knowledge. This portrait of Claggart's depraved obscurity is ironically reflected in the narrator's own strategic evasion into a tone of objective scholarliness. The shift from "inside" to "outside" serves as a disavowal of knowledge—proof of ignorance in the act of research.

Forster and Crozier neatly telescope this dense literary moment into that one cryptic sentence of Vere, collapsing "depravity according to nature" with the fear of mutiny (as an irrational action) into the cipher of "Greeks and Romans." Vere, not privy to Claggart's schemes (as was Melville's omniscient insider), speaks of a troubling precondition of the ship and crew. In the next scene, however, Claggart sings, "Would that I lived in my own world always, in that depravity to which I was born" (act 2, scene 2), thus dropping the second crucial reference to Melville's disquisition. Claggart embodies the trouble mentioned by Vere, the specific form not yet known, but generally understood.

Billy Budd is a figure of purity and youth. As a foundling, he is without specific age, parentage, or birthplace. His shipmates give him infantilizing alliterative nicknames such as "Baby" and "Beauty," and when emotional he becomes inarticulate, frozen in a preverbal stage. Melville describes Billy in both feminine and masculine terms. As feminine, Billy is "a rustic beauty transplanted from the provinces and brought into competition with the high-born dames of the court" (299) and "a beautiful woman in one of Hawthorne's minor tales. . . . No visible blemish indeed, as with the lady; no, but an occasional liability to a vocal defect" (302).[98] As masculine, Billy is "a fine specimen of the *genus homo,* who in the nude might have posed for a statue of a young Adam before the Fall" (345). These descriptions set up queer erotic equations—the interloping rustic, the lady with a hidden flaw, and the naked prelapsarian Adam; all seem to be liminal identities, precariously poised between activity and passivity. In Melville's homoerotic triangle, Claggart and Captain Vere are active in both word and deed, while Billy cannot speak in his own defense; nor can his one action, a savagelike physical strike against Claggart's false accusations, go unpunished. With this killing blow, Billy and Claggart change places, and Vere must condemn Billy's action as a threat to social order.

For the opera, Forster and Crozier give Billy a more masculine finish.

Though the nicknames remain, there are no descriptive references to femininity, and they add a fight scene in which Billy gives one of Claggart's henchmen a drubbing for pilfering his kit bag. Captain Vere, however, betrays a mark of femininity in his devotion to "culture," also encrypted in his reference to Plutarch. In the second half of the nineteenth century, culture was a "feminized concept" in association with the Aesthetic movement, which was, as Joseph Bristow writes, "characterized by the foppish arrogance of the oversensitive writer" such as Oscar Wilde. Bristow notes that Forster's narratives often show a tension or polemic between a cultured style of manhood and an athletic or brutish style, worked out through implicit expressions of "desire between men of differing masculine types." Just as Plutarch, starting from the homosexual dyad of Plato, reimagines erotic love as a heterosexual dyad, so Forster "continually imagines circuits of sexual desire in primarily gendered terms, where connection is seen as the complementarity of feminine and masculine virtues."[99]

Desire flows initially from Claggart, climaxing in his so-called "perverted" accusations against Billy, for which Billy, dumbstruck by his stutter, in turn strikes and silences Claggart. Melville's narrator contemplates the change of place between Claggart and Billy—how victimizer becomes the victim, and how the primitive judgment meted out to Claggart must, in light of the martial code, transform his guilt to innocence (354). In the opera, however, it is Claggart and Vere who change places, and this shift becomes a focus of musical contemplation.[100] Vere, too, has been "struck" by Billy, penetrated by his verbal flaw, for Vere is unable to speak in Billy's defense, though he believes Billy to be fundamentally innocent (act 3, scene 2). Furthermore, Vere seems to have inherited Claggart's menacing desire. Britten and his librettists have Vere's final speech (act 3, scene 2) echo, rhetorically and musically, that of Claggart's earlier ambivalent soliloquy (act 2, scene 2). Claggart sings, "beauty, o handsomeness goodness, you are surely in my power tonight, and I will destroy you"; Vere sings, "beauty, handsomeness, goodness, it is for me to destroy you." These phrases are sung to the same basic melody but are separated by a half step, that paradoxical degree of the closest melodic and farthest harmonic relation. Furthermore, at these parallel moments Britten has Claggart and Vere sing in each other's symbolic key signatures.[101] Claggart's soliloquy (example 4a) appears in C major, the key of Vere, though his melody is full of flats, which points to his own key of F minor. Vere's later echo (example 4b) appears in F minor, though his melody, similarly, points to his own key, but with limited success. Both soliloquies end with self-identifying statements recited on the symbolic tone of the other. Claggart sings, "I, John Claggart, Master-at-Arms upon the *Indomitable*" on C (example 4c), while Vere sings "I, Edward Fairfax Vere, captain of the *Indomitable*" on F. Both statements, however, end in F minor (example 4d). Claggart and Vere are revealed as each other's double. In Jungian terms, Claggart repre-

Example 4. Benjamin Britten, *Billy Budd,* op. 50 (1951).

a. Act 2, scene 2, *animato*

(continued)

sents Vere's "shadow": Vere, ostensibly bound by law and fueled by panic, fulfills Claggart's menacing desire for Billy.[102]

The ethical conflict of *Billy Budd,* worked out through the story's homoerotic matrix of imbalanced power relations, pits the greater good of a current social order against the verity of a moral order beyond the social, a

Example 4 *(continued)*

b. Act 3, scene 2, *stringendo*

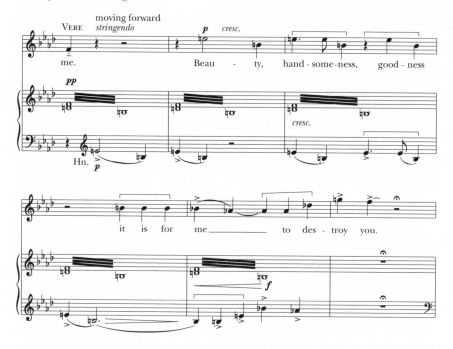

moral order embodied and even named as "truth" in the figure of Vere, but also sacrificed with Billy. Billy consents to be disciplined and sacrificed. According to Melville's story, Billy's lack of "mechanical spasm in the muscular system" (376) on the gallows indicates not only the thoroughness of his consent, but also his own self-mastery. Melville dwells on the vision of Billy's *stiff* body, retreating again to a scholarly register through the reported and almost Platonic dialogue of ship's purser and surgeon. These two characters debate the cause of this phenomenon. The purser attributes the lack of spasm to Billy's "will power," whereas the surgeon suggests that "'Budd's heart, intensified by extraordinary emotion at its climax, abruptly stopped.'" When the purser asks "'was it a species of euthanasia?'" the surgeon tellingly replies, "'*Euthanasia,* Mr Purser, is something like your *will power:* I doubt its authenticity as a scientific term. . . . It is at once imaginative and metaphysical—in short, Greek'" (377, emphasis in the original). "Greek" here is presented as a system of thought in opposition to the rigors of scientific thought—in short, philosophy. Billy's corporeal "will power" can only be understood within Greek philosophy, which regarded his unresponsive body as an object of admiration. Billy's stiff figure signals his virility, cor-

Example 4 *(continued)*

c. Act 2, scene 2, *adagio*

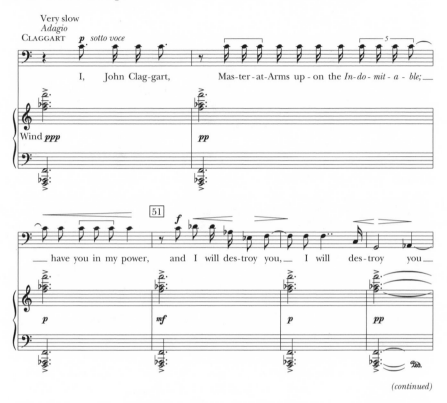

(continued)

recting his troublesome passive consent. Indeed, it is only through his consent that we can fully appreciate his manhood.

The moment of Billy's verbal consent we neither read nor hear. Captain Vere tells Billy Budd the verdict and punishment behind closed doors. Melville has his narrator once again step outside the "inside narrative" and imagine rather than describe the encounter:

> Captain Vere in end may have developed the passion sometimes latent under an exterior stoical or indifferent. He was old enough to have been Billy's father. The austere devotee of military duty, letting himself melt back into what remains primeval in our formalized humanity, may in end have caught Billy to his heart, even as Abraham may have caught young Isaac on the brink of resolutely offering him up in obedience to the exacting behest. (367)

Britten represents this unseen scene, ending act 3, in a long series of sustained chords, alternating orchestral timbres of woodwinds, brass, and

Example 4 *(continued)*

d. Act 3, scene 2, *a tempo*

strings like the rocking of the sea, terrifying yet calming in its inevitability. In this way, Britten and his librettists replace Melville's disingenuous imaginings with a blank canvas for the imaginings of the audience. It is this blank canvas, however, that Britten filled in one year later with his second canticle *Abraham and Isaac.* There he would use Melville's reference for further meditation on the ethical dilemma of a youth's consent, and that consent as a source of both admiration and erotic fascination.

. . .

For his setting of the story of Abraham and Isaac, Britten adapted a medieval Chester miracle play.[103] This play, which itself fills in the blank emotional canvas of the biblical story (Genesis 22), dramatizes the psychological torment suffered by both Abraham and Isaac as a result of Abraham's acquiescence to God's command to sacrifice his only son, Isaac. The canticle presents an erotic triangle analogous to that of *Billy Budd:* Isaac replaces Billy and Abraham replaces Vere, and, along these lines, God replaces Claggart (which seems blasphemous). But God's cruel and ultimately spurious request sets in motion the same ethical dilemma as did Claggart's counterfeit charges against Billy, that is, the necessity to sacrifice innocence for a "greater good," with religious order and obedience to God in this case substituting for martial law and social order.

The homoerotic element in *Abraham and Isaac,* scored for two voices and piano, is brought to the fore by the canticle's associations with *Billy Budd.* An additional erotic charge was provided by the choice of singers. The canticle was first performed in January 1952 by Britten on piano, the tenor Peter Pears (Britten's longtime lover), and the contralto Kathleen Ferrier. In 1961, the same year he revised *Billy Budd,* Britten and Pears recorded the canticle with the boy alto John Hahessey;[104] and that same year, he incorporated music from the canticle into his *War Requiem.* Thus it seems that *Billy Budd* and *Abraham and Isaac* were always linked in Britten's mind, even a decade after their debuts.

Britten uses the two voices for God's beckoning, entwined melodic lines full of resonant perfect intervals flowing in unmeasured recitative, like early medieval polyphony (example 5).[105] This sound establishes an aural intimacy that continues even after the bonded voices dissolve into father and son. Britten sets God's double voice as sensually pleasurable, even seductive, despite the severity of the request. Who wouldn't want to obey this God? The odd melodic benevolence encasing such onerous words in part reflects the medieval drama's mingling of New Testament allusions with Old Testament story. The narrator, called the Expositor, glosses the story as follows:

> By Abraham I may understond
> the Father of Heaven that can fond
> with his Son's blood to break that bond
> the Devil had brought us to.
> By Isaac understand I may
> Jesus that was obedient ay
> his Father's will to work alway
> and death to underfo.[106]

Example 5. Benjamin Britten, Canticle II: *Abraham and Isaac,* for alto, tenor, and piano, op. 51 (1952): "God Speaketh."

Thus, just as Britten made Captain Vere a double of Claggart through shared music, so Abraham and Isaac together appear to be a double of God. The honeyed voice of God, Himself a blend of Father and Son, is twinned by the dovetailing voices of father and son at the first 6/8—a horizontal rendering of the prior divine organum.

If, in the medieval drama, Abraham represents God the Father who sacrifices his son, then the terrifying Old Testament God who calls for the sacrifice would seem to align with the murderous throngs in the Passion of Jesus, which parallel abstract martial law and order in *Billy Budd*. All these forces can be understood as representing social exigencies that require sacrifice. In *Abraham and Isaac*, obedience to God, a coercion of seduction rather than intimidation, registers as the elder male's consent to sacrifice his beloved son, but the dramatic and musical momentum of the canticle climaxes with the beloved son's consent to be sacrificed. After an extensive agitated exchange, which dissolves into the shyly resolute *a cappella* statement "Father, seeing you mustë needs do so, Let it pass lightly and over go" (example 6), Isaac suddenly sings a major ninth leap from c^1 to d^2, an ecstatic vocal gesture over a first inversion minor seventh chord, broken and widely spaced in a manner that recalls the wide-spaced arpeggios of God's music. In answer to this melodramatic request for fatherly benediction, Abraham imitates Isaac's vocal leap, and he concludes this episode with his own *a cappella* statement, a stunning pentatonic "recitative" that narrates the most vivid moment of this ethical dilemma, the binding of Isaac's body ("Come hither, my child, thou art so sweet, Thou must be bound both hands and feet"). The naïveté of the music, along with the mixed rhetoric of love and discipline, produces a moment of queer melodrama, which recalls Melville's sexually charged description of Billy's stiff body, acquiescent but endowed with Greek "will power." Indeed, a haze of God's alluring music (at the 6/4) leads us to this exquisite act of bondage ("Come hither, my child, thou art so sweet, thou must be bound both hands and feet"), eroticizing the sacrificial body, just as Melville had done. The ethical dilemma of a youth's consent is here reconfigured (and Christianized) as sacrifice, and then again erotically recuperated through a further imagining of this sacrificial consent as a physical discipline. So disciplined, the consenting youth becomes an object of admiration, more so than the father, who has himself consented to God's will.

. . .

Through the various triangle structures that link *Billy Budd* and *Abraham and Isaac*, we can map onto the canticle an allegory of the oppression of the individual by social forces. Taking note of how Britten filled in the blank left by Melville (the moment of the youth's consent), first with his own blank in the opera, and later with this canticle, we can read this filling-in as an allegory for Britten's discipline of his own sexuality in 1950s England. For most of his

Example 6. Benjamin Britten, Canticle II: *Abraham and Isaac,* for alto, tenor, and piano, op. 51 (1952): "Here Isaac asketh his father's blessing on his knees."

Example 6 (continued)

HENCE ISAAC RISETH AND COMETH TO HIS FATHER, AND HE TAKETH HIM, AND BINDETH
AND LAYETH HIM ON THE ALTAR TO SACRIFICE HIM, AND SAITH:

professional life Britten performed and lived with his lover Pears, comfortably, though perhaps warily, according to the incoherent rules of the "open secret." Philip Brett, using Britten's life and work as a model, has written on how music can function as a policing force, helping to conceal homosexuality by providing a cover for non-normative behavior. Within the popular discourse of essentialism, Brett argues, "musicality" operates in the same semantic field as "homosexuality": musicians have natural musical talent and homosexuals natural sexual proclivities, and both identities deviate from a norm. Brett writes, "though it is highly 'specialized,' and sometimes 'despised,' musicality does not denote a noticeably 'punished role,' but rather a privileged one." Later he notes that "for the musician in general, and particularly for the gay or lesbian musician, there is an involvement in a social contract that allows comforting deviance only at the sometimes bitter price of sacrificing self-determination."[107]

In his great pacifist statement, the 1961 *War Requiem,* Britten uses a melody from the canticle as the subject of a lengthy fugue at the *Quam olim Abrahae* of the Requiem Offertory, the invocation of God's promise to Abraham to lead his seed to salvation. This fugue prefaces a setting of Wilfred Owen's poem "The Parable of the Old Man and the Young," a bitter and ironic retelling of the Genesis story in which Abraham (who represents warmongering heads of state) slays Isaac (the seeds of Europe) in spite of God's proposed alternative of the ram.[108] For the *Quam olim Abrahae,* Britten takes the melody that Isaac sings as he gathers sticks for the sacrifice of what he thinks will be a lamb ("Father, I am all ready," mm. 50–52) and literally subjugates Isaac's naïveté to traditional Germanic (read: authoritarian) contrapuntal techniques in what might be read as an ironic display of musical (self-) mastery to preserve the thin veil of ignorance.

As Philip Brett has noted, Britten relied heavily on the willful ignorance of British society, and especially that of critics who "embraced a strategy of choosing an approach to the themes of Britten's operas that would mask, parry, or render ridiculous their homosexual content."[109] To suggest that *Abraham and Isaac* should be included here not only as having homosexual content, but also as being very much about homosexuality, may well invite resistance in light of our cultural antipathy toward confronting the play of sexuality—not to mention overtones of incest, sadomasochism, and pedophilia—in Judeo-Christian stories and images. And no doubt it was this very antipathy that both Britten and Melville counted on when they chose the Abraham and Isaac story to imagine the unknowable exchange between Billy and Vere.

With its ties to *Billy Budd, Abraham and Isaac* appears as one of Britten's most concise musical explorations of the ethics of the consent of a youth to an adult male. This issue of consent, however, ramifies on a second level: the consent of postwar homosexual British citizens to be silent for the sake of social benefits. While struggling with the composition of *Billy Budd,* Britten wrote to a friend, "it is a strange business this, creating a world which finally ends by dominating oneself." There is a telling ambiguity in his words, one that confuses the fates of Billy and Britten.[110] Yet Britten's use of music to create that world provides us, the listeners, with a disquieting pleasure at the moment of this self-mastering consent to self-sacrifice. It is both his confession and our experience of what Foucault argued was unthinkable for the ancient Greeks—namely, the erotic gratification of the passive partner: Billy, Isaac, and ultimately Britten himself.

CRAFT AS CONFESSION

Britten biographer Humphrey Carpenter calls moments of *Abraham and Isaac* "self-parodying melodrama" and reports that "Britten seems to be amused by Isaac's attempts to wriggle out of what is coming." In a letter, Britten describes Isaac as "using every wile to try & escape. . . . I don't think there'll be a dry eye in the place————!"[111] Britten's interpretation of Isaac as "wily" casts a playful light on the story, one that accords with Foucault's understanding of ancient Greek erotics and the expectation of the youth's resistance. But Britten's almost cynical confession of planned theatricality bespeaks a shrewd awareness of how to touch the audience with a tearjerker.

If the comment by Britten betrays a cognizance of the melodrama of his canticle, then it also speaks indirectly to his compositional craft, that is, his mastery of a particular language and its affective power. Few would dispute that composers and performers learn a craft through rigorous training as apprentices, whether inside or outside a conservatory or music school. Even ears are "trained" or "educated." Technical mastery, however, stands in a binary relationship to the perceived prerequisite of natural talent. Popular accounts of Mozart, for example, describe how his prodigious talent allowed him to compose entirely in his head, without the aid of preliminary sketches, and how he wrote down his compositions quickly, with few or no corrections.[112] In this narrative, utter fluency with his craft places Mozart above craft*work,* his manual labor presumably inconsequential to artistic content. Evidence of the labor in composition, however, has also been assimilated to narratives of natural genius. Beethoven's copious sketches and corrections reveal not only a composer's workshop, but also his celebrated "titanic struggle" with the craft, popularly mythologized as his conquest of chaotic or obstinate raw material. This portrait was further strengthened by the fact of his deafness.[113] In such an account, acquired techniques alone are not sufficient against untamed musical elements, nor do they compensate for tragic physical disability.

Yet the rhetoric of natural musicality converges with essential formulations of homosexuality under the shared rubric of "deviance" from a non-musical, heterosexual norm, as Philip Brett has shown. Thus on one hand "musicality" can function as a social lubricant for queer identity, a "natural talent" that annexes sexual deviance, while on the other hand "musicality" can become a social sign of sexual deviance. The eclipse of sexual deviance by musical talent, however, is rarely complete. In music criticism, the focus on technique as opposed to talent often signals a suspicion of sexual deviance. The article on Tchaikovsky in the third edition of the *Grove's Dictionary of Music and Musicians* (1927), under the heading "Qualities of the Composer," disparages his lack of coherent compositional method, claiming, "His constant fluctuation between old and new forms of expression seems to argue a lack of strong intellectual conviction. . . . [W]hen we come to estimate his place in the history of music, we cannot forget that a more logical continuity of development, closer concentration, more searching self-criticism, more ruthless elimination of all that is merely facile and sentimental, have always been the characteristics of supreme genius." Later the author writes, "The chief defect of his instrumental writing—the repetition and development *ad nauseam* of an idea which is too thin to bear such over-elaboration—is even more obvious in his songs."[114] About Maurice Ravel— a self-styled aloof dandy whose only emotional attachment was reportedly to his mother—one critic snipes, "To hear a whole program of Ravel's works is like watching some midget or pygmy doing clever, but very small, things within a limited scope. Moreover, the almost reptilian cold-bloodedness, which one suspects of having been consciously cultivated, of most of M. Ravel's music is almost repulsive when heard in bulk; even its beauties are like the markings on snakes and lizards."[115] Similarly, Brett notes the questioning of craft in the reception of Benjamin Britten's music, placing the remarks in the context of the "open secret":

> On the one hand Britten's music was characterized as "mere cleverness," "devilish smart." On the other it was accused of sentimentality. Behind both attitudes, of course, lay the unspoken fascination with Britten's homosexuality, both labels being the reverse sides of the oppositions craft/cleverness, sincerity/sentimentality, which belong among a whole plethora of binarisms that Sedgwick has claimed as "epistemologically charged pairings, condensed in the figures of 'the closet' and 'coming out.'"[116]

The more a composer's non-normative sexuality is apprehended by the public, the more the composer's talent will be understood to be flawed, giving way to artifice and technique. According to his critics, Tchaikovsky's much-admitted "sincerity" and impulsive emotionalism ultimately devolves into self-indulgent repetitions that shred and deplete originality. Tropes in music criticism of cleverness, sentimentality, or superficiality reveal an epistemological anxiety. How does one distinguish artificiality, imitation, or exaggeration from an original that is always already deviant? Nowhere is this anxiety more apparent than in Hans Keller's 1948 essay "Britten and Mozart: A Challenge in the Form of Variations on an Unfamiliar Theme," which compares the two composers' biographies, compositional techniques, and reception histories. Not only does Britten appear as a "variation" of Mozart displaced by a few centuries, but Keller concludes (remarkably) that "the only deep-rooted musico-characterological difference between Britten and Mozart is that the one is often strongly inspired by nature while the other is an indoor composer."[117] (Could it be that with this confirmation of Britten's closeness to nature—he is an outdoor type in comparison to Mozart, the indoor type—Keller hoped to redress the *contra naturam* of Britten's sexual preference?)

Here, with debates about originals and imitations, themes and variations, begin fundamental questions about representation and queer identity, intersecting with what Foucault calls technologies of sign systems. These questions will be the focus of the next chapter.

3

Queer Ears and Icons

sign systems

This chapter will consider how music operates as an aspect of what Foucault calls the "technology of sign systems, which permits us to use signs, meanings, symbols, or signification." The technology of sign systems does not refer to semiotics—how sign systems work—but rather to how relationships of power are implicated in the assignment of meaning to abstract sounds and symbols. I will, however, offer some comment on how and why musicians as "icons" become an integral part of the sign system of queer identity; further, I will discuss how musical icons, along with music in general, can serve as strategies of self-representation for gays and lesbians—and this in confrontation, as well as dialogue, with the normative function of sign systems.

The technology of sign systems is dynamically related to configurations of power; the significance of icons will reflect various configurations, frequently being specific to generation, gender, race, and class. Judy Garland, for example, held no meaning for self-identifying queers of the 1990s (as did, for example, Madonna), and she seemed to have little appeal for lesbians, pre- or post-Stonewall. Judy Garland's victimhood and emotionalism represented subversiveness only to urban closeted gay men; those same aspects simply reinforced or amplified systematic gender oppression visited upon lesbians. The study of icons can thus become a juggling act of variables, and a comprehensive treatment is far beyond the scope of this book. My objective here is to articulate some basic principles of how and why musicians come to signify queer identities, how such signs, or icons, have operated in the past and continue to operate today.

The word icon (*eikon* in Greek) means "image," a visual representation that prompts the viewer to recall and ponder something beyond the icon itself, such as an abstract idea, a set of actions, or a group of people. In current popular and scholarly usage the word "icon" most often refers to famous real or fictive personages (such as Madonna or Barbie dolls) or person-types (such as cowboys) who are understood by their audience to organize a cultural identity. We would not know what that "cultural identity" was without looking at an icon. They define each other.

The icon as an object of individual fantasy and identification, however, is necessarily malleable. In her book *Barbie Culture,* Mary F. Rogers writes, "icons become such because of their versatility, thick folds of meaning . . . and open-ended nature. In a sense, then, a cultural icon is paradoxical. At one and the same time it evokes commonality and differences. It offers a shared point of reference for society's members while adapting itself to the cultural differences built up among them."[1]

This paradox of cultural icons—how they evoke both commonality and difference—may provide access for persons of queer identity to meanings originally developed out of normative identity; in other words, the icons of queer culture are celebrated as much for their difference in gender and sexuality as for the fact that these differences circulate within dominant culture, similarly constituting and representing those cultural identities. The distinction between queer icons and mainstream icons is not fundamentally the icons themselves; indeed, many queer icons come from the same pool of high-profile personalities of mainstream culture, especially musicians and actors. Rather, the distinction resides in the relationship of those two populations to representation itself, to the possibility of encoding identity in a legible sign.

TECHNOLOGY OF SIGN SYSTEMS

Foucault's own theorizing about signification and communication is perhaps most evident in *The Order of Things,* in which he argues that since the end of the Renaissance, the relationship of words to things has been one of ordering. Prior to the seventeenth century, Foucault argues, words were bound to things through a "similitude," the idea that the word somehow *resembled* the thing to which it referred. Language, both spoken and written, participated in a vast web of resemblances and cross-references, such that "nature and the word can intertwine with one another to infinity, forming, for those who can read it, one vast single text."[2] The later disenchantment of words—their shift from resemblance to representation—rendered language a system of signification in which, to use the terms of linguist Ferdinand de Saussure, the sign became divisible into component parts arbitrarily linked: the concept of the thing (the signified) and the word (signifier).

Key to *The Order of Things* and Foucault's other writings on language is Saussure's formulation that "each language articulates or organizes the world differently. Languages do not simply name existing categories; they articulate their own."[3] This view positions the speaking subject vis-à-vis language not as the powerful creative and self-actualizing force governing meaning, but rather as a decentered effect of a social process. Jonathan Culler summarizes, "all that is relevant [to language] are the distinctions and relations that have been endowed with meaning by a society." He states further, "when one speaks, one artfully 'complies with language.'"[4] Foucault blended Saussure's theories of language with the philosophical and hermeneutical tradition that can be traced back to Friedrich Nietzsche's *On the Genealogy of Morals* ("there is no 'being' behind doing, effecting, becoming; 'the doer' is merely a fiction added to the deed"),[5] but also to social theorists such as Foucault's onetime teacher Louis Althusser. Indeed, Althusser's idea of interpellation, whereby individuals are called into subjectivity by social forces as represented in the ideological state apparatus, also shows the influence of Saussure's decentering of the subject in relation to socially preordained structures of signification. Thus Foucault argues that language precedes the subject with ready-made identity categories and modes of expression through which subjectivity is not only articulated, but fundamentally shaped—what Judith Butler calls Foucault's "linguisticism . . . whereby language effectively brings into being that which it names."[6]

Foucault confronts an ontological crisis of the subject in the simple utterance "I speak." He writes, "'I speak' refers to a supporting discourse that provides it with an object. That discourse, however, is missing; the sovereignty of 'I speak' can only reside in the absence of any other language. . . . And the subject that speaks is less the responsible agent of a discourse . . . than a nonexistence in whose emptiness the unending outpouring of language uninterruptedly continues."[7] To gloss Foucault, I turn to a passage from Judith Butler contemplating the instability of the lesbian subject. Like Foucault, Butler asks "can the [lesbian] 'I' ever repeat itself, cite itself, faithfully, or is there always a displacement from its former moment . . . ?" She goes on to say, "if the 'I' is the effect of a certain repetition, one which produces the semblance of a continuity or coherence, then there is no 'I' that precedes the gender that it is said to perform; the repetition, and the failure to repeat, produces a string of performances that constitute and contest the coherence of that 'I.'"[8] Both Foucault and Butler posit that the subject (the "I") is void of specific content, for the very assertion "I speak" or "I am a lesbian" taps into the preexisting ideological content of language. For Foucault's subject to be sovereign (that is, self-governing and self-constitutive), the "I" must be outside the language that precedes it; for Butler's subject to be stable, the "lesbian I" must enact a single performance, or performances that are thoroughly identical, even in time. These are impossible conditions, of course, and they call attention to another aspect of sign systems, namely their purpose to create an illusion of fixity to inherently unstable and socially constituted conditions of being.

Butler states that repetition is both a stabilizing and destabilizing force.

On the one hand, the accumulated force of similarities in performance generates the sense of a prototype; on the other hand, performances at variance with one another disturb the sense of a prototype, rendering the prototype a phantasm. Butler, thinking about gender, goes on to say, "it seems there is no original or primary gender that drag imitates, but *gender is a kind of imitation for which there is no original;* in fact, it is a kind of imitation that produces the very notion of the original as an *effect* and consequence of the imitation itself. . . . In other words, heterosexuality is always in the process of imitating and approximating its own phantasmatic idealization of itself—*and failing*" (emphasis in the original).[9] For Butler, the gender of an individual is neither inherent nor stable, but rather it is produced by repetitive performances in imitation of the phantasms of heterosexuality. Signs such as "I" or gender are phantasms, which present themselves as robust by the force of repetition.

Saussure argues that concepts (signifieds) represent arbitrary divisions of a continuum of possibilities, and that the sounds or written images (signifiers) that denote these concepts are likewise arbitrarily matched to signifieds. But he also recognizes a class of "motivated signs." These are linguistic signs that are not entirely arbitrary, but rather share a mimetic relationship between signifier and signified (such as the onomatopoeic "bowwow" signifying a dog's bark) or descriptively combine signs that create a relation between the sound sequence and the concept, such as "typewriter."[10] When one moves beyond linguistic signs to other modes of representation, the "motivation" linking signifier and signified may be strengthened. For example, Culler summarizes, "an icon involves an actual resemblance between the signifier and the signified: a portrait signifies the person of whom it is a portrait less by an arbitrary convention than by resemblance."[11]

Cultural icons, then, could be considered a type of motivated sign insofar as the relation between the celebrity and his or her fans is one of resemblance, or the desiring of such, psychically enacted through identification or emulation. Since cultural icons are socially authorized as prototypes of gender and sexuality, individuals in this sign system remain decentered. The phantasmatic prototypes and the imitations that swirl around and destabilize "the subject" are, nevertheless, constituted as meaningful by the interpreting subject, just as the icon renders the subject, or, more specifically, the subject's interpretation of self, more legible. In other words, the Icon begets its icons.

Musical icons, I propose, enjoy an extra degree of resemblance or "motivation" as signifiers of queer subjectivity, for music, extralinguistic and nonvisual, has often been considered—indeed celebrated as—ineffable. As such, music can be understood as resembling queer subjectivity: music's position outside language resembles the impossibility of signifying subjectivities that lie outside normative heterosexuality. In this chapter I will show how a number of musical icons function as a means of negotiating the crisis of representation for gay, lesbian, and queer subjects. I will first look at the notion of music as a means of self-representation through the medium of "melodrama," and also the nineteenth-century queer icon of a melodramatic Sappho signifying a male "wish to be a woman." Then I will turn to three of the most famous gay and lesbian icons of the post-1950s era, Judy Garland, Melissa Etheridge, and Madonna. Each represents queer subjectivity to the mainstream, and to gays and lesbians, through various resemblances; each disrupts the technology of the sign—Judy Garland as a failed signifier, Melissa Etheridge as an imaginary signifier, and Madonna as a polymorphous signifier.

MELODRAMA

In the course of the nineteenth century the German philosophers Schopenhauer and Nietzsche turned to music—especially "absolute music," or music without words—as a vehicle for thinking about the relationships between the external world and the internal world of self-consciousness.[12] Early in the century, Hegel had considered such music to be an inferior art form because it was nonconceptual, hence its meaning was indeterminate and always bound to the senses and emotions of individual listeners.[13] The promotion of music to the highest form of art by the later philosophers has to do in part with their reevaluation of feeling and sensuousness, and a valorization of the ineffable. Feelings, emotions, were celebrated as the nonverbal, prereflective basis of subjectivity that makes philosophical reflection possible. To think about (absolute) music was to think about subjectivity, or, rather, to confront specifically those aspects of subjectivity that defied description in language.

For Schopenhauer and Nietzsche, all art is Dionysian because it instigates a cycle of creation and destruction of reflective thought. Andrew Bowie notes that "the process of 'infinite reflection' in Romantic art is associated with music because of music's dependence upon the passing of time for the different moments of a piece of music to become unified into a whole. . . . What this whole signifies, though, cannot be articulated in a definitive way."[14] Yet absolute music does *represent:* it represents the inarticulate whole, the unsayableness of subjectivity, the irreducible sonic excess of language, the Romantic "infinite reflection." Music is the *melodrama* of Dionysus.

The term "melodrama" derives from two Greek words: *melos,* meaning limb, honey, musical phrase, or song; and *drama,* meaning deed, action, or staged action. The dual signification of the Greek word "drama" as real but also represented action—act and enactment—was played out in nineteenth-century "melodramatic" plays and literature, characterized by sensational incidents, a strong polarity between good and evil, and bald appeals to the emotions. Literary critic Peter Brooks describes melodrama as a mode of imagination that, through excessive, intense, and extravagant forms of representation, exerts pressure on surface actions to advance a drama of ethics. In other words, the melodramatic mode of expression creates a parable of moral struggle out of banal gestures, statements, and scenarios. In this parable, "what one lives for and by is seen in terms of, and as determined by, the most fundamental psychic relations and cosmic ethical forces."[15]

Brooks asserts that the "desemanticized language of music" is embedded in melodramatic literature. "Style, thematic structuring, modulations of tone and rhythm and voice—musical patterning in a metaphorical sense— are called upon to invest the plot with some of the inexorability and necessity that in pre-modern literature derive from the substratum of myth."[16] The representational and emotional excesses of melodrama, according to Brooks, arose in reaction to the rationalism of the eighteenth century. Music took the place of myth in modern literature, replacing the inexorable of the sacred with the ineffable. Thus the "melo" of melodrama signifies the excess of meaning that connects the narrative of emotional realities to cosmic ethical forces. The *melos* is the real *drama,* the action that reveals the "enactments" or representations of larger forces at work behind banal gestures.

We can see the essence of melodrama in Radclyffe Hall's novel *The Well of Loneliness* (1922), about the emotional travails of a female "sexual invert" named Stephen. In one of the few peaceful episodes in the story, the simple act of listening to a beggar's song becomes laden with metaphysical significance. Hall writes, "They would not understand the soft Spanish words, and yet as they sat there they could but divine their meaning, for love is no slave to mere language. Mary would want Stephen to take her in her arms, so must rest her cheek against Stephen's shoulder, as though they two had a right to such music, had a right to their share in the love songs of the world."[17] Here the foreignness of the language transforms a song with words into absolute music. This pure music, then, expresses the ineffability of the love between Stephen and Mary, and their own foreignness to "love songs of the world." No matter what language, they will be outsiders. Mary's resting her cheek on Stephen's shoulder, a naïve—and thus also banal—gesture, becomes an act of defiance, a claim of cosmic rights in the face of hegemonic heterosexuality.

SAPPHO AND THE MELODRAMATIC MAN

Stephen and Mary are not just foreigners to the world of heterosexual lovers, but also to the phallocentric social order that rarely acknowledges the reality of women's same-sex desires and practices.[18] They are, in fact, foreigners even to their own signification in the figure of Sappho. Today Sappho occupies an exalted position in lesbian history, but it was male homosexuals who, in the nineteenth century, first established her as an icon of homosexual desire. Prior to the nineteenth century, male appropriations of Sappho worked to assimilate her to a normative heterosexual model, beginning with Ovid, who imagined Sappho to be lovers with Phaon.[19] The assimilation strategy of Ovid held sway during the neoclassical intellectual movement in early modern and modern France, where Sappho became a national obsession for the literati. Ovid's story of Sappho was taken as authentic biography in the seventeenth and eighteenth centuries, and this elevation from fiction to fact served as a means of attenuating the homoeroticism of her poetry.

Nineteenth-century German scholars broke with the Ovidian tradition by creating a chaste Sappho, who, according to Joan DeJean, originated with historian and philologist Friedrich Gottlieb Welcker. In his 1816 study of Sappho, Welcker argued that Sappho could not be homosexual because as a woman she could not possibly experience the ennobling homoerotic bond that was a part of the Socratic tradition. For Welcker, a "female variant" of *pederastia,* the ideal homosexual love, was intolerable; but neither did Welcker want to support a reading of her poetry as associated with "the basely sensual heterosexual eros."[20] This ambivalence led Welcker's disciples to configure Sappho as chaste, and thus they banished Sappho from both homo- and heterosexuality. They even Christianized Sappho by associating her with the Virgin Mary.

In contrast to the German tradition of scholarship that Christianized Sappho stands the French and English tradition that appropriated the sexualized lesbian subject position to express male same-sex desire. In France, the lesbian poems in Charles Baudelaire's 1857 *Les Fleurs du Mal* (Flowers of Evil) repositioned Sappho as homosexual, but they also portrayed her as a *femme damnée,* simultaneously heroic, tragic, and predatory. Baudelaire's Sappho had a vampiric unquenchable thirst for a love that was condemnably sterile.[21] This donning of the lesbian Sappho's subjectivity was also taken up by the English poet Algernon Charles Swinburne. Richard Dellamora, drawing on the work of Isabelle de Courtivron, argues that for these sexually ambiguous writers, identification with Sappho and lesbian desire provided "a field in which to play out male confusion about and discontent with prescribed roles for men and women." He writes, "lesbian fantasies allow male writers to indulge what de Courtivron calls the 'wish to be a woman.' Through lesbian personae, men cross over into the forbidden territory of feminine feeling and bodily sensation. . . . But crossing into Lesbos, the land of women, connotes as well transgression, sin, and the concomitant experiences of guilt, suffering, and even eternal death."[22] The male poet's "wish to be a woman," or, more specifically, the "wish to be Sappho," is both the wish to explore sensuality and sentimentality forbidden to men, and "a means for men to own their desire for other men."[23] The phallic femininity of a vampiric Sappho became iconic of male same-sex desire at Oxford during the 1860s, in the context of the intellectual and aesthetic "revival" of ancient

Figure 2. Simeon Solomon, *Sappho and Erinna in a Garden at Mytilene,* 1864. Watercolor on paper. Tate Gallery, London. Photo: Tate Gallery, London / Art Resource, NY.

Greek ideals by writers and artists such as Walter Pater, Swinburne, John Addington Symonds, and artists such as Simeon Solomon.

Greatly influenced by the writings of art historian Johann Joachim Winckelmann, these Oxford revivalists posited that the androgynous figures in ancient Greek sculpture represented ideal beauty in antique thought—an ideal they also believed was later emulated in the works of Renaissance artists such as Leonardo da Vinci.[24] The paintings of Simeon Solomon, one of the few in the Oxford circle to acknowledge his sexual desire for men (he was eventually disgraced by a trial in 1873), exemplify this revivalist ideal. Drawing upon Greek myth for his subject matter, he peopled his paintings with smooth hermaphroditic figures. In his 1864 watercolor *Sappho and Erinna in a Garden at Mytilene* (figure 2), inspired in part by Swinburne's Sapphic poems, androgyny takes the form of action. Two women sit on a marble bench in a classical verdant garden; Sappho, with a garland about her head (a sign of honor that places her alongside celebrated Greek men) has caught Erinna in an intense embrace. The recent lunge of Sappho's body is revealed in the position of her legs—splayed, bent, twisted, and penetrating the space of Erinna's lap. She has forced Erinna's knee upward into an erect position. The erotic energy of the lunge is also registered in the luxuriant draping of the dresses; the upward sweeping fold of Sappho's gown leads the viewer's eyes to the loins of Erinna, where her dress gathers beneath her hand and falls in a line of circular creases down her leg.[25] Sappho's head is in profile to the viewer, her eyes closed as she kisses her beloved. Meanwhile, Erinna stares at the viewer, eyelids heavy with ardor or quiet resignation, her right hand caressing or arresting Sappho's left hand, which pulls her dress down from her shoulders. The viewer, as an interloper, catches the two women at the precise moment of their transgression.

Writing about this painting, Swinburne describes the pair in opposing, heterosexualizing terms:

> The clinging arms and labouring lips of Sappho, her fiery pallor and swooning eyes, the bitter and sterile savour of subsiding passion which seems to sharpen the mouth and draw down the eyelids. . . . The face and figure beside her are souless and passive, the beauty inert as a flower's; the violent spirit that aspires, the satisfied body that takes rest, are here seen as it were in types; the division of pure soul and of mere flesh; the powerful thing that lives without peace, and the peaceful thing that vegetates without power.[26]

For Swinburne, the scene is post- rather than pre-orgasm, for the surge of passion has passed with the moment of sterile contact. Sappho is the pure soul, aspiration, and the restless spirit of masculine nature, while Erinna is mere flesh, powerless and idle.

What preceded this frozen moment? How can a "peaceful thing that vegetates" motivate such transgressive, transgendering behavior? Later in the same essay on Solomon, Swinburne describes the painter's art as "music made visible." He writes, "in pictures where no one figures as making music, the same fine inevitable sense of song makes melodies of vocal colour and symphonies of painted cadence."[27] In *Sappho and Erinna in a Garden at Mytilene,* no overt music making is depicted, though music subtly penetrates the scene. Sappho's lyre sits in the lower right-hand corner, leaning against a pedestal upon which rest a scroll of paper, a pen, and an ink jar. These symbols of her musical and poetic identity appear close by, as if rivals with Erinna for Sappho's attention and embrace. Indeed, it seems as if her fit of passion came upon her in mid-composition, causing her to swivel about in a violent redirection of her erotic energy. The juxtaposition of the lyre with Erinna not only renders the lyre as the phallic instrument of Sappho's sexuality, but also suggests that both are co-conspirators in Sappho's perverse desire. So, too, Swinburne's description of Solomon's visual "musicality" renders this picture, in particular, perversely melodramatic: the *"meloi"* are displayed in the *limbs,* contorted and entangled like polyphonic melodies, while the *"drama"* is an enactment of phallic sexuality depicted as the intrusion of knees and arms.

JUDY GARLAND / SAPPHO REDUX

In 1963, on the ninth episode of her television show, a forty-one-year-old Judy Garland sits close beside a twenty-one-year-old Barbra Streisand. Their arms are entwined as Judy glances bashfully up at Barbra and then vacantly out to the audience before beginning to sing very softly, "Forget your troubles . . ." Barbra answers her with equal delicacy, "Happy Days . . ." The dovetailing continues:

(Judy) . . . come on get happy . . .

        (Barbra) . . . are here again . . .

we're going to chase . . .

        the skies are bright . . .

all your blues away . . .

        and clear again . . .

They each sing their own signature "happy" songs in the inverted, melancholic tempo that defined Barbra's famous torchy rendition of "Happy Days."

Mel Tormé recounts that the merging of the two songs was Judy's idea for Barbra's guest spot on the show, and that the two legendarily temperamental divas felt "instant warmth" for each other.[28] In the duet sequence they look relaxed and comfortable singing together despite their contrasting styles, Judy characteristically anticipating the beat and Barbra frequently delaying her entries, as if an afterthought. The effect is powerfully tender, as if the elder Judy were carefully scooting her nearly monotone melody out of the way to allow the showier music of her younger partner—and heir as gay icon—to shine. Indeed, we, the audience, witness a passing of the "torch" in this performance, from the elder icon to the younger. At the beginning of the second verse Judy briefly leans against Barbra and seems to smile in response to what she hears from her. As the music builds with a crescendo their hands clasp tight (figure 3). Barbra sings, "so let's tell the world . . . about it now."

Nearly one hundred years after the unveiling of Simeon Solomon's *Sappho and Erinna in a Garden at Mytilene,* Judy and Barbra enacted a similar scene of *meloi* entangled; Judy, like Sappho, served as a melodramatic icon of queer identity for the homosexual male. These two icons, however, did

Figure 3. Judy Garland with Barbra Streisand, *The Judy Garland Show*, 1963. Photo: Gabi Rona; Motion Picture and Television Photo Archive.

not function in the same way. Sappho, as a lesbian, was projected as imbued with phallic power, and therefore as active, even predatory. She was male homoerotic desire in female form, with female emotions. Judy Garland, who was not a lesbian, and whose image was in part constructed by Hollywood, was not imbued with phallic power (with one notable exception, discussed below), nor, however, was she passive. She did not signify male homoerotic desire; rather, she signified the whole condition of male homosexual identity in the mid-twentieth century.

The adult Judy Garland was frequently marketed as frail and lonely. On the back cover of Judy Garland's 1957 album *Alone*, the descriptive blurb encapsulates the pathos that would become legendary.

> Here is the music of aloneness . . .
> Sung with a heart-catching blend of tenderness, torchiness, and irrepressible vitality by the incomparable Judy.[29]

This pathos would also fuse her to the identity of gay men prior to the gay liberation movement. She is tragic in her fundamental solitude, heroic in her fortitude, unique in her very essence.

Judy Garland seemed to personify melodrama. Her movies are often marked by banality infused with cosmic emotionalism, and her career was a string of nostalgic repetitions and imitations. When she was well into her early twenties, MGM still cast her as a lovesick adolescent, even after giving her adult roles. Later, for her concerts and television show, she relied heavily on re-creations of musical numbers from her films. Thus Judy Garland's status as an icon cannot be separated from the context of Broadway musicals and their Hollywood counterparts, as these melodramas served the imagination and coping strategies of white homosexual adolescent boys and men of the 1950s, '6os, and early '70s.[30]

According to D. A. Miller, the appeal of Broadway musicals to latent homosexual adolescent boys of this era is the discontinuity between the drama and the music, the fantastical interruption of stories of heartache and frustration by musical numbers. For the boy with "diffuse sentimentality," as for the characters of the show, the songs "had the same miraculous effect . . . that of sending the whole world packing."[31] Interrupting harsh reality for a song represented defiance, and an exaltation of "personal will." Miller summarizes, "the true content of show-tune transcendence is simply the strength to endure a depressive status quo."[32] Elsewhere he describes the Broadway song as "transcendental longing,"[33] somewhat analogous to the German Romantic "infinite reflection" as an endless process of examining the unsayable of subjectivity.

In a somewhat different interpretation, John Clum argues that the celebration of sensual pleasure, heightened theatricality, and "often parodic presentation of gender codes" provided gay adolescents, such as himself, with an escape from "the masculine rites that disinterested and threatened us."[34] Clum, too, reads the preoccupation with musicals as a sign of defiance—here a defiance of gender norms through the creation of an alternative masculine rite of reveling in unmasculine sensual and emotional display, much as Sappho provided nineteenth-century writers.

This meaning of defiance, whether as a fantastical stopgap for heartbreaking reality or an escape of gender norms, may have been integral to the intention of the composers and producers of Broadway and Hollywood musicals, for they were mainly outsiders to the status quo. Gerald Mast notes that, "those who would create the twentieth-century American musical and shape the histories based on it were Jewish or gay or both."[35] Notable homosexual or bisexual composers, directors, and producers include Cole Porter, Lorenz Hart, Noël Coward, Stephen Sondheim, Leonard Bernstein, Arthur Laurents, Jerry Herman, Vincente Minnelli, and Roger Edens. But Miller remarks, "the historical uniqueness of the Broadway musical among 'the signs' [of the homosexual] consisted in the fact that it never looked like one."[36] Musicals, after all, celebrate the heterosexual couple, their romantic struggle for union and their ultimate success. As a foil to the ideal heterosexual couple there often appear homosexual allusions and avoidances. For example, the effete, dandyish masculinity of Fred Astaire was buttressed as heterosexual by the appearance in supporting roles of men who were either more effeminate than Astaire or strategically impotent within the plot. Fred Astaire also rarely danced with a male "buddy," as the more macho and athletic Gene Kelly frequently did.[37] Astaire's style of masculinity was too sexually ambiguous to risk it. Judy Garland's image, too, projected an ambiguous and ambivalent presentation of gender and sexuality.

Garland was not the classic Hollywood beauty of her on- and off-screen rival Lana Turner. Her adolescent roles cast her as the ordinary (if not asexual) girl next door (usually within a small town) with the extraordinary voice.[38] Indeed, young Garland here seemed to embody the double entendre of the "extra," both intensifying and surpassing the ordinary. The contradictions of this image reached a height in *The Wizard of Oz* (1939), in which the "ordinary" Kansas farm girl Dorothy is configured as an outsider, unrecognized, misunderstood, unprotected from danger by her parents, and harassed by Miss Almira Gulch, who threatens her with punishment by the state authority (the sheriff). Dorothy sings the central number of this escape fantasy, "Over the Rainbow," only to find later that her fantasy world is filled with variously deficient "queer" types of males, including the brainless Scarecrow, the heartless Tin Man, and the "sissy" Lion. None of these are appropriate as a romantic interest, a fact that seems to support the reverse fantasy to return "home." Thus Dorothy is caught in her struggle against banality and her own desire for it. She articulates an ambivalent relationship to "ordinariness" and normalcy that resonates with many gay, lesbian, and transgendered populations.[39]

Film critic Richard Dyer has noted that "not being glamourous is to fail at femininity, to fail at one's sex role. [Garland] might be valued for her peppy singing, but pretty much as one of the boys."[40] He goes on to argue that many of her roles convey her "in-betweenness" in terms of sexual maturity ("Too old for toys / Too young for boys").[41] In her later movies, this "in-betweenness" became an indeterminacy of sexuality and gender, which fed the characteristic self-deprecating humor that aligned her image with "camp." Camp is often described (most notably in a famous essay by Susan Sontag) as a sensibility or behavioral strategy characteristic of homosexual men. It is a deliberately self-conscious performance, theatrical and artificial, in a context that is otherwise serious, natural, or even banal. Camp shares with melodrama excessiveness as a mode of imagination or a register of performance, accommodating but at the same time subverting mainstream norms.[42] But camp and melodrama differ fundamentally in that camp blends seriousness with irony, bringing together multiple cultural references that set up humorous intertextual resonances that emerge from a melodramatic foundation. Readers of *The Well of Loneliness* were not invited to laugh at the plight of Stephen and Mary, but viewers of the adolescent Garland in *Babes in Arms* (1939) cannot help but smile during her mid-song pouting and lovesick soliloquy, which she addresses to a photograph of the always less-than-masculine Mickey Rooney:

> I know I'm no glamour girl . . . But maybe someday you'll realize that glamour isn't the only thing in this world. If your show's a flop you'll find you can't eat glamour for breakfast. Anyway, I might be pretty good-looking myself when I grow out of this ugly duckling stage. And you're no Clark Gable yourself.

This over-the-top melodramatic moment has even greater camp value if the viewer understands the implicit reference to another Garland performance—the one that put her on the map in Hollywood. This is her performance of "Dear Mr. Gable (You Made Me Love You)," which she sang to a picture of Clark Gable, initially for a publicity birthday party in his honor; the scene was later re-created in *Broadway Melody of 1938*. Given that *Babes in Arms* was released the same year as the *Wizard of Oz* (1939)—at the height of Garland's popularity—this winking look back to her "humble" beginning enhances the irony and artifice of the self-deprecation.

Her last movie for MGM, *Summer Stock* (1950), consummates all three tropes of ordinariness, androgyny, and camp, and does so with a unique dose of phallic power, and even lesbian coding. At the beginning of the movie Garland is a short-haired, overall-wearing "maiden" farm girl (Jane) in an endless and sexless engagement to an allergy-ridden, father-dominated "sissy" (Orville). By the end of the movie she appears as a sultry cross-dressing dominatrix. There are many scenes in *Summer Stock* in which Garland is marked as "one of the boys," such as her barn-dance *pas de deux* with Gene Kelly, a "buddy" dance in which she meets the challenge of imitating his dance steps. More importantly, however, she is presented simply as "the real man," in contrast to Orville and to the entire troupe of performers brought to the farm by her aspiring actress sister. Garland shows them all how to do the hard work of feeding pigs, harvesting food, and gathering eggs (neither the virile Gene Kelly nor the effeminate Phil Silvers knows how to milk the cow).

In the famous "Get Happy" number,[43] she similarly commands the movements of the dancers, knocking them out of the way, initiating their steps with her hands, or walking nonchalantly among their prostrate bodies, one of which convulses at her feet. With her hair all but hidden under a black fedora, and her disproportionately long stockinged legs streaming down from a black suit coat that slyly functions as a *very* short skirt, she dances against a fantastical background of clouds in a bright orange sky among black-suited men who seem an eerie foreshadowing of her later gay entourage and concert audiences.[44] Her dance steps subtly reflect the masculine movements of the male dancers that surround her,[45] and these imitations resemble the earlier *pas de deux;* but here it is a show of easy mastery rather than mimicry. Garland further emphasizes her masculine cool by repeatedly pulling her fedora down over her brow, mobster style, shadowing her face as she sings and dances. She is no longer a worker; she is The Boss (figure 4).

Indeed, the tension of this "barnyard musical" story lies in the confrontation of two forms of gendered "work": farm work, commonly understood as masculine and licit, and theater work, feminine in its display and emotionalism, historically harboring illicit behaviors. Both forms of work and their associated populations are parodied and amplified by the contrast: the drabness and small-mindedness of the farm-town folk is set against the exaggerated gestures and youthful exuberance of the actors. Judy/Jane crosses over from one world of work and gender to the other. But gender here is complexly and campily related to sexuality, for the sexless butch farm girl becomes, at the end of the movie, an urban gay man, happily cruising among the male dancers.

To return briefly to that Sapphic scene between the two gay icons, Streisand and Garland: it was played to a studio audience that Mel Tormé described as always "heavily populated with homosexuals . . . Odd Fellows [who] had a predilection for La Garland" (here exhibiting his own familiarity with gay lingo).[46] No doubt, then, these audience members experienced a special pleasure as they superimposed their memory of the *en travesti* homoeroticism in *Summer Stock* onto the vision before them: two women—two icons—singing and clinging to each other.

That an ethos of "work" should drive the plot of *Summer Stock* is ironic given that MGM sacked Garland after completing the film, having had enough of her temperamental behavior and apparent waywardness. By all accounts, Garland's gay fans read her subsequent concertizing and television appearances in terms of her professional and personal difficulties. The perception of tragedy enhanced the meaningfulness of her singing: decades of drug addiction, disastrous relationships and marriages (some with gay or bisexual men), and paralyzing insecurities made her emotionally intense performances seem expressively authentic. The real Judy was the one on stage singing about her life, while the offstage Judy was barely living.

After 1950 and *Summer Stock,* Judy Garland rose to the status of a gay icon; there were multiple "comebacks," brilliant concerts alternating with ruinous flops. For many younger gay men today, Garland represents an embarrassing time of stereotypically flamboyant effeminacy and an identification with tragedy and victimhood.[47] The era of "the closet" came to a symbolic end with the Stonewall Inn riots on June 27, 1969, hours after Judy Garland's wake in New York. George Chauncey notes, however, that before Stonewall, Garland's concerts provided an important space for gay men to congregate in a critical mass and form a community, sowing the seeds of collective identity and "liberation" thinking.[48]

Figure 4. Judy Garland sings "Get Happy," from *Summer Stock*, 1950.
© Bettmann/CORBIS.

Nonetheless, signs of Garland as a gay icon in homophile documents
dated prior to her death are surprisingly difficult to come by. Dyer mentions
this fact as well, citing only one example, the British film journal *Film and
Filming*, which featured Judy Garland on the cover of its first issue in 1954 and
which "quickly established itself as a closet gay magazine." In the third issue
the editor wrote a piece about *A Star Is Born* (1954) entitled "The Great
Come-Back," at one point expressing his admiration for her courage.[49] The
next earliest example is perhaps her own aside in the 1963 movie *I Could Go
On Singing*: "I've had enough [martinis] to float Fire Island." Fire Island, with
its many resorts for vacationing New Yorkers, had a long-standing reputation
as a gay paradise.[50] Remarks about her homosexual fans occasionally appear
in reviews of her concerts throughout the 1960s.[51] One reviewer for *Time*
notes of her 1967 Palace Theatre concerts that

curiously, a disproportionate part of her nightly claque seems to be homosexual. The boys in the tight trousers roll their eyes, tear at their hair and practi-
cally levitate from their seats, particularly when Judy sings:

If happy little bluebirds fly
Beyond the rainbow,

Why, oh why can't I.[52]

The review goes on to quote two Manhattan psychiatrists who offer explanations for this "phenomenon." These explanations were quoted, and the
whole review lampooned, in a short editorial that appeared in the first issue
of *The Advocate* (then *The Los Angeles Advocate*):

> We imagined a senior associate assistant managing editor of *Time* reading his
> reporter's fresh copy, then shouting across the room, "Get a couple of head-
> shrinkers on the phone. Find out why the queers like Judy so much." . . . We
> gravitate toward superstars, one Doc says, because "these are people they can
> idolize and idealize without getting too close to. In Judy's case, the attraction
> might be made considerably stronger by the fact that she has survived so many
> problems; homosexuals identify with that kind of hysteria." Says another Mad-
> hattan psychiatrist, "Judy was beaten up by life, embattled, and ultimately had
> to become more masculine. She has the power that homosexuals would like to
> have, and they attempt to attain it by idolizing her."
>
> Back in the *Time* office, we imagined again, Brilliant Young Reviewer is sit-
> ting in the office of the SAAME (the one that yelled before). The Big One
> speaks, cigar clenched firmly between teeth, smoke curling lovingly around
> each word, "Good work, Grimsby! You really dug into the nitty-gritty and sent
> it flying up the flagpole."
>
> "Thank you, Miss Lovelace," replies Brilliant Young Reviewer, rolling his
> eyes, tearing at his hair, and levitating gracelessly from his seat.[53]

The imagined final scene between the young reviewer and the dominatrix
editor echoes the *Time* review. While, on one hand, the *Advocate* piece
spoofs pop-psychology theories about abject gay men and their "diva worship" of Garland, on the other hand, it turns the tables on straight culture,
suggesting that straight men also succumb to abjection and "diva worship,"
and that their divas can be masculine women, too. The editorial further
insinuates that the straight world is out of step with the current climate of
gay culture; the implication is that gay men, already in 1967, are distancing
themselves from the stereotypical identification with abjection and "that
kind of hysteria."

No other references to Judy Garland appear in *The Advocate* until September 1969, when an obituary proclaims, "One of the gay world's favorite
entertainers is dead. . . . In many gay clubs, the Judy Garland impersonation
has been a standard part of a dozen acts. Judy often visited one of the clubs
in Hollywood to see the show there; she loved the attention, and the audience loved to see her."[54]

Most surprising is where Judy Garland does *not* appear. The published
diaries of Donald Vining, which document many details of gay New York life

from 1933 to 1982, mentions Judy Garland only once, in the context of trying to get tickets to her concert (by contrast Greta Garbo is mentioned several times in nearly every volume, as are many operas and Broadway musicals).[55] Garland's name does not appear in the homophile magazine *One* (which began publication in 1953 out of Los Angeles), nor the *Mattachine Review* and the Mattachine Society newsletters published in Los Angeles, San Francisco, and New York. These publications were angling to assimilate gay male identity to the upper echelons of the dominant heterosexual culture, and thus generally shied away from any camp icons perceived as lower-brow and decidedly queer.

But Garland is noticeably absent from less assimilationist publications as well. Angelo D'Arcangelo does not mention her in *The Homosexual Handbook* (1968), nor in his *Gay Humor Book* (1972) (though in a list of gay bores, number eighty-three reads "Bores who sing along with Barbra Streisand records"). Bruce Rodgers's 1972 *The Queens' Vernacular: A Gay Lexicon* only obliquely refers to Garland in the entry "Dorothy and Toto," which he defines as slang for a couple with a dominating effeminate partner. Perhaps most surprisingly, Garland does not appear in a list called "The Camp Hall of Fame," nor among female singers who represent camp published in *The Camp Followers' Guide!* (1965). Barbra Streisand, however, is listed in both places.[56]

The Camp Followers' Guide! is a pop culture version of, and response to, Susan Sontag's 1964 academic article "Notes on 'Camp'" (alluded to above), and it includes and expands upon her list of camp items within its various essays. Though Sontag mentions neither Streisand nor Garland, Streisand appears four times in the *Guide* and Judy Garland only once, in an anonymous story that spoofs the pretentious appropriation of camp by straight bohemians. The scene, a dialogue between a girl named Greta and her friend Adolphus, takes place among what are described as "high-spirited people at a Bogart *feste*." Adolphus, who throws flirtatious glances at other male "culturati," at one point turns to his companion and asks, "Greta, do you *identify*?"

> "I mean, do you identify with like Judy Garland in *Shall We Dance?*"
> Great Galloping Toastrounds! Greta is blushing! "Well . . . sometimes," she says. "Occasionally one gets just a *tiny* bit involved. Of course, one's appreciation rarely descends to that level. After all, taste does not exist simply to dignify bad art."
> "Well, I identify with Judy Garland," says Adolphus. . . . "Sometimes I think I *am* Judy Garland. Nineteen-forty Judy Garland, of course."[57]

Judy Garland as a sign of gay identity is here being parodied as already passé among urban bohemians eager to display a camp sensibility, for Greta pronounces such emotional identification as beneath camp, as beneath that intellectually justified appreciation of "bad art." Similarly, the anonymous author sets Adolphus up as a poseur who misunderstands and mangles gay signification. Adolphus does not really know Garland's films (*Shall We Dance* is a 1937 Fred Astaire and Ginger Rogers movie), and his professed identification with the 1940 Garland, who was then at the height of her career, goes against the gay grain of identifying with the later period of her career when her hard life was more exposed. Upon seeing a boy and girl kissing in the ticket line, Adolphus, retching, shouts "'Give Camp . . . back . . . to the homosexuals,'" to which Greta responds:

> "Pull yourself together, chicky-baby," she says. "If, as Susie Sontag says, 'watching stag movies without lust is Camp,' then surely the same dictum can apply to watching public copulation ditto."[58]

Greta comforts Adolphus by saying, "'It's all right, chicky, they're *Pop*.'" The author then remarks, "Greta has read Susan Sontag, all right."[59] The joke is that the butch-coded Greta—no doubt a reference to the lesbian icon Greta Garbo—assures the sissy-coded Adolphus of his camp and homosexual authenticity through *theory*, since he seems ignorant of gay *practices*.

Homophilic writings from the mid- to late 1960s suggest a more slippery and critical set of meanings attached to Garland as a gay icon than is usually put forth.[60] Like the appropriation of Sappho by writers and artists in the mid-nineteenth century, identification with Garland by gay men a century later might also have involved a "wish to be a woman," or, more specifically, a "wish to be a woman torch singer" as a gender-critical stance that allowed for the vicarious experience of emotional and sensual display. But, as indicated by Adolphus's outing proclamation, "Sometimes I think I *am* Judy Garland. Nineteen-forty Judy Garland, of course," it would be crazy to wish to be the tragic and miserable Garland of the fifties and sixties; *The Advocate*'s parodic response to *Time*'s psychological profile of Garland fans also reflects this attitude, as does the scene in the 1968 play *The Boys in the Band* (the title of which comes from a line in Garland's famous film *A Star Is Born*), in which Michael sings the opening lines from "Get Happy" and then quips "what's more boring than a queen doing a Judy Garland imitation?"[61] By 1972, it seems, the answer would be a queen imitating Barbra Streisand.

This play, along with Garland-mourning "queens," served as the principal objects of derision in a remarkably long essay published in *Esquire* just six months after her death. This article documented "The New Homosexual," who preferred drugs to drink, machismo to camp, and Jim Morrison to Judy Garland. One young man, when asked if he knew any "homosexuals of the type depicted in *The Boys in the Band*," replied that six years ago (which would have been 1963) he had been asked to dinner by "one of them," claiming "The Beatles were still new then, but very big, and—you won't believe this— *he had never heard of The Beatles!* He had this old Ethel Merman record. And Judy Garland—everything of Judy Garland. She was interesting, but I mean, who wants to *listen* to that stuff? It's all external, while rock is, you know, internal. That theatrical music is kind of a denial of sex, while rock is *pure sex*" (emphasis in the original).[62] Thus, by the time that Judy Garland emerged *in writing* as a gay icon, she already symbolized a moribund and disembodied gay past whose soundtrack of "theatrical music" had somehow locked its queer listeners in the closet, perpetuating their sexual self-denial despite Garland's famous self-indulgences. For the generation that came of age in the 1970s, Garland, who was without question an icon of social deviance, did not signify the new defiant, sex-positive attitude of gay men.

Nevertheless, the funeral of Judy Garland has often been connected to the Stonewall riots, the moment when gay politics became defiant. It is this connection—Garland as somehow sparking resistance to oppression—that gives us a clue about her early, undocumented appeal as a gay icon, before young gay writers sought to distance themselves from older gay Garland fans.

Judy Garland's unpredictable performances, her no-shows, her serial marriages, and her perpetual comebacks, represented the conundrum of queer subjectivity—Foucault's voided "I," a subject susceptible to ideological pressures yet stubbornly resisting them. Indeed, Garland did not bend under pressure, she collapsed, and in so doing she was a force of disruption. If nothing else, she exemplified instability; in terms of signification, she enacted the melodrama of poststructuralist linguistics, that is, the precarious relationship between signifier ("Judy Garland," the movie star) and signified (Judy Garland, the subject), and the susceptibility of the whole system to failure. For only through repeat performances does language create a signifier that produces and regulates the signified, just as, according to Judith Butler, physical bodies are made legible for us through imitative performances that generate a phantasm of gendered identity.

In Judy Garland's post-MGM performance career, the signified intruded upon the regulatory aspects of the signifier; Judy Garland disrupted the phantasm "Judy Garland." Yet that phantasm was already a disruption, already publicly constructed as "in-between." The "Judy Garland" who on screen problematized ordinariness, maturity, and femininity became the Judy Garland who continued to show the fault lines between the signifier and signified. For those who identified with Judy Garland during her lifetime, she may have represented resilience born of misfit tragedy (the prevailing conclusion of later reminiscences and interpretations);[63] she may also have represented resistance through failures and a refusal to behave, to fulfill expectations.

During her November 16, 1964, concert at London's Palladium Theatre, the crowd called out "Rainbow" after nearly every song. Judy responded by chiding them: "In a couple of minutes, really!" . . . "Oh, not yet" . . . "Why don't you be quiet while I'm talking to you? I'll do 'Over the Rainbow,' I promise." At the end of the concert, she finally began the much-awaited number, and, knowing that her voice was giving out, she made the crowd sing it, as if to say, "I'm tired of being 'Judy Garland'! You sing *the song;* you be 'Judy Garland.'" She then turned the song into a comedy, badgering the audience as they had badgered her: "Oh, I've sung this song for so many years. Sing it with me. You can sing it better than I can. Come on, come on." . . . "Keep singing, you're marvelous!" . . . "Don't get scared." Garland even mocks the sentimental music of the bridge, singing the notes of a string phrase purposefully out of tune. In this way, the oft-repeated performance of "Over the Rainbow" became not the hoped-for and expected emotional climax, but rather a moment of camp, a consciously failed imitation of the melodramatic original, in front of an imploring audience.

This *resistance* to dominant culture, as well as *resilience* against its barbs, makes the connection of Garland's funeral to the Stonewall riots more compelling. At least one drag queen participating in the riots unequivocally admits to having been grief-stricken over Judy that night, and in the mood to vent.[64] Just as Judy Garland failed to fulfill her contractual obligations, refused expectations, and behaved badly as "Judy Garland," so, too, did the rioting drag queens fail to behave as expected, as passive victims, during a routine police raid.

Despite her gender-bending and even lesbian-coded images, lesbians did not, by and large, adopt Garland as an icon. Her on-screen emotionalism, as well as her off-screen declarations that women should be subordinate to their husbands (despite her actual behavior toward her own husbands), did not offer anything particularly transgressive or empowering for women wanting to imagine a different world order.[65] One older friend of mine was stuck on Garland's daughter Liza Minnelli, who starred in the gay-sympathetic 1970 movie musical *Cabaret,* arguing that she was not so fragile as her mother. I must confess that from the age of eight or so, I was smitten by Judy Garland— the Garland of the 1930s and '40s, of course. It began with the delight of recognizing "Dorothy" in another movie while flipping through channels one Saturday morning. The movie was *Babes in Arms,* precisely at the song "I Cried For You," which contains the camp soliloquy quoted above. I was captivated by her rich, silky mezzo voice, her emotional catches of breath, and her heartbreak: "I cried for you, now it's your turn to cry over me." I did not know anything about her personal struggles (and I had only an inkling about my own to come), but her voice and melodramatic flair struck me as an alluring sensuality and paralyzed me every time she came on the screen. Watching old MGM musicals on television was also one of the few bonding activities I shared with my older sister, whose eyes were glued to Fred Astaire and Gene Kelly while I gazed at Judy Garland. In those moments, we were not rivals.

A SISTER OF DOROTHY: MELISSA ETHERIDGE AND THE
MELODRAMATIC LESBIAN PHALLUS

Melissa Etheridge was born and raised in Leavenworth, Kansas, a town of prisons inside a state that, thanks to *The Wizard of Oz,* is itself associated with imprisoning black-and-white normalcy and disruptive cyclones. Etheridge's success story can easily be told as the other happy ending to that movie—the one in which Dorothy leaves in a cyclone and does not return home, but stays in glamorous Oz, soaking up the adoration of munchkins. Etheridge moved to the Los Angeles area in the early 1980s to break into the music business. She played mostly in lesbian bars until she was discovered in 1986.

In the late 1990s, when I asked my twenty-something students "What musicians are lesbian icons?" they immediately answered Melissa Etheridge ("of course"), though Ani DiFranco came in a close second. When I asked my thirty-something friends the same question, they deliberated between k. d. lang and Melissa Etheridge, considering who came out first. Forty-something friends mentioned Meg Christian or Cris Williamson ("of course"), lesbian musicians of the 1970s who wrote explicitly about lesbian experiences. This age group tended to regard Etheridge as a second-generation icon—not a pioneer, but undeniably the most visible lesbian singer.[66]

By the year 2000 Melissa Etheridge had seemingly been anointed the number one lesbian icon by mainstream gay and popular music media. That year *The Advocate* stated that she has graced their cover five times, "more than any other person in our 33-year history"[67] (she has made two more *Advocate* covers since then, for May 8, 2001, and January 20, 2004), and the magazine named her "Person of the Year" in 1995. The lesbian glossy magazine *Girlfriends,* which began in 1993, featured her in three cover stories (January/February 1996, October 1999, and August 2001). She made the cover of *Rolling Stone* twice (June 1995 and February 2000), which is considered a career milestone and the music industry's stamp of approval. In 1993, after coming out, her fourth album, *Yes I Am,* went platinum within the year; her videos enjoyed heavy rotation on VH1, and her singles were played frequently on Top 40 radio. She won a Grammy award for "Best Rock Vocal Performance, Female" in 1993 and 1995, and an ASCAP award for "Songwriter of the Year" (1997). She has even been incorporated into images of male-dominated national pastimes: baseball and cars. Etheridge sang the national anthem for game six of the 2001 World Series, and she is the January picture in the *Rolling Stone* 2004 calendar of "Rock Stars with Cool Cars" (sponsored by Chevrolet).[68] In short, Melissa Etheridge is the first out lesbian mainstream rock and roll superstar, surpassing the slightly earlier mainstream crest of k. d. lang. She has garnered far more popular attention than the increasing number of self-identifying lesbian and bisexual performers such as Ani DiFranco and Me'Shell NdegéOcello or individuals in the groups Luscious Jackson and Sleater-Kinney, who work with independent labels and perform in underground club or college networks.

As a lesbian icon ensconced in the mainstream, how and what does Melissa Etheridge represent? Judith Butler proposes that lesbian subjectivity cannot, in fact, be signified within patriarchal culture, within a world of baseball and cars, without a degree of fantasy. In the psychoanalytic theories of Freud and Lacan, the power to produce and control signification resides in having the principal object of desire, which is "the phallus," understood as an abstraction of the male genitals that functions as a symbol. According to Lacan, the phallus is produced through a narcissistic visual encounter with the body through "the mirror stage" of childhood development, when the child (always male in theory) idealizes the body parts he sees in the mirror. In other words, the phallus becomes an "imaginary effect" of having a penis.[69] Through this narcissistic reduction of masculinity to the penis, the phallus also comes to symbolize the primacy of the male gender. The penis/phallus becomes the privileged signifier of the self; women are also signified in terms of the phallus—the phallus they lack.

Butler points out, however, that phallic signification depends upon the phallus being transferable and displaceable onto other body parts and other bodies, which destabilizes its original connection to the penis.[70] Signification of lesbian subjectivity can take place, Butler argues, because of an imaginary form she calls the "lesbian phallus." It is an impossible configuration of "sex" and signification because the lesbian exists outside the phallic economy of heterosexuality. But such a signification is nonetheless thinkable as *the unthinkable*. Butler argues that the "exclusionary [heterosexual] matrix by which subjects are formed thus requires the simultaneous production of a domain of abject beings, those who are not yet 'subjects,' but who form the constitutive outside to the domain of the subject."[71] "Lesbian phallus" brings together as one both abject being and sovereign subject: "lesbian" signifies an abject being outside subjectivity (and thus outside signification and language), while "phallus" insists on the status as a subject (and thus regulating signification and language). Thus "the lesbian phallus . . . [is] an apparently contradictory signifier which, through a critical mimesis, calls into question the ostensibly originating and controlling power of the Lacanian Phallus."[72]

Butler also notes that "symbolization depletes that which is symbolized of its ontological connection with the symbol itself."[73] In other words, in order for a sign to work, it must be understood as not identical with the object being signified. This could explain the tendency toward the choice of women as gay male icons. Sappho, Judy Garland, Barbra Streisand, Bette Midler, Madonna: all these icons signify while leaving the signified at a distance, allowing a critique of gender that nevertheless keeps gender boundaries safely secured. But what happens when a lesbian signifies lesbians? Butler argues that "the phallus is bound to the penis, not through simple identity, but through determined negations."[74] She is interested in that (ironic) negation that makes possible alternative morphologies such as the "lesbian phallus." If the phallus negates the penis, then does a lesbian icon negate real lesbians? Here the lesbian position outside the phallocentric system of signification is a boon, for thus lesbian signification can take place as *virtual reality,* a realistic representation of unrepresentable reality. Indeed, most lesbian icons are lesbians—or virtually so, as in the case of Katherine Hepburn.[75]

Recall that German Idealist and Romantic philosophers thought that music represented the unsayable of subjectivity. But what about the unsayable subject? I will argue here that Melissa Etheridge and her music can be understood as expressing the tension between the unsayability of lesbian subjectivity, its situation outside signification, and a post-1970s insistence by lesbians that their icons say something—with candor, no less. Etheridge works as a lesbian icon because she has the power of the lesbian phallus; she is the unthinkable, abject-phallic subject shadowing the celebrated one, "singing her life with his words," and even his voice.[76]

Honest Abjection

"*Honesty,* that's the word!" So one friend and Etheridge fan summed up her primary impression of Etheridge's music. It is an impression that appears consistently in the comments of her fans, frequently in combination with more descriptive words such as "real," "raw," "core," "bare." Being perceived as honest is a common trait among musical icons of lesbian identity, initiated by the explicitly lesbian lyrics of Christian and Williamson, who were writing within a tradition of political folk music and second-wave feminism of the 1970s, which emphasized gender differences (see chapter 4). In the early 1990s Ani DiFranco continued this tradition of folk music and explicit lyrics. She revised women's music by incorporating the vigorous rhythms and caustic delivery of post-punk rock styles and writing distinctly third-wave feminist lyrics, which express a suspicion of any attempts to categorize sexuality and gender.

Though touted as honest, Etheridge does not sing about lesbian love explicitly; she avoids gendered pronouns (except when describing rival female lovers), addressing her songs to an unmarked "you." This gives listeners both a sense of constant personal revelation, and a paradoxically revealing concealment of the beloved's gender. Thus her songs could be heard as a description of heterosexual romance, her object of desire a man who is tempted or stolen by another woman. As long as the categories remain pure, without bisexuality in the mix, the rhetoric of homosexual and heterosexual love songs can sound the same.

The perception of Etheridge's honesty is strengthened, however, by lyrics that portray Etheridge as self-deprecating ("dysfunctional," as one fan described to me), wallowing in heartbreak and groveling before the beloved who has spurned her. A case in point is the 1995 song "I Want to Come Over," a song filled with images of stalking ("I know you're alone, I watched the car leave"), emotional manipulation ("I know you're weak, I know you want me"), and outright begging ("I want to come over, to hell with the consequence").[77] Sometimes themes of unrequited or fleeting love and triangulated relationships are couched in terms of a Faustian pact. In "Bring Me Some Water," she sings

> Can't you see I'm burning alive
> Can't you see my baby's got another lover . . .
> Baby's got my heart and my baby's got my mind
> But tonight the sweet Devil, sweet Devil's got my soul.[78]

Though Etheridge has many fans who believe she sings of universal human emotions, others feel she expresses something "core" about the lesbian romantic experience. The sense of a disclosure of specifically lesbian love succeeds, in part, because of the close relationship between the idea of confession and deviant sexuality (discussed in the previous chapter). In other words, abject, confessional lyrics reveal sexual deviance.

In interviews, promotional material, and her autobiography, *The Truth Is . . . My Life in Love and Music,* Etheridge markets herself as a heart-on-the-sleeve rocker. The press release for *The Truth Is* describes her as "garnering . . . public adoration for her uncompromising honesty." Etheridge describes her own performances as intimate, even sexual, exhibitions, as the quote below suggests.

> When I write a song from my gut, when I write it from everything deep inside of me, I get such a response, and people know that's where it comes from. It's not that "Like the Way I Do" is such a great song. But it comes right from my center. It burns inside me, and people love that hot place. . . . I invite the audience to share the intimacy of the song. I let the fire grow and my passion spills over until I just can't take it any more and I have to let go.[79]

Etheridge (like Garland) performs in such a way that she seems to expose her inner self and true feeling; in other words, her performances are paradoxically put forth as a display of authenticity and honesty, and not as "performance" at all. Etheridge's fans frequently describe conversion experiences inspired by seeing her in concert, specifically remarking on the energetic performances and the air of candor in her banter between numbers. One lesbian fan, who initially did not like her first album, describes seeing her at a small club in Chicago in the fall of 1988, saying, "She was phenomenal—I went from condescension to ardent fandom in the span of a few minutes. . . . I have faithfully bought all her albums and listened to some of them a lot, and I've probably seen her five or six times."[80] Subsequent to the epiphanic experience of her live performance, then, Etheridge's albums may sometimes figure as souvenirs of an original apparent intimacy between icon and fan, signifier and signified.

The perception of honesty in Garland's concert performances depended upon the notion that they were analogous to the aspect of performance that described the everyday lives of closeted gay men of the 1960s. This included an emphasis on outer style over inner content, or, better, an encrypting of inner content in a flamboyant "performative" outer style. Such an ironic twist to the perception of honesty more aptly describes the lesbian singer k. d. lang and her early gender-bending play within country music and rockabilly. Although k. d. lang came out before Etheridge, proving herself more the "pioneer," lang has not had the enduring profile of Etheridge as a spokesperson for lesbian causes, due in part to the perception of artifice in her suspiciously impeccable singing craft, her flitting from country music to torch songs to pop covers. In sum, lang, too, seems to emphasize outer style over inner content, and thus appeals to a more "arty" crowd, as one Etheridge biographer explains. Etheridge draws the distinction between lang and herself in terms of the normal versus the queer, writing, "k.d., in my eyes, is a personality, an unusual chanteuse kind of androgynous something else. I have always been the working woman's singer. . . . Mine is heartland music. My audiences are very mixed. So I worried, *If I come out, will it make me strange?*" (emphasis in the original).[81]

By way of contrast, many lesbians hear in Melissa Etheridge's music an undecorated and uncompromising expression of the reality of lesbian love, its pathos and melodrama. Though lang's collection of torch songs on her 1992 album *Ingenue* described a similar experience of love, Etheridge's musical style, and especially her voice, tap into a mainstream musical encoding of abjection—indeed, one already established as phallic abjection.

The Voice as Lesbian Phallus

Butler writes that "the process of signification is always material; signs work *by appearing* (visibly, aurally)" (emphasis in the original).[82] But how can a sign appear aurally? In chapter 1, I discussed how the singing voice has historically given rise to cultural intrigue and anxieties about physical and psychical integrity, from the queer allure of the Sirens, to Ovid's Orpheus, whose singing triumphs over death itself, to the worries of Augustine over the thin line between heightened devotion and sensual entrapment in the chant. If there is any phallic object that might be considered fundamentally lesbian, it is the singing voice—phallic power that has disappeared into a cavity (with teeth, no less). This phallic voice operates through a stealthy penetration of the ear, uniting one cavity to another.

The phallic transfer to the voice, disruptive of heterosexuality, is most obvious in castrati, male singers in the seventeenth and eighteenth centuries whose genital "power" was sacrificed to achieve a more penetrating voice of the female register. Star castrati, who played both male and female roles, enjoyed the adulation of both men and women. Homoerotic titillation haunts these male performers (aural for women, visual for men), requiring opposite modes of accommodation: men must suspend their disbelief in the visual, while women must suspend their disbelief in the aural.[83] Roland Barthes, reading Balzac's *Sarrasine* (a story about the title character's infatuation with the castrato Zambinella), writes, "Music, therefore, has an effect utterly different from sight; it can effect orgasm, penetrating Sarrasine. . . . It is Zambinella's voice that Sarrasine is in love with: the voice, the direct product of castration . . . since it is both linguistic and musical, unites in the one plenitude both meaning and sex."[84] Thus the *castrato,* aurally feminine but visually masculine, penetrates the listener with the feminine voice—a female, if not lesbian, phallus—rendering the listener (here male) feminine as well. In this sense, paradoxically, the two men are engaged in lesbian sex.

For many of her fans, Etheridge's voice is the instrument of revelation and the object of desire. In her 1998 article on Melissa Etheridge as *The Advocate*'s "Person of the Year," Judy Wieder writes, "Many have heard the call to freedom in Etheridge's raucous vocals . . . her leather lungs have roped in fans as diverse as actor Juliette Lewis ('Melissa sings like we all dream of singing') and Janis Ian ('The first time I saw Melissa perform at the Bluebird Café, I said, "I have just seen the first female stadium act." ') to say nothing of Sting, Brad Pitt, and, of course, Springsteen."[85] Other musicians, such as Don Henley and her bass player Mark Brown, claim that hearing her voice on the radio compelled them to meet and work with her. Actress and friend Laura Dern has flirtatiously remarked about Etheridge, "She's got that lusty man/woman sound in her voice that I love and respond to on a raw level."[86] One fan described her voice to me as "guttural, sensual," part of the "core" that can be heard in her songs; another fan, in an online Q&A with Etheridge, admitted to vocal emulation: "I've tried forever and I can't get that same smoky voice you have."[87] Indeed, Melissa Etheridge has earned industry accolades for that voice; she won both her Grammys for "Best [Female] Rock Vocal Performance." As a beacon for other musicians, the presage of gender-crossing stadium-rock stardom, the object of private desire and public recognition, Etheridge's voice itself has become an icon, signifying and locating her communicative power.

In her autobiography, Etheridge admits "my sound wasn't exactly what was happening in the music scene at the time. Groups like the Eurythmics, Flock of Seagulls, and Culture Club were on the radio, and I didn't sing, or look, like that at all."[88] All the groups she mentions used gender-bending images inherited from the cross-dressing of glam and unisex fashions of punk rock, combined with danceable grooves of disco. The play with androgyny and irony in much of 1980s new-wave pop opened mainstream doors to queer identities, at least as a source of cutting-edge fashion and provocative sensibility. The early 1980s also saw the increased popularity of new leather-clad and guitar-wielding women rockers, such as Chrissie Hynde of the Pretenders and Joan Jett. Melissa Etheridge's musical style, however, resembles neither the synthesizer-driven dance pop of the Eurythmics and Flock of Seagulls, nor the punk-influenced guitar rock of the Pretenders and Joan Jett. Though acclaimed as a "rocker," the majority of Etheridge's studio recordings emphasize her acoustic rhythm guitar; few songs feature an electric guitar solo or a heavy drum groove. But neither does she sound like the folk-influenced 1970s "women's music" singer-songwriters such as Joni Mitchell, or her mainstream (though lesbian coded) pop-folk contemporaries such as Tracy Chapman and the Indigo Girls. Rather, by her own admission, her conservative and nostalgic "heartland rock" style resembles that of Bob Seger, Bruce Springsteen, and John (Cougar) Mellencamp, staples of mainstream, "classic rock," and Top 40 radio formats since the mid-1970s.[89]

This rock idiom (often hailed as "pure" rock)[90] uses a basic rhythm and blues ensemble (guitars, drums, keyboard, and maybe a saxophone) to accompany lyrics that evoke small (Midwestern) towns and working-class perspectives, frustrations of life and love, and escapism into drink, cars, or girls. Blues- and Bob Dylan–influenced vocals, raspy and unpolished, further add to a sense of authenticity, signifying raw feeling. Indeed, like Judy Garland's torch songs, these rock ballads convey, in Richard Dyer's words (referring to Garland), "an emotional register of great intensity," bringing together contrasting qualities of suffering and survival, vulnerability and strength, and even authenticity and theatricality. Voices catch, break, and shout with abjection or an exuberance tinged with melancholy; melodic and harmonic invention and soloistic virtuosity take a back seat to hooks, standard progressions, and rhythmic guitar playing. Generally missing is any sense of irony that might turn the surface of these melodramas into a camp critique of gender or sexuality. In the escape-fantasy classic "Born to Run" (1975)—a rock and roll "Over the Rainbow"—Bruce Springsteen sings the bombastic lines "just wrap your legs 'round these velvet rims, and strap your hands 'cross my engines."[91] Listeners may smile at such an unsubtle expression, at the exposure of a male fetish for motor vehicles, and at the conflation of engines with masculine (phallic) power. But this humorous moment reinforces the pathos of the underlying narrative, in which youthful (masculine) energy has no place to go. The projection of earnestness and the avoidance of irony shores up the integrity of masculinity despite the theatrical display of emotion.

Melissa Etheridge comes across as a phallic icon in part because she takes on this register of masculine emotionality available within the conservative rock ballad style. The resulting gender critique—the "wish to be a man"—is conveyed clearly by her musical language and lyrical images. In her favorite show-stopping song "Like the Way I Do" (1988), Etheridge sings passionately to her beloved in chest-thumping warrior images:

> Don't you think I know there's so many others
> Who would beg, steal, and lie, fight, kill, and die
> Just to hold you, hold you, like I do.[92]

The thrust of these lyrics is further projected by the percussive bass line, vigorous acoustic rhythm guitar, and her trademark voice, which modulates in texture from slightly husky to coarse-grain sandpaper, approaching Janis Joplin's split-tone wails. She delivers the words with theatrical emphasis (what one writer dubbed "a subtlety-be-damned style" of "over-the-top" singing),[93] spitting out hard consonants, smearing sibilants, and distorting vowels. In short, this is "muscle music," more specifically "vocal muscle music" of the style of those male rock balladeers to whom she is frequently compared.[94]

On the softer side, her song "You Can Sleep While I Drive" (1989), described by one critic as "a feminine version of Bruce Springsteen's 'Born to Run,'"[95] is a classic drive-away fantasy, though instead of emulating Springsteen's jubilant escapee, she sings as a lovelorn desperado:

> Come on baby let's get out of this town
> I got a tank full of gas with the top rolled down
> There's a chill in my bones
> I don't want to be left alone
> So baby you can sleep while I drive.[96]

Her more theatrical vocal mannerisms are here kept to a minimum; still, the soft, slow delivery calls attention to an edgy waver in her voice, while the slightly clipped phrase endings seem to rein in the "vocal muscle," resisting lyricism. This, again, casts Etheridge's "honest expression" as masculine pathos—emotion necessarily contained, but barely.

Melissa Etheridge's voice has phallic significance as the isolated, unseeable body part that organizes and confers meaning to her body in relation to other bodies. As Laura Dern's remark reminded us, Etheridge's voice, like the Sirens' song, has the power to call into question the heterosexual matrix. Coming from a lesbian but emulating masculine melodrama, this voice also unites (always phallic) meaning and (always feminine) sex. It is the castratolike plenitude of her voice that occasions the contradictory critical reception of her music as "cliché-ridden but painfully genuine";[97] in other words, as a rock balladeer she is an ordinary "everyman." As a lesbian, she is authentic in her "wish to be a man." The "wish to be a man" is not, of course, Freudian "penis envy," an abject sense of lack; rather, it is the wish of artistic fantasy, enhancing self-expression.

Certainly Baudelaire, Swinburne, and Solomon were selective in their "wish to be a woman," glad to be men thinking "in drag," imagining emotional opportunities through the appropriation of a lesbian subject-position but safe from the reality of *being* a woman (let alone a lesbian woman). Thus the gay male "wish to be a woman" is always ironic—a superficial wish that takes refuge (and pleasure) in the Teflon coating that inhibits the signifier (in this case, "woman") from ever adhering to the signified (in this case, the male artist). But is the lesbian "wish to be a man" similarly protected? Given the entrenched polarity of genders and consequent power imbalance favoring men, the lesbian "wish to be a man" hardly seems ironic or transgressive. What lesbian does not fantasize about having more power, whether it be physical, economical, political, social, or personal? Neither the lesbian community nor heterosexual society comfortably tolerates a lesbian's blatant desire for masculine power, let alone celebrates this power and supports it financially. Lesbians, on one hand, might see in the "wish to be a man" a dangerously self-negating acquiescence to oppressive patriarchal culture; patriarchal culture, on the other hand, has condemned the idea of a lesbian "wish to be a man" in imagines of lesbians as predatory vampires or as murderers. As Butler observes, "the phallus enters lesbian sexual discourse in the mode of a transgressive 'confession' conditioned and confronted by both the feminist and misogynist forms of repudiation: it's not the real thing (the lesbian thing) or it's not the real thing (the straight thing). What is unveiled is precisely the repudiated desire, that which is abjected by heterosexist logic and that which is defensively foreclosed through the effort to circumscribe a specifically feminine morphology for lesbianism."[98]

Do the phallic performances of Melissa Etheridge enact an escape from regulatory iterations of heterosexuality? I believe the answer is no, for the reason that Etheridge as a lesbian icon represents not the desire to escape or confound normalcy through the fissures of signification (as Garland did), but rather the desire *to signify* normalcy in spite of those fissures. In other words, she signifies the desire not to be "queer," not to be outside social norms.

Etheridge's *mainstream* success may result, in part, from a purposeful suspension of disbelief in the "lesbian phallus," in its impossibility. As abject being (that is, lesbian), Etheridge fulfills the position of an outsider to the patriarchal subject position; but as an imagined "normal" or "mainstream" lesbian (that is, a lesbian subject that *can* emerge within a phallocentric symbolic order), Etheridge's "lesbian phallus" allows for the mainstream to co-opt and make intelligible the outside as well. This tango of disbelief and belief in the "lesbian phallus" in reference to Melissa Etheridge became especially agitated with regard to the paternity of the children she parents with her now ex-partner Julie Cypher.

For three years, during two pregnancies (Cypher's) and births, Melissa

Etheridge was dogged by questions of paternal identity. But the questions sometimes took a peculiar form, revealing a certain level of anxiety about the disappearance of the paternal figure. *Time* magazine columnist Joel Stein asked, "It is a man, right?" David Letterman quipped, "Now, I'm no geneticist, but in some regard there must have been Daddy somewhere" (thereby collapsing the biological function of fertilizing an egg with the social function of parenting).[99]

In 1996 a columnist for the *San Diego Union-Tribune* asked jokingly if the father of Etheridge's first child was Michael Jackson, thereby betraying the anxiety—frequently expressed—about queer sexual fertility by equating the technical impossibility of a child begotten from two women with the mainstream incredulity concerning Jackson's masculinity (and heterosexuality).[100] The caption on the *Rolling Stone* cover revealing Etheridge's and Cypher's sperm donor reads, "The Name of the Father and the Making of a New American Family." This is a reference, perhaps unwitting, to the "name-of-the-father" in Lacanian psychoanalytic theory, a metaphor that describes a child's entry into symbolic and social systems. The "name-of-the-father" represents an internalization of a disciplinary framework ("the law") associated with the role of father within the family, as authorized within a patriarchy. As a wedge between the primary duality of child and mother (self and other), the father symbolizes "the law" that forces the child to differentiate from the mother. Indeed, comprehension of "the father" as a third, abstract component allows for the development of symbolic thinking (that is, the entry into language) and a legible subjectivity that is either male (identified with the father) or female (identified with the mother). The "name-of-the-father" also elicits the incest taboo (forcing a renunciation of the mother) while socially defining and legitimizing kinship ties.

Butler writes, "what constitutes the integral body is not a natural boundary or organic telos, but the law of kinship that works through the name."[101] David Crosby was announced as "the name of the father" of Etheridge's and Cypher's children, and thus his naming, and his name, granted Etheridge a guest pass into patriarchal subjectivity through a series of substitutions by way of a musical kinship. Crosby, who as a founding member of the Byrds and later of Crosby, Stills, and Nash, is an august figure of mainstream folk-rock; he shares with Etheridge a common denominator—not only music per se, but also the specific musical idiom of folk-influenced rock. Crosby's gender substitutes for that of Etheridge, while Etheridge's age substitutes for that of Crosby, resulting in a curious joint custody of the paternal position. In her autobiography, Etheridge at one point describes Julie Cypher as "the mother of my children"—not "the mother of *our* children" or "the other parent of my children"—and this classic objectifying and proprietary phrase reveals another aspect of Etheridge's lesbian phallus; here, as the "imaginary effect" of David Crosby's penis, Etheridge's lesbian phallus is easily absorbed into the patriarchal order.[102] *The Truth Is* contains a telling photo of Etheridge, her face deep in concentration, as she reads a book entitled *Husband-Coached Childbirth*.[103] Why, one has to wonder, did she not feature herself reading a book on lesbian parenting?[104]

Moreover, a household cannot tolerate two father figures. When Etheridge's daughter asked why her daddy does not live in the family's house, Etheridge explained that "he doesn't live in our house so that I can live here."[105] Should Crosby and Etheridge live in the same household, they would be locked in a curious Oedipal struggle in which Etheridge, the younger lesbian lover, becomes the murderous impotent son, and Crosby, the older biological father, becomes the potent father who shatters the fantasy of sexual union between son (Etheridge) and mother (Cypher). Only through Crosby's absence from the household can the disbelief in Etheridge's lesbian phallus be suspended, allowing Etheridge and Cypher to be legible as a father and mother.

Throughout her autobiography, Etheridge writes that in her music can be heard the gap between her publicized domestic entry into the status quo and "the truth" of domestic troubles. Two 1999 interviews in *The Advocate* also reveal this tension. In June she proclaimed:

> There's something about having all your dreams come true. In 1994, '95 with the music . . . I got it all. . . . [W]hen [her second child] Bailey was born in '97 it was clear. This is the purpose of my life. And puts everything in place.[106]

But in September she remarked:

> The biggest misconception that people have about me is that I'm in this perfect relationship with perfect children and that I'm just fine. That's not true. . . . My relationship with Julie requires a great deal of work, and sometimes it is crisis. I'm just trying to be truthful.[107]

The context for these quotes is important: the first belongs to an interview focused on her role as a mother, while the second is a promotional interview for her album *Breakdown;* darkest in theme and richest in its use of instruments, the album was released after a four-year hiatus. As a mother, Melissa refers to the heterosexual ideal that children and nuclear family provide correct order and purpose for a woman's life. As a musician, by contrast, Melissa refers to the "truth" of melancholy and frustration—her signature themes, to be sure, but now taking on new meaning in light of her prominent "fatherhood."

The song "Enough of Me" seems most pointedly directed at this frustrated ideal, with verses that refer to a "domestic war" between lovers, a beloved who is compared to emotionally distant parents, and a refrain of melancholic resignation: "there is no other." The verse is sung to one of her most delicate, most thoughtful melodies, and she sings it in a voice that is smoother than usual, accompanied only by acoustic guitars and an understated electric bass. The chorus, however, is classic anthem rock, thick with drums, electric guitars, and masculine-style boasts such as "I turned your dreams into lightning," each of which is followed by the plaintive heartland-rocker refrain, "Ain't that enough?"

The bridge between verse and chorus is the most dramatic and curious part of the song. It begins softly, with short statements by the voice answered by the bass guitar. As the flow of statements accelerates, the volume and thickness of the musical accompaniment increases. This transition between the contemplative verse and the assertive chorus is also reflected in the lyrics, which present a mix of masculine and feminine associations.

> I gave you my soul
> And every ounce of control
> I gave you my skin and my original sin
> (alternate line: I gave you my shame and my eternal flame)
> I gave you my pride, and my side, oh my pride, ain't that enough?
> (alternate line: I gave you my need, and my seed, oh my need, ain't that
> enough?)[108]

While "original sin," "shame," and "need" are commonly associated with women, "control," "pride," and "seed" are commonly associated with men. This last reference to "seed" once again positions Etheridge as father, while "soul," "side," and "eternal flame" have a biblical air; the lyric "I" becomes Adam, sacrificing the rib from his side, and Etheridge as seed-bearing father becomes Father, creator and sufferer.

The disjunction between Etheridge's seemingly successful imitation of the heterosexual nuclear family and her continued musical expressions of melancholy work together to communicate crushing disappointment, frustrated desire, and, perhaps, a subversive pleasure in the confession of it all. Her lyrics capture the lesbian longing for arrival into subjectivity and representation, the "American dream" of living in prosperity with our one true love. They also capture the impossibility of that arrival. But are not such struggles generic to all "marriages"? To what extent are Etheridge's troubles specifically lesbian troubles? In her autobiography, Etheridge reports that in 1999, after nine years together, Julie announced to her, "I'm just not gay."[109] It is also true, of course, that many long-term heterosexual relationships end with one partner announcing, "I am gay." In both scenarios, the burden of failure is placed on homosexuality and its essential incompatibility with marriage and the nuclear family.

The demise of Etheridge's relationship with Cypher provided the impetus for her autobiography, and the context for her seventh album of tragic love ballads, *Skin* (2001). During her years with Cypher, Etheridge, as an icon of lesbianism *for the mainstream,* could placate mainstream anxiety about the potency of deviant sexuality precisely because she could be read as an imitation of a masculine norm of the heterosexual "heartland"—which, like the castrato, titillates through a suspension of disbelief. As a lesbian icon *for lesbians,* she could disrupt the norms of the heterosexual heartland simply by presenting a lesbian version of them. In songs such as "Enough of Me," she also conveyed "the trouble with normal," its disappointments and deficiencies.

In a 2003 interview, however, Etheridge disparaged her relationship with Cypher as not normal enough; she claimed that, despite twelve years together and two children, they were not sufficiently committed to get married. Earlier in 2003, Etheridge proposed to and "married" actress Tammy Lynn Michaels. In the interview Etheridge unabashedly refers to Michaels as "my wife," and Michaels plays the traditionally submissive, sacrificing role to the hilt. She is fulfilled by mothering Etheridge's children, and by making sure Melissa has what she needs. She even hints that her career aspirations will take a backseat to these simple pleasures.[110] "She's an old-fashioned girl," Etheridge told the Associated Press in February 2004. Michaels, it should be noted, is thirteen years younger than Etheridge. In that same interview, Etheridge, when asked about their age difference, quips, "'It's in the rock 'n' roll handbook . . . Hit 40, get divorced and marry the young actress."[111] Out of this domestic bliss came Etheridge's more exuberant album *Lucky,* described by Michaels as "a kegger party!"[112] Where Etheridge once captured a melancholy, if not an ambivalence, in the emulation of heterosexuality, she is now fully invested. With a younger wife in tow, Etheridge forges ahead to write frat-house rock.

MADONNA: DOROTHY IN OZ

> I have always identified with Madonna. I love how free she has been in her own sexuality and style. And constantly pushing the envelope, which always made me seem more normal.
> *Melissa Etheridge,* Rolling Stone *interview, July 2001.*

If Melissa Etheridge has earned a guest pass into the patriarchy, then Madonna has earned a guest pass into the queer community. No one has worked harder to be a gay icon than Madonna, and she has done so by using every possible taboo sexual fantasy in her videos, performances, and interviews. This concern to shock the public with her image is in sharp contrast to the sound of her music, which is radio-friendly pop. Designed primarily for dancing, and sung with a light, girlish voice (usually enhanced with reverb or multitracking), her songs are, if anything, antimelodramatic: they lack the heft and richness of expansive lyrical melodies, as well as the ease and freedom of soulful improvisatory embellishments. The discrepancy between Madonna's mainstream music and the assault on the mainstream by her public image thus sets up a Siren-like dynamic. Mainstream listeners are pulled in by Motown and techno-inspired dance grooves and the occasional contemporary R&B or Latin-flavored ballad, only to crash on the rocks of her salacious interviews, concerts, and videos. Her videos alone feature a long list of transgressions: miscegenation ("Like a Prayer," "Secret"), homosexuality ("Justify My Love"), voyeurism ("Open Your Heart," "Justify My Love"), sadomasochism ("Express Yourself," "Justify My Love," "Human Nature"), masturbation (every scene of solitary writhing, especially "Like A Virgin" and "Take A Bow"), blasphemy ("Like A Prayer"), fascism ("Express Yourself"), murder ("Bad Girl"), the insane ("Nothing Really Matters"), and pederasty ("Open Your Heart," "Like a Prayer," "Cherish"). She even flirts with incest in "Oh Father." Nearly every image is saturated with provocative sexuality.

Madonna's hypersexuality has had particular resonance with gay men, whose post–liberation era culture of the 1980s tended to be organized around subcultures of sexual fetishes, often associated with particular masculine body types or costumes: SM leather apparel, military or police uniforms, T-shirts and jeans (associated with physically fit bodies), cowboy boots and hats, and flannel (associated with hirsute bodies). Madonna's myriad sexual costumes communicated a sex-positive message, the height of which coincided with the emergence of AIDS and the conservative Reagan-Bush administration. In sum, Madonna flaunted a flamboyant sexual expression characteristic of gay subcultures.

Michael Musto's 1995 panegyric to Madonna, "Immaculate Connection," documents her importance for gay men as a mainstream figure who interceded on their behalf. He also documents an ambivalence over her exploitation of gay culture.

> We're mad at her for ripping us off, but somehow thanking her for noticing us, legitimizing us, pulling us by our bootstraps up out of hiding and into the public pleasure dome of security and success. . . . Deliriously, we imagine we're sitting *with* her in the arena—not cheering from the bleachers, but laughing alongside her on stage and sharing the kudos from the throngs who recognize that we're a big part of her triumph.[113]

This fantasy of recognition and intercession rewrites those Judy Garland concert reviews deriding her emotionally overwrought "boys in tight pants." Madonna is not just nodding to her gay fans with a sly aside about Fire Island; she has appropriated their power to offend via sexuality, and she has used this power as a means of self-promotion with a degree of success that no other mainstream performer has yet achieved. Musto goes on to say, "We finally seem willing to release Judy Garland from her afterlife responsibilities of being our quintessential icon. And in the land of the living, career stagnation has robbed Diana, Liza, and Barbra of their chances. . . . [Madonna] isn't afraid to offend straight America, if it does the rest of us some good."[114]

Straight America's reaction to Madonna is not just one of offense, but equally one of fascination, kept fresh by her never-ending changes in the configuration of gender and sexuality—that of her audience as well as of herself. The song "Express Yourself" (1989), for example, presents multiple registers of representation that pander to multiple fetishizing gazes in quick succession, thereby facilitating their collision. The song is Madonna's version of Aretha Franklin's feminist favorite "Respect" (1967): it includes the core admonition "express yourself, respect yourself" introduced by a gospel call ("Come on girls, do you believe in love? Well I got somethin' to say about it, and it goes like this"), along with synthesized horn lines and a backup chorus exhorting women not to go for second best ("make him express how he feels, then you'll know your love is real"). In the video (directed by David Fincher), inspired by Fritz Lang's *Metropolis* (1926), Madonna first appears as a scantily clad boy-toy of a business tycoon (and tyrant); then as a cross-dressed Garbo-esque version of that tycoon, gyrating above the laborers; and finally as a shackled, crawling submissive femme. Madonna's many incarnations in this video reference the story of *Metropolis*. In the movie the heroine, Maria, preaches peaceful resistance to the oppressed workers, but an evil scientist creates a robotic twin of Maria, who incites violence in the workers. As the riotous Maria, Madonna, in her tycoon drag, performs a crotch-grabbing dance in front the workers, mimicking dance moves and gestures made famous by Michael Jackson in his videos of the same decade. The parody is thick here: Jackson's crotch grabbing and athletic moves, through which he mimics the virility his body clearly lacks, become far more potent and virile when performed by Madonna as her own "self-expression."

Interspersed throughout the video are shots of hunks—bare-chested, clean-shaven working men who could have been clipped from the classified pages of *The Advocate*. They do coordinated calisthenics, or operate cogs and wheels in a perpetual rain. Madonna's varied autoerotic dancing eventually calls forth (only) one of the hunks; he moves trancelike toward her boudoir. Though she sings, "roses are the way to your heart, but he need start with your head," the male self-expression called forth by Madonna is unfettered brute sexuality: the sweaty hunk pulls Madonna onto the floor. Men and women, both straight and gay, all find something to admire and salivate over in this video, and all are perhaps left more than a little ambivalent about her politics. Musto writes, "reinventing herself constantly, in the way the rapidly aging MTV generation seemingly requires, she's elevated 'What next?' to an art form . . . isn't she just using us to advance her own notoriety?"[115] Musto and many other gay writers conclude that such positive exploitation—offering queer sexualities as "permissible"—is ultimately a good thing, as long as she continues contributing to the fight against AIDS.[116]

Madonna's relationship with lesbians, on the other hand, has been fickle. In videos, publicity photos, and interviews between 1988 and 1991,[117] Madonna flirted with lesbian chic—a growing trend in pop music—even though she denied more than once the rumors of actual same-sex sexual liaisons that she indulged earlier.[118] Beginning in 2000, Madonna returned to same-sex erotics as a strategy to rally public interest. Indeed, Madonna's lesbian self-reinventions are her version of the comeback. Lesbian erotics appear in her video for the song "Music" (2000), and in her 2001 tour performance of "What It Feels Like for a Girl." In 2003, when sales of her *American Life* album were flagging, she engaged in a brief but infamous kiss with Britney Spears (twenty years her junior) on the Video Music Awards show[119] and a near-kiss in the video for their duet "Me Against the Music." In 1963, Judy Garland presented Barbra Streisand as her protégée as songstress and gay icon; in 2003, Madonna instated Spears as her protégée in same-sex erotica and icon of polymorphous sexuality.

Lesbians admire Madonna's unfettered sexuality, her switches between butch and femme styles, as well as her intrusion into patriarchal power. The Netscape business poll for July 23, 2001, asked respondents to vote for the best strategist among Bill Gates, Dick Cheney, and Madonna, thus ranking Madonna's cultural muscle with the world's number-one computer magnate and the most powerful U.S. vice president in history. But many lesbians also feel discomforted by her use of sex to reap social and economic rewards. This seems to play into, rather than resist, patriarchal sexual objectification of women.

The various lesbian reactions to Madonna can be better understood if situated in the context of the several "waves" of feminism. The suffrage movement, from the late nineteenth century through the 1920s, constituted the first wave. The women's liberation movement, growing out of the civil rights movement and the New Left in the mid-1960s, was the second wave; it produced numerous streams of feminist ideology that reviewed gender roles in both heterosexual and homosexual contexts. Finally, third-wave feminism, heavily influenced by queer theory and AIDS activism, is both pragmatic and postmodern in its approach to gender and includes a particular concern with sexuality.[120] Madonna's foregrounding of sexuality falls into the category of third-wave feminism, with its edgy, in-your-face tactics. This type of feminism glorifies rebellion, whether it is directed at the patriarchal status quo or at second-wave feminism's monolithic critique of gender, tendency toward "victim politics," and suspicion of non-normative sexuality.

For second-wave lesbian feminists and those less inclined toward sex radicalism, Madonna might be seen as a guilty pleasure rather than an icon. This is evident in Karlene Faith's 1997 book *Madonna: Bawdy & Soul*. Faith, a criminologist and lesbian feminist active in the 1970s, is particularly seduced by Madonna's gender critique. On one hand, Faith applauds Madonna for her parodies of traditional gender roles, performances that "cannot be contained by any politic";[121] on the other hand, Faith criticizes Madonna for preserving the nonegalitarian, gendered role-playing "that characterizes mainstream heterosexual imagery."[122] Similarly, Faith sees Madonna's first decade of videos and publicity stunts to be about "overcoming inhibitions about Sex and the Body,"[123] but Faith draws a political line at depictions that suggest pornography, sadomasochism, or pedophilia. According to Faith, a fundamental contrast between third- and second-wave feminists is this: those whom Faith calls "self-identified sex radicals of the 1990s" defend "any sexual practice in principle"[124] in the name of freedom of expression and the pursuit of happiness, whereas for Faith and 1970s radical lesbian feminists, nonegalitarian role-playing, even with mutual consent, works to legitimize hierarchical power relations. Thus all artistic or fantastic explorations of hierarchical power relations are morally suspect. While Faith can enjoy parodies of such power relations as parodies of gender, she refuses to acknowledge that, as David Halperin says, "hierarchy itself is *hot.*"[125]

Madonna's force as an icon for gays and lesbians may well reside in her representation of sexual fearlessness and fluidity; nonetheless, her excursions into soft, stylish butch personas, her kissing the next-generation female music superstars, are dismissable because she is safely ensconced in heterosexuality, as sexual object and also as wife and mother. Madonna and Etheridge became celebrity moms within months of each other in late 1996 and early 1997. Madonna did not marry the father of her first child, and the politics of family that this decision ignited was on a par with the redefinition of family that Etheridge's and Cypher's lesbian parenting provoked. But after the birth of her second child (August 2000) and her marriage to the child's father, film director Guy Ritchie (December 2000), Madonna began to model the roles of mainstream wife and mother as vigorously as she once modeled independence and sexual freedom.[126] In this context, her post-marriage lesbian flirtations can seem a curious relic from the past, from Madonna's years of youthful (queer) immaturity.

On a few occasions, however, Madonna has presented an alternative to the presumed heterosexual matrix—an alternative by way of narcissism. The video for "What It Feels Like for a Girl," directed by her husband, casts Madonna as a leather-clad female Robin Hood with tattoos and bruises, guns and Camaros. An elderly woman, whom she "liberated" from an old-folks home, rides as a catatonic "shot gun" while Madonna commits gratuitous acts of violent mischief against men—smashing into cars of leering boys, breaking up their street games, stealing their money to give to a fast-food waitress. This video plays in bars to a dance mix with a brisk, pounding bass beat and bubbling techno grooves, to which is added sampled and looped phrases from the vocals. The album version, however, is a mid-tempo ballad with a warm synthesized ethereal background and light hip-hop beat accompanying Madonna's dry, unenhanced voice.

> Strong inside but you don't know it
> Good little girls they don't show it
> When you open up your mouth to speak, could you be a little weak.[127]

The lyrics describe what, in 1929, Joan Riviere called "womanliness as masquerade," an inner wish for masculine power disguised by an outer mask of womanliness that serves to avert retribution from men.[128] Madonna's two versions of this song, one overly feminine and the other overly masculine, are both parodic. Ultimately, however, both point back to herself: they presume not a status quo (heterosexual) audience, but specifically *her* audience, which has its own sexually diverse status. Her third presentation of this song, performed in concert, took a queer turn. Madonna sang the song in Spanish while being passed among salsa-dancing soft-butch women, clad in muscle shirts, with greased-back hair to mimic male Latino youths. As in the scene from *The Well of Loneliness* described earlier, foreign language (here also Spanish) signifies a sexuality beyond normative language, yet appropriated as a part of a general cast of exoticism, and therefore made comprehensible.

The two videos for the song "Music" present further evidence that Madonna, at least by 2000, presumed an alternative, Madonna-oriented audience for her art. The television version is simply a montage of Madonna's earlier videos. As an illustration of a song about the power of music, this video rather boldly conflates "Madonna," the icon, with that power. These old images of Madonna, however, serve as a masquerade for the new images banned from broadcast. In the banned video, Madonna, dressed as a Texas oil tycoon with cowboy hat and big jewelry, goes out for a night of carousing with two gal pals. The offending moment is when they stop at a club and stuff dollars into the G-strings of a female erotic dancer. Just as in "What It Feels Like for a Girl," men get short shrift; they are characterized as buffoons locked outside the women's world of sensual delights. Though Madonna exchanges one lustful glance with an Asian woman in the club, the women depicted in the video are far from lesbian. They are, in fact, cartoonish, as the embedded cartoon segment reveals. Madonna becomes a musical superhero, smashing thugs and flying among neon signs that flash her own song titles. As the saying goes, it's her world, and we're only in it for a minute.

Perhaps the song and video that most presumes her *queer* audience is "Don't Tell Me" (2000), directed by Jean-Baptiste Mondino (he was also the director of the 1990 video for "Justify My Love," which garnered so much attention with its scenes of polymorphous sexuality). Here Madonna, in a cowboy hat and leather chaps, dances in the foreground, while four rugged cowboys form her chorus line as they all perform an intricate Western line dance. In many ways, the scene harks back fifty years to Garland's "Get Happy" number, in which the gay icon was similarly surrounded by gay-

Figure 5. Madonna, "Don't Tell Me" video, 2000. Directed by
Jean-Baptiste Mondino.

coded dancers, but here the set, with a desert highway and big sky projected
onto an exposed background screen, spoofs old Hollywood movies. At first
the men, who are dressed in jeans and various Western-style shirts, appear as
projections on the screen behind her, but moving parallel to her moves.
Later they appear with her in front of the screen, now dressed as she is, in
black leather chaps and black tops. Just as in Garland's chorus line, they fall
about her at various times in choreographed adoration (figure 5).

The song opens with an acoustic guitar hook that abruptly stops and starts
like a faulty disc player, out of time and in the middle of a phrase. With the
repeat of the hook, however, the musical segments and abrupt silences fall
into a meter, forming the underlying groove of the song. It is a brilliant sonic
construction, a postmodern collision of acoustic warmth with cold digital dis-
section represented by interspersed silence. This technofolk song perfectly
matches the constructions of Americana dissected in her video.

Kitschy symbols of Americana are the marketing theme of the album
Music; Madonna seems to be pointing out the intersection of Americana with
gay subculture—which was never more apparent than in *The Wizard of Oz.* If
this Madonna-Garland-Oz connection seems far-fetched, it is made less so by

the picture that lines the *Music* jewel box; there, behind the CD bed, is a picture of a ruby slipper—actually, a ruby pump—lying in the hay.

. . .

In this chapter I have focused on three musical icons of queer identity. As icons, they help organize and represent gay and lesbian subcultures, and they show how those subjectivities, which are not provided for in normalizing systems of signification, nevertheless do circulate in and around normative culture. To the mainstreams of both heterosexual and homosexual culture, Judy Garland represented tragic queerness, and her comeback performances, in light of her personal hardships, represented resilience in the face of oppression. She also represented resistance; specifically, she represented resistance to predictable repetitions of behavior that allow for stable representation at all. Garland frustrated the public consumption of "Garland," and in so doing she may have served as a motivator, if not a model, for strategic resistance taken up by gay activists after her death.

Melissa Etheridge's imitations of mainstream male identity, her performances as heartland rocker and patriarchal placeholder, have been juxtaposed with her endless songs of frustrated desires. Throughout her career she has represented both the idealized entry into normalcy and the ambivalence that disrupts the idealization of that normalcy. As icon, Etheridge depicts the lesbian in a continual orbit around heterosexual subjectivity.

Garland as well as Etheridge act as icons by expressing for their audiences desires that lead across genders, although they do so in different ways. In the case of Garland's gay fans, identification with her effected a critique of heterosexual masculinity, a "wish to be a woman" that recalls nineteenth-century male aesthetic identification with Sappho. In the case of Etheridge, her own performance of the "wish to be a man" allows her to take on an imaginary morphology with phallocentric signification and a patriarchal subject position.

Madonna's performances often express the wish to be both man and woman, to simultaneously be the subject and object of desire. Her greatest achievement as an icon of (polymorphous) sexuality has been to recognize and play to the gay gaze almost as much as any other. Her videos and sapphic comebacks increasingly presume a Madonna matrix rather than a heterosexual one, a world that is populated by an audience of diverse sexualities. She acts out an ideal of gender and sexual fluidity that appeals to many gay men and lesbians as a liberation from stereotypic and simplistic categories that work toward discrimination. But Madonna's conscious antinormative performances of gender and sexuality reveal the extent to which the ideal of fluidity can double back to an original narcissism—one that, based on self-idealization and self-reference, may ultimately result in insignificance. If, as Faith declares, "Madonna cannot be contained by any politic," then she may, indeed, impact none.

Both Etheridge and Madonna make music that appeals well beyond gay and lesbian audiences. Yet the sounds they make, whether Etheridge's acoustic-guitar rock ballads or Madonna's electronics-driven dance music, have historical roots in queer communities that formed in the 1970s. Elements of Etheridge's sound and ethos can be traced from lesbian women's music, and Madonna's from lavishly produced gay-centric disco. In the next chapter I will explore such "homomusical communities" in terms of Foucault's "technology of production."

4

Homomusical Communities
production

Music makes the people come together,
Music makes the bourgeoisie and the rebel
Madonna, "Music" (2000)

Musicians "make music": they set in motion sound waves that produce some-thing, but that something has no physical substance. Lovers "make love": they too produce something that has no physical substance. Once "made," and assuming the involvement of at least two persons, the intangibles "music" and "love" often have consequences—influencing or even regulat-ing behavior, defining relationships of power, opening up channels of mate-rial and economic exchange. Making music changed dramatically with the technological development of amplification and recording: music became a thing that could be "played" by anyone, regardless of their musical skill.

In this chapter, I consider music in recorded format—discs and tapes—as a commercial product; specifically, I explore the role of this product in constructing, transforming, and organizing queer identities during the 1970s. In this role, the musical commodity of the album generated kinship and articulated desire in lesbian and gay communities, thereby illustrating Foucault's concept of technologies of production in the construction of sub-jectivity. Technologies of production describe the ways in which things, as well as our production, transformation, and manipulation of them, are used to scrutinize and modify ourselves. Foucault notes that this modification can be understood "in the obvious sense of acquiring certain skills but also in the sense of acquiring certain attitudes."[1] It is with the "technology of produc-tion" that Foucault's use of the word "technology" (the science of applying systematic practices, or techniques, in certain domains of thought and behav-ior to understand the self) intersects with the common understanding of "technology" (the science of applying knowledge to practical purposes, especially in the development of machines). The central question here is how did the production of recorded music, enabled by advances in record-ing technology, affect practices of thinking about and modifying the self?

Recording technology opened up new dimensions in marketing music to a mass audience, and also new dimensions in the use of music, by producers and consumers, to form and inform community by fortifying or crossing over social categories of class, race, gender, and sexual identity. Recordings (on vinyl, tape, or compact disc) can be considered a stand-in for the performer, who is the real focus of attention and object of desire, even fantasy. But records, and especially albums of songs, can themselves be objects of desire. They can be eagerly awaited, and played repeatedly; album covers and liner notes can be contemplated and touched. As a commodity produced and distributed to a mass market in a capitalist economy, recorded music offers itself as an object of analysis in terms of its social work.

Following on the heels of (and also continuing) the civil rights movement and sexual revolution of the 1960s, the 1970s witnessed the rise of leftist countercultural movements, some organized around the protest of the Vietnam War, others around high social and political ideals. These anticapitalist New Left movements appeared at the same time as exponential commercial expansion and corporate consolidation in the music industry.[2] Not only did pop superstars perform in sports arenas and stadiums (rather than the concert halls used in the past), but their albums also sold in previously unheard-of numbers—millions within a year of their release. Album covers became more elaborate and clever, adding to the allure of the product as well as the performer(s) behind the product. Andy Warhol's design for the cover of the Rolling Stones' *Sticky Fingers* album (1971) featured a photograph of the crotch of a man clothed in jeans, with a real zipper affixed to the cardboard. Warhol's cover uncovered the product itself as a sexual object: desire to unzip the album cover was irresistible.

By the early 1970s, the music business had become a multi-billion-dollar industry that operated through complex corporate structures. Ten major record companies controlled the production and distribution of popular music, with only two companies, CBS and Warner-Elektra-Atlantic (WEA), accounting for 40 percent of the total market.[3] As the name Warner-Elektra-Atlantic illustrates, major companies at first distributed and then absorbed the many independent labels that had formed in the late 1960s. Radio stations began to carve up audiences in terms of particular markets and demographics. FM radio, once the outlet for progressive and experimental programming, increasingly began to resemble AM formats, which were organized around a single style (such as pop-rock, soft rock, hard rock, or soul) and a heavy rotation of forty or fewer top-selling songs interspersed with commercials. As a result, the radio listening experience became narrow and homogenized.

Given the corporate stronghold on the music industry, it is not surprising that independent recordings distributed through underground networks held meaning for subcultural identities. I focus on two such recorded repertories here: "women's music" produced by lesbian feminists, and disco music produced by gay men. Women's music and disco each defined a communal space: for the lesbian community, that space consisted of music concerts and festivals; for the gay men's community, it was composed of discotheques and clubs. Taken together, these spaces provide a context for understanding the production and consumption of the recordings.

In this chapter, I will be looking at what the recordings are saying, as well as what the discussions about the recordings say. Lesbian-feminist, gay, and even mainstream newspapers and magazines reveal an intense debate surrounding these recorded repertories; it was a debate about the public image of lesbians and gays and their community, about constructions of same-sex desire, and about the public consumption of those constructions. It was a debate that took place separately, within the different homosocial communities, but which nevertheless similarly concerned race, class, and gender.

PRODUCT TO THE PEOPLE

The story of women's music begins with the politics and sounds of the Old Left labor movements of the 1930s and '40s, which flourished in American cities, especially New York. Drawing upon the Marxist idea that revolutionary power lay in the hands of the proletariat, the Old Left romanticized rural life and advocated the creation of "a new social order" and a "new folk community" based on egalitarianism and, importantly, awareness of class-based oppression. In order to propagate these views, musicians such as the Almanac Singers and Woody Guthrie co-opted the musical idioms of rural and traditional communities and used politically explicit lyrics to instill working-class consciousness, or "folk-consciousness," in middle-class intellectuals. The result was the creation of a genre best described as "urban folk music," of which Guthrie's song "This Land Is Your Land" is perhaps the best-known example.[4] Combining simple chord progressions and repetitive lyrics, this song conveyed notions of social equality and communal property: "From the redwood forests to the Gulf stream waters, this land was made for you and me."

Throughout the 1950s and '60s the left's increasing concentration on global humanitarian and sociological issues replaced concerns about local economics and labor. This shift caused the left to attract larger numbers of students, and eventually the movement came to be called the New Left, giving the next generation of urban folk musicians—Pete Seeger, Phil Ochs, Joan Baez, and young Bob Dylan—a mass market. The shift also associated "downwardly mobile" acoustic sounds with anticonsumerist and antiestablishment politics. In this way, folk music provided leftist political movements with an alternative to the technological materialism of pop and rock.

The philosophy of the New Left was influenced by the work of Herbert

Marcuse, a Marxist critical theorist. Marcuse was associated early in his career with the exiled members of the Frankfurt Institute for Social Research, which included Adorno and Horkheimer. After World War II Marcuse remained in the United States, where he strove to broaden Marxist critiques and reconcile them with aesthetics and Freudian psychoanalysis in order to develop mechanisms for social change. In the mid-1960s Marcuse rejected the Marxist vision of social revolution as springing from the working class because he felt that this class had been thoroughly indoctrinated with capitalist ideals through mass media and through state and industrial management. He turned instead to "nonintegrated" countercultural populations such as radical intellectuals, students, minorities, and women.[5] Marcuse believed that art and aesthetics could reconcile sensuality with reason; that such reconciliation could transform social reality by turning nature from an antagonistic force into an object of contemplation; and that labor as production of material wealth could thereby be redirected to the freeing up of space and time for the "freely evolving potentialities of man and nature."

In his 1972 book *Counter Revolution and Revolt,* Marcuse proclaimed the women's liberation movement as the radical force working to weaken "primary aggressiveness which, by a combination of biological and social factors, has governed the patriarchal culture." He envisioned an "ascent of Eros over aggression, in men *and* women" through "nonviolent, nondomineering" behavior and values. "This means," he argued, "in a male-dominated civilization, the 'femalization' of the male"[6] (note that Marcuse did not say "feminization"). But Marcuse also feared that cultural revolution was always threatened by co-optation: "ecology, rock, ultramodern art are the most conspicuous examples."[7] In his earlier book, *One-Dimensional Man* (1964), Marcuse had blamed the failure of populist revolution on "technological rationality," by which he meant a means-ends arrangement of thoughts and actions, a focus on instrumentality that subjects individuality to social administration and control through economic pressures, and the creation of false needs and desires only met through material consumption.[8]

In the late 1960s, sexism pervaded the "progressive" cultural and political movements; male "free love" hippies, civil rights activists, and New Left "politicos" tended to treat their female counterparts poorly, caring little about their ideas, concerns, or unwanted pregnancies. This sexism eventually galvanized radical women to organize separately. These second-wave feminists argued that gender was analogous to class, and that women constituted a class that was subject to systematic oppression within the patriarchy. But ideological differences soon emerged among women's groups in the early 1970s, resulting in the formation of several strains of feminism. Radical feminists believed gender differences to be social constructions and saw activism as its central work. Liberal feminists sought to reform the old democratic system. Cultural feminists, evolving later from radical feminism, believed that men and women were fundamentally different and saw a separatist counterculture as the goal. "The personal is political" is a slogan that originated with the New Left but came to characterize both radical and cultural feminism: radical feminism used the slogan to invite women to investigate the gender dynamics in the details of their behavior; cultural feminism used the slogan to prescribe behavior.[9]

Lesbianism became a divisive issue among women's liberation factions between 1969 and 1973. It was disparaged by both liberal and radical feminists, who feared an emphasis on sexuality would undermine their credibility. Furthermore, it was widely believed that gendered role-playing—one partner playing the "butch" and the other the "femme"—was endemic to lesbian relationships. In 1970 lesbians began to organize chiefly around Rita Mae Brown, who founded the Radicalesbians to sensitize feminists to lesbian causes through insurrections and writings.[10] As a bridge builder, the group found itself in a complicated position, arguing, on one hand, for the inclusion of lesbian sexuality as a feminist cause, while, on the other hand, deemphasizing that sexuality as only part of a more comprehensive same-sex-oriented identity. The Radicalesbian paper "The Woman Identified Woman" argued that the label "lesbian" is part of the "male classification system of defining all females in sexual relation to some other category of people," but maintained that "until women see in each other the possibility of a primal commitment which includes sexual love, they will be denying themselves the love and value they readily accord to men, thus affirming their second-class status."[11] Only this thorough "woman-identification," which necessarily took place outside of compulsory heterosexuality, held the promise of liberation and therefore could present a political choice. Other lesbian-feminist writings of the time similarly strove to distance lesbianism from genitally oriented "sexuality," which was male-identified, using terms such as sensuality, communication, closeness, pleasure, and even "nonprofit."[12]

Between 1971 and 1973, lesbian-feminist collectives began to agitate for, and experiment with, separatism. Washington, D.C., was the home of the extreme separatist lesbian group the Furies and their influential eponymous newspaper, and also the point of origin for Olivia Records. The slogan "Feminism is the theory; lesbianism is the practice" circulated in women's liberation groups, antagonizing some and empowering others, but at any rate adding to the increasing polarity of cultural feminist ideology.

Cultural feminism contrasted markedly from other forms of feminism by reasserting the biological differences between men and women and arguing that the unity of womanhood ought to override other "male-imposed" divisions of race, class, and sexuality. Jane Alpert, Robin Morgan, Mary Daly, and Rita Mae Brown, cultural feminism's chief spokespersons, advocated the development of women's arts, religions, and communities, even calling for the "restoration" of matriarchy.[13] In her 1973 book *Beyond God the Father,* theologian Mary Daly drew heavily on Marcuse's ideas, especially those in *One-Dimensional Man,* arguing that women need to create a "new space" outside the patriarchal morality and its "technical knowledge, [which] . . . degrades its object and dehumanizes the knowing subject."[14] She notes, "Marcuse, for example, encourages the building of a society in which a new type of human being emerges," and that this "human being of the future . . . would have a new sensibility and sensitivity, and would be physiologically incapable of tolerating an ugly, noisy, and polluted universe."[15] Later she comments on Marcuse's notion of capitalism creating false material and intellectual needs that lead to "repressive satisfaction," writing, "Although his intent and context clearly were not precisely the same as those reflected in this book, there is a coincidence of insights. The rituals of patriarchy *do* create false needs, such as the need to lean on father-figures instead of finding strength in the self, or the need for compulsive 'self sacrifice' because one is brainwashed into thinking that one is sinful."[16] Daly goes on to explain that nonrepressive satisfaction can only be gained through alternative women-centric cultural systems, rituals, and modes of communication, which she calls "new sounds of silence," "the vibrations of which are too high for the patriarchal hearing mechanism."[17]

But it was music, not silence, that became a primary vehicle for communicating and organizing this new cultural politic. The album *Mountain Moving Day* (1972) represents an early attempt to record a form of separatist popular music. Released on the independent label Rounder Records, which specialized in folk, blues, and bluegrass styles, it brought together the songs of two groups, the Chicago Women's Liberation Rock Band and the New Haven Women's Liberation Rock Band, each band taking one side of the album. The liner notes to the album lays out these bands' musical and political agendas:

> All of us wanted to create a new kind of band and a new kind of music. . . . We knew what we didn't want: the whole male rock trip with its insulting lyrics, battering ram style and contempt for the audience. . . . We knew that we wanted to make music that would embody the radical feminist, humanitarian vision we shared. . . . What we all want to do is use the power of rock to transform what the world is like into a vision of what the world could be like.[18]

As early as 1971, feminist articles decrying rock as sexist, vulgar, materialistic, and egotistical began appearing in mainstream publications, using the common epithet "cock rock" to neatly summarize these qualities. For these writers, rock was masculinist music, conveying masculine values and "a million different levels of women-hating." Women, these writers complained, were denied access to electric guitars and drums on the grounds that these instruments were "unfeminine" and that "women aren't aggressive enough to play good, driving rock."[19] Lyrics and performance postures came under the fiercest attack; the liner notes to *Mountain Moving Day* list offensive songs such as the Rolling Stones' "Under My Thumb" and "Back-Street Girl" and James Brown's "It's a Man's Man's Man's World," and they describe offensive theatrics such as the "bumping and grinding" of Mick Jagger, the "raping and burning" of guitars by Jimi Hendrix, the "whacking-off on stage" of Jim Morrison, and the strict hierarchy of rock star, backup band, and audience.

The mission of the Chicago Women's Liberation Rock Band, founded in 1970 by Naomi Weisstein as the "agit-rock arm" of the Chicago Women's Liberation Union, was to separate the energy of rock music from the sexism of rock culture, "to make a collective, non-assaultive joyful rock music."[20] Their goal was to establish an "alternative, feminist, socialist" culture as the "Queen pin in the achievement of social change."[21] Though their songs and political writings were not concerned with lesbianism, the band sprang from the desire to build a women-identified culture that would open up previously closed opportunities for women, including work in sound engineering and arts management.[22] At that time, and well into the next decades, women met with serious discrimination on all levels of the music industry; they were virtually shut out of executive and technical positions.[23] Furthermore, female performers often found themselves boxed into softer pop styles and sexualized images.

The Chicago Women's Liberation Rock Band reveals an early turn toward rock music as an appropriate medium for a feminist message. They provided preexisting songs with new lyrics, parodied macho rock poses, and broke down the barrier between performer and audience by keeping the house lights on, soliciting comments between songs, and conducting sing-alongs. In a collectively written article on their music, they admit that "we chose rock because it is so popular"; they wanted to take advantage of its reputation as "the new insurgency, that it was dangerous to the powers that were." But they also wanted to divorce its lyric content from "the drive and the energy, the electronic sounds, the real technical and human magic that our society is able to create." Their hope was to "demystify the priesthood of the instrument and the amplifier" for women,[24] not only by playing electrified guitars and keyboards, but also by having women as their sound technicians.

About the music itself, they remark, "one can't make revolutionary rock without the rock itself—the musical form—changing."[25] None of their statements offer anything more explicit about their reconception of the rock sound, but the four original songs on their side of *Mountain Moving Day* may be taken as examples of it. The songs range from mid-tempo folk-rock with lengthy instrumental jams that recall the Grateful Dead ("Secretary" and "Mountain Moving Day"), to an old-timey rag ("Papa"), to traditional twelve-bar blues ("Ain't Gonna Marry"). Evidence of electrification is kept to a minimum; the jam in "Secretary" features an acoustic lead guitar, and although the lead guitars in "Mountain Moving Day" are electric, no distortion nor any of the other guitar effects that were common in guitar-based rock are used. This "pure," nonaggressive soft rock is sometimes coupled with caustic lyrics:

> Rolling Stones, Blood Sweat & Tears,
> I've taken that shit for too many years,
> Papa don't lay those sounds on me,
> I ain't your groovy chick.[26]

Early feminist complaints about rock music had primarily singled out the sexist lyrics, although traces of hostility toward the music itself can be found as well. In a 1971 review of the women-fronted rock group Joy of Cooking, Lynne Shapiro writes, "what impresses me most about the group is while the beat is energetic and stirring, it is subtle. There is no raucous guitar twanging or piano banging—often the mainstay of macho rock groups."[27] Ruth Scovill, paraphrasing a 1976 comment by women's musician Margie Adam, writes "eventually it became evident that women needed to say more, both with lyrics and musical form, than was possible within the rock format."[28]

By 1978, the influence of feminist criticisms of rock could be seen in some academic sociological analyses of popular culture. In an article entitled "Rock and Sexuality," Simon Frith and Angela McRobbie, using Marxist theory, argue that rock turns leisure into a consumption of sexuality, and thus serves as the principal medium for conveying a particular convention of male/female roles in sexual activity. They cite two extremes. One extreme, identified as "cock rock," presents male "wild" sexuality through "sexual iconography," using guitars and microphones as phallic symbols. They go on to describe the music as "loud, rhythmically insistent, built around techniques of arousal and climax." The other extreme, identified as "teenybop," presents female "passive" sexuality as male sexuality domesticated—romantic and emotionally vulnerable. Rock ballads—soft, "less physical music"—play on "notions of female sexuality as serious, diffuse, and implying total emotional commitment."[29]

Frith and McRobbie adhere to second-wave feminism's focus on gender differences: if loud rock drums and electric guitars were indicative of masculine sexuality, then a "less physical," less "insistent" rhythm and softer electric or acoustic guitars were indicative of feminine sexuality. Given that the feminist debate tended to polarize genders, neither feminist nor feminist-influenced analyses considered rock to be itself a complex discourse of gender. The routine citations of artists such as Mick Jagger, Robert Plant, and Jimi Hendrix as examples of "cock rock" neglect the many ways in which these performers can be read as androgynous, or even feminized.[30] Similarly absent from these criticisms is any mention of rock's African-American roots, and the ways in which Jagger, Plant, and Hendrix (Janis Joplin, too, though she is rarely mentioned in feminist critiques of rock) also crossed racial categories.

Yet the issue of race in such criticisms of rock was conspicuous to women of color. Linda Tillery, an African-American women's musician, responded to the charge "that rock and jazz aren't good musical idioms for women":

> I get extremely angry when people tell me that rock—really what they're talk-
> ing about is rhythm-based music—is not a good way for a woman to go. The
> music I grew up with and that I understand most is music created by my ances-
> tors, my family. Blues, rhythm and blues, and jazz are part of our tradition, and
> I resent the fact that anyone would say these are not good idioms for women.
> That's telling me that I shouldn't express my own culture, that some other tra-
> dition would be more appropriate for me. And that, to me, is racist.[31]

Tillery associates rock as a discourse of race primarily because of its rhythmic roots in the music traditions of the African diaspora. But the use of the
electric guitar—a primary feature of African-American music since the
1940s—often appears to be more problematic than the music's rhythmic
drive. Not only was the instrument phallic but it was also an emblem of technology, and it symbolized the misogyny of the music industry in general. One
reviewer of the "all-electric women's band" Be Be K'Roche, writing in 1977,
remarks, "It's not an easy task to define what women's music is, what separates it from men's music, especially for women in electric bands. It sometimes seems that many women have been conditioned to turn off to 'that
kind' of music, having seen all that raw power so badly abused by our male
counterparts."[32] Thus the very presence of the electric guitar is enough to
call into question the women-identified nature of the music. Given the emergence of rock from the electrified rhythm and blues of African-American gui-
tarists such as Muddy Waters, this bias against electric guitars can also be
understood as having the racist consequences that Tillery describes,
although even she seems reticent to argue this point.[33]

Mountain Moving Day was an important early use of rock music to forge
and disseminate the sound of a new, alternative women's culture, but it was
folk music that came to dominate recorded women's music from 1973 to
1978; specifically, it was white American urban folk music, with its emphasis
on words and accessibility, that had served as a consciousness-raising tool for
both the Old and New Left. Indeed, the origins of recorded women's music
lie in the money of white, politically left, middle-class women, who invested
in the project of their own self-expression.

Folk singer Alix Dobkin is credited with creating the first album of
"women's music." She could be called its first star. Together with flautist Kay
Gardner and bassist Patches Attom, Dobkin formed in 1973 the group
Lavender Jane. Within a year they had released an album entirely produced

and nationally distributed by women. Although the group's name seemed innocent enough, in fact "Jane" referred to Jane Alpert, the leftist crusader who went underground for participation in several bombings of military buildings in 1969. While hiding from the F.B.I. Alpert joined the separatist feminist cause, condemned the left as sexist, and wrote the influential militant track "Mother Right," which *Ms.* magazine published in 1973. "The music of Lavender Jane," Dobkin writes, "followed the same feminist analysis and point of view."[34]

Dobkin describes the origin of the album *Lavender Jane Loves Women* in her 1975 collection of writings and songs.

> *Lavender Jane Loves Women* was launched on a Lesbian Lifespace cruise during a balmy September night in 1973. It was a festive evening in New York City for five hundred or so Dykes partying on the Hudson River, dancing to live music by The New Haven Women's Rock Band. . . . It was there that I was approached with concrete offers to help finance a Lesbian record. . . . About a dozen women loaned us enough [money] to get us into the studio by October.[35]

With $3,500 in personal loans, Dobkin and her group set about recording, producing, and distributing an album of songs, most of which had explicit lesbian content. They used women sound engineers, photographers, and studio musicians, and they used their lesbian underwriters as chorus and distribution agents. The album was completed and released in November 1973.[36]

Dobkin's stated goal was "to institutionalize Lesbian culture": she wanted "Lesbians to have tangible musical proof of their existence," and she wanted to concretize a subject position that had up to that point been relegated to the ephemeral moment of concert performances.[37] More than literature or graphics, "tangible" lesbian music was to be the new material imprint and "record" of lesbianism. Lesbian music as a "cultural product" could repeatedly define any given space and time according to that particular subject position, without the expense or restricted accessibility of a concert. Dobkin admits that she initially did not think "past record production." The need to become "business women" was an afterthought; she had to sell records in order to pay back the loans—not to mention realize her goal of getting her "pioneering product onto Lesbians' turntables." For Dobkin, with her background in Jewish leftist and communist organizations, the significance of such a product was less the display of independent economic power and more the goal of outreach and cultural confirmation.

Dobkin's musical record of lesbianism reflected her concert repertory of Scottish, American, and Balkan folk songs (the latter being a particular specialty of hers), along with original numbers with explicitly lesbian and separatist lyrics. Much of *Lavender Jane Loves Women* today comes across as an exercise in unrestrained sentimentality and righteousness, sometimes delivered with humor, as in Dobkin's clever reworking of the leftist folk song "Talking Union" into "Talking Lesbians." There is an amateurish quality—perhaps conscious—to the performances: intonation and tuning waver, and the arrangements are limited to those few musicians at hand, which included a guitarist, flautist, bassist, and sometimes cellist. But this rough-and-ready sound adds to the sense that the music represents the unbridled expression of highly motivated musicians.

The last song on the album combined Dobkin's political and ethnic interests in a musical-political tour de force. According to the album's liner notes, she "lifted" the melody for "View from Gay Head" from the Balkan song "Savo Vodo" (though only the first phrase of Dobkin's song bears any resemblance to "Savo Vodo").[38] The music in general provides a curious contrast to the militantly separatist words; it features warm cello and flute countermelodies that engage musical codes of pastoral innocence with a hint of classical music stuffiness. While the chord changes map out four-bar phrases, the vocal melody overlaps with these variously, creating a metrically flexible, declamatory effect. In her songbook, Dobkins described the lyrics as her "first venture into Lesbian consciousness set to music." The words actually recount topics and conversations from a separatist consciousness-raising ("c-r") discussion group: each verse names a woman ("Liza wishes the library had men and women placed separately," "Carol is tired of being nice"), and the refrain features a chorus of women singing of separatism ("Lesbian, Lesbian, Let's be in no man's land"). The topics of each verse follow logically, touching first on a sense of "us" and "them" (verse 1), then anger about the absence of women in history (verse 2), anger about submissive habits of behavior (verse 3), women's anger as beautiful (verse 4), and a commitment to separatism (verse 5). The personal names ground the lyrics in a sense of reality and community: this anger is not just Dobkin's, but also that of a host of women—Cheryl, Mary, Liza, and Carol, to name but a few.

As the song progresses the verses get increasingly acrimonious and, with the last verse, even castrating. It is here that we can see the influence of Jane Alpert. I quote the verse below as it is published in Dobkin's songbook (though the emphasis is added):

> The sexes do battle and batter about
> The men's are the sexes I will live without
> I'll return to the bosom where my journey ends *where there's no*
> *Penis* between us friends. Will I see you again when you're a [Lesbian?]

According to the rhyme scheme the line break should be:

> I'll return to the bosom where my journey ends,
> Where there's no penis between us friends.

As Dobkin printed the lyric, however, the word "penis" takes an exalted position at the beginning of a line. "Penis" also signals the emotional climax in the recording; Dobkin punches out the word with a sudden shift from singing to speaking. Thus the desire for the radical removal of the penis ironically promotes the penis as the organizing force for lesbian separatism. The verse is awkward and ungrammatical to be sure; it stands as a rough-hewn political statement, made all the more powerful and threatening by a deceptively polished and sweet musical encasement from which sharp edges protrude.

THE BUSINESS OF WOMEN'S MUSIC

Dobkin's "Project #1" (as she called it) was simply to get the album distributed to as many women as possible. The founders of Olivia Records, however, had quite a different set of goals in mind. After the lesbian-feminist Furies collective disbanded, some former members continued to publish their newspaper, contemplating in this forum the complexities of feminist political commitment and the material class-based issues of survival, these being the very issues that had torn the original collective apart. The May 1973 issue of *The Furies* featured a bold, controversial article entitled "Building Feminist Institutions" by Lee Schwing and Helaine Harris, who advocated the formation of feminist businesses (euphemistically called "institutions"). Schwing and Harris called feminist business "part of the solution of our goal to achieve power for women." They noted that "it was oppressive for middle class women to work at 'downwardly mobile' jobs, if other opportunities were open to them. Why should a middle class woman be 'poor by choice' alongside a working class woman 'poor by caste' when she could be working at a job that would help support both of them."[39] Theoretically, feminist institutions established by women with economic means would offer economic self-sufficiency to the women's community as a whole, and that would allow the enactment of structural economic changes. This vision of "sharing the wealth" seemed to place a new emphasis on materialism. The critique of capitalism as exploitative was exchanged for an exploitation of capitalism as the way to empowerment and liberation. Schwing and Harris considered feminist capitalism a "step towards a feminist society."[40] By creating an alternative economic network, feminist business would close the distinction between labor and activism. Such closure, however, was inconceivable within the left; it was the opposite of Marcuse's vision of the women's liberation movement as a triumph of the aesthetic over the aggressive. The article also caused a rift within the staff of *The Furies;* it was published along with a rebuttal written by two other members, Loretta Ulmschneider and Deborah George. Ulmschneider and George criticize Schwing and Harris for their idealism and lack of analysis, and they warn that it will be middle-class women who create the businesses, and it will be they who benefit most.[41]

The aesthetic did, nonetheless, play an important role in the new feminist economics, and music was the product of choice to initiate the real goal of feminist business. Harris, along with Furies members Ginny Berson and Jennifer Woodul, cast about for an appropriate feminist institution to found. Eventually, they joined forces with local folksinger Meg Christian and members of the Radical Lesbians of Ann Arbor (which included Judy Dlugacz).[42] Together they established the Olivia Records collective (they had considered calling it Siren Records!) in January 1973. By August of 1974 the national feminist magazine *Off Our Backs* published a "debut" article entitled "The Muses of Olivia: Our Own Economy, Our Own Song." In this interview, Harris notes that "the disappointment that some of us have had in the women's movement is that we've not been able to sustain ourselves in different types of alternative institutions that we've begun, such as day-care centers—a lot of it having to do with not having a partial capitalist business sense to keep it going, not being able to salary ourselves, always being volunteers . . . and burning ourselves out."[43] In the same article Ginny Berson describes the impetus behind Olivia Records, claiming, "We wanted to set up some sort of economic institution which would both produce a product that women want to buy and also employ women in a nonoppressive situation—get them out of regular jobs. Second, we wanted to be in a position to be able to affect large numbers of women, and that had to be through media. The medium that was most accessible to us, was the easiest way for us to get something out to large numbers of women, was music."[44] When asked about the issue of profits, Berson noted that money earned from selling records would go to salaries, equipment, and training rather than to shareholders, and that people's earnings would be based on need rather than "male societal values" such as fame. Most striking in this interview is Berson's discussion of the function of concerts as promotional rather than communal events, as "a way to raise money for Olivia and to raise money for women musicians who right now do not have many opportunities to sing for women and make any money for it."[45] This article is the first of many published between 1974 and 1978 in which Olivia Records figures as the center of a fierce ideological battle within the women's liberation movement about the ethics of feminist businesses.[46]

In an issue of *Off Our Backs* (1976), Brooke L. Williams and Hannah Darby published a scathing critique of feminist businesses entitled "God, Mom, and Apple Pie." They charged that such businesses, along with the cultural feminist ideology that supports them, offer only delusions of political participation, economic power, and egalitarian structures, while in fact exploiting women in low-paying jobs, turning feminism into a commodity and feminists into a market, falling into unavoidable hierarchical organization. Williams and Darby argued that feminist business had "enormous power over determining the movement's public image and recruitment—power that is neither delegated nor controlled by the women's movement itself."[47]

The implications of this last point are tremendous: in effect, the public image of (lesbian) feminism will be shaped by market forces, or, in other words, by whatever sells. Olivia Records collective member Jennifer Woodul responded to the criticisms of Williams and Darby in a counterarticle in which she argues, among other things, that the product—especially the musical product—can transform the subjectivity of the buyers. Her argument relies in part on the association of women's music with "consciousness-raising" folk music. She also suggests that feminist businesses such as Olivia Records act as a sort of money-laundering operation, washing the capitalism out of profit margins by keeping the socialist ideal of redistributing wealth as their goal. She writes, "Olivia's survival is vital to the economic future of all of us; it must succeed. And we want this music to reach beyond the feminist community we're in touch with now. Both because we feel that music is an effective way of reaching other women, and because we're trying to make a big business, one that brings *new* money into the feminist community—not just circulates what we have among ourselves again and again" (emphasis in the original).[48] For Woodul, buying an Olivia Records product could change attitudes, reconstitute subjectivity, and perhaps even rescue capitalism from the patriarchy. This notion of feminism as "big business" should have sent shudders down the spine of any follower of Marcuse. Woodul seemed to be arguing from a position of "technological rationality"; Olivia Records and its musical product were creating a "false need" within the movement through the conflation of consumerism and political action.

The debate in *Off Our Backs* spread to another feminist record label, Kay Gardner's Urana Records (formed in 1975), which operated on the East Coast and presented "a women's business" that was "very different from many other women's businesses." What Gardner described is in direct contrast to the egalitarian ideal behind Olivia Records: "We're a corporate structure, with a president, vice president, and a secretary-treasurer. . . . We didn't found ourselves, as Olivia did, as a collective. We founded ourselves as two women who wanted to put out a product and be covered and protected by the corporate structures. Then we evolved into more than that. We're really a business, with the major impetus and interest being women's music." Ironically, Gardner combines this patriarchal pragmatic business sense with a mystical view of women artists and musicians as gurus for the movement, claiming that the woman artist is "aware of what's happening before the rest of the world is aware of it and works her art to say what's happening. A movement is happening in women's music that is becoming powerful."[49] Gardner's contradictory descriptions of her business and her product provide further evidence of Marcuse's nightmare "technological rationality," which seemed to have crept into the business of women's music; it is a rationality that divides an analysis of the product from an analysis of the production process—precisely the thinking that Marcuse blamed for the failure of populist revolution in *One-Dimensional Man*.

SELLING LESBIANS

At about the same time that *Lavender Jane Loves Women* first hit lesbian turntables in early 1974, Olivia Records released, as a fund-raiser, a 45 rpm single on which Meg Christian sang "Lady" by Carole King on one side, and Cris Williamson sang her own song "If It Weren't for the Music" on the other. The idea of founding a feminist record company had apparently come from a chance remark made by Williamson (who already had a number of commercially released albums to her name) during a radio interview on a show hosted by Meg Christian and Ginny Berson.[50] But it was Christian who eventually recorded Olivia's first full-length album of songs, *I Know You Know* (recorded in 1974, released in March 1975).

Like Dobkin, Christian began as a folk musician. She moved to Washington, D.C., in 1969 after studying English literature and classical guitar performance at the University of North Carolina at Chapel Hill. Eventually she narrowed her repertory to songs with feminist and lesbian themes, including parodic covers of old rock and roll and Motown songs. Her classical guitar skills were prominently featured in her arrangements; they were also highlighted, as part of her musical persona, in interviews, on the cover of *I Know You Know* (where she is listed as playing "classical guitar" for each song), and in her songbook and "scrapbook" for the album. In the introduction to the songbook, Kate Winter writes about taking lessons from Christian, claiming that Meg "had studied classical guitar and still included classical pieces in her practicing, although she didn't perform them. Her method of teaching was to start with basic classical training and theory as the foundation for dealing with contemporary music. I was too impatient and unwilling to work hard enough to go that route."[51] Indeed, and in contrast to Dobkin's ragged but honest product, Olivia Records touted Meg Christian as a *serious* musician who complemented their goal of making "*high quality* women's music" (emphasis added). They proudly proclaimed Christian's album as "first-rate technically as well as musically," since their ultimate goal was to demonstrate competence in all aspects—musical, technical, and business.[52]

Like the album, the songbook, published in 1975, represents a high degree of technical competence, even though it appears egalitarian. Christian provided detailed melodic transcriptions of every song, including both notated and tablature versions of instrumental interludes, instructions for finger-picking patterns for the right hand, the melody work of the left, and discussions of the capo and transposition, as well as her nomenclature for simple chords and chords with added notes. The idea was to give those women who wanted to learn *exactly* the songs on the album all the necessary information. In spite of the disclaimer that simplified and personalized versions are just as valid, the result is a fetishizing of detail that seems to enjoin the user to practice and learn the authentic recorded version.

The New Woman's Survival Sourcebook (1975) features an article by Woodul (an "infomercial," really) on the genesis of Olivia Records and Christian's *I Know You Know*. Woodul writes, "we knew her music had an irresistible appeal—we could trust it and it spoke to us. (Looking back, I could say that it expressed female experience and values that we all shared—but we hadn't analyzed it then. We just loved to hear her sing and play.) And we saw the same kind of communication happen when other talented women performed their own beautiful women-identified music."[53]

This quote points to the crystallization of a "mainstream" style of women's music (that "*we* just love to hear"), one formed, perhaps, more by default than by design, but one that nonetheless had a lasting impact on both internal and external evaluations of women-identified music. While the first version of the sourcebook, *The New Woman's Survival Catalog* (published in 1973), features a full-page advertisement for *Mountain Moving Day*, with extensive quotes from the album's liner notes, the second sourcebook, published two years later, documents a shift in the constitution of women's music, for it features a two-page article on Olivia Records and a full page of record advertisements with brief written portraits of a number of prominent "women-identified" singer-songwriters. These include Meg Christian, Cris Williamson, Willie Tyson, Casse Culver, Alix Dobkin, and the experimental composer and flautist Kay Gardner. By contrast, the New Haven Women's Liberation Rock Band and Be Be K'Roche appear on another page in a much smaller section labeled "feminist music groups" (the Chicago Women's Liberation Band had disbanded in 1973), along with twelve other outfits collectively described as ranging from "rock and roll to folk-jazz to ragtime." The mention of rock seemed to require clarification, for the description goes on to say, "Each group explicitly rejects prevailing sexist-macho musical values and is committed to providing a woman-identified alternative."[54] The allocation of space reflects primarily whether a musician or band had recorded an album, thus marking a clear division between those with a product and those without one. Furthermore, the hierarchical nature of the advertisements reveals the predominance of singer-songwriters, whose styles were derived from folk music and soft rock, over groups of musicians, whose styles were derived from jazz and rock. In the course of two years, then, the rock album *Mountain Moving Day* had disappeared from the women's music chart; nor does the second sourcebook list any racially or ethnically marked group.[55]

. . .

Christian's album *I Know You Know* begins with the celebratory "Hello Hooray" by Rolf Kempf. The song was recorded by Judy Collins in 1968, and this recording likely served as Christian's source.[56] But it was also recorded by heavy metal shock rocker Alice Cooper in 1973 to quite a different effect.[57] All three musicians used this song as the first track of their album, taking advantage of the song's opening lines:

> Hello Hooray, let the show begin, I've been ready.
> Hello Hooray, let the lights grow dim, I've been ready.

In this, as in many of the songs on *I Know You Know,* Christian's idiomatic guitar arrangements and skillful playing are foregrounded in the mix, while piano, bass, and other supporting instruments form a softer haze, thickening the texture. "Hello Hooray" opens with a quick, high-register fingerpicking pattern, which cleverly creates an air of excited anticipation to suit the words—indeed, to suit the sentiment of the whole album as a triumph of women's culture and feminist business, as well as the hope of a bright new future for lesbians. The chorus features a rousing declaration of self-empowerment through music.[58] Cris Williamson and Aleta Greene (the only African-American woman among the Olivia Records collective members pictured on the back cover) join in with rousing, gospel-like responding vocals. Their wordless "Ah" initially enhances the "I" of Christian's lead vocal, then they finally unite with her "we" in the final line:

> I've been waiting so long,   for another song
>
> (ah————————so long)
>
> I've been thinking so long,   I was the only one
>
> (ah————————so long)
>
> We've been hoping so long,   for another song.
>
> (we've been hoping—so long)

It is a highly effective opener for Olivia Records' first musical product, matching the concept of "another song" (women's music) with the spirit of "coming out" ("thinking . . . I was the only one"). This coming out of women's music is affirmed and supported by a heavenly choir of women's voices. The "only one" begs the question "only one of what?"—to which the rest of the album gives a complex answer. Indeed, this first song about singing sets the stage for the many self-referential song titles, including "Valentine Song," "Song to My Mama," "Morning Song," and "Ode to a Gym Teacher." On one level this collection is as much about being an *album* of songs—and not the "only one" in Olivia Records' future—as about being a woman, a lesbian, or a feminist.

Many of the songs on the album focus on the personal struggles of lesbians, with lovers, family, and, occasionally, the world at large. Surprisingly few of Christian's songs on *I Know You Know* use gendered pronouns. This may seem at odds with her militant politics; by all accounts Christian was considered an ideological purist among women's musicians in the mid-seventies, resolutely refusing to perform for mixed-gender audiences or with male musicians and recording only for companies owned and operated by women.[59] Her focus on explicitly lesbian concerns, however, clearly defined "women's music" as "lesbian music," and lesbianism itself as political action.

Christian was occasionally criticized in the feminist presses for her confessional romanticism (she admitted in a 1973 interview to being uncomfortable singing "blatantly political songs").[60] The albums that Cris Williamson recorded with Olivia Records addressed women's spiritual and emotional life, rather than global women's issues. In contrast, Holly Near, who was not an Olivia Records artist, recorded music that mostly concerned women in the context of global politics, workers' rights, and political prisoners. In 1977, Olivia Records would come under fire for the lesbian-centric themes of their records. One commentator on the feminist politics of Olivia Records remarked:

> Ultimately the area in which Olivia's politics are most important is the records themselves [as opposed to their business practices]. The political emphasis there seems to be lesbianism, or pro-lesbian statements. . . . But is lesbianism a political goal? a feminist goal? and is it sufficient to have as a goal? Politics and lesbianism do not necessarily go hand-in-hand. . . . [Olivia Records] rarely get down to the nitty gritty of economic, racist, or political oppression outside of lesbianism.[61]

Olivia Records' products, then, constructed "women" not only as objects of desire, much like mainstream pop music, but also as subjects of desire, specifically in the image of white, middle-class lesbians. This desire of women for women, according to Olivia Records, was itself a feminist position, a politics of sexual identity; according to other feminists, it was no politics at all.

Christian's first album attempted to record the political and emotional horizons of a queer sexual identity for lesbian audiences. The title, *I Know You Know,* directly engages the epistemology of the closet with its revelation through elision. It comes from one of two songs ("Scars" and "Song to My

Mama") that directly confront issues of oppression (of lesbians). In contrast to Christian's impish smile on the cover, lending a mischievousness to the phrase, its lyric context is, in fact, a sobering one: "Mama, Mama, well I know you know, but you couldn't survive, if I told you so." This is the only song with anything like a "driving beat," pounded out on closed hi-hat cymbals or the guitar. Each verse begins with this beat as the only accompaniment to Christian's naked vocal address, "Mama, Mama." Her guitar playing is also strongly rhythmic, much like that of Melissa Etheridge, but here the pounding beat sounds as an emblem of mother-daughter tension within the constraint of coded communication. Some of the lyrics and rhymes are strained—such as "is there something buried in your old widow's mind, that blesses my choice of our own kind"—but some moments are arresting for their expression of internal conflict and bitterness:

> But maybe once a year,
> When I'm a little tight,
> I'll feel fresh regrets and write,
> Some cryptic thank yous . . . [62]

Christian's "mother figure" could, in fact, stand for many women in the feminist movement who put pressure on lesbians to desexualize their subject position. This situation was still very much in evidence four years later, as a liner note on Holly Near's "coming out" album, *Imagine My Surprise* (1978), bears witness. Near, who was Christian's lover at the time of the album's making, writes, "One surprise was discovering that for many women, lesbianism is more than 'sexual preference' as it is often so narrowly defined. For me it opened many doors . . . emotional, spiritual, cultural, political."[63]

But Near's abstract view of lesbianism as more a political position than a sexual identity does not match the sentiment of *I Know You Know.* Many of those songs explore very specific emotional details of same-sex *desire,* such as the youthful crush on a gym teacher, or the gray area between shared and separate property within a lesbian relationship, as expressed by the delicately melancholic "Morning Song." Here, Christian describes a simple domestic scene, watching cats play early in the morning, but follows this with the lyric: "And we keep saying two are mine, and two belong to you."[64] This could be read as merely a whimsical moment, but a deceptive cadence over "two belong to you" subtly spotlights the sadness that can attach to the amorphousness of lesbian relationships, in which lovers struggle for definition—without the social institution of marriage that guides, sanctions, and supports heterosexual couples. In effect, this song addresses the unrepresentability of lesbianism within patriarchal social structures: how do two women, sexually and affectively conjoined, living under one roof, symbolize their relationship?

THE POLITICS OF INSTRUMENTAL MUSIC

The last track on *I Know You Know* combines Judy Mayhan's folk song "Freest Fancy" with a Renaissance English lute piece called "Kemp's Jig." The jig provides both the accompaniment to the song as well as an instrumental interlude between the two verses; for the interlude Christian lowers the seventh degree and adds ornaments to each repetition, creating an "early music" feel. As she explains in the songbook, "fancy" was a term used in Renaissance England for a type of lute piece with dance rhythms. "Well, it turned out," she writes, "that all the fancies I found were either too hard or in the wrong key. So I had to settle for a jig."[65] This she slowed to half speed to accompany the song. In Mayhan's song, "fancy" describes the love object ("you are my freest fancy, my craziest dream"), but in Christian's version, the "fancy" also refers to the instrumental interlude and its moment of pure musical "freedom"—Christian's musical love object. The interlude clearly serves as a demonstration of her musical depth and competence, but it is also a moment that ventures precariously into "abstract" and "elitist" musical waters.

Perhaps more antagonistic to feminists than the rhythmic drive and electric guitars of rock were wordless musical solos that seemed to have no political content and smacked of narcissistic showmanship.[66] In a 1982 interview, Christian herself spoke about the pressure to write "issue" songs that "stifled" her interest in writing instrumental music ("why, an instrumental doesn't *say* anything!"), and her related worries about the elitism of labels such as "artist" and her identity as a "composer."[67] The mistrust of purely instrumental music is also in evidence in the defensive tone of the liner notes for Kay Gardner's 1975 album *Mooncircles,* a collection of meditative instrumental music that features her own flute playing. Here, Gardner argues for an essential and historical connection between femaleness and instrumental forms, writing, "The concept of music having a biological function diverges sharply from the respected tradition of social protest music from which much of women's music derives. . . . But *[Mooncircles]* is above all not a nostalgic flight away from the pain of reality but rather a journey into awareness of the strength and wholeness of our heritage."[68]

Hints of bias against instrumental music show up in concert reviews for the pianist Margie Adam. These frequently criticize her apparent self-involved music and performance. As one 1974 review noted, "you might get just a little annoyed at all the sighs and breath-catching in-between songs. . . . Margie's pretty much on her own particular trip, and while the poetry and sounds she has arrived at so far are well worth our attention, she still has to visit a few outer planets before we women can be sure she's the superstar we want."[69] In 1974, Adam had the potential to be the musical "superstar" lesbian feminists were searching for; three years later, it was clear she had fallen well short of the mark. A review of her 1977 concert listed various complaints and disappointments and claimed that some women "feel that while prais- ing the work of women as a collective, etc., Margie is pursuing her own goals, and in turn, moving away from the women's community." One measure of this "moving away" seemed to be her wordless pieces. The review continues, "Some women felt that Margie was antagonistic toward [the sign language interpreter] Jayne's presence on stage. . . . They felt that by playing long musical passages, Margie was able to force Jayne off the stage, thus bringing attention back to her."[70] Such reviews illustrate how wordless music could be read as self-indulgent, and could seem to fracture community with individu- alism, bringing this product of cultural feminism dangerously close to the mainstream products of the patriarchy. On the surface these charges seem petty and ridiculous, but the current of anxiety underlying them runs deeper than Margie Adam's performances. The debate over the propriety of word- less music within women's music mirrored the debate about the ethics of feminist business and women's music: in both debates the issue was the nature and content not only of political action, but of lesbianism itself. Word- less music came close to expressing sexuality without politics—pure les- bianism, or, worse, pure narcissism. If lesbianism was to have any political value, it had to be written about, sung about, and, more importantly, pack- aged and sold with other things.[71]

Wordless lesbian music was acceptable, however, if it was made by women of color. Olivia Records did not produce albums by minority women until 1978, when they released two albums by African-Americans, one funk- influenced collection by percussionist Linda Tillery, and another eclectic collection by keyboardist Mary Watkins. The white folk-music mainstream of women's music was gently mocked in a review of Watkins's album that appeared in *Off Our Backs,* which read, "For a long time most people thought that women's music was synonymous with white American folk music. The image: a white woman, twenty-eightish, seated on a wooden stool . . . [with] her guitar, one microphone, a glass of water. . . . And for a large part that image was real." The reviewer goes on to note that women who "don't fit that bill: women of color and white women who probably can't even fake it through the first stanza of 'Blowing in the Wind,'"[72] will make different music. The reference to race is obvious, but the reference to class is subtle, lodged in the association of the urban folk music of the political left with the middle class.

While, according to the reviewer, the funk style of Linda Tillery's music appealed to the "black music listening audience," Watkins's album was directed to another audience, the "sophisticated jazz listening crowd."[73] By implication, this audience was different from that for Tillery's "black music" album; Watkins's "sophisticated" audience could be black or white, but they were most definitely middle class—perhaps even upper middle class. Of the seven pieces on Watkins's album, only three are songs with words. The lyrics are about lesbian love and community; they do not mention race, although all three fall within the "black music" categories of soul or funk.[74] The four instrumental pieces include a light blues number ("Back Rap"), two pieces of easy-listening pop ("A Chording to the People," and "I Hear Music"), and an experimental jazz-rock fusion composition ("Witches' Revenge"). It could be argued that the politics of race is expressed in the music of these four pieces, in the African-American roots of jazz and rock and the tradition of instrumental improvisation within those styles. Indeed, the *Off Our Backs* review has nothing but praise for these pieces, but not explicitly because of the politics of race embedded in them. That politics is wholly contained in the race of Mary Watkins. "It's a real treat for me," the reviewer concludes, "to see Olivia Records recording such fine Black women's music." The album, as commercial product, itself served a political purpose: it expanded the "women" of women's music to include "black women." That it also expanded the "music" of women's music to include "black music" was, ultimately, of less political value.

PROBLEMS WITH SUCCESS

Beyond all expectations, Olivia Records sold more than ten thousand copies of *I Know You Know* within the first year, entirely through a grassroots network of women fans who volunteered to act as regional distributors. This network had been gained through a rigorous cross-country tour. About six months after the release of that album, Olivia Records released Cris Williamson's *The Changer and the Changed,* which became their all-time bestselling album. In 1976 the four "big names" in women's music—Meg Christian, Margie Adam, Holly Near, and Cris Williamson—launched a "Women on Wheels" tour that began drawing audiences of women in the thousands. Many in these audiences would go later that same year to the first separatist Michigan Womyn's Music Festival.[75]

By this time, however, Margie Adam, the pianist for Olivia Records' first two releases, had formed her own label, Pleiades Records; Holly Near had several years earlier formed Redwood Records with her parents. In her autobiography Near recounts the many conflicts of ideology and business tactics among the four musicians (now representing three record labels), conflicts that not only prohibited them from recording the concerts but also bred a sense of "mistrust."[76] After only one year the women's music "industry" had become mired in capitalistic competition. At one point Olivia Records even attempted to monopolize the network of volunteer distributors, but the latter eventually formed their own separate organization, the Women's Independent Label Distributors (WILD).[77]

Over the next several years, both Olivia and Redwood Records, for financial reasons, abandoned their efforts to underwrite the production of unknown (and struggling) female musicians and concentrated on producing albums by their top-selling stars. Despite the steady attempt to integrate African- and Latin-derived musical styles such as jazz, funk, salsa, and rock—especially into festival programs—the market for the recorded product remained largely white, middle class, and aesthetically conservative. Tillery and Watkins, as well as Sweet Honey in the Rock, sold poorly in comparison to Christian, Near, and Williamson.[78] Shortly after producing the second record of Sweet Honey in the Rock in 1978 (an experience that, according to Near, was fraught with racially inflected ideological conflicts) Near reorganized Redwood Records to function more as a management firm for her own recordings and concerts and less as a record company for new, diverse talent.[79] By the early 1980s, Olivia Records, now financially insecure, had also been reorganized into a more efficient, hierarchical structure. A subsidiary label, Second Wave, was created, which would carry more nonpolitical, nonseparatist artists who often used male musicians. That the new label was called Second Wave was ironic since the term had been applied to the forms of feminism of the 1970s that had mounted a materialist criticism of gender. But even Olivia's Second Wave shied away from harder-edged rock sounds; Olivia rejected Melissa Etheridge's audition tape in the early 1980s.[80]

In "God, Mom, and Apple Pie," the authors argued that feminist businesses "serve as scouts" for larger corporations, and that was exactly what developed in the late 1980s and early 1990s within the music industry. As Olivia Records was capsizing, only to be reborn as a lesbian cruise and vacation package company (full circle from Lavender Jane's portentous first gig on a lesbian cruise!), lesbian-coded female singer-songwriters hit the mainstream big time, many on major labels or healthy independents. From the "out and proud" artists Phranc (Island Records) and Two Nice Girls (Rough Trade) to the bisexual Ani DiFranco (on her own Righteous Babe label) to the "keep 'em guessing" artists Tracy Chapman (Elektra), Michelle Shocked (Polygram), and Indigo Girls (Epic)—the last of whom eventually came out—all mixed the low-tech acoustic sounds and the androgynous, comfortable-clothes look of 1970s women's music with a dose of punk attitude often directed at the earnestness and essentialism of cultural feminism.[81] Phranc challenged the butch phobia of cultural feminism with her flattop hair, and combined a seemingly irreverent humor that poked fun at cause-oriented songs of women's music ("Female Mudwrestling," "Handicapped [Parking Zone]") with an homagelike faithfulness to its folk song roots. Two Nice Girls promoted themselves as philosophically rebellious and musically tied to rock; in concert they would turn guitar-based "cock rock" numbers (such as "Purple Haze" by Jimi Hendrix) into vocal folk songs, scat singing Hendrix's famous opening melodic riff, thereby drawing upon a long tradition in women's music of reclaiming or mocking mainstream rock. But they would also write songs using awkwardly set, curiously insipid lyrics that recalled the roughness of Alix Dobkin, suggesting either a hint of satire or entrenchment in a tradition.[82] In the 1990s, Ani DiFranco wrote songs blasting the narrow-mindedness of both straight and gay communities, while Chapman, Shocked, and the Indigo Girls explicitly distanced themselves from "lesbian music," insisting—as they still do—that their music is for the masses. At the height of lesbian chic in the popular music of the 1990s, the two biggest lesbian artists, lang and Melissa Etheridge, became top sellers despite, or perhaps because of, their stylistic distance from folk music. But both the country music of lang and the heartland rock of Etheridge share with folk music a pretense to grassroots origins, as well as a strong association with white audiences.

Many lesbians of my generation and younger, coming out in the 1980s and '90s in college and even high school, flatly rejected women's music as part of a reevaluation and critique of cultural feminism's construction of "womaness" and women identification. The new generation of third-wave feminists, heavily influenced by the libertarian, in-your-face attitudes of the punk rock culture, queer theory, and AIDS activism, saw cultural feminism as having made too many concessions to the straight, white, and middle-class power base. This new generation of feminists nevertheless revived the grass-roots feminist business of women's music and Olivia Records with the "riot grrrl" scene, which formed in Washington, D.C., and Olympia, Washington, in the early 1990s. The name pokes fun at feminist respellings of "women" as "wimin" or "womyn." These women musicians played a furious punk-derived rock and preached feminist and antihomophobic messages. They also formed support networks, organized training workshops, and founded independent labels, all of which were maintained through underground publications ('zines) and minifestivals.[83]

Third-wave feminists criticized cultural feminists for deemphasized sexuality, for redefining lesbianism as "warm and fuzzy" sensuality (or, as Holly Near proclaimed, something other than sexuality), and for dismissing butch-femme lesbian identities as aping heterosexual gender roles. Women's music seemed stuck on "expressive realism," portraying lesbianism as melancholic emotionalism and infantile crushes, generally lacking in irony and expression of more robust sexuality.[84]

One exception to this tendency to downplay sexuality within the context of women's music was Kay Gardner. In a 1977 interview she described her use of "circular forms" in her instrumental music as "being directly related to the biological difference in sexual expression between men and women." She goes on to say that "the orgasmic climax in men is a release at the *end* of a buildup of tensions and energy. On the other hand, the orgasmic climax for women is in the middle of her sexual expression with the afterplay being as important as the foreplay, and with the potential of beginning the cycle again immediately, thus creating the circular form" (emphasis in the original).[85] Gardner is clear: her music is a sonic portrait of sex and orgasm— indeed, potentially multiple orgasms! We might expect such an explicit mapping of sex onto music for the bump and grind of (male) rock and roll, but it seems a stretch for meditative flute music. Nevertheless, Gardner insists on the language of sex and orgasm for her women's music, rooted in biological difference.[86]

When asked what she thought about disco music, Gardner replied, "there's a driving rhythm behind it. I don't put that down, but I'm saying that music reflects what the atmosphere is."[87] That atmosphere was the urban dance clubs, whose clientele was largely gay and minority in the early and mid-1970s, before the disco craze hit the suburban mainstream with the movie *Saturday Night Fever* (1977). Women's music and disco were, in many ways, opposed to each other in sound and idea. While the artists and producers of women's music and disco in part defined their music against mainstream music, they also replicated, in a fashion, the gender differences described by Frith and McRobbie; lesbian women's music seemed to communicate emotionality and diffuse sensuality, while gay male disco seemed to communicate raw physicality and promiscuous sexuality.

For many urban gay men, disco music became a determining factor in their experience of community and communal identity—an identity that, through disco music, became more evident in mass culture in general. Gay men were also implicated in the backlash against disco. Similar to women's music, then, disco participated in the production of gay identity and its public image; discussions of disco registered debates about the appropriate expressions of gender, the visibility or invisibility of race, and the construction of desire. The following discussion focuses on the reception in mainstream and gay presses of disco in general and of the Village People and Sylvester in particular. The macho of the multiracial Village People and the effeminacy of the African-American singer Sylvester together highlight the intersection between the politics of gender and the politics of race in the gay community of the late 1970s.

DISCOSEXUALITY

The front page of the *Chicago Tribune* for Friday, July 13, 1979, reads "Mob Scene Ends White Sox Double-Header," and the featured photo essay in the sports section contains the headline "Discophobia Out of Control." On July 12, the infamous "bad boy" morning show host Steve Dahl, of WLUP-FM, had arranged a "Disco Demolition" between the games of a White Sox doubleheader with the Detroit Tigers at Chicago's Comiskey Park. In one of countless gate gimmicks used by the White Sox to draw fans to their games, game-goers were to bring disco albums to sacrifice to a mid-field explosion and bonfire. With a disco album, White Sox fans would be charged only 98 cents at the gate (WLUP's dial position was 97.9). The definitive moment was to bring together Dahl, wearing army fatigues, and a blond model named Lorelei, proclaimed the "goddess of the fire," to blow up a crate of some ten thousand records in what was touted as a "ritual burning of disco records." As the photo caption reads, "the idea was to demolish a pile of disco records in a symbolic cooling down of disco fever." The various *Tribune* stories report that fifteen thousand more people showed up for the event than the park could accommodate, causing mayhem before the first game. After the ritual explosion, the crowd turned into a mob, chanting antidisco slogans, shouting obscenities, beating up ushers, throwing records and firecrackers, and eventually tearing up the field so badly that the second game had to be cancelled.[88]

Such violence, such consolidated and ritualized hatred, usually has as its target a community or category of people who are perceived as threatening to the well-being of another community. African-Americans, emancipated by President Lincoln and the defeat of the South in the Civil War, threatened white economic and political supremacy, thus becoming the target of the ritualized violence of the Ku Klux Klan. Disco, through its association with racial and sexual minorities, also became a target in a war of words and songs that thinly veiled racism and homophobia. The November 12, 1979, issue of the *Village Voice* reported that a Detroit DJ put together an antidisco vigilante group called, with chilling flippancy, the Disco Ducks Klan.[89] For some, the name may have been excusable as an example of wordplay typical in antidisco promotions. The name Disco Ducks Klan stems from a play on the title of a 1976 novelty song "Disco Duck" by Rick Dees; "ducks" not only rhymes with "Klux" but also stands for it, as in "clucks." Moreover, the sinister allusion to the Ku Klux Klan was borne out in the group's intentions: the DDK had planned to invade a disco wearing white sheets, but the riot at Comiskey Park changed their minds.

That *music,* not people, was the stated target on July 12, 1979, only served to cover up the underlying social issues. That "disco" stood for "gay" more specifically was evident in the *Chicago Tribune*'s own description of the event as "Discophobia," inspired by the term "homophobia." Soon after his triumph at Comiskey Park, Steve Dahl recorded a parody of Rod Stewart's disco hit "Do Ya Think I'm Sexy?" (1979). Dahl called his song "Do Ya Think I'm Disco?" which makes more sense if the title is decoded as "Do Ya Think I'm Gay?" This, it seems, was a central question and concern for straight men in the 1970s, one that disco music directly provoked. The mingling of race baiting with gay baiting in discophobic campaigns played to white (male) fear that black and Latino men were, in fact, *more* masculine and sexually predatory than they were. If black and Latino men could be linked to disco, then their masculinity could be called into question, and straight white men (represented by rock) could be assured of their supremacy.

In his scrutiny of the "discophobia" phenomenon, *Village Voice* writer Frank Rose reports the often-cited criticisms of disco, explaining, "Rock fans say disco sucks because it's 'mindless' and 'repetitive,' because it's 'plastic' and synonymous with gold chains and polyester, perfect hair, pulsating lights and sex, sex, sex. Also, it comes from New York. It is spread via media image. It is monolithic. . . . Like defenders of the nuclear family, rock fans felt their backs to the wall. They imagined themselves in extinction, and they started lashing out."[90]

As this quote suggests, disco was often described as a disease, a *homoge*-nizing and feminizing musical infection. Rod Stewart, once the epitome of hard-drinking bluesy rock and rollers, is a case in point; his sudden trans-formation into a glam-dressing disco giant was understood by fans and crit-ics as a betrayal. Rose goes on to note that "rock fans' disparaging charac-terization of disco as music for gay people seemed linked to their perception that it hasn't got balls—a quality they interpret to mean aggressive power chords and masturbatory guitar solos. At the same time they resented it for pressuring them to be sexual."[91] Rose, in a passage that recalls feminists' cri-tiques of "cock rock," here describes a complaint of straight men that itself comes close to those feminist critiques: disco is an assault of oppressive sex-uality. Disco forces "real men rockers" to have sex without balls—to be the passive sexual partner, and thus to be forced into gay sex.

But in what way were rockers compelled into discosexuality? The answer is simply that the music industry, motivated by profits, made disco "mono-lithic" and hegemonic. In contrast to women's music, which never reached a mass market, the craze for disco sent shock waves through the recording industry and mainstream culture—shock waves that turned many (cock) rock radio stations into (gay) disco formats. In the mid-1970s, the major labels suddenly found themselves in stiff competition with independent labels that produced wildly successful albums using ad hoc collections of musicians rather than a stable cadre of stars and touring acts.

The history of disco began with the use of recorded music as a cheap form of entertainment in bars, "after-hours" clubs, and private parties. Many such venues were gathering spots for communities at the margins of dominant culture: homosexuals, African-Americans, and Latinos. The recorded music coming from jukeboxes in bars was eventually replaced by live "disc jockeys," or DJs, who acted as a musical master of ceremonies. The musicians on the records were quickly upstaged by the dexterity and ingenuity of the DJs, whose "mixing" entailed the creation of a seamless flow of songs carefully planned to produce an emotional and physical "trip" for the dancers.[92]

Early 1970s soul music, particularly that produced by Kenny Gamble and

Leon Huff for the Philadelphia International label, formed the basis of the disco sound. This sound was characterized by clean, crisp rhythmic guitar lines, opulent orchestrations, smooth vocals, and, above all, a clearly defined and unwavering 4/4 meter, uninterrupted by fills or solos, and not syncopated, as in funk. The meter was usually emphasized by a heavy bass-drum kick on all beats, sometimes with sixteenth-note subdivisions carried in the hi-hat. This combination of a heavy bass beat and shimmery subdivision became emblematic of disco and its infectious physicality: the bass beat anchors the body to the floor, while the subdivisions in the hi-hat give the illusion of speed and airiness.[93] The rhythmic consistency of disco made for easier mixing by DJs. With this new consumer in mind, record producers began to extend instrumental breaks, further reducing the role of the singers.

Disco singles enjoyed skyrocketing success throughout the second half of the 1970s. By the summer of 1979, disco had indeed taken over much of music industry production and radio play. The July 14 issue of *Billboard* (two days after the "disco demolition" in Chicago) devoted more than thirty pages to disco, containing articles with titles such as "No Surprise: Disco Hogging N.Y. Arbitron" (Arbitron was a company that rated radio stations based on a correlation of radio formats, audience numbers, and audience profiles), "Fatal Prognosis Wrong, Patient [Disco] Alive and Well," and "[Disco] Music Rejuvenates Pop Trends." A few months earlier *Rolling Stone* had devoted nearly the entire April 19, 1979, issue to disco.

With the rise of disco came the apparent fall of the star system. *Billboard* also included in their July 14, 1979, issue an article entitled, "Dearth of Superstars Dims [Disco] Industry Future: Producer Rather Than Artist Is Star." Here writer Radcliffe Joe reports on the record companies' concern over the problematic facelessness of disco, claiming, "Among industryites it is often referred to as concept [or] 'manufactured' music. The producer has an idea. He takes his concept into the studio, and more often than not, with the help of an aggregate of studio musicians, he translates his concept into musical reality. The artists are often little more than convenient vehicles through which the producer reaches an audience."[94] Joe articulates here an anxiety about how disco challenges notions of "artistry." Disco producers are somehow not "artists" because their musical ideas require mediation; and those mediators, who are traditionally called "artists," do not in fact express their own ideas in disco songs. While there was nothing new about singers singing other people's songs, nor about celebrated producers exerting disproportionate power and control over the artists they produced, somehow disco seemed to disrupt the illusion of sincere artistic expression, offering instead a strangely diffuse multiple subjectivity. While dancing, the song's audience may shift their identification of the expressive agent from singer, to producer, to DJ.

MAKING GAY MEN

Although the figures of the producer and the DJ, formerly behind the scenes, seemed to be replacing the rock star, one French music producer, Jacques Morali, worked against this trend by "manufacturing" a singing group that would give a face to disco—a face that would be clearly gay. He put together an interracial group of six well-muscled men dressed as ultra-macho stereotypes: cop, leather-clad biker, cowboy, Indian, soldier, and construction worker. These were the Village People. The Village People get the most attention in Radcliffe Joe's article because they did succeed in becoming the disco "superstars" that he felt the industry so badly needed. Their only real challengers were a handful of African-American women, most notably Donna Summer, and the white Australian group the Bee Gees. Just months before Joe's *Billboard* article, the Village People had achieved the industry's mark of success by appearing on the cover of *Rolling Stone* for the magazine's April 19 disco issue. With hints of both xenophobia, homophobia, and admiration, Joe writes, "French producer Jacques Morali devised an even more ambitious plan for a concept record. Behind the idea was the elevation of the homosexual male to a macho-type image. He teamed up with [producer Henri] Belolo to put the idea into production. The Village People group was later assembled and the now-famous 'Macho Man' was recorded. The rest is industry history." Joe later concedes that the Village People are also exceptionally entertaining performers, claiming "their flair, their outrageously camp costumes and the obvious and timely message they deliver all meld to make them a phenomenally marketable product."[95] For Joe, Morali's "ambitious plan" was not primarily musical, but instead suspiciously political: the Village People's record "Macho Man" would, much like Meg Christian's *I Know You Know*, raise the consciousness of its consumers, gay and straight, and deliver the "timely message" of gay macho.

Although "Macho Man" was not the Village People's first record, as Joe implies, it did seem to be Morali's initial concept for the group. In a 1978 interview for *Rolling Stone*, Morali described how he drew inspiration from visits to New York's West Village gay discos, where he saw dancers variously costumed as American masculine stereotypes. He said, "I think in myself [*sic*] that the gay people have no group, nobody, to personalize the gay people. . . . I never thought that straight audiences were going to catch on to it. . . . I wanted to do something only for the gay market."[96] The macho look had taken gay urban enclaves by storm beginning in the mid-1970s (garnering the nickname "clone"), displacing other queer and stigmatized articulations of masculinity such as androgyny and effeminacy. What Morali intended to do for the gay market was to put this relatively new face of the gay consumer on record covers and eventually on stage.

In his book on "gay macho," Martin P. Levine argues that the masculine clone emerged from a reformist branch of gay liberation that urged a separation of homosexual practice from gender identity, with a separatist ideology that paralleled that of many lesbian feminists. He writes, "Militant chauvinism reorganized the cultural meaning of homosexuality, which allowed gay men to express masculine demeanor and interests. . . . Gay men had become real men, and in their affect, attire, and attitudes celebrated their newfound masculinity—and nowhere more than in sexual self-celebration."[97] Despite their generally middle-class backgrounds, the gay macho clones adopted a downwardly mobile look: short hair, jeans and plaid shirt or T-shirt, work boots, and an overworked body of muscles. They also adopted "downwardly mobile" practices: cruising, "tricking," misogyny, and racism.[98]

For the Village People's first album cover, then, Morali assembled just such a shirt-and-jeans crowd to pose in a bar, with only a few hats giving a hint of the characters to come. Accessories such as hard hats, cowboy hats, handkerchiefs, and keys were already part of the gay scene as a new type of campy masculine drag,[99] while leather biker wear (with connotations of SM) and uniform costumes (police, soldier) signified particular nonclone subcultures within gay macho identity. That these further nuanced masculine identities lived in the margins of clone culture can also be gathered from the Village People's first album cover, in which a "leather man" appears blurred in the background on the front cover and lurks in the shadows on the back cover; the policeman is not represented, while the soldier is represented by an African-American man wearing a U.S. Navy T-shirt that bears the sexually suggestive slogan "Strike Hard, Strike Home." Uniform fetishes remained unrepresented on the cover of the Village People's second album, which includes their hit song "Macho Man." Instead, lead singer Victor Willis appears in a sparkling jumpsuit, perhaps representing an astronaut's garb, but with a heavy dose of George Clinton's cosmic funk costumes. The stable presence and costume of Felipe Rose, the "Indian" (by all accounts the bar dancer who first inspired Morali), epitomized the campiness and cartoonishness of these gay macho types. His Hollywood-style getup—war headdress, face paint, and beaded loincloth—mixed camp humor with gay male self-involvement and the media's eroticization and colonization of racial and ethnic otherness. Felipe is listed in the album credits as providing background vocals as well as "foot bells" for the songs.[100]

The Village People's first album (1977), with eponymous title, contained two extended songs on each side, each with geographically specific gay associations. The "East Coast" side featured the songs "Fire Island" (a popular gay resort area) and "Village People" (referring to the Greenwich Village gay enclave). The more popular "West Coast" side featured a medley called "San Francisco/In Hollywood," which served as a musical model for the later "Macho Man." Initially, the Village People were popular with gay audiences.

The music critic for *The Advocate* described the Village People as "the first big disco group to be openly gay." He commented further that "if you haven't already been dancing to their 'San Francisco/In Hollywood' medley, you haven't been going to discos."[101] But as the Village People became popular with straight audiences (despite their continued development of overtly gay themes), their favor with gay audiences decreased. Their second album, *Macho Man* (early 1978), contained the three hit singles "Macho Man," "I Am What I Am," and "Key West." Gay and gay-friendly presses began to react with suspicion and skepticism. Guy Trebay of the *Village Voice*, reviewing a concert, lamented that "on two consecutive nights—at a gay dance bar—these six men posing as homosexuals played to an audience that was 90 percent straight. 'It's the weirdest thing,' someone said, 'the lead singer isn't gay. I seen him kissing girls in the corner between sets last night.'"[102] In a mostly positive article appearing in *The Advocate* (1978) entitled "Prophets or Profits? The Village People," Charles Herschberg documented the initial rush of pride that gay disco audiences felt when they heard the first album with references to "gay places," an apparent homage to disco's gay roots. But Herschberg goes on to say, "how much of Village People is a well-timed lavishly promoted commercial venture, and how much of it is the loving work of prophets who can bring people together by putting it all out in the open with dance, music, lyrics and style from a gay perspective, will be revealed as time discos on."[103] It is clear that Herschberg wants the latter to be true, and he seems to ignore the group members' ominously vague comments such as "our message is love" and "we're a call for freedom and liberation" that foreshadow their later apolitical position. In an interview for *Rolling Stone* that same year, David Hodo (the construction worker) revealed that profit, or at least a desire to maximize their audience, was winning over prophet, saying "We're not a protest group, we're not a gay-liberation group. If anything, we call ourselves a people-liberation group, because we don't play gay discos. We play straight discos because our straight audience won't go to a gay disco. But the gays will come to a straight disco."[104]

The year 1979 witnessed a complete break between the Village People and their gay fans on both coasts. Andrew Kopkind reported in the *Village Voice* that neither "Macho Man" nor "Y.M.C.A."—their two biggest hits—were played in New York's hottest gay discos. Kopkind's comments reveal the new feeling of insult: "For gays, the line 'I want to be a macho man' from the mouths of these butch-impersonators is a bit like 'I want to be white' if it were sung by Stevie Wonder for a black audience."[105] *The Advocate* published an article with a damning series of quotations from interviews conducted between early 1978 and late 1979 that illustrate the dramatic backpedaling of both Morali and the singers regarding their gay image. According to the article, "slowly, subtly, imperceptibly—in the revolutions of each new LP, in the evasions of each new press release—something happened. The Village

People became the Osmond Brothers from Oz. Opprobrium became appropriation. . . . They weren't ours anymore. They belonged to 13-year-old girls in Grover's Corner and Garden City. . . . Are they still us? . . . Were they ever?"[106]

The conversion of the song "San Francisco" to "Macho Man" is symptomatic of the group's public shift from its homoerotic deployment of "American blue-collar machismo" to a repackage of that machismo for mass suburban consumption. These two songs are identical in their hook and general sonic map: both open with exactly the same driving rhythm track, and a triangle marks the subdivisions of the beat, with soft pitches of conga drums spicing the pounding bass. In "Macho Man," however, the beat is ratcheted up several degrees more than in "San Francisco." Both songs also begin with the same extended break, which serves as the hook—jabbing choral interjections in a minor mode, overlaid or dovetailing with the lead singer's improvisatory vocals. "San Francisco" begins after three measures of introduction, with a chorus of male voices that call out well-known gay areas of the city—Folsom Street (leather clubs), Polk Street (male hustlers), and Castro Street (the clone ghetto). In "Macho Man," this specifically gay urban geography is relocated onto the self: the shouts of "Fol-som" become shouts of "Bo-dy," and the lead vocal's phrase "all the way to Polk and Castro" (two streets that, incidentally, do not intersect) becomes "wanna feel my body, baby." The verses also present a striking transformation of theme. "San Francisco" celebrates uninhibited individualism:

> Dress the way you please
> and put your mind at ease
> it's a city known for its freedom

"Macho Man," on the other hand, describes lockstep image consciousness:

> Every man wants to be
> a macho, macho man
> to have the kind of body
> that's always in demand.

The refrain of "San Francisco" includes interjected slogans like "San Francisco . . . you've got me," "city by the bay," and a mock-gospel "take me to the water" that make it sound more like a campy touristic paean than a disco song. In "Macho Man," this refrain is turned into an equally campy paean to ideal masculinity, "Macho, macho man, I've got to be a macho man." Thus the inherent self-interest of gay macho identity literally mapped out and celebrated in "San Francisco" becomes, in "Macho Man," male narcissism for the mainstream.

As one *Village Voice* critic observed, the Village People "turn camp into mainstream show biz shtick. Morali succeeded by appealing to America's obsession with packaging."[107] Although this same critic declares that the selling of gay macho as disco showbiz "liberated Main Street," we can also understand the mainstream success of the Village People in terms of Marcuse's critique of the mass media. Driven by capitalistic forces, the media participates in the construction of gender and sexuality, and it exerts control over public opinion and taste. Beginning with "Macho Man" from their second album and continuing with their later hits, most notably "Y.M.C.A." (1978) and "In the Navy" (1979), the Village People presented urban gay macho identities as banal media products. Under different conditions or direct contact, these identities might have posed a threat to middle-class suburbanites; as part of the packaging of frothy disco songs, these identities were inherently disposable. Indeed, the music industry depends upon the loss of desire for today's products so that they can be replaced by those of tomorrow. In buying Village People records suburbanites in no way contributed to gay pride or liberation; they only escaped into the reassuringly momentary world of the latest thing in overproduced masculinity.

MIGHTY REAL MEN, AND THE QUEENS BEHIND THEM

The overproduced masculinity of gay macho seemed to provide a haven for gay men in general—a haven, that is, from the stigma of effeminacy that plagued them. But in the late 1970s, the "village" that was the gay community was not at all safe from internal strife. In an early 1979 interview for *The Advocate,* the African-American gay disco star Sylvester observed about San Francisco, "Gay people . . . keep screaming for equal rights from straights and they can't even get themselves together because they're discriminating in cliques within themselves. We will never become one as long as the Folsom queens don't like the Castro queens, and the Castro queens don't like the Polk queens, and blacks don't like whites and whites don't like blacks and it's all segregated and fucked up like that."[108] The macho model of masculinity was apparently as divisive as it was cohesive for the gay community, in San Francisco and New York alike. The highbrow glossy magazine *Christopher Street,* modeled on *The New Yorker,* published in early 1978 an article entitled "Where Have All the Sissies Gone?" in which writer Seymour Kleinberg attacked what he called the "relentless pursuit of masculinity" as "in fact eroticizing the very values of straight society that have tyrannized their own lives." The resulting tension, he argues, has led to misogyny, bigotry, and "sexual libertinism," specifically masochism. He writes, "in the past, the duplicity of closeted lives found relief in effeminate camping; now the suppression or denial of the moral issue in their choice is far more damaging. The perversity of imitating their oppressors guarantees that such blindness will work itself out as self-contempt. . . . The new bars are often private clubs

as much for the sake of legally barring women as for screening male cus-
tomers. Their atmosphere is eerily reminiscent of the locker room."[109]

Two mid-1990s commentators on disco and the gay community have
probed this crystallization of gay macho urban identity through the disco bar
and disco music and have come to very different conclusions. Walter Hughes
likens the obsession with dancing to the obsession with other physical disciplines in the gay community, such as bodybuilding, which he sees as an eroticization of subjugation. Like Kleinberg, Hughes views the gay identity under-
written by disco as inherently masochistic through "an implicit parallel
between the beat and desire"; in other words, gay men identify as a slave to
both. He writes, "by submitting to its insistent, disciplinary beat, one learns
from disco how to be one kind of gay man; one accepts, with pleasure rather
than suffering, the imposition of a version of gay identity."[110] Implicit in
Hughes's formulation is an understanding of disco as an ideological tool, a
discursive practice that constructs the gay male subject—just as Simon Frith
and Angela McRobbie described rock music as an ideological tool that organizes gender and sexuality.

Gregory W. Bredbeck also considers disco an ideological tool, but for him
the construction of gay identity is in fundamental opposition to the ideology
of the status quo. Using Althusser's scene of interpellation along with Benedict Anderson's theory of "imagined communities," Bredbeck argues that
gay discos set up a microstructural "interpellative node" that becomes the
site of "subcultural generation."[111] Disco, as if operating on a different hailing frequency, calls the gay listener into a specifically queer subjectivity, one
that is, for Bredbeck, resistant to domination.[112] Like Kleinberg and Hughes,
Bredbeck believes that subjectivity to be macho and phallocentric, but he
sees this as liberating. Gay macho, for him, is masculinity set free from its heterosexual reproductive function, and hence from "the bourgeois and domestic frame that typically marks and contains it."

As Bredbeck surveys "gay seventies revisionism" and nostalgically looks
back at 1970s disco, the Village People emerge as the "apotheosis" of this
queer interpellation, his gay heroes of "antibourgeois eroticism." Bredbeck
attributes to them an explicit marketing of "gay promiscuity," which he sees
as revolutionary.[113] Yet male promiscuity is hardly a revolutionary concept,
and the easy link of promiscuity with consumption and disposability, neatly
packaged together in the gay macho of the Village People, may have not only
fueled exclusionary practices—by race, class, or gender (including effeminacy)[114]—but also helped conservative politicians ignore the AIDS crisis in
the 1980s as the isolated problem of an entirely disposable queer population.

Bredbeck is seduced, I believe, by the commercial success of the Village
People and their dissemination of gay macho identity. This can be read in
retrospect as a supreme joke on conservative Middle America—a great gay

hijacking of suburbia—if we neglect the processes that attend that success, namely the public relations program that vigorously straightens out the ample gay codes in their songs, and the inherent misogyny that allies gay and straight macho men.

. . .

Misogyny may explain Bredbeck's relegation of Sylvester, who was famously effeminate, to a footnote. Sylvester is also routinely omitted from surveys and encyclopedias of rock and pop music, whereas the Village People are apt to appear as the representative of disco's "gay element."[115] None of my students know who Sylvester was, nor does he mean much to my younger queer professorial colleagues. They may have heard his 1978 hit songs "You Make Me Feel (Mighty Real)" or "Dance (Disco Heat)," but few have seen his videos or album covers or remember his remarkable appearances on *American Band Stand, The Tonight Show,* or *The Dinah Shore Show.* Born Sylvester James in 1946 in Los Angeles, Sylvester was hailed as a gospel-singing child prodigy, but his predilection for designing and wearing women's clothes in high school bounced him out of school and into L.A.'s drag queen cliques. His interest in performance led him to San Francisco and the psychedelic, orgiastic theater troupe called the Cockettes. Sylvester soon became the star attraction of the troupe, singing the classic blues of Bessie Smith and Billie Holiday in what would become his trademark falsetto, and dressing in period drag. From the Cockettes Sylvester went on to record several R&B albums in the early 1970s with a group called the Hot Band. It was an incongruous pairing of a feminine black falsettist and an all-white, long-haired bunch of good ol' boys. Sylvester did not think much of disco at first, preferring to perform styles that were closer to gospel and blues. But disco, with its glamour and escapism, proved to be the musical environment capacious enough to accommodate Sylvester.[116] Sylvester became a remarkable phenomenon: an openly gay, African-American disco star. He spoke with a pronounced lisp, liberally peppered his sentences with the word "fabulous," and performed in elaborate gender-bending costumes. He nonetheless achieved remarkable success with three Top 40 hits. Furthermore, his success lasted well into the 1980s.[117] Long before the media embraced mainstream gay men in *Will and Grace* or *Queer Eye for the Straight Guy,* and just before the post-punk gender provocations of Boy George, Annie Lennox, and others in the 1980s, Sylvester paved their way by publicly insisting on an identity that broke every rule of gender, sexual, and racial normalcy. For straight and gay disco historians, then, Sylvester poses a problem: his version of black gay male masculinity on the one hand points back toward pre-Stonewall stereotypes for which femininity denotes homosexuality, yet on the other hand his insistence on "old-fashioned" effeminacy in the face of rampant and commodified gay macho exposed the latter as a rival *drag* that unsettled prior constructions of desire and identity.

In *Mother Camp: Female Impersonators in America,* Esther Newton studies female impersonators and their central role in homosexual subcultures in the late 1960s. The "problem" that male homosexuals pose for dominant culture is rooted in the common belief that "male-female sexual relations" are "the only 'natural' model of sexuality." Newton argues that the "moral transgression" of male homosexuality is not their rejection of women, but the fact that "at least one of the men of a homosexual pair must, then, be 'acting' the woman: passive, powerless, and unmanly."[118] It is the passive partner and his effeminacy that defines—from the perspective of the heterosexual status quo—the identity of the homosexual community as a whole. It can be argued, then, that the core of male homosexual identity is inextricable from "femaleness" due to the gendering of sex roles. Thus the figure of the drag queen—the gay man who voluntarily places himself in the role of woman— is emblematic of the homosexual subculture regardless of the actual percentage of drag queens within the homosexual population.

Kleinberg notes that prior to the new emphasis on virility then emerging in the late 1970s, effeminacy was integrated into the structure of desire. He writes,

> while there is still much role preference for passivity, it no longer has the clear quality it had in the past. Then, gay men made unmistakable announcements: those who liked to be fucked adopted effeminate mannerisms; those who were active tried to look respectable. . . . Today to replace the usually reliable information that straight or campy behavior conveyed in the past, gay men at leather bars have taken to elaborate clothing signals: key chains or handkerchiefs drooping from left or right pocket in blue or yellow or red, all have secret meanings.[119]

In his 1979 interview for *The Advocate,* Sylvester also remarks on the internal "cultural clash" that occurred in the reorientation of gay male desire toward the idealized active "straight" member. He says, "Queens are strange; they all do the same thing, but everything depends on what you wear. . . . You're still gay, you still do the same things that the person does who's in a dress. . . . I would always meet men who would be attracted to the costume and then want me to fuck them in drag—'butch boys,' you know."[120] The attempt to decenter the drag queen from gay identity by substituting masculine types does not, in fact, win automatic acceptance from the straight mainstream. Newton writes, "gay men are kidding themselves if they think the deeper stigma of homosexuality can be eliminated while the antagonistic and asymmetrical relations between men and women persist. . . . So long as current models of sexuality persist and predominate, gay men will always be 'like' women."[121]

Sylvester's most famous song, "You Make Me Feel (Mighty Real)" (1978), seems to speak directly to the fraught situation of gay men in the late 1970s. The song was his second to appear in the Top 40, following on the heels of his first hit, "Dance (Disco Heat)." Unlike the lush orchestral fills and accompaniment of East Coast disco, the texture of "You Make Me Feel," produced by Patrick Cowley, consists of bubbling electronic beats, synthesized strings, and a crisp hi-hat offbeat pattern, a style of disco close to that of European producer Giorgio Moroder (who was best known for his work with Donna Summer). The verse sets the scene of dancing at a disco:

> When we're out there dancing,
> on the floor, darling,
> and I feel like I,
> need some more, and I
> feel your body, close to mine

The song builds up to the climactic refrain line as the initial chanting of an insistent plea ("make me feel, mighty real, make me feel, mighty real") is transformed into a soaring gospel statement against the mesh of synthesized beats and strings: "You make me feel, mighty real."[122]

The word "real" describes a quality of being that is essential, authentic, verifiable, not artificial. To "feel real" is to feel authentic; feeling "mighty real" suggests that there are gradations of authenticity and essence, that it is possible to feel more or less real. Sylvester, through a whir of synthetic strings and drumbeats, sings passionately of feeling real in falsetto, in the same register as a woman's voice. His voice is comparable to those of popular black female disco singers such as Gloria Gaynor, Donna Summer, and Cheryl Lynn. Lynn also sang of realness in "Got to Be Real" (1978), a funky midtempo disco song:

> What you find, ah,
> what you feel, now,
> what you know, ah,
> to be real.[123]

The "what" that is "real" here is "our love," determined through finding, feeling, knowing. In Sylvester's song, the "what" that is real, or feels real, seems to be Sylvester himself. Lynn's "Got to Be Real" features real guitars, real drums, real horns and strings, and a real female vocalist. In contrast, Sylvester's "You Make Me Feel (Mighty Real)" seems a sonic portrait of the not-real; we hear an artificial black female disco singer accompanied by artificially synthesized instruments.

The verbal hook of Sylvester's song depends upon a connection between emotions and ontology—one *is* what one *feels*. Aretha Franklin sang in 1967 "you make me feel like a natural woman," a lyric that readily springs to mind in conjunction with Sylvester's song. Judith Butler has noted that this lyric implies a state prior to or different from feeling "like a natural woman," a "not feeling like a natural woman" or a feeling like an "unnatural woman." Butler comments, "the effect of naturalness is only achieved as some consequence of that moment of heterosexual recognition. After all, Aretha sings, you make me feel *like* a natural woman, suggesting that this is a kind of metaphorical substitution, an act of imposture, a kind of sublime and momentary participation in an ontological illusion produced by the mundane operation of heterosexual drag."[124] Only through an "invocation of the defining Other,"[125] the "you" in "you make me feel," does the "me" come into being, or, rather, my feeling "like a natural woman." "You" must refer to a "natural man," or someone who "feels like a natural man," in order to produce the parallel effect of a "natural woman."

In the 1960s, a "natural woman" in African-American slang meant a heterosexual woman, as did a "real woman" in the 1970s and later.[126] Thus when Sylvester sings "you make me feel mighty real," we could be hearing him sing "you make me feel like a natural woman" in vocal drag, for Aretha Franklin and Sylvester share not only a vocal style derived from hard gospel, but also a vocal register. The male falsetto voice in African-American gospel and soul music had a long history by 1978 and was not in itself a marker of effeminacy or artifice, but rather an ideal romantic or earnest voice, marked as emotionally sincere. This association of a high register and emotionality transfers feminine vocal effect onto a masculine body, but the resulting vocal construction has been "naturalized" within popular music to the male (and specifically to the African-American) body.[127] In other words, it is vocal drag that is no longer drag but completely assimilated within the musical construction of heterosexual romantic love. Thus Sylvester's voice is as "real" as Aretha's is "natural."

The "drag effect" of Sylvester's falsetto, then, depends upon the context of 1970s gay macho, the dominant configuration of desire in the discos. There, Sylvester's falsetto could be heard as feminine vocal drag. Sylvester himself thought of his falsetto as a type of drag; in concert he would momentarily sing in chest tones and then quip, "you see, I can be butch too, when I want to be."[128] This routine refers back to those female impersonators and vocal impressionists who would periodically break the illusion mid-song for comic effect.[129] "You Make Me Feel (Mighty Real)," then, might be heard as camp, as comic as well as nostalgic, insofar as the meaning of "real" shades into "natural woman." Thus "you make me feel mighty real" could mean "you make me feel like a passive partner"—the masculine sexual preference (according to Kleinberg and Sylvester) that, given the hegemony of gay macho, could no longer be communicated through the signals of effeminacy.

The promotional video for "You Make Me Feel (Mighty Real)" strengthens the song's association with drag, for Sylvester appears in different guises, each corresponding to a different section of the music. As he sings the first verse, Sylvester descends a staircase in a long V-neck smock, black leather pants and jacket, a feminine relaxed-curl hairdo, and makeup. With the next verse, Sylvester wears male costume: white pants and suit jacket, short hair. For the climactic refrain, Sylvester becomes someone else—a glorious sequin-covered African queen with flowing tunic, turban, tassels, and bracelets. This last costume connects gay drag to the look of African-American musicians who blended ancient Egyptian or other African fashions and images with those of the "space age," such as astronaut jumpsuits, glittery fabrics, and cosmic designs. These musicians sometimes also took on the identity of aliens from outer space—an identity born from alienation from a white-dominated society. The jazz musician Sun Ra had cultivated an astro-Egyptian image since the early 1960s by wearing an Egyptian headdress and a long robe, and by insisting he had come from Saturn to save the black population of America. With his band The Intergalactic Research Arkestra, he produced a frenetic free jazz that often featured his own long solos on some of the earliest Moog synthesizers.[130] George Clinton famously combined an alien identity with his avant-garde funk. Like Sun Ra, he donned wild costumes, and he often sported a wig of long blond hair. In his 1975 song "Mothership Connection," Clinton ("Star Child") comes to earth to "reclaim the pyramids" and throw a salvational party. Sylvester's 1982 album *All I Need* features a cover illustration of Sylvester made to look like Cleopatra.

Sun Ra's astro-sexuality was ambiguous; he had a slightly effeminate manner and a clear penchant for dressing up, and he lived communally with male members of his orchestra. He claimed, however, to be celibate, having transcended sex. George Clinton and other funk musicians turned this ethos of sexual purity into one of pure sexuality. Disco shared in the pure sexuality of funk, in its infectious beat, suggestive lyrics, and party ethos. More important, disco took from African-American futurism both its escapism and its ideal of self-creation. The disco club was a seemingly otherworldly, cosmic space, filled with flashing lights and a twinkling mirrored ball, which stood in stark contrast to everyday experiences. The disco club also provided a space in which flamboyant costumes—all a kind of drag—could mean resistance.

Revisionist histories of gay disco marginalize Sylvester as a curiosity, but in the context of disco music both his look and sound were close to the center. Although the bars of the 1970s may have reinvented the locker room, the gay macho facade of the Village People was not typical of the disco consumed by gay men. Rather, in spite of misogyny and bigotry within the gay community, the most popular disco "voice" was that of African-American women. This fact is usually explained as due to an affinity gay men had with African-American women: both were classes of socially and politically oppressed persons. As one New York DJ remarked, "Gays like to hear black women singers;

they identify with the pain, the irony, the self-consciousness. We pick up on the emotional content, not just the physical power."[131]

It is curious, however, that this identification seems to go no further than the consumption of dance music; it does not result in any political action. Walter Hughes sees this cross-identification of gay men with female disco singers as perpetuating the racist idea that African-American women are both powerless and sexually predatory, at once socially disenfranchised and sexually enfranchised.[132] Seen in this way, African-American women could be understood as displacing the drag queen at the core of urban gay identity. The African-American woman as a fully naturalized and racially remote Other stood at a safe distance from macho white "clone" culture, disguising and deflecting the drag queen core. The female "disco diva" bore no particular relationship to gay male structures of desire, and only metaphorical rather than ontological relationships to gay identity; that is, gay men are "like" African-American women as victims of oppression, but their gendered identity is not directly implicated as it is with the "drag queen."

This displacement of the drag queen by the African-American "natural woman" is evident in the reception of Sylvester, both in the 1970s and later. In a 1979 concert review Robert Christgau focuses on the quality of Sylvester's voice in comparison to those of other male falsettists and women soul singers, specifically his famous backup vocalists Martha Wash and Izora Rhodes, African-American women collectively called "Two Tons o' Fun" (they later went on to have their own disco recording career as "The Weather Girls"). Referring to the falsetto tradition in soul, Christgau notes that while "the typical 'love man' sings in a woman's normal register but has no interest in her normal dramatic breadth," Sylvester's aspirations were "to sing like a woman," to "access the gamut of a woman's [voice]"—in other words, a vocal drag more "real" than that of a straight male singer. As the review progresses, however, it becomes evident that even while lauding Sylvester's expressive goals, Christgau doubts he can "pass." He writes:

> when Sylvester ventured beyond his bursts and croons into songs that required more detailed emoting, his voice still lacked luster. But the amazing thing was that Sylvester implicitly conceded this—that's why Martha Wash and Izora Rhodes were there. . . . At the close of a rather colorless version of "A Song for You," he stopped and announced, "This is the part I like." After a brief pause, Wash and Rhodes went into a celestial harmony. Everyone else liked that part too.[133]

Thus Christgau's critical analysis cuts Sylvester off from both genders, segregating Sylvester (because of his "aspirations") from the falsetto soul tradition of African-American men while insisting that he is musically handicapped by his maleness; his "falsetto," Christgau argues, cannot match the natural emotional expression of "real women's voices." Christgau perceives the backup singers as the "core" of Sylvester's music and their voices as the "goal," displacing whatever may be unique about his identity as a falsettist/drag queen with their more clearly gendered identity. And, according to Christgau, Sylvester seems to endorse this displacement by giving the backup singers center stage.

Hughes's later article on disco makes this displacement even more evident. It is in the context of African-American female disco stars that Hughes mentions Sylvester, whose identity as a gay black man, he argues, "stands at the origin of the disco tradition" yet is "rendered invisible if not impossible by the dominant culture's potent alliance of homophobia and racism." Hughes reads Sylvester through the lens of Donna Summer:

> "You Make Me Feel (Mighty Real)" performs the representative hypostatization of his gay identity. His impassioned repetition becomes as orgasmic as Donna Summer's in "I Feel Love," insisting that, for the gay black man, the realization of the self can have the ecstatic force of a revelation. . . . This is "gay" realness that flickers into being with a "touch" and a "kiss"—at the moment of homosexual physical contact. According to Sylvester, we "feel" real the way Donna Summer claims we "feel" love, as a heightened erotic sensation, not as an essential state.[134]

For Hughes, Sylvester seems to function as a variation on, or imitation of, the African-American female vocalist central to disco, and the fact of his actual maleness and gayness simply draws a clearer arrow to gay male identity as the "real" commodity behind the disco songs, for such songs generate homoerotic desire and contact.

Wash and Rhodes do not sing on "You Make Me Feel (Mighty Real)," and their absence is significant, for without them we hear Sylvester's "realization of the self" without compromise. What makes Sylvester's performance of this song erotic, incarnational, and revelatory—and thus so poignant—is that he reclaims effeminate gay masculinity as a definitive position: he is the identifiable gay black man because he is effeminate.

Sylvester, as an effeminate gay black man, presented his homosexuality to the world at large not as a "flicker" but rather as the seemingly problematic "essential state." The ideal of the white, gay macho man stood as a rejection of that abject state; it also created discriminatory practices. In particular, the entrances to dance clubs became sites for the practice of racism, elitism, and internalized homophobia, as Sylvester himself related in a 1979 interview. He reported, "Once I went to a particular bar and I had on a pair of those plastic Greek fishing shoes, which are considered open-toed shoes, and they let me in with no hassle. There were two black kids standing with the same shoes on, and they wouldn't let them in. I immediately went off and screamed and read them and refused to go in myself after they'd said I could."[135] Dress codes effectively allowed doormen to control the color and the gender expression of the crowd; they made sure the crowd did not "become too black," nor too effeminate. Sylvester skated past the gatekeepers only because of his status as a star, as an object of a particular kind of desire. The interviewer went on to ask if "what is taken for discrimination isn't often sexual preference." This is a remarkable question, one that reveals an easy accommodation between commodified forms of desire and racism. "Everything's based on sex [in the gay community]," Sylvester answered. "It's out of proportion as far as other aspects and things people have."

He described the San Francisco scene as one in which nearly all social encounters are predicated upon sexual desirability—a sexual consumerism that precludes "equal communication on issues and levels that have nothing to do with sex." Sylvester, however, proclaimed, "I can go out and have a fabulous time anywhere and not be the least bit interested in anyone sexually, but I can still enjoy myself because I'm around a variety of people."[136] It seems contradictory, perhaps, for a famous gay disco singer who sings about bodies pressed close, of heat, of wanting, and who once belonged to a notoriously salacious theater group called the Cockettes, to advocate for a desexualized experience of gay community, for a pure appreciation of cultural variety. In this Sylvester approaches the ideals of his lesbian feminist contemporaries, especially Holly Near. But Sylvester's comments stemmed, of course, from the racism and the misogynistic, internalized homophobia that resulted from the narrow organization of community around desire, and the organization of that desire around an image that came directly from the mainstream media (classic Hollywood beefcake). Although Sylvester's songs could articulate that desire, he himself could neither represent it, nor change it.

Sylvester's successes in the late 1970s foreshadowed an increase in the number of effeminate men (some of whom were African-American) in dance and pop music of the 1980s. Boy George perhaps compares most closely to Sylvester in his unabashedly gay look and demeanor, but there were also top-selling straight-acting stars in this camp, such as Michael Jackson and especially Prince, whose early albums feature his Sylvester-like falsetto and who used disco's sexual glamour to push the boundaries of pop from soulful crooning to orgasmic cries. With a seeming vulnerability, conveyed in songs and album covers, Prince invited all women to be the butch to his femme. Similarly, the gay macho look of the Village People was carried on into the 1980s by Freddie Mercury of Queen (who will be discussed in the next chapter). Nearly thirty years after the popularity of Sylvester and the Village People, both gay masculinities—the mincing comedic queen and the macho hunk—can now be openly represented on network television, as in the sitcom *Will and Grace* and the reality program *Queer Eye for the Straight Guy*.

These two successful shows, however, also reflect the continuing, troubling construction of gay identity as white and elite.

. . .

Though the centrality of sexual pleasure and escapism conveyed through disco music and its club context seems diametrically opposed to the consciousness-raising and culture-building aspirations of Olivia Records and women's music festivals, the production and dissemination of gay masculinities through key gay-coded disco artists had a comparable impact in forming the public face of gay identity within and outside the gay community. Just as the early albums of women's music came to stand for the stereotype of 1970s lesbian feminism—puritanical desexualized essentialism—disco music came to stand for the stereotype of 1970s gay male culture as decadent, superficial, and homogeneous.

Women's music and disco were products of a relatively new politics, one that applied the discourse of the political left and civil rights to gender and sexual identity. These recorded repertories in turn conveyed a sexual identity politics that could seem more a capitalistic enterprise than a subversive action—a politics that carved up the larger queer community into target audiences based on demographic profiles of race, class, and gender. The 1970s was, in general, a time of sharp focus on these components of identity as ways of organizing politics and culture, as well as markets. While women's music and disco helped railroad lesbians and gays into problematic separatism and destructive factionalism, these products also helped them confront and critique their newly emerging public face. The homomusical communities of the 1970s were, in a way, a cultural rehearsal for gays and lesbians as they prepared to move openly, in ever-increasing numbers, into the world at large. The process of this movement into the world is the subject of the final chapter.

5

Flights of Fancy

power

Foucault describes "technologies of power" as practices that "determine the conduct of individuals and submit them to certain ends."[1] He first worked out this idea of technologies of power in *Discipline and Punish: The Birth of the Prison*, where he studied disciplinary practices designed to produce docile, governable bodies. Foucault believed that practices of domination emerged as technologies of power in the eighteenth century and can be traced in multiple institutions, such as prisons, the military, and schools. All three use strict codes of conduct, surveillance, and physical control to keep peace and ensure governability.[2]

The idea of technologies of power that discipline the body appears in his next major work, *The History of Sexuality, Volume I: An Introduction*, but here Foucault prefers the word "discourse" to techniques. Relationships of power and domination, he argues in this study, are masked as issues of knowledge, and specifically knowledge of sexuality. Like the regulatory techniques of power he described in *Discipline and Punish*, the discourse that brings together power, knowledge, and sexuality does so through various "discursive elements," such as confession, marriage, education, science, and psychoanalysis (and I include music). These elements have "tactical functions" that "come into play in various strategies."[3] Foucault saw the seventeenth century as the time when sexuality became the principal domain of the discourse of knowledge and power (or this technology of power), and he saw the eighteenth century as the time when, parallel to the disciplinary institutions studied in *Discipline and Punish*, clear strategies for the deployment of this discourse emerged. One strategy was the division and codification of adult sexual behavior into two opposing categories: the socially normative and the pathologically perverse.[4]

Socially normative sexuality, Foucault argues, came to be represented by "the Malthusian couple," the heterosexual dyad whose sexuality was regulated through marriage. Marriage binds the couple to the social body as a whole—that is, the nation-state—in a relationship of responsibility for sexual reproduction as well as sexual restraint.[5] In other words, marriage ensures the governability of bodies, and in return the married couple is given fuller rights and benefits of citizenship. Moreover, marriage also works to fortify patriarchy by stabilizing gender and gender roles. The word "marriage" historically specifies the conjoining of two families through the legal (and often sacralized) union of a man and woman. The Defense of Marriage Act (DOMA), signed into law by President Clinton in 1996, worked to secure that meaning in the United States in the face of state governments, such as that of Vermont, that granted marriagelike legal status to same-sex "civil unions." At the time of this writing (the election year 2004) gay marriage is a hot political topic; the Massachusetts Supreme Court ordered the granting of marriage licenses to same-sex couples in November 2003, which inspired President George W. Bush to propose a constitutional amendment banning gay marriage (this would be redundant in light of DOMA).

If the institution of marriage defines sexual and social normalcy, then "coming out" can be considered its parallel in queer identity. Since the 1970s, and perhaps earlier, coming out stories have formed a staple of queer conversation and the *sine qua non* of signposts in queer identity. Like marriage, coming out marks an individual's entry into the social, into community. The perpetual recounting of those stories is ritualistic; the similarities of personal narratives and emotional reactions generate a sense of cohesiveness, of shared experience. This ritual of self-exposure should be distinguished from the idea of confession as discussed in chapter 2; it is not a weekly rehearsal or reminder of a pathology from which the individual strives to "recover." Rather, coming out is a ritual proclamation of sexual eligibility closely related to marriage. Indeed, the phrase "coming out" originally referred to the ceremonial introduction of young women (or debutantes) into the world of adulthood. To "come out" was to proclaim formally the marriageability of a young woman, to advertise her sexual availability. To "debut" or to "be a debutante" were early names for this process of sexual revelation in both heterosexual and homosexual society. In heterosexual society, one debuted at a masquerade ball; in homosexual society, one debuted at a drag ball.[6]

Historian George Chauncey has noted the shifting semantics of "coming out" since its pre–World War I reference to an initiation into a community. By the 1950s "coming out" referred to a solitary process of self-understanding (one was usually "brought out" by an initiatory sexual experience); after Stonewall, "coming out" once again took on the connotation of a social proclamation, but this time in front of representatives of the dominant culture rather than the community of peers.[7] By the 1970s, coming out had thus become a two-stage metamorphosis, from the cocoon of "the closet" (itself a postwar concept), where one's sexuality supposedly developed and fomented in isolation, to an individual action of emerging from one's prior containment. At that time, coming out as gay or lesbian was proclaiming the opposite of marriageability: it was an automatic disqualification from it, if not a conscious rebellion against it.

Foucault's *History of Sexuality, Volume I* was in part a critique of the identity politics of the late 1960s and 1970s and its potential to lead to self-limiting and exclusionary practices.[8] Understood in this way, his analysis of sexuality as the glue binding power and knowledge has many implications for rethinking coming out as a strategy for criticizing an identity based on a discourse of sexuality, rather than a strategy for constituting one. For Foucault described both macro- and microstructures of human relations ("verbal communications . . . amorous, institutional, or economic relationships") as "relations" or "games" of power that are necessarily "mobile, reversible, and unstable." "In power relations," he writes, "there is necessarily the possibility of resistance." Resistance works toward freedom from domination.[9]

The state neither recognizes nor regulates the social identity of "being out," as compared to "being married," and this can empower coming out with the potential to be a continual process of questioning: How does our culture equate sexuality and identity? What are the consequences of such an equation? Coming out, then, can be thought of as a resistant deployment of sexuality, a performance that interrupts other discursive practices that work to normalize heterosexuality. It is, quite literally, an act of hubris; the English word "out" is related to the Greek word *hybris,* meaning insolence, as well as wantonness.

The musical compositions, performances, and interpretations in this chapter are "about" coming out, not into tidy identities through instituted channels, but rather into the messy contestations of sex and gender. They are examples of queer identity tactically enabled by music, acts of hubris by men who use music to escape marriage, interrupt heterosexuality, and critique masculinity; they are musical announcements of an availability to some other unruly identity.

I will focus specifically on musical examples on either end of what might be called the "epoch of sexual discourse"—when, as Foucault points out, "modern societies . . . dedicated themselves to speaking of [sex] *ad infinitum,* while exploiting it as *the* secret."[10] Foucault sees this trajectory as beginning in the late seventeenth and early eighteenth centuries, with the rise of bourgeois society and a vicious antagonism among Reformation and Counter-Reformation forces within Western Christianity. The "frankness" of discourse about sex that Foucault attributes to the prior epoch went increasingly "underground," refined and sublimated into abundant metaphors and allusions.[11] The seventeenth-century English "catches" and George Frideric Handel's early Italian cantatas provide examples of this movement from "frankness" to sublimation in the "early days" of the "epoch of sexual discourse." On the other end of this epoch, in the twentieth century, Foucault notes that a "rupture" in the history of sexuality occurred when "the mechanisms of repression were seen as beginning to loosen their grip; one passed from insistent sexual taboos to a relative tolerance with regard to prenuptial or extramarital relations; the disqualification of 'perverts' diminished, their condemnation by the law was in part eliminated."[12]

Late twentieth-century chatter about sex and sexuality has reached a critical din in popular music such that the last several decades have witnessed a rapid recycling of themes. But like original documents successively photocopied—from Queen to Marilyn Manson, from *The Rocky Horror Picture Show* to *Hedwig and the Angry Inch*—the gender-and-genital-based sexual discourse of the earlier epoch has become increasingly distorted with each recycling. Indeed, these successive distortions, while still shocking, nonetheless work to degrade, in turn, the primacy of gender and sexuality to identity. This perhaps signals the effective end of the "epoch of sexual discourse," and the beginning of a new set of questions.

CATCHING CUCKOLDS AND HERMAPHRODITES

Historians of sexuality since Foucault have corroborated his proposition that there was a steep rise in intolerance for sodomitical and same-sex activity in the second half of the seventeenth century. The rise in intolerance was, in part, a response to an earlier rise in the accommodation of such activities in the taverns and "molly houses" of urban areas, as well as in artistic and Arcadian societies in aristocratic circles.[13] This is not to say, as Foucault seems to suggest, that a period of "tolerance" preceded the later injunctions against sodomy; rather, legal and religious rhetoric simply became more explicit in its focus on "sodomy" as a specific category of sexual activity that ultimately posed a threat to natural, social, and religious law. "Sodomy" was frequently used as a synonym for "debauchery," which encompassed a wide range of excesses, including drink, idleness, gluttony, and whoring. The terms "sodomy" and "buggery," when used to denote a sexual act, pointed as much toward the act's potential to lead to social disorder as to the perversity of the sexual act itself. Depending on the views of the magistrate, sodomy could include bestiality, homosexual or heterosexual anal penetration, pederasty, or even nonpenetrative sexual acts. The charge of sodomy was also used as a tool for political sabotage and xenophobia, hence early modern English writers commonly associate sodomy with social and political undesirables, including Papists (especially the Jesuits) and foreigners (especially Italians, but also Spaniards, Turks, and even Russians).[14]

Henry Purcell's tavern song "The London Constable" (published in 1685) includes the following exchange:

> *Constable:* "Whence come you sir? And wither do you go? You may be, sir, a Jesuit for ought I know."
>
> *Citizen:* "You may as well, sir, take me for a Mahometan!"
>
> *Constable:* "He speaks Latin: secure him, he's a dangerous man!"
>
> *Citizen:* "To tell you the truth, sir, I am an honest Tory, but here's a crown to drink, and there's an end of the story."[15]

Both men are drunk, the constable described as a "midnight magistrate with a noodle full of ale" and the citizen so implicated by his wandering around at midnight, which was a popular theme of tavern songs. The comical string of misrecognitions and the final monetary solution satirizes the persuasiveness of money and drink over the generalized paranoia about the infiltration of devilish forces—here Catholics collapsed with Muslims or "muhammadans," both of which were frequently linked with sodomy.

Drink was always an occasion for male solidarity, and in Restoration England the tavern provided a primary site for male homosocial and even homoerotic activities. Some taverns may have specialized in catering to homosexuals as early as the late sixteenth century.[16] Misogyny was also part of the masculine world of the tavern. The character of the midnight wandering drunk featured in many tavern songs became associated with Purcell himself and the legend of his death. John Hawkins recounts that Purcell died of an illness incurred because his wife had locked him out of the house after a bout of late-night drinking.[17] The misogynistic implications to this legend are clear: it is not Purcell's drinking that killed him, but rather his wife's intolerance of his wanton behavior. We might see this legend as a parable for the historical shift described above, wherein the tavern's accommodation of sodomitical behavior was met with institutionalized social intolerance.

Along with drinking there was singing. Without a doubt, tavern songs musically inscribe what Eve Sedgwick calls "male homosocial desire"—affective social relationships among men (whether hostile or affectionate) that forge "the structures for maintaining and transmitting patriarchal power."[18] A substantial repertory of songs published from the mid-seventeenth century on (with and without music) evokes, eroticizes, and satirizes the intense homosocial bonding in tavern culture. Many of these songs, including "The London Constable," are catches, intricate melodies to be sung as a round, or canon, for three or more voices. The name "catch" stems from the fourteenth-century Italian *caccia* and French *chace* (both meaning "hunt"), which are playful canonic musical genres. They require a certain degree of singing skill, if not also musical literacy, to perform. The catch of the seventeenth-century catch was the revelation of double entendres in the context of the full-voice statements. Strategically placed rests and notes of long duration allowed for the formation of phrases and sentences, often lewd, among the voices; the listener literally catches new meanings in the words as

Example 7. John Hilton, "Here Is an Old Ground" (1652), from *The Catch Book*, ed. Paul Hillier.

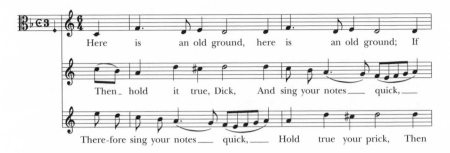

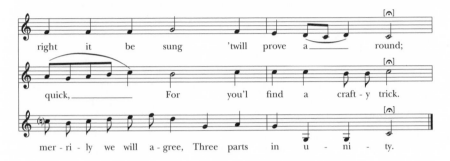

they are sung in canon. John Hilton's 1652 "Here Is an Old Ground" (example 7)[19] is a self-referential catch whose words point to the "crafty trick" embedded in the music should the named singer Dick perform his part correctly ("Hold true your prick"). "Dick" in the sixteenth and seventeenth centuries was a generic if slightly pejorative name for a lad or fellow, and "prick," as today, was a slang term for the penis, though it was also a term for written music. Against the low notes that appropriately set the word "ground" and a middle-register melisma over "quick," the words "Dick," "prick," and "trick" pop out of the texture as the highest notes, giving the round an off-color spin.

The other trick of this catch is the integration of an old popular melody called "Browning" in the top voice (the "old ground" referred to in the lyrics), which was set by numerous composers as a song with various words, or as an imitative theme in instrumental consorts. Thomas Ravenscroft used the tune in a three-part round with the words "Browning, Madame, Browning, Madame, so merrily we sing Browning Madame." The melody in this catch, however, more closely matches the version preserved in William Byrd's five-part consort setting, which carries both the titles "Browning" and "The Leaves Be Green." One of the manuscripts for Byrd's consort setting preserves the following set of words for the tune: "The leaves be greene the nuts be browne, they hang soe high, they will not come downe."[20] Should the "Dick" who sings Hilton's catch recall the tune and words from these or other contexts, the catch in meaning results in a brash celebration of a nexus of "pricks"—on one hand musical notation, which allows for the transmission and transformation of "old grounds," and on the other, the anatomical "prick," which defines the social environment of the music.

This pun directs our attention to the social operation of these catches, namely the fortification of the male homosocial world. Several theme complexes in this repertory point toward a musical contemplation of gender and sexuality in a playful, half-revealing manner such that plausible deniability is retained. Songs of male bonding, dominating masculine women, and hermaphrodites offer critiques of married life, but with sharp edges smoothed over by clever musical and verbal twists that delight the senses as well as provoke winks and nudges. The words to Purcell's catch "A Farewell to Wives" (1684) epitomizes the theme of male bonding:

> Once in our lives, let us drink to our wives,
> Tho' their numbers be but small:
> Heav'n take the best and the Devil take the rest,
> and so we shall get rid of them all.
> To this hearty wish let each man take his dish,
> and drink, drink, drink till he fall.[21]

The performance of this catch yields no revelation of second meaning; the words are quite clear in their misogyny and antimarriage sentiment as the singers merrily drink a toast to the distribution of their wives to heaven and hell. The song promotes the idea that men do and should prefer the company of other men to their wives; indeed, they dream of getting rid of their wives altogether.

But the second line of "A Farewell to Wives"—"Tho' their numbers be but small"—discloses a curious demographic profile. Quite a few of the drinkers, we learn from this lyric, were bachelors. Bachelors occupied a precarious position in seventeenth-century England. On the one hand they were praised as naturally and circumstantially more charitable, while on the other they were condemned as "woman haters" and it was implied that they were sodomites. Sir Francis Bacon (1561–1626), who was a favorite of King James I (1566–1625) and whose homosexual proclivities are well documented (as are those of His Majesty),[22] writes against marriage in his *Essayes or Counsels, Civil and Moral* (1601), a book that circulated in various published editions throughout the seventeenth century. I quote from a 1664 London edition:

> Certainly the best works, and of greatest merit for the publick, have proceeded from the *unmarried* or *childless Men,* which both in affection and means have married and endowed the publick. . . . But the most ordinary cause of a *Single*

Life is Liberty, especially in certain self-pleasing and humorous minds. . . .
Unmarried Men are best Friends, best Masters, best Servants, but not alwayes
best Subjects; for they are light to run away, and almost all fugitives are of that
condition.

Because of the flight risk, Bacon admits that "for Souldiers, I find the Gen-
erals commonly in their hortatives put Men in mind of their *Wives and Chil-*
dren. And I think the despising of *Marriage* amongst the Turks, maketh the
vulgar Souldier more base."[23]

That unmarried men do not make the most loyal subjects (and that, by
extension, soldiers should be married) is historically borne out by the many
homosocially and homoerotically inclined men who served as spies.[24] These
potential spies were also spied upon, especially by Edward (Ned) Ward, who
published a monthly magazine from 1698 to 1709 called *The London Spy*.
Ward claimed his intention was to expose the "Vice and Villainy" of London's
taverns and brothels, though the magazine reads like a gossipy travel diary.
Such sensationalistic exposés of vice-ridden taverns circulated throughout
the eighteenth century and into the nineteenth century. One 1813 tract by
Robert Holloway bears a title that titillates with promises of up-to-date information on the practices of sodomites (also called "mollies"): *The Phoenix of*
Sodom, or the Vere Street Coterie. Being an Exhibition of the Gambols Practised by the
Ancient Lechers of Sodom and Gomorrah, embellished and improved with the Mod-
ern Refinements in Sodomitical Practices, by the members of the Vere Street Coterie, of
detestable memory.[25] The Vere Street Coterie referred to the clientele of a particular "molly house" called The Swan; molly houses were taverns and private
clubs where men dressed as women, took women's names, and even performed mock weddings. Over a century before the publication of Holloway's
tract, Ward had written about molly houses in *The London Spy*. His descriptions of tavern life frequently included scenes of singing, and he even published song lyrics.[26]

A married man could, with impunity, desire to be unmarried, to be free,
but to become a "woman hater" crossed an important line and would
exclude him from the musical male camaraderie of the tavern. In the play
The Woman Hater (1607), by Francis Beaumont and John Fletcher, the misogynist Gondarino was particularly distinguished as hating music as well as
women.[27] An anonymous song (song 9) in a 1672 collection of lyrics for
songs and catches, compiled by "a Person of quality," contrasts the singing
"Lover" with "the woman-hater."

A Lover I am, and a Lover I'll be,
And hope from my true Love, I shall never be free.
Let wisdom be blam'd in the grave woman-hater,
Yet never to love, is a sign of ill nature.[28]

"Ill nature" may here bear the connotation of *contra naturam,* a phrase used to condemn sodomitical acts since the Middle Ages. A 1707 broadside entitled *The Woman Hater's Lament* provides some evidence that the term "woman hater" signaled a sexuality rather than simply an attitude toward women, for it calls woman haters "mollies" and sodomites. The social problem of woman haters, however, was still primarily conceived as a threat to the institution of marriage rather than a perverse sexuality: a married man who buggered a servant was less deplorable than a woman hater.

Nevertheless, marriage and women were often savaged together in catches and songs that portray wives as scolding and cuckolding. Sedgwick notes that " 'to cuckold' is by definition a sexual act, performed on a man, by another man"; that is, the husband is cuckolded by the man who has sex with his wife. The prevalence of this theme—almost an *idée fixe*—of the cuckolded husband in the songs and literature of this time offers an early example of how "heterosexual love" was used "as a strategy of homosocial desire" in which one man is constructed as "active" and knowing while the other becomes "passive" and ignorant in their bond. This male-male relationship, Sedgwick explains, "is not detrimental to 'masculinity' but definitive of it."[29]

Yet time and again in tavern songs the husband is called a cuckold on account of his wife's scolding. It is she who becomes the active male in cuckolding her husband. Purcell's "Jack, Thou'rt a Toper" (from the play *Bonduca* [1695] and published independently in 1701) is a case in point.

> Jack, thou'rt a toper: let's have t'other quart;
> Ring, we're so sober, so sober, so sober 'twere a shame to part.
> None but a cuckold bully'd by his wife for coming late, fears a domestick strife.
> I'm free, and so are you too;
> call and knock! Knock boldly, the watchman cries "Past two o'clock."

In performance, Purcell has each male singer (whose state of drunkenness is illustrated by what is effectively a stutter in the second line) experience the wife's bullying as they sing "coming, coming, coming" for four bars of quick eighth notes, as if answering her call (example 8).[30] When all three voices sound, we hear a catch of meaning in measures 2–4, as a cascade of phrases from top to bottom says: "thou'rt," "a cuckold," "so are you" (see top system). Thus the three singing men are made to accuse each other of being the cuckold as they sing of their own imagined freedom.

Bullying, cuckolding wives sometimes merge with wives who show a degree of masculinity that calls into question the masculinity of their husbands. The anonymous catch "When Wives Do Hate the Husbands Friends" describes in the first stanza a veritable battle of the sexes, which results in a literal travesty of nature in the second stanza:

Example 8. Henry Purcell, "Jack, Thou'rt a Toper" (1695), from *The Catch Book,* ed. Paul Hillier.

When Wives do hate the Husbands friends,
As jealous of some fearlesse ends,
And still an angry look she settles,
As if of late she 'ad piss'd on Nettles;
Ware ho, ware ho; for then of force
The Mare will prove the better Horse.

When Women will be ever nice,
Foolish, Proud, and Manly Wife,
And their wanton Humour itches
To wear their Husbands widest Breeches:
Ware ho, ware ho; for then of force
The Mare will prove the better Horse.[31]

Here, as in Purcell's "Jack, Thou'rt a Toper," scolding and cuckolding go hand in hand, but now they are divided into two separate profiles of female dominance. The first stanza presents a variant of the "scolding wife" trope; the wife is not upset by the late hour of the husband's return from a night of drinking, but rather she seems to have a more abstract hatred and jealously of the husband's friends. The male homosocial world of the tavern—a world rife with eroticized male rivalry—is set up as the wife's direct rival, an alternative to the fraught, heterosexual domestic one. This curious competition seems to require that the "mare" prove the better horse so that the husband's own masculinity can be rescued from debauchery. The second stanza presents a variant on the "cuckolding wife" trope; oversexed women behave and even dress like men. Together these two stanzas imply a relationship of cause and effect: if men spend too much time with their friends to the neglect of their wives' sexual appetites, then their wives will become more manly than they.

This anxiety, that a man's homosocial proclivities will actually transgender women, is taken to a limit in songs that feature a woman who can do without a man, or a woman who can be a man. The song "A Maiden of Late," included in the same 1672 collection as "A Lover I Am," tells of "sweet Kate" who "would have a Child without help of a man." I quote two of the eight stanzas below:

To a Doctor she came,
A man of great fame.
Whose deep skill in Physick report did proclaim,
Quoth she, *Master Doctor, shew me if you can,*
How I can conceive without help of a man.

Then listen, quoth he,
Since so it must be,
This wondrous strong Med'cine I'll shew presently:

> Take nine pounds of Thunder, six Legs of a Swan,
> And you shall conceive without help of a man.[32]

The subsequent stanzas continue the fantastical list of ingredients for this alchemical recipe, each stanza concluding with some version of the incantatory refrain. With its humorous impossible concoctions (such as "the wool of a Frog, the Juyce of a Log"), the song assures men of their place in procreation, although it likewise plays on their anxious fantasy of being magically, or worse, medically, superseded.

Fantastical procreation is also the theme of William Lawes's catch "Dainty Fine Aniseed Water Fine" (1652; also published in 1663). Though in performance this song does not feature any catch of meaning, the lyric leads the singers into a world of bizarre gender and sexuality.

> Dainty fine Aniseed water fine,
> Dainty content and your money again:
> See, here comes *Robin* Hermaphrodite,
> Hot waters, he cryes for his delight:
> He got a Child of a Maid, and yet is no man
> Was got with childe by a man, and is no woman.[33]

Aniseed water was an aid for expelling gas, and "hot water" refers to an alcoholic beverage. The two waters—one for output and one for intake, as it were—reflect the double nature of the hermaphrodite, who begets a child as a man, and is also begotten with a child as a woman. Given the homosocial context of this song, where the singers themselves would be calling for "hot waters," the lyric implies that the hermaphrodite could be anyone in the tavern. The song could be a seventeenth-century version of the twentieth-century gay joke: What's the difference between a gay man and a straight man? The answer: a six-pack of beer. Hot waters blur boundaries, loosen inhibitions, and allow homosocial bonding to slide into queer explorations.

The lyric's matter-of-fact inquiry into the nature of a hermaphrodite betrays a fascination with that body's impossible potency. The figure of the hermaphrodite captivated the imagination of seventeenth-century Europe; it appears in moralistic, scientific, pornographic, and literary writing. The anonymous author of the *Wandering Whore* (1660), a tract railing against sexual libertinism, used the term "hermaphrodite" to describe someone akin to the woman hater, writing, "There are likewise hermaphrodites, effeminate men, men given to much luxury, idleness, and wanton pleasures, and to that abominable sin of sodomy, wherein they are both active and passive in it."[34] Here the ability and desire to switch gender roles in the sexual act defines hermaphroditism rather than a superfluidity of gendered anatomical parts. In her study of the hermaphrodite in early modern natural philosophy, Ruth Gilbert notes that studies of hermaphrodites routinely combined an interest in physical anomalies, human biology, scientific taxonomies and sexual excitement. The hermaphrodite had been popularised as a subject of scientific enquiry in the studies of Jacques Duval (1612), Gaspard Bauhin (1614), and Jean Riolan (1614) as well as the medical works of Jacob Rueff (1554) and Ambroise Paré (1573). Apart from Bauhin's each of these works was published in the French vernacular and was either translated into English or transmitted into English texts.[35]

Gilbert argues that the New Science and natural philosophy of the seventeenth century, articulated most clearly in Francis Bacon's *The Great Instauration* (1620), emphasized visual proof. This generated descriptions in exhaustive detail, which "marks the confluence between the methodologies of early modern science and the techniques of pornography." Here, *scientia sexualis* and *ars erotica* colluded in the enterprise of describing and displaying the hermaphrodite.[36]

At least two English-language literary treatments of the hermaphrodite predate the first publication of Lawes's catch: a translation of the myth of Hermaphroditus in Ovid's *Metamorphoses* attributed to Francis Beaumont, and John Cleveland's poem "Upon an Hermophrodite," both published in 1640. Cleveland's poem in particular transmits concepts of the hermaphrodite that we will meet again in this chapter. Cleveland likens Adam prior to the making of Eve as having "both Sexes thus ingrost." He continues:

> When Providence our Sire did cleave;
> And out of *Adam* carved *Eve,*
> Then did man 'bout wedlock treat,
> To make his body up compleat
> Thus Matrimony speaks but *Thee,*
> In a grave solemnitie;
> For man and wife make but one right
> Canonical *Hermaphrodite.*[37]

This theory of marriage as an attempt to regain an original hermaphroditic wholeness is likely drawn from Aristophanes' myth of love in Plato's *Symposium,* in which humans, having once existed in a state of bonded pairs (both heterosexual and homosexual), now seek their other half. But Cleveland's poem veers away from this romanticized view of the hermaphrodite to a comical description of double genderedness, including self-courtship:

> How many melting kisses skip
> 'Twixt thy Male and Female lip? . . .
> When musick doth thy pace advance,
> Thy right leg takes the left to dance,
> Nor is't a Galliard danc'd by one,
> But a mixt dance, though alone:

> Thus every heteroclite part
> Changes gender, not the heart.[38]

Rather than abhorrence at the opportune switching of gender roles, as in the *Wandering Whore,* Cleveland imparts a hint of envy, for the hermaphrodite is a self-contained sexual and social being in which both genders exist in perfect agreement; there is no scolding, no cuckolding.

. . .

William Lawes's catch about "Robin Hermaphrodite" bears witness to the circulation of this hermaphrodite fascination (if not envy) in the male homosocial world of the tavern—a musical parallel to the scientific and literary explorations of the hermaphrodite's intoxicating double nature. In the tavern, this hermaphrodite mingled with scolding and cuckolding wives who similarly traverse or combine genders; these characters, extragendered Others, point to the precarious nature of masculinity, especially within marriage. The frequent combination of scolding and cuckolding, fantasies of wanton wives donning breeches and maidens preferring an alchemical cocktail to a cock for procreation, grabs that definitive place of action away from men. Indeed, those catches with a particular catch of meaning in performance work their cleverness through a turn taking of activity and passivity, the cycling of double entendres evinced in one singer's words by those of another. Thus tavern songs, and especially catches, probe and prick at masculinity in its married state, showing it to be vulnerable. Yet bachelorhood did not necessarily afford safe haven from the emasculation of marriage. To be labeled a "woman hater" could imperil a man, make him vulnerable to suspicions of committing the capital offense of sodomy. In this light, the figure of the hermaphrodite in Lawes's catch, who enjoys his "hot water" as any good fellow, presents a fantastical and perhaps somewhat enviable personage who could be both the active male and active female in a cuckolding, and for whom marriage was always already redundant. "When thou joyn'it hands," Cleveland writes of the hermaphrodite, "my ear still fancies / The Nuptial sound, I *John* take *Frances.*"

"THE PHOENIX OF SODOM"

Although the cuckolding portrayed in tavern songs and catches reveals an anxiety about the precariousness of masculinity in marriage, such songs also demonstrate the playfulness that characterizes homosocial environments. Without the presence of women, men tend to play around with masculinity, making it more elastic in order to accommodate forms of male-male erotic and even sexual activity packaged as boasting, teasing, and (at its worst) hazing. To sing and laugh about cuckolding—for one man to say in jest "I know more about your wife than you do," or, more to the point, "I am screwing you by screwing your wife"—in effect celebrates erotically charged relationships among men that are created by marriage.[39] It is a musical-sexual discourse of knowledge and power that binds men together more strongly. Sedgwick has described this paradoxical situation as "the radically disrupted continuum, in our society, between sexual and nonsexual male bonds." She summarizes, "For a man to be a man's man is separated only by an invisible, carefully blurred, always-already-crossed line from being 'interested in men.'"[40]

Marriage was but one early modern context that led to practices of male bonding and games with gender that were facilitated by music. In a context without marriage, where bachelorhood was tolerated or sanctioned, male bonds and same-sex attractions could be musically reimagined in terms of creative invention and erotic fantasy rather than cuckoldry. The early Italian compositions by George Frideric Handel (1685–1759) with texts by Cardinal Benedetto Pamphili offer just such a window into music's tactical deployment within a decidedly homosocial and homoerotic environment. Here music helped in an erotic game of power between two unmarried men, patron and artist.

Recent scholarship has traced the many implications of same-sex desire in Handel's biography and music, pointing specifically to his early Italian cantatas as expressive of the homosocial and homoerotic social milieu in which he lived and worked.[41] In her study of Handel's Italian chamber cantatas, Ellen T. Harris documents that many of his patrons, such as Cardinal Pamphili and Cardinal Ottoboni in Rome and Prince Ferdinand of the Medici family in Florence, were known to have homosexual attractions, especially to castrati. These inclinations were sometimes encoded within the Ovidian "literary heritage" of the poetry and amplified in Handel's dramatic musical settings. Pamphili, who was quite possibly Handel's first Italian patron, authored a number of poems set by Handel in 1707. Harris interprets one of these—*Hendel, non può mia musa* (June 1707)—as betraying Pamphili's own attraction to Handel. This can be seen, she argues, in the cardinal's comparison of Handel to Orpheus, whose double fame as divine musician and originator of same-sex attraction would have been well known from Ovid. In *Hendel, non può mia musa,* as Harris has uncovered, Pamphili employed phallic double entendres in the "animate and inanimate objects that Pamphili lists as attracted to Orpheus—'birds,' 'wild beast,' 'tree trunk,' and 'rock.'"[42] Through these sexual metaphors, Pamphili's poem suggests that Handel, like Orpheus, was able to attract men—even older men, such as the cardinal, who felt themselves to be past love. An anecdote recorded by Handel's later librettist Charles Jennens recounts the composer's dismissive reaction to the poetic flattery in *Hendel, non può mia musa;* Handel called the cardinal "an old Fool."[43]

Hendel, non può mia musa may have put Handel off with its direct flattery and thinly veiled eroticism, but only a month after composing that chamber cantata, Handel set another of Pamphili's classically themed poems—one that conveys a similar message of sexual flattery but with far more subtlety—*Tra le fiamme* (July 1707), which concerns the story of Daedalus and Icarus.[44] Because Handel set this poem for solo voice, obligato viola da gamba, and orchestra, Harris mentions this cantata only briefly in her study, but it warrants a close examination in light of her findings, for *Tra le fiamme* deploys earlier erotic interpretations of the myth as a strategy for conveying same-sex passions in a way that differs markedly from the strategies found in the chamber cantatas.

In ancient Greece, the Athenian Daedalus represented the archetypical artist and craftsman. The Greek noun and adjective *daidalos* meant "artistic" or "cunningly wrought," and Daedalus was credited with innovations in sculpture; specifically, he was said to have been the first to open the eyes, to place arms and legs in more natural positions, and even to have created statues that moved.[45] The most famous and elaborate account of Daedalus and Icarus is transmitted in two works by Ovid: book 8 of the *Metamorphoses* and book 2 of the earlier poem *Ars amatoria*. In the *Metamorphoses,* Daedalus first appears as the creator of the famous labyrinth on Crete, which was built to hold the dreaded Minotaur (eventually killed by Theseus). Father and son are forcibly detained on that island by King Minos, and so Daedalus plots an escape by air.[46] Ovid writes, "Then he turns his heart to arts unknown; he makes nature new" *(ignotas animum dimittit in artes naturamque novat).*[47] This phrase is key, for the only thing that transforms in this story—transformations being the theme of the *Metamorphoses*—is nature, which Daedalus renovates by building birdlike wings for humans. He sews hollow reeds together, covers them with feathers, and affixes them to the skeletal structure with wax. Ovid compares the sloping shape of the wing to the reed instrument that shepherds play, a panpipe, whose origin he described in book 1. Like Daedalus building his wings, Pan secures the reeds of his pipe with wax. At this point in Daedalus's story, the *Metamorphoses* offers poignant details of Icarus playing with the feathers and wax, hindering Daedalus and unknowingly fingering the implement of his own death. This is a foreshadowing that Pamphili paraphrases in his poem. In a scene reminiscent of Abraham and Isaac, Daedalus becomes filled with trepidation, admonishing his son to fly "in the middle" *(medio)*—not to descend low, where the water from waves could weigh down his wings, nor to soar high, where the sun could scorch them. Daedalus then tearfully affixes the wings to Icarus's arms and kisses him before they both alight into the air.[48] Icarus, exuberant in his flight, swoops upward, close to the sun. The sun melts the wax and Icarus plummets, featherless, into the sea.

The components of the story as told in the *Metamorphoses* do not differ significantly from those in the earlier *Ars amatoria;* indeed, Ovid even paraphrased himself here and there. The *Ars amatoria,* however, is a didactic poem intended to teach young lovers about seduction and adultery. In its own time it was considered morally subversive, and it was cited as the reason that the emperor Augustus banished Ovid from Rome.[49] Nevertheless, like the *Metamorphoses,* the provocative poem enjoyed a healthy tradition of translation, commentary, and adaptation from the Middle Ages onward. The story of Daedalus and Icarus opens book 2 (of three) as a double allegory: on one level Daedalus represents Ovid as the poet and teacher, while Icarus represents the readers as students; on another level, the story explores the ambivalent position of the artist (Daedalus/Ovid), whose ingenious and bold creations (Daedalus's wings/Ovid's poems) threaten to break natural bonds (between father and son/art and nature).[50] Icarus, in this poem, epitomizes human impulsiveness and audacity, passionate abandon that leads to dire consequences. His story, then, is a cautionary tale; it warns young lovers to avoid rash behavior in the pursuit of love.[51] Unlike the later, post-exilic *Metamorphoses,* there is no foreshadowing of doom nor the pathos of tearful kisses.

From the late fifteenth to the late seventeenth century, Italian poets integrated the myth of Daedalus and Icarus within the discourse of courtly love; they compared Icarus's glorious flight to the lover who is emboldened to act by his passion. More specifically, these poems frequently associate Icarus with the phoenix, a birdlike creature that, in ancient Near Eastern and Greco-Roman fables, would throw itself into a fire to be rejuvenated. In the sonnet "Avventurate, ma più audaci piume" (Fortunate, but more daring feathers), by Tommaso Castellani (Venice 1549), the male lover is likened to Icarus (line 3); both suffer from a dangerous, if not fatal, attraction. The lover uses his wings to fan the flames of this passion and, unlike Icarus, he is reborn in those flames like a phoenix.

Ma quel, ch'ad altri nuoce è sol radice	But that which does harm to another is only the source
del vostro ben; però movete el vento	of your well-being; so stir the wind
per accrescer la fiamma, che vi giova.	to increase the flame, for it aids you.
Onde poi quella nostra alma fenice	In that way that phoenix soul of ours renews,
le gran forze d'Amor; l'altrui tormento	in its own flame, the great forces of Love
ne proprio ardor, se stessa e voi rinova.	others' torment, itself, and you.[52]

John H. Turner comments that these poems convey the typical convention of courtly poetry, namely an "almost masochistic delight in the abject submission," through the image of Icarus's fascination "with the very source of [his] own peril."[53]

Giovanni Battista Marino (1569–1625) published the little verse "Icarus in cera" in a 1636 collection of poems about imaginary paintings and sculptures. Here Marino deftly compresses both the courtly Icarus and the artistic Daedalus interpretive traditions into a circular labyrinth of meaning. Edward Sherburne translated the poem into English in 1651. I give both texts below.[54]

La cera, che fatale	What once did unto thee impart
Icaro, ti diè morte,	The means of Death; by happy Art
Ecco con miglior sorte,	Now thee restores to life again:
Per man di dotto artefice scolpita	Yet still remember to refrain
Hor ti rende la vita.	Ambitious Flights; nor soar too nigh
Ma guardati da'rai	The Sun of an inflaming Eye;
Del Sol doue tu vai;	For so thou may'st, scorcht by those Beams,
	In Ashes dye, as once in Streams.
Che s'egli auien, ch'ei ti distrempi l'ale,	
Senza risorger mai	
cenere ricadrai.	

Icarus's phoenixlike resurrection is effected through the very material (wax) that caused his demise by melting from the sun. But more importantly, Icarus is revived through an artistic rendering (in other words, by Daedalus), and his new formation in wax ultimately places Icarus once more in front of the "inflaming Eye" of the viewer, the devastating look of the beloved so prevalent in courtly love poetry. Just as Daedalus crafts both death and resurrection, Icarus has been crafted as both imperiled subject and imperiling object of the gaze, for the moral of this verse is directed at the reader/viewer, who is reminded by *looking* that not all bold lovers can rise from the ashes.[55]

The Daedalus and Icarus myth may not seem a likely candidate for encrypted homoeroticism, but, as Marino's poem suggests, something erotic obtains to visualizing Icarus. The story of Icarus and Daedalus was the subject of many European artists from the sixteenth through the eighteenth century who found in its imagery an opportunity to explore the relation between two male bodies, often in contrasting states of motion.[56] Peter Paul Rubens chose the frequently depicted climactic moment for his famous 1636 oil sketch *The Fall of Icarus* (figure 6). The sketch shows Icarus poised to plummet headlong from the air, back arched with his chest to the viewer, as Daedalus glides by, confident in flight but helplessly watching his son's fall. Even in this moment of horror, Rubens eroticizes Icarus by depicting his tunic as mere drapery on his groin, his clothing violently disheveled by his twisting body. Just as Icarus is suspended on the brink of falling, so the viewer is on the brink of seeing his genitals; we are invited to imagine the fall, and the falling away of the cloth that would follow, through which we take measure of his corporeal heft.

The theme of the winged Icarus before flight is surprisingly common in

Figure 6. Peter Paul Rubens, *The Fall of Icarus*, ca. 1636. Oil on panel.
Royal Museums of Fine Arts of Belgium, Brussels.

the visual depictions of this myth, despite its lack of dramatic action.
Anthony van Dyck chose another popularly depicted moment in his
Daedalus and Icarus (ca. 1620): it is the moment when Daedalus warns a
winged Icarus to stay the middle course (figure 7). As in the Rubens painting, drapery is gathered precariously around Icarus's groin, but here it
amplifies the smoothness of his naked skin. The white, youthful torso of
Icarus dominates the painting. His naked chest is thrust out, his lips pout,
and his eyes stare directly at us, as if in mild defiance of the confines both
of his father's request and of the painting itself. Yet he seems all too vulnerable to the potential doom that Daedalus, from the shadow of the boy's
wings, communicates with gesture and furrowed brow. The viewer is immediately attracted to the youth's body, but not in a vision of eroticized terror;
rather, it is a vision of the classical ephebe, the androgynous, impetuous
beauty on the brink.

Figure 7. Anthony van Dyck, *Daedalus and Icarus,*
ca. 1620. Oil on canvas. Art Gallery of Ontario,
Toronto. Gift of Mr. and Mrs. Frank P. Wood, 1940.

The same moment in the myth is depicted in Andrea del Sarto's *Icarus*
(Florence, ca. 1507; figure 8). A winged Icarus stands naked on a rock in the
center of the space, with one hip raised above the other, his body forming a
gentle curve. Scholars have noted that his pose seems to have been modeled
on Michelangelo's famous erotic sculpture *David,* but Icarus's head is disproportionately small compared to his torso; his genitals are at the center of
the image.[57] His mother is the one who indicates that he should choose the
middle path; her finger points to the middle of his torso, as if it were a map.
Indeed, against the background of land, sea, and sky, her finger points out
for the viewer exactly where he should fly, and identifies his body with that
middle path. His father, however, grips him by the arm, preventing his
imminent flight; like the Icarus of van Dyck, the boy is shown in a state of
voluptuous potency, ready to go, on the brink of unruliness.

A white marble bas-relief of Daedalus and Icarus at the Villa Albani in
Rome offers another homoerotic visual study of Daedalus and Icarus at the

Figure 8. Andrea del Sarto, *Icarus,* ca. 1507. Oil
on panel. Palazzo Davanzati, Florence. Photo:
Alinari / Art Resource, NY.

point of their greatest physical potential (figure 9). Daedalus, in profile, sits
at a workbench fabricating a wing, his hand grips a tool (an *ascia*) in mid-
action, and his eyes focus on his invention. Icarus stands idly by with his
wings strapped to his chest, watching his father and delicately fingering the
wing upon which his father works. The scene corresponds to the moment in
the myth when Icarus interferes with his father, fingering wax and wings. His
body, with its softly muscled contours, is positioned so that it faces the viewer,
although his head is turned toward Daedalus. The sculptor has placed him
leaning on a pedestal, one hip thrust upward as in the del Sarto painting,
accentuating the pelvis and creating a gentle curve out of his body, which
visually parallels the shape of the wings—the ubiquitous erotic serpentine
line that fascinated eighteenth-century art historian Johann Joachim Winckelmann.[58] It seems here as if the viewer is invited to compare and eroticize
these two male figures, the adult in action and the ephebe in repose, an
erotic pairing that is a motif in classical art.

Figure 9. Daedalus and Icarus, Roman
marble relief. Museo di Villa Albani, Rome.
Photo: Alinari / Art Resource, NY.

This relief is, in fact, the product of a fusion of ancient and mid-eighteenth-century ideals, for only the torso of Icarus—roughly from the upper thighs to the chin—are antique; the rest had been restored, perhaps for Albani's collection, based on a second-century-C.E. "red porcelain" (*rosso antico*) bas-relief of the same scene. The more complete relief, which is also part of the Albani collection, features a younger-looking Icarus, without wings, and an older-looking Daedalus, whose back is more bent, limbs more frail. Thus the eighteenth-century restorer closed the age gap between the father and son, and amplified the erotic potency of both.[59]

Cardinal Alessandro Albani was a collector of classical antiquities who in the mid-eighteenth century commissioned the villa that housed these pieces. He was also the patron of male scholars and connoisseurs who flocked to the Villa Albani and created what G. S. Rousseau describes as an "unrivaled nervecenter for combined antiquarian and homosocial activity." He goes on to say, "In the unique atmosphere of this Roman villa, many homosexual aesthetes, in addition to Winckelmann, the bisexual Mengs, and the homosocial Richard Payne Knight, discovered their artistic and erotic sides conjoined."[60] At the Villa Albani, for example, Knight began to plan his book *A Discourse on the Worship of Priapus* (1786), "the first extensive treatment of phallic symbolism, an Enlightenment landmark in the development of sexual symbols."[61] Winckelmann also made the villa his home; it was the place where he wrote his monumental *Geschichte der Kunst des Altertums* (1764). Through this and other works, Winckelmann's richly erotic descriptions of the "hermaphrodite" as the ancient Greek and Roman ideal—the composite of both sexes yielding an ideal beauty—were highly influential, especially in the burgeoning literature of *Bildung. Bildung* is a word and concept that became prominent in German literature in the late eighteenth and early nineteenth centuries. In literature it was associated with the ideals of autonomy and humanistic progress, yet it could also be associated with religious mysticism, which calls autonomy and progress into question.[62] Many writers on *Bildung* in the decades around 1800 believed that the theater and visual arts (and less frequently music) could enable self-realization. Winckelmann's writings inspired a fashion for androgyny in contemporaneous German literature and art (notably in the works of Johann Wolfgang Goethe, Wilhelm von Humboldt, Friedrich Schiller, and Friedrich Schlegel), as well as in the works of the later nineteenth-century Oxford Hellenists such as Walter Pater.[63]

Cardinal Albani's patronage of Winkelmann and others is the most famous eighteenth-century example of how the alliance between art, classics, and homosocial networks facilitated contemplations of gender and creative homoerotic expressions. Fifty years earlier, as Harris's study documents, Cardinal Pamphili's patronage of Handel and others yielded a similar alliance, producing similarly creative homoerotic expressions.[64]

Pamphili's *Tra le fiamme* fused the courtly Icarus of poets with the eroticized Icarus of the visual artists in a reimagining of Icarus's flight as a homoerotic flirtation. The first aria sets up the parallel between the heart that is deceived by a beautiful face and the fatal attraction of a moth to a flame:

Tra le fiamme tu scherzi per gioco,	Among the flames you play for fun,
o mio core, per farti felice,	oh my heart, seeking happiness,
e t'inganna una vaga beltà.	and a fair beauty deceives you.
Cadon mille farfalle nel foco,	A thousand moths fall into the fire,
é si trova una sola fenice	but there is only one phoenix,
che risorge se a morte sen va.	who can rise again, after succumbing to death.[65]

The courtly Icarus tradition is evident in his use of the phoenix trope, but it should also be noted that Pamphili's adopted Arcadian name was Fenicio Larisseo, incorporating *fenice,* the phoenix.[66] The reference to the phoenix, then, links Pamphili himself to Icarus. A passage from the second recitative, however, identifies the phoenix with Daedalus: "There have been many Icaruses, but only one Daedalus" *(moti gl'Icari son, Dédalo un solo)*—a line that echoes the earlier "thousand moths . . . one phoenix" image in the first aria. It is Daedalus who rises like a phoenix from flames of passion, while Icarus succumbs to fatal attraction; Daedalus can rejuvenate himself through his art, while his art lures many Icaruses into certain immolation.[67]

Only the first recitative paraphrases the *Metamorphoses'* foreshadowing of doom when Icarus interferes with his father's work (the scene depicted in the Albani bas-relief). The rest of the poem, however, does not tell the story in a linear fashion but rather presents a series of reflective stanzas that focus on Icarus's exuberance in flight, as the A section from the second aria illustrates:

Pien di nuovo e bel diletto	Filled with a new and sweet pleasure,
sciolse l'ali il giovinetto	the youth let free his wings,
é con l'aure gìa scherzando	already frolicking with the breezes.

In the third aria, Pamphili offers a curious moral to the story:

Voli per l'aria chi può volare	Leave flying through the air to those who can,
scorra veloce, la terra, il mare. . . .	let them run quickly over land and sea. . . .
Voli ancor l'uomo ma coi pensieri	Let man also fly, but with his thoughts,
che delle piume *ben* più leggieri e più sublimi il ciel gli diè.	which, more swift and more sublime than feathers, heaven gave to him.

The tragedy of Icarus's fall has been nearly erased from the story; there is no description of Icarus's terror, nor a mournful aria from Daedalus on his son's death. Pamphili's poem seems not so much a parable about man's hubris in his attempts to defy natural or divine law, but rather a little lesson in distinguishing between reality and fantasy—one that itself revels in the fantasy of hubris, of being *out* of nature's constraints.

As with *Hendel, non può mia musa,* some of the images in this poem carry sexual innuendos. Phoenix and flames can stand for sexual excitement, *diletto* (delight) for sexual pleasure, flight for an erection. We might also understand the word *morte* (death) in the line "*é si trova una sola fenice, che risorge se a morte sen va*" (but there is only one phoenix, who can rise again, after succumbing to death) as a metaphor for orgasm; the words "morte" and "morire" could mean submission generically or, more specifically, submission within a sodomitical sex act.[68] The use of death as a metaphor for orgasm is widespread in sixteenth- and seventeenth-century poems and song. Occasionally the idea of resurrection appears in the same context to suggest unquenchable sexual appetite.[69] These double entendres form a semantic background to Pamphili's lyric. Clearly Pamphili followed the Italian poetic traditions, but, notably, without a metaphorical link to a female beloved. Within the male homosocial realm of Pamphili's court, then, patriarchal masculinity could stretch to encompass the role of the daring, inventive lover, as well as the resourceful, beguiling beloved.

That Pamphili may be referring to Handel as the beloved object of his sexual desire is further suggested by an overlap between the rhetoric of *Tra le fiamme* and that of certain excerpts from Pamphili's libretto for the oratorio *Il trionfo del tempo*, composed a few months earlier. Following her discussion of the erotic flattery of *Hendel, non può mia musa*, Harris quotes passages from the oratorio's allegorical figures Pleasure and Beauty, which she believes "doubtless [refer] to the 22-year-old Handel." One exchange contains images in common with *Tra le fiamme* (in bold):

Pleasure:

Un leggiadro **giovinetto**	A graceful **youth,**
Bel diletto	Awakens **sweet delight**
Desta in suono lusinghier.	With enticing tones.
E vuol far con **nuovo invito**	And with **new allurements**
Che l'udito	He would make listening
Abbia ancor il suo piacer	Have its own pleasure.

Beauty:

Ha della destra **l'ali,**	His hand has **wings,**
Anzi **fa con la mano**	Or rather he **makes with his hand**
Opre **più che mortali.**	Music **more than mortal.**[70]

A winged youth, new exquisite pleasures, masterful hands that transform raw material into divine art: these passages from the oratorio in tandem with *Tra le fiamme* offer more evidence of flirtation. Music, according to the oratorio, is Handel's pair of wings. According to the poetic and visual tradition associated with Daedalus and Icarus, wings signify potency, both erotic and artistic. In the cantata, Pamphili indirectly compares the young composer to the archetypical artist-craftsman who made those wings. Much like Orpheus, Daedalus defied the laws of nature with inventions that invite flights of fancy, and that seem to promise phoenixlike rejuvenation. But Pamphili, rejuvenated as Icarus in the throes of a dangerous passion, knew full well that only Daedalus would remain unscathed.

In her study of Handel's chamber cantatas, most composed early in his career, Harris focuses on those in which the lyric subject is female (or, in Harris's terms, cantatas for a "woman's voice"), making the important observation that "Handel's cantatas for women strikingly adhere to an earlier, seventeenth-century concept of the cantata (and opera) as recitative monologue (or dramatic recitation) interrupted by lyrical passages."[71] The free, irregular forms of both the micro- and macrostructures of these cantatas signify the unruliness of women's passions, epitomized in the dramatic laments of abandoned women. Harris goes on to note that "From the outset, the cantatas for men are structurally simpler and more modern; based on the recitative-aria pair, they include, with the rarest exceptions, only *da capo* arias. Not only do they all end with an aria, but *Tra le fiamme* even builds an aria frame with the repetition of the *da capo* from the opening aria to end the cantata."[72] She convincingly argues that "Handel found the breadth and depth of his own expressive voice by trying on the voices of abandoned women."[73] It is, however, in the ultramodern *Tra le fiamme* (one of Handel's earliest cantatas for voice and instruments) that Handel explores the construction of his own desire with reference to the story of Daedalus's artistic and technological feat.

The unusual return of the *da capo* from the opening aria is key to an assessment of Handel's "voice" in this third-person narrative. Indeed, a stream of vigorous, tuneful arias dominates this cantata, cushioned by short, modulatory *secco* recitatives. Handel's music for the first and most substantial aria (it is nearly four times as long as the other two arias) cleverly generates a complex atmosphere of exuberance and fragility with its juxtaposition of the solo treble voice (probably performed by a *castrato*) and the solo viola da gamba (or viol). The viol was falling out of favor with composers of the period, especially in Italy. Rome, however, was an exception, and Pamphili's retinue of musicians included a viol player named "Monsieur Sciarli" who likely performed *Tra le fiamme*. By the eighteenth century German composers often used the viola da gamba, which had a light and dry, reedy tone in comparison to the warmer violin and cello, for special effects, or in association with a solemn affect such as lamentations and sacred contemplations. Handel's oratorio *La Resurrezione* (spring 1708) also calls for an obligato viola da gamba, which Lucy Robinson describes as "in keeping with the German association of the viol representing the solace of the Resurrection."[74] In *Tra le fiamme,* Handel dispensed with such weighty cultural filiations, exploiting instead the instrument's feathery timbre to translate aurally the feeling and motion of flight.

Viol and voice appear in the first aria as equal partners in a duet, or as two different extensions of one body. Handel (Daedalus/beloved) animates the voice and viol, which signify Icarus (Pamphili/lover), sometimes with a humorous twist, as in the opening ritornello. The ritornello, scored for two violins, two recorders, and a continuo group, features the viola da gamba playing a solo full of upward leaps and zigzagging descendents, which get higher with each repetition (example 9). It is Icarus as a fledgling, determined but uncertain in his first chance at flight.

The voice and viol enter together, without accompaniment, in measure 22, and this sets up their intimate association, which continues throughout

Example 9. George Frideric Handel, *Tra le fiamme* (1707), "Tra le fiamme," mm. 8–15.

the cantata as they flutter about each other exchanging turns and trills or join together to fly in parallel third formations. In this first aria, Handel places one such intimate flight of voice and viol over the word *inganna* (deceives) (example 10)—a grand melisma that begins with fitful flapping (mm. 78–79) and opens out to glorious swooping (mm. 81–84). We can hear recklessness in this gesture, a blissful ignorance of danger, or perhaps that masochistic delight in self-deception described by Italian Renaissance poets.

The sensual abandon of the first aria becomes a more youthful abandon in the second ("Pien di nuovo e bel diletto"), with swift transitions back and forth between grandiose, assertive dotted rhythms and buoyant triplets. Although this aria describes the heady pleasures and exciting dangers of flying high on (love's) wings, the voice and viol surprisingly do not take off together in extended solos. The vocal melismas on *scherzando* (frolicking, playing) in the A section and *mormorando* (murmuring) in the B section begin instead with a series of false starts that combine an octave-leaping dotted-note figure (coordinated with an attack on the bass-note pedal) with incrementally ascending triplets. Once the triplets get off the ground, the viol enters, followed by a violin solo, as if to suggest that the young fledgling glides on an updraft of air (example 11).

By way of contrast, the third aria has extensive solo sections for voice and viol (and sometimes flutes); the viol plays a dark and furious *perpetuum mobile* against stabbing violin arpeggios. The voice weaves in and out, sometimes joining in the viol's efforts, at other times gliding on its energetic gust of music. The resulting mood seems to suggest a curious musical overstatement of the lyric's mild injunction to leave the real flying to real birds, and to be satisfied with the more sublime flight of thought. The middle section is mostly without bass support, and without the viol; flutes and voice are suspended in the upper register, "ungrounded" in their flight (example 12). An abrupt silence ends this section; it is the only moment of pause in the *perpetuum mobile* of the aria, perhaps signaling the moment of Icarus's fall. Indeed, the words of this middle section describe the flight of imagination that is permitted to humans by heaven; once these words are stated, the incessant physical motion momentarily ceases. What Handel seems to be expressing in this final aria is neither the exuberance of the courtly Icarus (as in the first aria), nor the erotic impetuousness of the youthful Icarus (as in the second aria), but rather Daedalus's own vigorous struggles against the limits of nature.

The final, third recitative, before the return of the first aria, echoes the sentiment of the third aria, but, rather than an admonishment, it presents a simple description of what man does (or, perhaps, what a man such as the cardinal does): with his thoughts anchored to the ground, he flies with wings of fantasy *(con ali che si finge)*. But, having thus dryly proclaimed that imagination is the only real means of flight and pleasure, Handel then returns to the opening *da capo* aria. With its text about moths and flames, and its

Example 10. George Frideric Handel, *Tra le fiamme* (1707), "Tra le fiamme," mm. 75–90.

(continued)

Example 10 *(continued)*

exuberant intimate flights of voice and viol, this return represents the reju-
venating flame from which the phoenix will emerge. That flame is the content of the fantasies that allow men to fly, that is, dangerous erotic attractions. It is also Handel's statement about artistic power. With the novelty of
the large-scale *da capo* form, Handel resurrects artist and audience and sends
them on infinite flights of fancy and hubris.

Nearly a century before Handel's cantata, Francis Bacon published his *De
sapientia veterum* (1609), which was translated into English as *The Wisdome of
the Ancients* by Arthur Gorges (1619). The English version circulated in subsequent editions well into the late seventeenth century. In this book Bacon,
much like Joseph Campbell, examined ancient myths for their messages
about moral action. The myth of Icarus he understood to be a parable for
choosing the "middle way" between excess and defect. Bacon, however, finds
Icarus's "youthful excesses" more commendable than the "defects" of age. As
Gorges translates, "youth commonly makes choyse of the better, defect
being alwayes accounted worst, for whereas excess contains some sparks of
magnanimity, and like a bird claimes kindred of the Heavens, defect onely
like a base worm crawls upon the earth." But he goes on to say that "there
must be moderation used, that this light [from the sun] be subtilized *[sic]* . . .
and not destroyed by too much fervency. And this much every man for the

Example 11. George Frideric Handel, *Tra le fiamme* (1707), "Pien di nuovo e bel diletto," mm. 12–16.

most part knows."[75] Moderation, for Bacon, is the harnessing of excess—its *subtle* use.

If, as Harris argues, Handel in 1707 routinely expressed dangerous passion in the medium of the voices of abandoned mythological women, and in the dramatic realism of an earlier arioso style, then *Tra le fiamme,* with its modern large-scale formal design and its focus on the more controlled, "artificial" affective statements of the arias, says something quite different about that same topic. Simply put, it engages fantasy over realism, pleasure over suffering; Handel "subtilizes" (to borrow from Bacon) the erotic excesses of Icarus

Example 12. George Frideric Handel, *Tra le fiamme* (1707), "Voli per l'aria chi può volare," mm. 38–46.

Example 12 *(continued)*

sie - ri che del-le piu-me più leg - gie-rie più sub-li - mi il ciel gli diè.

using music, and more generally all art, as the "middle way" for the expression of homoerotic desire. This means of negotiating dangerous attraction—Freud would call it sublimation—anticipates the aesthetes and the antiquarians, such as Winckelmann, who would gather in the villas of Italian cardinals and mingle their homoerotic attraction with their study of ancient Apollos.

COMING OUT INTO THE MIDDLE

Winckelmann described beauty as "nothing other than the middle between two extremes. Just as the middle path is always the best, it is always the most beautiful."[76] This idea of beauty, Winckelmann believed, was embodied in the hermaphrodite, the middle between male and female. It was the androgynous figures in classical statues, many depicting male youths or ephebes, that attracted his attention and gave rise to his theories. Catriona MacLeod has studied the aesthetic of androgyny during the Enlightenment and Romantic periods, and she sees a parallel between Winckelmann's aesthetic theory of the beautiful androgyne and his own approach to life as "a mode of existence through art that is neither simply active nor simply passive, neither wholly 'male' nor wholly 'female.'"[77] Winckelmann was fascinated with the indeterminate genders of ancient statues; he believed such statues presented, to the keen observer, examples of dynamic metamorphosis. Describing one statue, he writes, "The face of this young hero is completely *feminine* when one looks at it *from below;* and it seems that something *masculine* is mixed in with it when one looks at it *from above.*"[78] Yet the hermaphrodite in real life was, and still is, a monstrosity to most viewers. So, too, was the hybrid Minotaur contained within Daedalus's labyrinth. MacLeod suggests that Daedalus looms in the background of Winckelmann's thinking, as a "mythological analogue" to himself and his androgynous aesthetic.[79] For Winckelmann, the "middle way" was not the careful path, the means of avoiding danger or conflict; rather, it was the path that emerged from passion and confrontation. "In order to find the middle," he wrote, "one must know the two extremes."[80]

Winckelmann cut an impressive figure for several generations of aristocratic and upwardly mobile bourgeois youths. These young men sojourned to Italy to become his pupils in a rite of passage through aesthetic education. His own rags-to-riches biography—"as a schoolboy he had been forced to supplement the family income through singing"[81]—gave him a mystique that was as much a Siren song as the ancient art about which he wrote. Winckelmann consciously hoped to channel the energy of sexual awakening in his young students into aesthetic contemplation by encouraging and describing a relationship of desire between the observer and the art object.[82] Goethe, who wrote about Winckelmann (but who had little, if any, direct contact with the man himself),[83] absorbed many aspects of his theories about achieving Enlightenment through the aesthetic encounter. He integrated these influences into his monumental *Bildungsromane, Wilhelm Meisters Lehrjahre* (1796) and *Wilhelm Meisters Wanderjahre* (1821, revised 1823). As previously mentioned, these novels and their many imitations concerned the psychological growth and spiritual progress of a young man who begins, metaphorically, as an androgynous, sexually "mobile" ephebe, "between a female, childish past and a male, adult future, eternally receptive to *Bildung.*"[84] The youth then navigates the perilous road to aesthetic maturity and (hetero)sexual definition. In Goethe's *Wilhelm Meisters Lehrjahre,* Wilhelm's *Bildung* is effected to a large extent through encounters with a parade of androgynous women to whom he is strongly attracted (Mariane, Mignon, Therese, and the "Amazon" Natalie). The human visual quandaries of gender presented by these women add to the entanglement of real life and theater at the heart of this *Bildungsroman.* The young Mignon, the central one of these figures, initially changes gender before Wilhelm's eyes, like Winckelmann's statue. This is reflected in the pronouns of the text: Mignon is "she" in one sentence and "he" in the next (see book 2.4). Although Wilhelm decides early on that Mignon is a girl, Mignon resists this gender designation until the end of the novel, when she becomes mortally homesick for Italy. It is the call to Italy, the adopted home of Winckelmann and destination for young men seeking *Bildung,* that feminizes her. Whereas Winckelmann saw the androgyne as the aesthetic endpoint and a metaphorical guide for life, Goethe developed a progress narrative in which the androgyne was a stage on the way to normative gender and heterosexuality.

. . .

Rock and roll songs may seem far removed from nineteenth-century *Bildungsromane,* but many songs share with them the topos of a male subject, frequently androgynous, who undergoes an education and transformation through art, or, in the case of rock and roll, music. Beginning with the mascara and pompadours of Little Richard and Elvis Presley in the 1950s, rock musicians have long presented themselves as conundrums of race and gender for adolescent contemplation. The quintessential model for a rock and roll *Bildungsroman* is Chuck Berry's "Johnny B. Goode" (1958), which tells of the education and maturation of a young "Johnny" who reaches the peak of his sexual and economic powers through his guitar and rock and roll music. This tale has been passed down not only in numerous covers and self-reflexive spin-offs, but also in the many rock movies of the 1960s starring Elvis Presley. The plots of these movies often recall the narrative of Elvis's own life: a young nobody with musical talent is discovered, and he is transformed by music into a powerful, sexual adult. Darker versions of this core rock and roll narrative emerged later in concept albums such as Pink Floyd's *The Wall* (1979). Since the late 1990s, the popular television series *VH1's Behind the Music* has managed to reduce the biographies of rock stars to a concise narrative formula: an epic struggle from rags to riches, through the trials of drugs and debauchery, and finally the redemption of sobriety, age, and a newfound artistry supposedly deepened through adversity.

Glam rock began to rewrite the end of the story by imagining that the male subject undergoes a metamorphic corruption of masculinity. Emerging in the early 1970s in the wake of the "sexual revolution," glam rock incorporated aspects of gay subcultures—drag, camp, androgyny, bisexuality—as an antagonistic response to the commercialized sincerity of blues- and folk-based hippie bands, the machismo of heavy metal, and the pretentiousness of "art rock." The pioneering glam rocker Marc Bolan of T. Rex affected an eighteenth-century fop style, with long curly hair, women's frilly shirts, makeup, and a sprinkling of glitter on his face. His music combined effeminate low-volume vocals, a slow funky beat, fuzzy guitar timbres, and image-rich lyrics full of sexual innuendo. As musicians such as David Bowie, Roxy Music, and Queen merged glam with art rock, songs and albums began to express more fantastical self-creation through epic stories and elaborate theatrical performances. In these narratives, putatively "normal" but vaguely discontented young men transformed into androgynous space aliens (Bowie), queer aristocratic bohemians (Queen and Roxy Music), or something more nightmarish, in the case of Alice Cooper. The wildly successful cult movie *The Rocky Horror Picture Show* (1976) belongs here as well, with its celebration of polymorphous perversity and transvestism and a motto that could have come from the mouth of Daedalus: "Don't dream it, be it."

In the next section, I will examine four such stories of queer rock and roll *Bildung*, metamorphoses through music that immolate the masculine subject and bring out from its ashes something quite different: a new, indeterminately gendered subject. In the first a poor boy becomes a bohemian ("Bohemian Rhapsody"); in the second, suburbanites become transvestites *(The Rocky Horror Picture Show);* in the third, a "worm-boy" becomes the Antichrist (Marilyn Manson's *Antichrist Superstar*); and in the fourth, a transsexual becomes an unnamable, self-gendered glam rock star *(Hedwig and the Angry Inch).*

A Sojourn to Italy: "Bohemian Rhapsody"

With its eclectic mix of music styles, hints of homoeroticism, and campy (if not downright goofy) nod to Italian opera, Queen's "Bohemian Rhapsody" seems an unlikely song to have become the anthem for suburban teenage boys. Yet after its initial release in late 1975, the song reached number one in England, where it stayed for a record-breaking nine weeks.[85] The band also had wild success in Japan. In 1992 "Bohemian Rhapsody" enjoyed a phoenix-like resurrection when it was featured in the movie *Wayne's World*. During this second life, "Bohemian Rhapsody" reached number two on the American charts, climbing higher than it had in 1976, when it peaked at number nine. The song was, and still is, an emblem of 1970s excess and bombast; it was the most expensive single song ever produced, and it was long, clocking in at six minutes—twice the normal playing time.

From the very beginning of the band's career, lead singer and songwriter Freddie Mercury (born Farookh Bulsara) liberally sprinkled gay innuendos throughout his lyrics and song styles. The name Queen, for example, mixes campy gay slang with images of royalty and aristocracy.[86] Further images of precious refinement were given voice in Mercury's nostalgic British music hall numbers, such as their first big hit "Killer Queen" (1974) and especially "Old Fashioned Lover Boy" (1976). These vaudeville-style songs call to mind the 1920s dandy, along with his female counterpart, the flapper. According to the memoirs of Mercury's personal assistant, sexual references lay close to the surface of many lyrics. Mercury would first compose phrases with off-color "dummy" words and then clean them up later: "Guilt stains on my pillow" began as "Cum stains on my pillow," "Radio Ga Ga" as "Radio Ca Ca," and "Staying Power" as "Fucking Power."[87] It is easy to imagine how something similar could be true for "Bohemian Rhapsody."

The word "bohemian" has long been a catchall word for people who live outside the norm on the margins of mainstream society, typically artists, writers, and musicians who were also sexual "free spirits." Mercury intended "Bohemian Rhapsody" to be a "mock opera," something outside the norm of rock songs, and it does follow a certain operatic logic: choruses of multi-tracked voices alternate with arialike solos, the emotions are excessive, the plot confusing. An opening chorus draws the listener in with a question that seems equally appropriate to *Tra le fiamme* or *Wilhelm Meisters Lehrjahre*: "Is this the real life, is this just fantasy?" We are on another musical flight of fancy, another sublimation of passions, as the first aria suggests:

> Mama, just killed a man
> Put a gun against his head,
> Pulled my trigger, now he's dead.[88]

This might be a simple story of murder, but it also seems to be a melodrama of homoeroticism. Guns, after all, are phallic; the phrase "*my* trigger" clearly locates "the gun" on the body. The lack of subject pronouns creates confusion over agency: exactly who has pulled the trigger? The son? The other man? The mother?—for the juxtaposition of sexual double entendres with "Mama" invites an Oedipal reading, in which the son has killed the father out of desire for the mother. The second verse of the aria seems to corroborate a sexual reading:

> Too late, my time has come,
> Sends shivers down my spine,
> Body's aching all the time.

We seem to be in a realm of both guilt and desire. For the many adolescents listening to this song, these phrases could describe the physical sensations of sexual awakening and the conflicting emotions that accompany them. If that sexual awakening is queer, then the greater the guilt and the need for confession.

The middle section of "Bohemian Rhapsody"—the operatic fantasy—is both a comic courtroom trial and a rite of passage.[89] Our young hero, having confessed his (sexual) crime to his mother, leaves home to "face the truth" and finds himself in a queer world of Italian opera. His voyage is represented by a melodious guitar solo that abruptly segues to a simple piano beat. This whole instrumental interlude recalls the same structural moment in the Beatles' own magnum opus "A Day in the Life" (1967), when the grand orchestral texture of the first dreamy section suddenly comes to a crashing cadence and is followed by a simple piano beat. In "A Day in the Life," this segue marks a shift from psychedelic ponderings ("I'd love to turn you on") to quotidian activities ("Got up, got out of bed, dragged the comb across my head"). The same piano beat in "Bohemian Rhapsody," however, becomes the accompaniment to music that emulates Gilbert and Sullivan, complete with patter recitative and choral interjections.[90] The scene begins with a barrage of random Italianisms and references to opera characters: silhouetto, Scaramouch, fandango, Gallileo, Figaro, magnifico, and, later, "Mama mia." In the trial, one chorus prosecutes, another defends, while the hero presents himself as meek though wily.

Solo: I'm just a poor boy from a poor family

Chorus: He's just a poor boy, from a poor family, spare him his life from this monstrosity

Solo: Easy come, easy go—, will you let me go—

Antiphonal Choruses: Bismillah! (No) We will not let you go (let him go) . . .

The music builds up to the climactic hard rock finale, announced by a cymbal crash, an energetic guitar riff, and hard rock beat. The hero turns defiant ("so you think you can stone me and spit in my eye") and emerges victorious from the trial by opera as a rock and roll rebel ("just gotta get right out of here").

If there is a lesson to be learned in this rite of passage, it is encrypted in the mischievous phrases we hear in the coda, which returns to the soft melancholic music of the opening aria: "Nothing really matters," "Any way the wind blows." Despite the song's outright goofiness, these statements add a level of complex resistance to the song's already charming subversion of macho rock and roll. Indeed, this resistance is its *Bildung.* I certainly heard it that way in high school. These words "brought me out," convinced me of the cosmic triviality of my concerns about being homosexual. The song delivered a slightly nihilistic but certainly devil-may-care message apropos to my internal prosecution, defense, and mental brinkmanship. But more importantly, the song suggests resistance through the adoption of a "bohemian" stance toward identity, which involves a necessarily changeable self-definition ("any way the wind blows").

Just as travels to Italy initiated the aesthetic education and psychosexual awakening of young men in the eighteenth century, here a sojourn into Italian opera might similarly initiate young men (and women) into the ways of a "bohemian" defiance of normative sex roles. In the late 1970s and 1980s, Mercury's stage act became more obviously influenced by gay-macho styles: he cut his long hair, grew a mustache, and wore leather biker outfits or muscle shirts. *Rolling Stone* reports that only with this new macho style did audiences in the United States begin to suspect that Mercury was gay, apparently not admitting the gay potential of the band's name (Queen), nor the gay influences in Mercury's earlier glam look and dandy music.[91] But despite Mercury's evolution from gender-bending glam rocker to strutting gay-macho stereotype, the queer excesses of "Bohemian Rhapsody," which reconfigured the masculine rock subject from guitar hero to opera queen, became integrated into the repertory of musical poses for young suburban men.

The song's suburban reception is both celebrated and spoofed in the 1992 movie *Wayne's World.* The movie tells the story of Wayne and Garth, two long-haired nerdy men of indeterminate age who live in Aurora, Illinois, a suburb outside Chicago.[92] Although they appear to have graduated from high school, their development has been arrested at a stage of adolescent aimlessness and rock-star worship. Wayne still lives with his parents, and Garth displays infantile nonverbal responses to women and strangers. In one of the movie's early character-establishing scenes, Wayne, Garth, and a few of their buddies drive around town listening to music in Wayne's AMC Pacer (an unusually wide but compact car that became an icon of 1970s suburbia). Wayne pops "Bohemian Rhapsody" into the tape player and the scruffy young men instantly begin to lip-synch the operatic middle section with great animation, vigorously bob their heads in time to the hard rock finale, and then turn calm and pensive—still dutifully mouthing the words—as the melancholic coda plays. We laugh at the time warp of the suburbs, whose young men are stuck in a 1970s adolescence; and we laugh at the goofy song and its ability to animate these beer-drinking, rock-loving, regular suburban "guys." The humor of the scene is amplified by a feeling of voyeurism; we witness an intimate moment of unselfconsciousness, of shared private pantomimes to this song. The young men look completely docile and content in the womblike car, safely contained in their homosocial world. We cannot help but recall our own pantomimes, and those of our friends, or wonder just how many suburban young men over the years, listening to Queen's "Bohemian Rhapsody," likewise became momentary opera queens before grabbing their air guitars at crotch level for the finale's famous riff.

Sexual Enlightenment at the "Frankenstein Place"

Suburban naïveté, queer sexual awakening, audience pantomime, and a celebration of androgyny all converge in the cult movie musical *The Rocky Horror Picture Show*. The movie began as a play (called *The Rocky Horror Show*) that was written by Englishman Richard O'Brien and first produced in London in 1973. For this play, O'Brien merged his experience in musical theater (he had appeared in London productions of *Hair* and *Jesus Christ Superstar*, both of which exploit late 1960s countercultural attitudes) with his particular interest in the phenomenon of late-night, science fiction, double-feature movie screenings. Such screenings, as Jonathan Rosenbaum points out, had a "cultish atmosphere, nurtured by the deep-rooted English tradition of the private club—a legal category to which some of the late-night London venues belonged."[93] The plot pays homage to the B-grade science fiction movies that anchored the cultish/clubbish experience, but also to movie musicals, teenage coming-of-age stories, and culture-clash movies such as *Rebel Without a Cause* (1955) and *Easy Rider* (1969).

A sexually uptight Midwestern American couple, Brad and Janet, fatefully encounter the aliens from the planet Transsexual, in the galaxy of Transylvania, and their polymorphously perverse transvestite leader Dr. Frank N. Furter. Dr. Frank N. Furter has just put the finishing touches on a perfect Adonis-like "man" whom he has created for his sexual pleasure. This encounter, which culminates in a musical chorus line number, awakens Brad and Janet sexually and, in the spirit of glam rock, liberates them from normative heterosexuality. The successful London play, which called for some audience participation,[94] was adapted for film by Lou Adler, who had earlier produced the "rockumentary" *Monterey Pop*. The movie version of *Rocky Horror* retained some members of the original London cast (Tim Curry and Richard O'Brien), and replaced others with up-and-coming American actors, including Susan Sarandon and Meatloaf (best known for his 1977 hard rock album *Bat Out of Hell*). Twentieth-Century Fox briefly released *The Rocky Horror Picture Show* in the summer of 1975, and then, after a careful marketing campaign, rereleased it in the spring of 1976 as—appropriately enough—a B movie for midnight showings in major cities.

A robust and highly organized cult formed around *The Rocky Horror Picture Show* in Los Angeles, where the play had an earlier successful run, and then, even more prominently, in the heart of New York's gay neighborhood, Greenwich Village, where the movie was screened at the Waverly Theater.[95] Over the span of several years, the largely gay audiences embellished—by popular account, spontaneously—the participation called for by the play with campy verbal wit, character drag, and burlesque props. This new style of interaction spread across the country and across demographics. At the height of the movie's cult popularity in the early 1980s, city dwellers and suburbanites, gays and straights, participated *together* in a ritualistic celebration of unfettered and undefined sexuality.[96] Audiences entered into the fantasy and ritual of the film through three channels: they dressed up and acted out the scenes along with the movie—a shadow performance that brought the monumental two-dimensional images to three-dimensional life; they engaged in unison verbal commentary, anticipating and responding to the screen dialogue or action; and they enacted moments in the film, or react to them, with props (for example, throwing dry toast in the air when Dr. Frank N. Furter raises his glass and announces "A toast"). National fan club newsletters, which began to appear as early as 1977, sometimes featured participation guides. In 1983 Lou Adler's Ode Records released *The Rocky Horror Picture Show Audience Par-Tic-I-Pation Album*, a double LP recording of the verbal responses at New York's 8th Street Playhouse in New York (which had taken over the Greenwich Village film screenings from the Waverly Theater in 1978). Such products standardized the responses to a limited but important degree; they fostered a familial feeling among cultists despite local inflections, and protected the original gay audience base from increasingly homophobic audience reactions.[97]

The film itself inspires repeated viewings and energetic, fetishistic audience responses by combining a frustratingly slow pace with a dense network of allusions to Christianity, ancient mythology, and, above all, Hollywood clichés and their self-conscious reversals. For example, the Frankensteinian "monster," Rocky, is a gorgeous blond muscle man, while the scientist Dr. Frank N. Furter appears as a monstrously bi-gendered creature.[98] This key reversal in turn sets up a scene ripped from Genesis, in which Janet, recently seduced by Dr. Frank N. Furter (whom the narrator later describes as "forbidden fruit"), herself seduces the intellectually infantile but physically mature Rocky—a B movie remake of the Fall of Adam and Eve.[99]

The plot bristles with emblems of Brad and Janet's metaphorical rite of passage and initiation into a world of unmanageable sexuality, a pilgrim's sexual progress echoed by cultists' designation of first-time viewers as "virgins." Brad and Janet's ordeal is treated with a heavy hand as "Enlightenment" by the movie and audience in the number "Over at the Frankenstein Place," which precedes Brad and Janet's entrance into Dr. Frank N. Furter's castle. Caught with a flat tire in a nighttime thunderstorm—while Nixon's resignation speech plays on the radio—Brad and Janet sing about the "light" they see in the windows of the "Frankenstein place," where they hope to make a phone call. It is in this scene that we learn not only of their Midwestern location, but of their status as suburbanites as well, for Janet clutches a Cleveland newspaper (*The Plain Dealer*) to protect her from the rain (while the audience likewise holds up newspapers and shoots squirt guns to simulate the rain). It is also a mark of the suburbanite that the vehicle of spiritual transportation should be a failed automobile, for suburbia owes its distinctive social ecology to the family car and the commutable highway. The song lyrics, however, turn this clichéd search for shelter into a metaphorical search for the "light in the darkness of everybody's life," the "sun and light" that must clear away "night's dreaming." The audience ignites cigarette lighters or turns on flashlights with every utterance of "light" in the chorus, extinguishing them with every utterance of "darkness," thus re-literalizing the song's metaphor, but also symbolically lighting the way for Brad and Janet to begin their spiritual/sexual rite of passage.

Two opposing ceremonies frame this rite. At the beginning of the movie there is a wedding, which designates the heterosexual status quo as the site of immaturity; at the end there is a musical floor show featuring a pool number (à la Esther Williams), which designates the fantastical and high camp movie musical as the baptismal font for sexual rebirth and maturity. Both ceremonies are characterized by careful orchestration and choreography, and both depict an ideal of social unity. In the wedding, two newlyweds (friends of Brad and Janet) emerge from the church into a shower of rice; the audience also takes part in this social ritual of matrimonial affirmation by showering itself with rice. And yet, for seasoned audience members, the dense visual references to American culture and later events in the film actually allow for an in-crowd reading against the *grain* of ritual participation. The images of American culture are conflicting: in one moment we see a billboard with the crass touristic slogan "Denton, Home of Happiness"; in another, the camera rests on the church custodians who at that moment duplicate Grant Wood's famous painting *American Gothic,* with all its rural dourness. (The painting also appears on one of the walls in the castle, right before the "Time Warp" number, which suggests that this dourness from outside—not the creatures within—haunts the castle.) Of course, the very term "gothic" gestures toward the literary genre in which the original *Frankenstein* is located. Early gothic literature used medieval ruins and shocking tales that insisted on the suspension of reason to shadow eighteenth-century Enlightenment ideals of rationality and order. Nineteenth-century Romanticism added idealism, horror, wilderness, and sexuality to form a literary genre characterized by emotional intensity and ethical extremes. For many, Mary Shelley's *Frankenstein, or The Modern Prometheus* (1818), with its macabre exploration of scientific irresponsibility and immorality, epitomizes this vein of writing. Suffering from guilt and revulsion, Dr. Frankenstein abandons his monstrous creation, whose loneliness and despair transforms into vengeful hatred, leading the monster to systematically kill those whom his creator loves, including, of course, his beloved fiancée. At the end of the novel, creator and creation are left in a perpetual hunt, forever doomed to remain each other's shadows.

Marjorie Garber reads Shelley's *Frankenstein* as "an uncanny anticipation of transsexual surgery," and she cites *Rocky Horror* as the evidence.[100] The opening scene of *Rocky Horror* also presents an uncanny doubling of actors who appear in eerily fleeting camera shots: the priest who has performed the wedding is none other than Tim Curry, who plays Dr. Frank N. Furter, the master of sexual ceremonies who ultimately undoes the sexual and protomarital knot of the suburbanites Brad and Janet. The church custodians who reproduced *American Gothic* likewise appear in parallel roles as Dr. Frank N. Furter's servants Riff Raff and Magenta. They are custodians of both Middle America's puritanical church and Frank N. Furter's libertine church. The dour gothic male Riff Raff in the end kills Dr. Frank N. Furter on account of his "extreme lifestyle," thus implementing the rigid morality alluded to in the visual reference to *American Gothic.*

A wedding functions as an initiation rite into the world of socially recognized adulthood and state-recognized citizenship. Inspired by their friends' marriage, Brad and Janet become engaged, thereby participating in imitative processes of compulsory heterosexuality. Seasoned viewers know, however, that the wedding in *Rocky Horror* marks the beginning of Brad and Janet's initiation into queer adulthood and citizenship, and this dual function of the wedding inside the movie is reinforced by a second, mock wedding between Dr. Frank N. Furter and Rocky, staged shortly after the monster's unveiling. The same wedding music and similar confetti-throwing guests accompany Dr. Frank N. Furter as he leads Rocky to their bridal suite and honeymoon night. Later that evening, Brad and Janet also become Dr. Frank N. Furter's "brides" when he seduces them one after the other. Rocky, Brad, Janet, and Dr. Frank N. Furter's one-time lover Columbia (now one of his groupies) end up in the floor show as a chorus line of Dr. Frank N. Furter replicas in transvestite uniform—pumps, black fishnet stockings with garter belt, sequin-covered corset, and Joan Crawford's standard heavy mascara and thick lipstick.

Most *Rocky Horror* fans admit that the principal attraction of the movie is Tim Curry's performance as Dr. Frank N. Furter. Curry achieves a perfect blend of the charismatic masculine power of Hollywood heroes with the mincing feminine delicacy and sex appeal of Hollywood heroines. Cultural critics disagree on which gender wins out in this bi-gendered superhero: Garber notes that the name Dr. Frank N. Furter, along with his costume, "make him the symbolic realization of the 'phallic woman,'" while Gaylyn Studlar emphasizes that Dr. Frank N. Furter's feminized maleness offers only superficial cover for his tyrannical and necessarily masculine phallic displays.[101]

Dr. Frank N. Furter's double-sexed body recalls the Greek images of a bearded Dionysus in a maiden's dress; both Dr. Frank N. Furter and Dionysus reproduce their playful disruptiveness by holding their similarly dressed followers in a choric trance.[102] Amittai F. Aviram notes that there are references to Euripides' *Bacchae* (circa 407 B.C.) throughout *Rocky Horror;* thus the floor show can be read in this context.[103] In the *Bacchae,* Dionysus comes to Thebes, his birthplace, to punish those who do not believe in his divinity by making them unwilling participants in a frenzied and violent dance. In *Rocky Horror,* Dr. Frank N. Furter devises the floor show to control his unruly initiates, for those whom he has bedded have nevertheless turned against him: Rocky and Janet have had a sexual liaison, Brad he suspects as a spy for the government (represented by the "intruder" Dr. Scott), and Columbia berates him for murdering her beloved Eddie (another of his former lovers whose brain he used for Rocky). The floor show, then, can be seen as a parallel to the Dionysian ritual in the *Bacchae:* it is coerced participation within the orgiastic ritual demanded by an angered god. In contrast to the violence unleashed in the *Bacchae,* however, the ritual in *Rocky Horror* unleashes only transsexual appetites.

Three numbers make up the floor show sequence. In the first, "Rose Tint My World," the four sexual initiates dance and sing in succession with highly individual movements and lyrics that summarize their confused states of mind. Columbia reminisces about being a "Frankie fan" and the sense of foreboding that she had when "he started working on a muscle man"; Rocky sings of being "seven hours old" and having an uncontrollable libido; Brad sings of his surprise at feeling sexy; Janet sings of being released from her inhibitions and having her mind expanded. The second number, "Don't Dream It," begins with an orchestral fanfare. A curtain opens onto Dr. Frank N. Furter's solo in front of an RKO radio tower. Here we have the god revealing himself in full form—that is, in the form of mythic Hollywood heroines such as Fay Wray, to whom he refers in the song. After singing a typical show-tune introductory verse, Dr. Frank N. Furter jumps into a swimming pool, the bottom of which depicts the scene from Michelangelo's Sistine Chapel ceiling in which God gives the touch of life to Adam. The initiates follow him there solemnly chanting the credolike refrain "Don't dream it, be it" and begin a watery orgy while they continue singing.

There is a progression from the individualism of the initial number (the song's refrain was "Rose tint my world, keep me safe from trouble and pain," which rewrites the idiom "Looking at the world through rose-colored glasses"), through the second number's chanted credo and baptismal orgy, to the third number and finale, "Wild and Untamed Thing," a hard-rocking ode to Dr. Frank N. Furter. For this last number, the initiates emerge from the pool and form a chorus line, moving in (imprecise) lock-step; all are wet and smeared with running makeup. The song shares the same "rose-tinted" refrain as the first number, but here the tint has been diluted and exposed as artificial. While the wetness of the dancers heightens their sexual allure (think clinging wet bathing suits), it also makes them appear bedraggled—how Esther Williams really would have looked once she left the pool.

The floor show sequence refers to a common device of Hollywood musicals, namely the insertion of a musical theater performance within the narrative, the organization of which often drives the plot itself, as in *Summer Stock,* discussed in chapter 3. This nesting of a fictional theater inside the real movie theater draws the real audience into the fantasy world of the movie. In most Busby Berkeley sequences, for example, the borders (and realistic restrictions) of the fictional theater immediately disappear within the impossibly elaborate song and dance numbers. The real audience becomes the ideal audience for the fantastical musical productions, able to view the geometric designs from above or to see Esther Williams's smile while she is underwater. References to the fictional theater audience sometimes appear as fleeting moments of applause—just enough to heighten the illusion of a wondrous and spectacular floor show. The floor show in *Rocky Horror* plays on this Hollywood gimmick with constant long shots of the stage from the back of the theater, but in this case it is an *empty* theater. We even watch from behind the dancers during Brad's solo, staring into the blinding floodlights out into a sea of tattered empty seats. This vision of desolation is a striking contrast to the utopian musical finale, for not even the Transylvanians who danced the "Time Warp" earlier are watching the performance.[104] The lack of audience enhances the ritual quality of the floor show to a certain extent: the separation of the initiates from the larger population is, of course, one key aspect of a classic rite of passage.[105]

These songs and dances constitute not merely a "show," but also critical moments of enlightenment. The empty seats, however, also function as placeholders for the movie audience, working not to draw them into the musical fantasy, but rather to keep them out.[106] This sets up a flow of desire on the part of the movie audience to be "inside." Indeed, the whole floor show sequence in *Rocky Horror* eerily prefigured the eventual behavior of the cult audience, their replication of characters in costume and their transformation of the entire movie into a doubling floor show. Their parallel pantomimed performances competed directly with the film, and the film itself became of secondary interest. As D. Keith Mano noted, writing for the *National Review* in 1978, "when a really fine Dr. Frank N. Furter singalike stood in his small flashlit pool, well, I found myself watching him, not the film. It was a valid performance. Who, you could justifiably ask, is lip-synching whom?"[107]

The movie does not end with the floor show, but rather with Dr. Frank N. Furter's martyrdom at the hands of Riff Raff. Columbia and Rocky are also annihilated, leaving Brad, Janet, and Dr. Scott "bewitched, bothered, and bewildered," writhing on the ground as the castle-turned-spaceship blasts off back to the planet Transsexual (perhaps a reference to Dorothy's flying house from the *Wizard of Oz*). It is a gloomy ending to be sure, but the audience knows that they will be back to see it all happen again, and that some Siren-like energy has been unleashed. The evidence of Dr. Frank N. Furter's effect on their world surrounds them as they leave the theater.

Between Pleasure and Pain

Monstrous supernatural or satanic forces unleashed into an unsuspecting suburban world form the basic plot of most gothic horror films. Indeed, Hollywood's horror can be read as a critique of suburban ideals, namely the investment in social containment and the presumption of a hermetic seal against the outside. Christoph Grunenberg points out that

> since George Romero's *Night of the Living Dead* (1968) horror has been situated in everyday suburban and small-town America. . . . Throughout the 70s and 80s films such as *Carrie* (1976, Brian de Palma), *A Nightmare on Elm Street* (1984, Wes Craven), *Poltergeist* (1982, Tobe Hooper) and the *Halloween* (1978, John Carpenter) and *Friday the 13th* (1980, Sean S. Cunningham) series have situated the bloody clash of the normal and pathological into a pastoral and idyllic America, ignorant of social, urban, or technological change.[108]

The Rocky Horror Picture Show's parody of horror films has all that genre's trappings, including a gothic castle in a rural setting and the confrontation of "normalcy" and "pathology." The "horror" in *Rocky Horror* is, on one level represented by Rocky, his technological construction; on another level the horror is represented by Brad. Technology, not nature, produces the muscled, masculine Adonis, while Brad, the "natural" man, is wimpy and powerless. But, in the end, both of these "men" readily give in to homosexual desire. Furthermore, neither the ideal nor the real version of masculinity compares in erotic potency to the androgynous Dr. Frank N. Furter.

Gothic rock began with the Doors and Jim Morrison's apocalyptic poetry, "Lizard King" alter ego, deep muddy vocals, and audience-antagonizing performances. Morrison took his inspiration from an experimental and interactive theater troupe called the Living Theater, founded and directed by Judith Malina and Julian Beck. During their performances the actors would taunt and harangue the audience, using tactics such as verbal retorts or even disrobing in order to provoke a response. American rockers Iggy Pop and Alice Cooper took the Doors' gloomy theatricality to the limit in the early 1970s, inciting audiences with gross-out antics and macabre stage shows. The expectation and instigation of audience responses in such theater performances and rock shows paved the way for the audience participation that grew around *The Rocky Horror Picture Show*.[109] *Rocky Horror*'s popularity also hit its peak during the emergence of punk rock, which continued to break down barriers between performer and audience—and also between genders, with its androgynous fashions and pan-aggressive music. Both punk and *Rocky Horror* raised the bar for ensuing generations of performers like Marilyn Manson, who took audience provocation and gender-bending to truly gothic extremes.

The music and performances of Marilyn Manson are frequently said to inspire horrific behavior among adolescents, most seriously the high school shootings in Springfield, Oregon (May 1998), and Littleton, Colorado (April 1999). Such specific connections have been challenged, however; some reports claim that none of these shooters was a Marilyn Manson fan.[110] Nevertheless, the persistent finger pointing, most notably in the U.S. Senate hearing *Music Violence: How Does It Affect Our Children* (November 6, 1997), betrays Manson's extreme challenge to mainstream social mores, and the mainstream's fearful reaction to that challenge. An in-depth discussion of the complex relationship between inflammatory popular music and antisocial behavior is beyond the scope of this book. Although I admit music's affective power, and do not dismiss the possibility of its motivational power, my project here is to deepen recent discussions of music and power by examining the queer attraction of Marilyn Manson as a potent yet *emasculated* musical subject.[111]

Marilyn Manson is the rock and roll alter ego of Brian Warner, a self-proclaimed bullied "geek from Ohio" who concatenated the names of Marilyn Monroe and Charles Manson for his stage name. "Marilyn Manson," then, serves as a pithy critique of the media that turns figures of both beauty and violence into pop icons. Indeed, Manson claims a general critical agenda for his music and pop persona: to examine and challenge mainstream American values, to champion individuality and imagination, and to get people to take responsibility for their actions.[112] He delivers this message of responsibility, however, in anti-everything lyrics and "death metal" music. His music combines self-consciously dreary gothic rock, characterized by minor modes, thin vocal timbres, and bass-heavy textures, with the power strumming, driving riffs, distortion, and gruesome visual theatrics of heavy metal (Alice Cooper, Kiss, Ozzy Osbourne) and the audience taunting and self-mutilation of early punk (Iggy Pop, Sex Pistols). Marilyn Manson entered the mainstream in 1995 with a cover song of the 1980s synth-pop hit "Sweet Dreams (Are Made of This)" by the Eurythmics, but his real success and notoriety came with his 1996 concept album and stage show *Antichrist Superstar.*

Antichrist Superstar is a satirical take on the rock theater show *Jesus Christ Superstar* (1970; lyrics by Tim Rice and music by Andrew Lloyd Webber); it also alludes to David Bowie's *The Rise and Fall of Ziggy Stardust* and Pink Floyd's *The Wall,* two semiautobiographical concept albums that follow the story of rock and roll *Bildung,* the transformation of a regular humble mortal to mythic rock god. In *Antichrist Superstar,* through a buildup of images rather than a clear narrative progression, we experience visions of the young Brian Warner, alias Wormboy, losing his innocence, gaining an exoskeleton, and then emerging as the Antichrist in the form of the antisuperstar Marilyn Manson. As Manson, this figure is a harbinger of the apocalypse, but he also becomes, on a metatextual level, a superhero fighting against the fascism of popular culture and Christian fundamentalism. "The beautiful people, the beautiful people," Manson screams, "It's all relative to the size of your steeple."[113]

The commemorative video of the *Antichrist Superstar* tour, called *Marilyn Manson: Dead to the World,* documents Christian groups picketing his concerts and fans emulating Manson in their pancake makeup, black lipstick, and self-lacerations. The film also offers the "behind-the-scenes" Manson, solemnly talking about mild childhood traumas or raging like a diva about failed strobe lights (this after an instrument-demolishing final set). These scenes are saturated with self-mockery and irony, as well as nearly every kind of body fluid and effluvium. We see Manson or his band members urinate, vomit, defecate, spit at and be spit at by the audience, wipe mucus from their nose on the wall, and cut themselves onstage to become drenched with blood and sweat. The missing liquid in this flood is semen: there is plenty of masturbation here, but the scenes of masturbation are all cheap and unsensual (but very sensationalistic) sight gags, such as a brief shot in which Manson rubs the Bible between his legs. One scene in particular offers the most telling statement about the place of sexuality in Manson's apocalyptic-satiric vision. A French prostitute sits naked on a bed making small talk with some band members while one of them lies passed out in a chair. In sum, this "rockumentary" presents an onslaught of bodies in a postphallic, postdesire, post-sexual state: ugly, porous, leaking, and numb.

Although Manson's bodies are sexually impotent, they are nonetheless powerful aesthetic subjects. His performances reconstitute masculinity within this discourse of postsexuality, bringing out, as a result, something quite startling. The performance of "Kinderfeld"—one of the most elaborately staged numbers in the show—portrays the moment of metamorphosis from Wormboy to demonic insect, the body transformed from the sexual to the aesthetic. Manson emerges from the shadows on metal stilts and elongated metal crutches, which appear to be organically connected to his limbs. His torso is wrapped tightly in a corset of sorts; straps dangle from the front, which gives the impression that his mummified body is unraveling. On his head sits a form-fitting cap with wires (or antennae) sprouting from the top. He is breathtaking, mesmerizing, lumbering slowly from one end of the stage to the other; he is an iron butterfly still shedding its former skin, waving its premature, handicapped wings.

The music for this song is a sonic portrait of menace, but one rich in sensual details. A heavy, slow bass groove supports a melody full of tritones and chromaticisms; phrases are punctuated by electronic buzzes and blips and humanoid laughing. Manson's voice sounds in an impressive number of guises here and throughout the recorded album: these include a near whisper that sporadically wanders into falsetto; electronically distorted low growls on which screams are at times superimposed; and timbres that begin smooth but end raspy. Indeed, there is a strange fragility to the identity of this voice; it is always mutating, never strongly defined in timbre or register. This idea of fragility is embedded in one humorously exquisite detail in "Kinderfeld": during an instrumental break Manson plays a little flute (electronically distorted in the recorded version). The pathos of the misplaced idyllic instrument is almost campy, signaling lost innocence with its fractured, flimsy melody. But the flute is a complicated symbol: not only idyllic but phallic as well, it is frequently used as an instrument of seduction in myths and legends. Marilyn Manson has certainly proven his powers of seduction, attracting not only devoted fans but also enraged Christian moralists and worried politicians, who inadvertently sail into his rocky shores and serve as his best (publicity) agents of darkness. But Manson, the singing, piping Siren, becomes the antiheroic Odysseus, strapped to metal poles, bound in a corset, spitting into a sea of kids who gleefully spit back, both performer and audience enthralled by the sadomasochistic exchange.

Foucault believed that sadomasochism represented a practice of resistance to the hegemony of phallocentric sex and sex appeal, a "desexualizing of pleasure" and a disassociation of pleasure from desire. For Foucault, sadomasochism potentially loosened the straitjacket of identities based on a fetishizing of genitals by fetishizing instead the performance and signifiers of power relations and non–genitally based erotic interactions.[114] As such, sadomasochism can be an ethical expression of freedom, an eroticization and performance of staged power relations, and a redistribution of bodily pleasure from the genitals to any location—even the ears. Manson's music provides the phallic penetration that his body, so thoroughly and artistically broken down, cannot. With frequently screamed choruses and heavily distorted vocals and guitar high in the recording mix, Manson's music—bordering on industrial noise—dominates its listeners, their bodies vibrating with excitation and distress.

Manson's performances provide a space in which to revel in the transgressive erotic pleasure of the emasculated body as an unlikely site of power and resistance. Like the Sirens, Manson calls to that ontological curiosity to get free of oneself—especially the self complacently bound up in oppressive configurations of masculinity, power, sexuality, and morality. For in Marilyn Manson's musical universe, you are either the bullied victim, the fascist bully, or, as the allegory of Manson as Antichrist relates, the former turned into the latter.

. . .

In 1997, the U.S. government mobilized one of its technologies of power, a Senate hearing, in an effort to curtail the effects of Manson's potent, emasculated body—a body that was verging on ungovernable. They believed, furthermore, that this ungovernability was spreading through countertechnologies of power, those of music and the music industry. The title of the hearing, *Music Violence: How Does It Affect Our Children,* inadvertently constructs music as a productive agent in and of itself, for without intervening and nuancing prepositions ("violence in music) or conjunctions ("violence and music") or even adjectival forms ("musical violence," "violent music"), "music violence" identifies a pernicious antisocial phenomenon, a contagion that spreads from performer to audience. Though the presiding senators take pains to explain that the hearing does not concern legislation, the very fact of a legislative body (or, rather, legislative bodies) defining a thing called "music violence"—and acting on it themselves—underlines the idea that music is potentially antagonistic to the state. As Senator Lieberman (D–Connecticut) explains:

> We are not talking here about censorship, but about citizenship. You and I are not asking for any government action or bans. . . . We are asking why [a] great company like Seagrams is continuing to associate itself with Marilyn Manson and the vile, hateful, nihilistic, and, as you will hear from Mr. Kuntz, dangerously damaging music, Marilyn Manson records. . . . I hope the corporate leaders of the industry . . . [will] draw some lines they will not cross just to make more money, because on the other side of those lines is damage to our country and our children and ultimately to themselves.[115]

Although Senator Lieberman cites lyrics from songs by Cannibal Corpse (produced by Sony) that are far more misogynistic and violent, such as "masturbating with a dead woman's head,"[116] Marilyn Manson's *Antichrist Superstar* serves as the primary exemplar of "music violence" and its challenge to citizenship—particularly and ironically the citizenship of "great corporations" like Seagrams,[117] but no less the citizenship of the musicians themselves (incidentally, no musicians were invited to speak at this hearing).

The heinousness of Manson is threefold. First, Manson's and Manson-like "vile material" has spread from urban to suburban and even rural (read: white) demographics. In his response to the testimony of the father of Richard Kuntz, a teenage Manson fan who committed suicide, Senator Lieberman remarks, "it is in the movies, and your son in Burlington, North Dakota, not in some dark alley in one of America's big cities, gets to tap into the lowest, most degrading aspects of our culture."[118] Second, Manson has launched a direct assault on Christianity. The song "The Reflecting God" receives the most attention in the hearing because it mixes satanic parodies of biblical references—such as "I say it is and then it's true" (a parody of Genesis) and "when I'm God everyone dies" and "you'll understand when I'm dead" (parodies of Christ's self-sacrifice)—with abstractly violent and nihilistic lines such as "One shot and the world gets smaller" and "Shoot motherfucker." The third charge against Marilyn Manson is his androgyny and emasculation. Senator Kent Conrad (D–North Dakota) sums it up as follows: "I think as the Chairman and the ranking members know, Marilyn Manson is a composite name. It combines Marilyn Monroe, who committed suicide, with Charles Manson, who is a mass murderer. I think that in itself says something about the mind-set of the performer."[119]

The androgyny of Marilyn Manson's name, the names of his band members (which follow the same pattern of derivation), and the dress of his followers comes up (or out) time and again in the hearing, from the mouths of politicians, parents, experts, and even a twelve-year-old boy. Indeed, homophobic panic bubbles to the surface in the statement by Dr. C. DeLores Tucker, chair of the National Political Congress of Black Women, in her description of the cover art of *Antichrist Superstar*. She says, "I just want to show you what this Marilyn Manson is all about. In this poster, he is with something [sic] I have never seen before, with two tubes extending from his genitals going into the mouths of two young people kneeling at his side." The kneeling "young people" are his band mates, and they wear oxygen masks with tubes attached to Manson's penis, covered to look like a miniature oxygen tank. In my opinion, the photo cleverly mocks how much popular culture lives and breathes the penis. Though she does not explicitly state it, Tucker insinuates that Marilyn Manson is "all about" homosexual pederasty through the homosexual association in the picture (i.e., the connection of one man's face to another man's genitals). She then argues that Manson panders to fourteen-year-old boys whose sexuality is unformed and implies that he influences them in the direction of homosexual perversity: "Manson has perfected his on-stage antics, which include performing oral sex on a male guest, or strapping on a dildo—d-i-l-d-o; and mimicking masturbation."[120] It seems that for Tucker, Manson's crime is one he shares with lesbians who use sex toys—namely, the displacement (or replacement) of the patriarchal phallus. That Manson should strap on a dildo is further evidence of his emasculated persona.

As if to illustrate the threat that Manson poses to young boys, the hearing wraps up with the statement of a twelve-year-old named Chad, whom Tucker has brought from Philadelphia. She introduces his testimony thus: "Marilyn Manson was in his neighborhood this summer, and the young kids were lined up—black males, in skirts—for a Marilyn Manson concert. So I think that it is relevant to hear from a child." Indeed, the young boy dutifully describes that "the males had on skirts, and they had devil signs and things like that," and "it was just an embarrassment."[121] Despite Chad's apparent disgust, it would seem that mere exposure to "males in skirts" potentially corrupts; the phrase itself seems to project the boy's own fate should he have any sustained contact with Marilyn Manson fans. The aspect of race here is significant, for the cross-racial horror serves to amplify the menace of Marilyn Manson and his transgression of socially structuring boundaries. White, middle-class, suburban teenagers constitute the main consumers of heavy metal and related styles of rock, and Manson's decrepit masculinity and voided sexuality would seem an even less likely attraction for urban black teenage boys. Thus the phrase "black males in skirts" is offered as the epitome of Manson's decadence that has extended to the furthest reaches of America, from the African-American neighborhoods of Philadelphia to the remote white town of Burlington, North Dakota.

Marilyn Manson's name sums up his "mind-set," his homosexual cover art is what he "is all about," and his spawn are "black males in skirts." Throughout the hearing, the senators assert that Manson's artistic expression is indivisible from his inner self; more importantly, that music can affect the inner self of the listener, that it can even influence the unformed sexuality of adolescent boys. These ideas about the power of art are worthy of Winckelmann and Goethe. But the *Bildung* that Manson's music offers has ominous consequences; the infractions of gender and sexuality made by Manson's aestheticized emasculated body threaten the nation with ever more unbounded, unruly subjects, necessitating federal regulation. Shy of making legislation that might impinge on First Amendment rights, or the profit margins of great corporations, however, the senators have no recourse but to become philosophers of citizenship, and in this they come very near to Plato's passages about the effect of music on the state in *Laws*, as discussed in chapter 1. Compare, for example, the following quotes from Plato and Lieberman, respectively:

Gripped by a frenzied and excessive lust for pleasure, they [composers] jumbled together laments and hymns, mixed paeans and dithyrambs, and imitate the pipe tunes on the lyre (700d). . . . This freedom will then take other forms. First people grow unwilling to submit to the authorities, then they refuse to obey the admonitions of their fathers and mothers and elders. As they hurtle along towards the end of this primrose path, they try to escape the authority of laws; and the very end of the road comes when they cease to care about oaths and promises and religion in general. (701b–c) [122]

We don't seem to blink when corporate citizens sell music to our children that celebrates violence, including murder of police and gang rape, and sexual perversity, including pedophilia. . . . these cultural indicators have very real implications. They bespeak a breakdown in the old rules and limits that once governed our public and private lives and the way we raised our children. We are left, I am afraid, with a values vacuum in which our children learn more and more that anything goes which I believe is at the heart of some of our society's worst social problems. [123]

Plato's "escape" from "authority of laws" and Lieberman's "anything goes" (an elliptical phrase made famous by gay songwriter Cole Porter) describe the epistemological fantasies allegedly engendered in the young by unregulated music. Like Icarus, who disdained natural laws with his impetuous flight, these musically miseducated youths disdain participation in human laws. For both Plato and Lieberman, music too easily leads to *Bildung* gone awry, unchecked aesthetic pursuits that incite transgression in the "coming of age" behaviors of youthful subjects. Ungoverned music results in a *generation* of Frankensteinian monsters, alienated from their parents/creators, themselves ungovernable.

Between Male and Female

If Marilyn Manson's *Antichrist Superstar* leads to the unnatural and antistate mayhem of "black males in skirts," then, by implication, only "natural" bodies that belong to one of two "natural genders" (and one race) are conducive to the state and citizenship. But what if the nation-state itself is "unnaturally" divided? And what if the human "natural state" is likewise unnaturally divided? These are some of the questions posed by *Hedwig and the Angry Inch*, an off-Broadway musical theater piece (1998) turned movie musical (2001) written by openly gay artists John Cameron Mitchell and Stephen Trask. The show probes and burlesques the intimate, constructed bonds between gender "citizenship" and national citizenship, both of which can be strategically circumvented through medical technology and musical celebrity. Through song lyrics and monologues in the play, enhanced by flashback shots and animation sequences in the movie, *Hedwig* tells the story of a young effeminate boy, Hansel Schmidt, growing up in Communist East Berlin, "a town ripped in two" in 1961 with the construction of the Berlin Wall.[124] As an adolescent, Hansel becomes the lover of an American serviceman who, with the assistance of Hansel's enthusiastic mother, persuades Hansel to undergo a sex-change operation so that they can marry and emigrate to the United States. Postoperative Hansel, now Hedwig, does then marry and emigrate; the "botched" gender-reassignment surgery, however, left an "angry inch" of the masculine member. The GI husband eventually leaves Hedwig in a Kansas trailer park, on the very day the Berlin Wall was torn down.

What, in this dire situation, does Hedwig do? Why, she becomes a glam-punk rocker, of course. Hedwig's act combines the rock cabaret of early David Bowie with the trashy transvestite look and raw proto-punk sound of the New York Dolls. At one point Hedwig recounts his childhood fascination with American rock and roll, which he listened to on American Forces Radio. He says he would "listen to the American Masters . . . Toni Tennille! . . . Debbie Boone! . . . and Anne Murray! . . . who was actually a Canadian working in the American idiom. Then there were the crypto-homo rockers: Lou Reed! . . . Iggy Pop! . . . and David Bowie, who was actually an idiom working in America and Canada."[125] Glam rockers, the crypto-homo "idioms" of identity, light the way for Hedwig's only hope for self-invention outside the laws of marriage and citizenship—laws that had already imposed the price of castration. As critic Eric Weisbard puts it, she becomes "one of those extra-gendered 'strange rock 'n' rollers.'"[126] Weisbard's reference is to "Midnight Radio," the last song in the show. In this song, Hedwig nostalgically lists herself among path-breaking female rockers such as Patti (Smith or LaBelle), Tina (Turner), Yoko (Ono), Aretha (Franklin), Nona (Hendryx), Nico— just as *Rocky Horror*'s "Science Fiction/Double Feature" nostalgically lists actors of cult science fiction movies. Indeed, references to classical and pop culture also saturate *Hedwig*. As with *Rocky Horror,* the plot pivots on Frankensteinian medical technology.[127] The dress-up cult of *Rocky Horror* finds its way into the movie in the depiction of Hedwig's fans who wear foam-rubber replicas of her Farrah Fawcett wig. But in *Hedwig,* the "creator" neither represents the hubris of unbridled science, as in the original *Frankenstein,* nor a pan-erotic demigod, as in *Rocky Horror,* nor, for that matter, a recovering bullied victim, as in *Antichrist Superstar.* Rather, the "creator" of *Hedwig and the Angry Inch* assumes ideological, mythological, and cultural forms.

The first song in the show, "Tear Me Down," establishes Hedwig's dual gender as an allegory for the split nation-state of Germany, which itself represents the world divided by the Cold War. An extended monologue, delivered by the transgendered backup vocalist Yitzhak during the break, explains:

The world was divided by a cold war,
and the Berlin wall
was the most hated symbol of that divide

Reviled. Graffitied. Spit upon.
We thought the wall would stand forever,
and now that it's gone,
we don't know who we are anymore.
Ladies and Gentlemen,
Hedwig is like that wall,
standing before you in the divide
between East and West,
Slavery and Freedom,
Man and Woman,
Top and Bottom.[128]

Here the Cold War is likened to the split of genders; it is an artificial division of the world into East and West based on political ideology, just as the social division between "man" and "woman" is itself an artificial divide. This geopolitical pretense—the analogy of East and West and male and female—are certainly hyperbolic, strained, even ironic. The binaries presented by Yitzhak's monologue as equivalent associate maleness not only with "top," but also surprisingly with "East" and "slavery," thus thrusting masculinity into the position of the exotic and the oppressed, roles usually reserved for the feminine.

The monologue also describes the identity crises that follow the collapse of those polarities, since the binary opposition of self/other is as fundamental to the idea of gender as it is to nation-states. How do we come back together, bridge East and West, after living and thinking separately for so long? And in terms of gender, what does coming back together mean? The fact that Hedwig's GI husband leaves her on the day that Germany moved toward reunification suggests that, at least for gender, the damage has been done: the tragic cut can never be fully healed. For masculinity, the uniting of the genders results ultimately in a dilution or even dissolution of phallic power—in castration, or rather half-castration, which is Hedwig's condition. As the song goes on to proclaim, "there ain't much of a difference between a bridge and a wall / without me right in the middle, babe, you would be nothing at all." A bridge and a wall are conceptually at odds: a bridge connects while a wall separates. The *ad absurdum* equations bespeak the failure of these analogies; their weightiness is always already mocked and ironic in the unnameable thing[129]—the angry inch—that haunts the utopian vision of reunification. When Hedwig's teenage lover, groping between Hedwig's legs, exclaims in horror, "What is that?" Hedwig replies, "That's what I have to work with."

Yet meaning and identity need not be structured solely by binary oppositions, a hetero-duality of polarized terms.[130] What about a homo-duality? Like shadowing like? *Hedwig* explores this prospect as well, through its adaptation of Aristophanes' speech in Plato's *Symposium* as the self-conscious metatheme of the story, and as the lyrical theme for the second song of the show, "The

Origin of Love." In the *Symposium,* when asked to reveal his opinion about the nature of love, Aristophanes answers with a myth about the original physical condition of human beings:

> There were three kinds of human beings, that's my first point—not two as there are now, male and female. In addition to these, there was a third, a combination of those two; its name survives, though the kind itself has vanished. At that time, you see, the word "androgynous" really meant something: a form made up of male and female elements, though now there's nothing but the word, and that's used as an insult. My second point is that the shape of each human being was completely round, with back and sides in a circle; they had four hands each, as many legs as hands, and two faces, exactly alike, on a rounded neck. Between the two faces, which were on opposite sides, was one head with four ears. There were two sets of sexual organs, and everything else was the way you'd imagine it from what I've told you. (189d–190a)[131]

These three sexes, children of the Sun (males), Earth (females), and Moon (androgynes), were a rebellious lot that insolently attempted to attack the gods. As a safeguard against their insurrection, Zeus split them apart and thus weakened their power. Apollo fashioned their wounded backsides into fronts so that when one half found the other "they would throw their arms about each other, weaving themselves together, wanting to grow together" (191a). Ironically, it was the freaky androgynes who, after the split, became heterosexuals.

Love, according to Aristophanes, stems from this divided state, and his myth accounts for homosexual as well as heterosexual desire. Indeed, Aristophanes holds male homosexual unions in the highest regard since they represent pure masculinity; these men will become the active citizens, participating most vigorously in the homosocial world of public life. His understanding of the nature of desire is not based on a heterosexual logic in which "opposites attract"; rather, the nature of desire is based on the circumvention or healing of an artificial split through the unification of two entities that are essentially the same. Indeed, heterosexuality here is collateral to a homosexual logic in which like attracts like. In *Hedwig,* however, sameness and difference as basic, heuristic categories themselves become scrambled. When Hedwig, the male-to-female transsexual character (played by a man), kisses Yitzhak, the former "drag queen" who is Hedwig's husband (played by a woman), the parallel and cross relations between the composite bio- and neo-genders, the "real" and "fictional" genders, create a union that is simultaneously homo and hetero—a perfect, undivided sphere like the original earth, original humans, and original love.

As previously mentioned, however, Hedwig also represents the pitfalls of both bio- and neo-gender, as well as both Cold War geopolitics and post–Cold War capitalistic globalization. Like Dr. Frank N. Furter, Hedwig is tyrannical, particularly toward her husband Yitzhak, who is a Croatian Jew and who serves as Hedwig's backup singer. Yitzhak's marriage to Hedwig replays Hedwig's earlier marriage, for just as the intersection of marriage and U.S. citizenship in immigration law required the "girlie boy" Hansel to become simply "a girl," Hedwig requires Yitzhak to give up his transgendered identity as a drag queen in exchange for marriage and escape from the Balkans. Hedwig holds Yitzhak's identity hostage by denying him both wig and passport, the symbolic and fetishized objects that denote and bestow citizenship of gender and nation.

Paradoxically, Hedwig's obsession with gender and national identity shadows his own postgender and postnation ontological "state," just as Hedwig and his band, The Angry Inch, shadow the androgynous gothic rock star Tommy Gnosis, Hedwig's one-time baby-sitting charge, lover, and musical collaborator. The name Tommy Gnosis combines the Who's messianic character, Tommy, from their 1969 rock opera of the same name, with the Greek word for "knowledge" (taken from the gnostic gospels, which includes the Gospel of Thomas). The character represents an innocent Adam who is sexually awakened by Hedwig *qua* Eve. In the biblical story (Gen. 3), the fruit of the tree of knowledge leads to a compelling recognition of sexual difference, which sets up a primary association of knowledge with sexuality. Hedwig feeds the boy the fruit of glam rock, those "crypto-homo" rockers David Bowie, Lou Reed, and Iggy Pop, who trigger an equally compelling confusion of sexual difference. Knowledge and sexuality are still linked, but Genesis's lesson of sexual difference is undone. Music propels the subject on a journey—a reverse *Bildung*—through heterosexual difference to sexual indeterminacy and ultimately to queer sexual union. In the movie, Tommy paraphrases the gnostic gospels: "When Eve goes back inside Adam and they become one, that's when paradise will be regained."[132]

Though acting as the agent of this postmodern "gnosis," Hedwig, like Eve, is initially exploited and cast off. Tommy steals Hedwig's songs, becomes a famous neo-glam rock star, and thus robs Hedwig of her only passport to a viable identity given her extragendered, extranational self. Like the tradition that figures Odysseus as the captor rather than the captured of the Sirens' song, here, too, phallic dominant culture seems to have triumphantly plundered queer identity for its energizing secrets. Those "crypto-homo" rockers—including Tim Curry, who played Dr. Frank N. Furter—have long since distanced themselves from their own queer idiom, and Mitchell and Trask's Tommy Gnosis does so as well.[133] *Hedwig*, however, ends not as a tragedy of unrequited gay or transgendered love, but rather as a rock and roll apotheosis of self-sufficient "wholeness"—working with what one has.

The finale of *Hedwig* begins with a rapid series of "outings": first Tommy Gnosis's gay past is exposed in the tabloids; then Hedwig finally liberates Yitzhak by giving him a wig. The most dramatic coming out occurs at the end of the punk-styled "Exquisite Corpse"—a song filled with *Frankenstein* images—when Hedwig tears away the female drag and symbolically embraces both genders. As Hedwig sings in the final song, "Midnight Radio":

> Know in your soul
> Like your blood knows the way
> From your heart to your brain
> Know that you're whole.[134]

Since Hedwig has lived as a female for most of the story, it is tempting to see the final gesture of self-outing as a recovery of the masculine half, or at least the troublesome inch. But the final song, "Midnight Radio," suggests something else, that Hedwig's unique gender may still have more in common with women despite that remainder of phallic identity. As mentioned earlier, this panegyric to "strange rock 'n' rollers" lists Patti, Tina, Yoko, Aretha, Nona, and Nico—not Lou, Iggy, and David—a list to which Hedwig adds *herself*. These women, working in a male-dominated musical "idiom," are the true transgendered heroes. The song not only redresses the masculinizing and misogynistic tendencies of rock and roll (glam rock included), but it also denies to the remaining angry inch of the phallus the power to define identity.

Like Manson's *Antichrist Superstar,* Mitchell and Trask's *Hedwig and the Angry Inch* harbors an antiassimilationist message via its critique of gender identification, especially identification with patriarchal masculinity. It can also be seen as the musical analogue to Foucault's exploration of the sadomasochistic subculture of the queer community as an alternative to genital-based sexuality. Hedwig, of course, has no "known" genitals, only an unnameable fragment, and music provides the means—indeed, the technology—for the realization of Hedwig's queer gendered identity. This ideal musical expression of inexpressible gender importantly does not dissolve or deny gender difference, but rather envisions a new type of coexistence that cannot be regularized and institutionalized.

. . .

The musical flights of fancy examined in this chapter can all be understood in some way as moments of coming out, of resisting technologies of power that regulate gender and sexuality and create governable bodies. At the beginning of this musical genealogy were the seventeenth-century catches, which critique marriage and betray a fascination with the extramarital body of hermaphrodites, and Handel's *Tra le fiamme,* which musically reimagined Daedalus and Icarus as escaping from the strictures of nature and realism into a world of perpetual homoerotic fantasy. At the end were Queen and *Rocky Horror,* which distorted the masculine rock and roll *Bildungsroman* with gender-disrupting journeys into Italian opera and the "Frankenstein Place," respectively, as well as Marilyn Manson's postsexual masculine body and

Hedwig's postgenital gendered body. In all of these cases, music is the vehicle for the deployment of queer identity, that is, music serves as a technique of questioning—even an erotics of questioning—the received categories of gender and sexual identity such that the map of identity is theoretically, if not actually, reconfigured and redrawn. And the new mappings explored in this chapter—created by *men,* gay, straight, and otherwise—work toward destabilizing phallic identity and reconfiguring masculinity, indeed, the exemplary phallic symbol, the penis itself. This seems a profound undoing of Augustine's predication of knowledge and power on male sexual impulses; if the phallus no longer organizes identity, then radically new social formations and dynamics can emerge.

But are we caught in a closed-circuit exchange in which the Sirens' song of illicit and dangerous queer identity ultimately underwrites the lawful status quo? Will those queer composite creatures, the Sirens, always have their songs captured, colonized, and commercially exploited? I think not. Myriad new out gay, lesbian, bi, queer, and transsexual musicians are closing the gap between privileged straight perspectives and subordinated queer expressions. Perhaps they are moving their receptive—if not utterly enthralled—listeners through a *Bildung* toward a mythological spherical state in which the beginning point of queer identity and the ending point of straight identity are indeterminable. Of course, music has obscured this border for centuries; it provides techniques for resisting the norms of gender and sexuality, whatever they may be.

Helping the young Tommy navigate through the murky waters of emergent queer identity, Hedwig sings, "you can follow my voice." Listening to the Sirens never fails.

NOTES

INTRODUCTION

1. The list of writing, visual arts, and music that use the myth of the Sirens for inspiration is vast. See s.v. "sirens" in Philip Mayerson, *Classical Mythology in Literature, Art, and Music* (Toronto: Xerox Corporation, 1971); and in Jane Davidson Reid, *The Oxford Guide to Classical Mythology in the Arts, 1300–1990s* (New York: Oxford University Press, 1993). See also Siegfried de Rachewiltz, *De Sirenibus: An Inquiry into Sirens from Homer to Shakespeare* (New York: Garland, 1987), written as a Ph.D. dissertation for Harvard University in 1983; Sabine Wedner, *Tradition und Wandel im allegorischen Verständnis des Sirenenmythos: Ein Beitrag zur Rezeptionsgeschichte Homers* (Frankfurt am Main: Peter Lang, 1994); Domenico Musti, *I Telchini, le Sirene: Immaginario mediterraneo e letteratura da Omero e Callimaco al romanticismo europeo* (Pisa: Istituti Editoriali e Poligrafici Internazionali, 1999); Jean Dorat, *Mythologicum, ou interprétation allégorique de l'Odyssée, X–XII et de l'hymne à Aphrodite* (Genève: Droz, 2000). For use of the story in more recent critical theory, see Maurice Blanchot, "The Song of the Sirens: Encountering the Imaginary," in *The Gaze of Orpheus and Other Literary Essays,* trans. Lydia Davis, ed. P. Adams Sitney (Barrytown, NY: Station Hill, 1981), 105–13.
2. See Max Horkheimer and Theodor W. Adorno, *Dialectic of Enlightenment,* trans. John Cumming (New York: Continuum, 1998), 43 and 36, respectively.
3. Ibid., 34.
4. Ibid., 34 and 59–60, respectively. For a discussion of the politics of gender, modernity, and bourgeois subjectivity in this text's treatment of the Sirens, see Barbara Engh, "Adorno and the Sirens: Tele-phono-graphic Bodies," in *Embodied Voices: Representing Female Vocality in Western Culture,* ed. Leslie C. Dunn and Nancy A. Jones (Cambridge: Cambridge University Press, 1994), 120–35.
5. See Adorno with George Simpson, "On Popular Music" (1941), reprinted in Theodor W. Adorno, *Essays on Music,* ed. Richard Leppert, trans. Susan H. Gillespie (Berkeley: University of California Press, 2002), 437–69. For an explanation of Adorno's thought, see Richard Leppert's introduction to this volume, 1–82.

6. Louis Althusser, "Ideology and Ideological State Apparatuses (Notes towards an Investigation)," in *Essays on Ideology*, trans. Ben Brewster and Grahame Lock (London: Verso, 1984), 48.

7. This stems from the work of Jacques Lacan, whose psychoanalytic theories of language heavily influenced Althusser. For a discussion of Althusser's concern with language in his formulation of "interpellation," see Judith Butler, *The Psychic Life of Power: Theories in Subjection* (Stanford, CA: Stanford University Press, 1997), 106–31, especially 112–16. Althusser, however, does allow that the hail can be a "verbal call or whistle" (48), though he offers no explanation of how the whistle conveys ideology by substituting for language.

8. See Terry Eagleton, *Literary Theory: An Introduction*, 2nd ed. (Minneapolis: University of Minnesota Press, 1996), 150.

9. Although Althusser believed that ideology and subjectivity are in actuality coterminous, the sequential aspect of his parable of hailing (which he dismisses as a matter of convenience) nevertheless divulges that the link between ideology and subjectivity is continuously renewed through sequential interpellations. It is at these moments of renewal that questioning can arise.

10. "Technologies of the Self" (1982), in *Ethics: Subjectivity, and Truth,* ed. Paul Rabinow, vol. 1. of *The Essential Works of Foucault, 1954–84*, trans. Robert Hurley et al., 3 vols. (New York: The New Press, 1997–2000), 224–25. See also his discussion of "techniques" and "technologies" of the self in Foucault, *L'herméneutique du sujet: Cours au Collège de France, 1981–1982* (Paris: Gallimard-Seuil, 2001), passim.

Foucault also mapped out these technologies in a 1981 essay, "Sexuality and Solitude," in *Ethics: Subjectivity, and Truth,* 177, in which he acknowledges a debt to the theories of Jürgen Habermas. Foucault may have appropriated the term "technology" from Habermas's essay "Technology and Science as 'Ideology,'" in *Toward a Rational Society: Student Protests, Science, and Politics,* trans. Jeremy J. Shapiro (Boston: Beacon Press, 1970), 81–122. In this essay Habermas reconceives "technology" as organically related to human behavior, that is, born from the desire to augment and replace human motor apparatus, expenditure of energy, senses, and intellection. Foucault transforms Habermas's notion of technology as an expression of instrumental rationality that seeks to dominate nature and overcome scarcity through the application of scientific discoveries into a notion of technology of human subject formation predicated on institutionalized means of control and domination of the subject, and resistance. Another possible source for Foucault's notion of technology, though unacknowledged, is the work of Marcel Mauss, who developed the notion of "techniques" to describe habits of physical behavior that are socially transmitted. For a discussion of Foucault's indebtedness to Mauss, see John Lechte, *Fifty Key Contemporary Thinkers: From Structuralism to Postmodernity* (New York: Routledge, 1994), 24, 27–28, and 112.

11. See Adrienne Rich, "Compulsory Heterosexuality and Lesbian Existence," in *The Lesbian and Gay Studies Reader,* ed. Henry Abelove, Michèle Aina Barale, and David M. Halperin (New York: Routledge, 1993), 227–54; and Gayle Rubin, "Thinking Sex: Notes for a Radical Theory of the Politics of Sexuality," in *The Lesbian and Gay Studies Reader,* 3–44. See also Gayle Rubin, "The Traffic in Women:

Notes on the 'Political Economy' of Sex," in *Toward an Anthropology of Women*, ed. Rayna R. Reiter (New York: Monthly Review Press, 1975), 157–210.

12. See William L. Leap, *Word's Out: Gay Men's English* (Minneapolis: University of Minnesota Press, 1996), 101–2.

13. *The Oxford English Dictionary*, 2nd ed., s.v. "queer" (Oxford: Clarendon Press, 1989), and Eric Partridge, *Origins: A Short Etymological Dictionary of Modern English*, 4th ed. (New York: MacMillan, 1966). Both Partridge and the *OED* state that the Scottish use precedes and has no connection to the German.

14. The *OED* cites the phrase " 'queer' in sexual behavior," from William Healy, *Practical Value of Scientific Study of Juvenile Delinquents* (Children's Bureau, U.S. Department of Labor, 1922), 8. See also George Chauncey, *Gay New York: Gender, Urban Culture, and the Making of the Gay Male World, 1890–1940* (New York: Basic Books, 1994), 15–16.

15. See Annamarie Jagose, *Queer Theory: An Introduction* (New York: New York University Press, 1996), especially 1–6, 72–100; and Michael Warner, *The Trouble with Normal: Sex, Politics, and the Ethics of Queer Life* (Cambridge, MA: Harvard University Press, 2000), especially 33–40.

16. Halperin, *Saint Foucault: Towards a Gay Hagiography* (New York: Oxford University Press, 1995), 62. See also Jagose, *Queer Theory*, 98; Sedgwick, *Tendencies* (Durham, NC: Duke University Press, 1993), xii.

17. Sedgwick, *Tendencies*, 8.

18. The classic article on this issue is Rubin's "Thinking Sex."

19. See Linda Martín Alcoff, "Who's Afraid of Identity Politics?" in *Reclaiming Identity: Realist Theory and the Predicament of Postmodernism*, ed. Paula M. L. Moya and Michael R. Hames-García (Berkeley: University of California Press, 2000), 337.

20. See Diana Fuss, *Identification Papers* (New York: Routledge, 1995), 2. Fuss attributes "the Self that identifies itself" to Jean-Luc Nancy. Psychoanalytic theories since Freud describe identity formation through a process of unconscious identification with, and internalization of, an "other." Diana Fuss writes, "identification inhabits, organizes, instantiates identity. It operates as a mark of self-difference, opening up a space for the self to relate to itself as a self, a self that is perpetually other."

21. Biddy Martin, *Femininity Played Straight: The Significance of Being Lesbian* (New York: Routledge, 1996), 69; see also 72–73.

22. Butler, *The Psychic Life of Power*, 86 and 95–96, respectively. For a critique of Butler and a detailed account of the debates surrounding identity politics, see Alcoff, "Who's Afraid of Identity Politics?" 312–44. Whereas Butler views social identities as primarily "injurious" and only paradoxically enabling resistance and resignification "by way of a necessarily alienated narcissism" (104), Alcoff views "identity" as less monolithic in meaning and effect. For her, "identity" can combine an imposed social category (interpellation) with lived experiences that are richer and more varied than "flattened, predetermined identities" (338). This allows an individual to take comfort and strength in community, to "actively engage in the construction of a self" (340), to accept, reject, or reinterpret interpellation. But she also notes that "the 'I' that chooses among these options is always already socially located" (341). Thus, even if an individual experiences

"identity" as flexible and dynamic, within the power structure that individual may still be viewed in terms of those "flattened, predetermined" categories.

23. Butler, *The Psychic Life of Power,* 94.

24. See Philip Brett, "Musicality, Essentialism, and the Closet," in *Queering the Pitch: The New Gay and Lesbian Musicology,* ed. Philip Brett, Elizabeth Wood, and Gary C. Thomas (New York: Routledge, 1994), 9–26, and Suzanne Cusick, "On a Lesbian Relationship with Music: A Serious Effort Not to Think Straight," in *Queering the Pitch,* 67–83.

25. Scholarship exploring music and gay, lesbian, and queer sexuality has grown exponentially since the early 1990s. Influential books and articles include Susan McClary, "Constructions of Subjectivity in Schubert's Music," in *Queering the Pitch,* 205–33; Mitchell Morris, "Reading as an Opera Queen," in *Musicology and Difference: Gender and Sexuality in Music Scholarship,* ed. Ruth Solie (Berkeley: University of California Press, 1993), 184–200; Wayne Koestenbaum, *The Queen's Throat: Opera, Homosexuality, and the Mystery of Desire* (New York: Poseidon Press, 1993); and Elizabeth Wood, "Sapphonics," in *Queering the Pitch,* 27–66. The most recent studies include *Queer Episodes in Music and Modern Identity,* ed. Sophie Fuller and Lloyd Whitesell (Urbana: University of Illinois Press, 2002), and Nadine Hubbs, *The Queer Composition of America's Sound: Gay Modernists, American Music, and National Identity* (Berkeley: University of California Press, 2004). For a thorough survey of this scholarship up to 2002, see the introduction to *Queer Episodes,* 1–21.

CHAPTER 1

1. Michel Foucault, "The Ethics of the Concern for Self as a Practice of Freedom," in *Ethics: Subjectivity and Truth,* ed. Paul Rabinow (New York: The New Press, 1994), 282.

2. Michel Foucault, "On the Genealogy of Ethics: An Overview of Work in Progress," in *Ethics: Subjectivity and Truth,* 266. For a fuller treatment of Foucault's ethics and its implications for music, see Peraino, "Listening to the Sirens: Music as Queer Ethical Practice," *GLQ: A Journal of Lesbian and Gay Studies* 9, no. 4 (2003): 433–70; see especially 435–36.

3. Foucault, "Technologies of the Self," in *Ethics: Subjectivity and Truth,* 225. See also Foucault, "On the Genealogy of Ethics," 263.

4. Foucault, "The Ethics of the Concern for Self," 282.

5. See Alexander Nehamas, *The Art of Living: Socratic Reflections from Plato to Foucault* (Berkeley: University of California Press, 1998), 177–79. See also Paul Veyne, "The Final Foucault and His Ethics," trans. Catherine Porter and Arnold I. Davidson, *Critical Inquiry* 20 (Autumn 1993): 1–9, especially 7–8.

6. Nehamas, *The Art of Living,* 178.

7. Foucault, "On the Genealogy of Ethics," 277.

8. Such myths are, of course, propagated by individuals who often reflect local concerns. See Simon Price, *Religions of the Ancient Greeks* (Cambridge: Cambridge University Press, 1999), for an excellent introduction to ancient Greek mythology and religious practices. Price notes (6) that a Panhellenic pantheon of deities, myths, and customs seemed to have been established by four important

works: Homer's *Iliad* and *Odyssey* (late eighth century B.C.E.) and Hesiod's *Theogony* and *Works and Days* (ca. 700 B.C.E.). He stresses, however, that "Greek myths were not rigid" and that "it is methodologically very important that we respect the individual telling or representation of myths" (15). A classic study of ancient Greek religion is Walter Burkert, *Greek Religion*, trans. John Raffan (Cambridge, MA: Harvard University Press, 1985).

9. See Burkert, *Greek Religion*, 182–89, for a discussion of the anthropomorphic nature of Greek gods. See also Price, *Religions of the Ancient Greeks*, 13 and 18–19.

10. For a discussion and examples of other classical depictions of the Sirens, see Diana Buitron-Oliver and Beth Cohen, "Between Skylla and Penelope: Female Characters of the *Odyssey* in Archaic and Classical Greek Art," in *The Distaff Side: Representing the Female in Homer's* Odyssey, ed. Beth Cohen (Oxford: Oxford University Press, 1995), 30–34 and plates 1–6, 39, 43–44, and 46.

11. See John Pollard, *Seer, Shrines, and Sirens: The Greek Religious Revolution in the Sixth Century B.C.* (London: George Allen & Unwin, 1965), 137–45.

12. Unless otherwise specified, all translations of the *Odyssey* are quoted from Homer, *The Odyssey: Translation and Analysis*, trans. R. D. Dawe (Sussex: Book Guild, 1993), 470–82. Dawe uses various typefaces to distinguish lines that he feels to be late interpolations. I have not called attention to these lines since they were transmitted in oral and written traditions despite ancient and modern arguments over their validity as "authentic." I have also standardized the transliteration of κ to *k*.

13. For my discussion of ancient Greek words I have relied on consultation with Pietro Pucci and The Perseus Digital Library (www.perseus.tufts.edu), which includes an online edition of Henry George Liddell and Robert Scott, *A Greek-English Lexicon*, revised and augmented by Sir Henry Stuart Jones (Oxford: Clarendon Press, 1940). For the etymology of Kirke, see also L. Darcey, "The Name of Circe and the Portolans of Archaic Greece," *Les études classiques* 53 (1985): 185–91.

14. The name Siren may also stem from the Semitic *sir,* meaning "song." For a discussion of other possibilities, see Pietro Pucci, *The Song of the Sirens: Essays on Homer* (Lanham, MD: Rowman and Littlefield, 1998), 8, n. 13; and Siegfried de Rachewiltz, *De Sirenibus: An Inquiry into Sirens from Homer to Shakespeare* (New York: Garland, 1987), 24. The following discussion owes much to these two studies.

15. For a discussion of the sexual connotations of these words, see Seth L. Schein, "Female Representations and Interpreting the *Odyssey,*" in *The Distaff Side: Representing the Female in Homer's* Odyssey, 21, and his "Introduction," in *Reading the Odyssey: Selected Interpretive Essays*, ed. Seth L. Schein (Princeton, NJ: Princeton University Press, 1996), 25–26; Pucci, "The Song of the Sirens," 198–99.

16. Pucci, "The Song of the Sirens," 196.

17. Translated in ibid., 1. I have made a minor adaptation; the opening epithet for Odysseus has been rendered by Pucci here as "skillful in telling stories" and elsewhere by him as "honored" (ibid., 191) and "famous for your stories" (see his *Odysseus Polutropos: Intertextual Readings in the* Odyssey *and the* Iliad [Ithaca, NY: Cornell University Press, 1987], 210). Dawe's translation is "much-praised Odysseus" (*The Odyssey*, 481). I have attempted to maintain the ambiguity of the epithet.

18. For a discussion of this scene, see Pucci, *Odysseus Polutropos*, 214–27.

19. Rachewiltz notes that the *Odyssey* is filled with images of knots and nets. See *De Sirenibus*, 24–25.

20. Ibid., 15–16. Rachewiltz notes that Odysseus listens with impunity and thus effectively steals the Sirens' song. The theme of Odysseus's thievery appears throughout the epic.

21. Pucci, "The Song of the Sirens," 196.

22. The red-figure bell krater is Greek, from the Italian colony of Paestum. See Buitron-Oliver and Cohen, "Between Skylla and Penelope," 32.

23. In book 8.537 Odysseus also describes the instrument of Demodokos as a *phorminga ligeian* (clear-sounding phorminx).

24. On women in the *Odyssey* see the essays in *The Distaff Side*. For a feminist reading of the *Odyssey*, see Barbara Clayton, *A Penelopean Poetics: Reweaving the Feminine in Homer's* Odyssey (Lanham, MD: Lexington Books, 2004); and Lillian Eileen Doherty, *Siren Songs: Gender, Audiences, and Narrators in the Odyssey* (Ann Arbor: University of Michigan Press, 1995). For a curious study that argues for a female authorship of the *Odyssey*, see Samuel Butler, *The Authoress of the* Odyssey, *where and when she wrote, who she was, the use she made of the* Iliad, *and how the poem grew under her hands*, 2nd ed. (London: Jonathan Cape, 1922).

    Ann Carson notes that for ancient Greek writers, *stoma* (mouth, lips, entrance) can refer to the orifice of vocal activity as well as sexual activity, and she discusses constructions of female speech and sound as the antithesis to masculine self-control. See "The Gender of Sound," *Thamyris* 1, no. 1 (Autumn 1994): 10–31.

25. See David M. Halperin, "Platonic *Erōs* and What Men Call Love," *Ancient Philosophy* 5 (1985): 161–204; see especially 163–66 and 176–77.

26. Page duBois, *Torture and Truth* (New York: Routledge, 1991), 75; see also 63–74 and 75–91, to which the following discussion refers. Carson argues that the connection of the female mouth and genitals points toward "women's allegedly definitive tendency to put the inside on the outside" and to discharge the unspeakable ("The Gender of Sound," 25–28; quote on 28). Thus women were associated both with interiority and its exposure.

27. Michel Foucault, *The Use of Pleasure*, vol. 2 of *The History of Sexuality*, trans. Robert Hurley (New York: Vintage Books, 1990), 8.

28. Foucault wrote about the Sirens' song in the midst of a discussion of Maurice Blanchot's writings in "The Thought of the Outside," in *Aesthetics, Method, and Epistemology*, ed. James D. Faubion (New York: The New Press, 1998), 160–63. He notes that Odysseus listens to a song that is only an elusive and fatal promise of a future song about his past identity. With its "speech that is indissociably echo and denial," the Sirens' dissimulating song effects what Foucault describes as a luring out of interiority and voiding of identity. For Foucault, this immobilizing void is the seduction of the Sirens' song; it is an attraction to an outside that will hollow out our identity. Though Foucault does not rigorously develop this point in his work, he is here describing a getting free of the self. He writes, "to lend an ear to the silvery voice of the Sirens . . . is not simply to abandon the world . . . it is suddenly to feel grow within oneself a desert at the other end of which (but this

immeasurable distance is also as thin as a line) gleams a language without assignable subject . . . a personal pronoun without a person" (both quotes from 163).

29. See Rachewiltz, *De Sirenibus*, 15–16.

30. In *Greek Religion*, Burkert writes, "an inalienable part of gods is, of course, their sexuality. The human man is defined by sexual activity; for gods, all human limitations fall away, and here, too, wish and fulfillment are one" (183).

31. Nietzsche's discussion of Apollo and Dionysus appears primarily in *The Birth of Tragedy*. For concise treatments of Nietzsche's views on Dionysus and Apollo see James E. Gibson, "Celebration and Transgression: Nietzsche on Ritual," *Journal of Ritual Studies* 5, no. 2 (Summer 1991): 1–13; and Lawrence J. Hatab, "Apollo and Dionysus: Nietzschean Expressions of the Sacred," in *Nietzsche and the Gods,* ed. Weaver Santaniello (Albany: State University of New York Press, 2001), 45–65.

32. See Thomas J. Mathiesen, *Apollo's Lyre: Greek Music and Music Theory in Antiquity and the Middle Ages* (Lincoln: University of Nebraska Press, 1999), 74–75, where he quotes an etymology of *dithyramb* by Proclus (412–85 C.E.). See also Walter F. Otto, *Dionysus: Myth and Cult*, trans. Robert B. Palmer (reprint Dallas: Spring Publications, 1981), 61–62; and Burkert, *Greek Religion*, 162–63. Burkert notes the myth's homoerotic implications (165). The double birth myth seems to have come from Thebes but was well known in other places.

33. For the geographical origins of Dionysus, see Otto, *Dionysus,* 52–64 and 74–76 (regarding his strange effects); and Burkert, *Greek Religion,* 162. In Euripedes' play *Bacchae*, Pentheus, in his first speech, calls Dionysus "new" (ll. 219 and 256) and tells of a foreign wizard (Dionysus in disguise) who proclaims Dionysus as a god (ll. 233–42). See Euripides, *Bacchae* (ca. 406 B.C.E.), trans. Paul Woodruff (Indianapolis, IN: Hackett, 1998).

34. The view of a polar Dionysus was first advanced by Otto in 1933, and it continues to be an influential paradigm. See Albert Henrichs, " 'He Has a God in Him': Human and Divine in the Modern Perception of Dionysus," in *Masks of Dionysus,* ed. Thomas H. Carpenter and Christopher A. Faraone (Ithaca, NY: Cornell University Press, 1993), 13–43, especially 29–31.

35. About women and maenads, see Otto, *Dionysus,* 134 and 171–80; Arthur Evans, *The God of Ecstasy: Sex-Roles and the Madness of Dionysos* (New York: St. Martin's Press, 1988), especially 11–18; and Clara Acker, *Dionysos en transe: La voix des femme* (Paris: L'Harmattan, 2002). About the effeminacy of the god and the transvestism of his male worshipers, see Evans, *The God of Ecstasy,* 19–24; Valdis Leinieks, *The City of Dionysos: A Study of Euripides'* Bakchai (Stuttgart: B. G. Teubner, 1996), 52–54; and Jan N. Bremmer, "Transvestite Dionysos," in *Rites of Passage in Ancient Greece: Literature, Religion, Society,* ed. Mark W. Padilla (Lewisburg, PA: Bucknell University Press, 1999), 183–200. See also Mathiesen, *Apollo's Lyre,* 78–79.

36. See Johannes Quasten, *Music and Worship in Pagan and Christian Antiquity,* trans. Boniface Ramsey, O.P. (Washington, D.C.: National Association of Pastoral Musicians, 1983), 35–36; and Mathiesen, *Apollo's Lyre,* 178–81 (for a discussion of *dithyrambs*, see 71–81).

37. See Leinieks, *The City of Dionysos,* 61–63; see also Thomas H. Carpenter, *Dionysian Imagery in Fifth-Century Athens* (Oxford: Clarendon Press, 1997).

38. For a concise discussion of active and passive sexual roles in classical Athens see David Halperin, *One Hundred Years of Homosexuality and Other Essays on Greek Love* (New York: Routledge, 1990), 30–36. Foucault explores ancient Greek homo-eroticism in *The Use of Pleasure,* especially 187–225.

39. See Michael Jameson, "The Asexuality of Dionysus," in *Masks of Dionysus,* ed. Thomas H. Carpenter and Christopher A. Faraone (Ithaca, NY: Cornell University Press, 1993), 44–64.

40. See Leinieks, *The City of Dionysos,* 277–302 and 327–49.

41. Warren D. Anderson, *Music and Musicians in Ancient Greece* (Ithaca, NY: Cornell University Press, 1994), 167–69.

42. Gregory Nagy, "The Name of Apollo: Etymology and Essence," in *Apollo: Origins and Influences,* ed. Jon Solomon (Tucson: University of Arizona Press, 1994), 3–7 (quote on 4). See also Walter Burkert, "Apellai und Apollon," *Rheinisches Museum für Philologie* 118, no. 1 (1975): 1–21.

43. Jon Solomon, "Introduction," in *Apollo: Origins and Influences,* ix–xii; see also Burkert, *Greek Religion,* 143–49.

44. On pederastic initiation rites see Bernard Sergent, *Homosexuality in Greek Myth,* trans. Arthur Goldhammer (Boston: Beacon Press, 1986), 7–54; see also 102–19 for a discussion of a myth in which Apollo serves as the *erōmenos* to the mortal King Admetus. The classic study of homosexual practices in Greece is Kenneth James Dover, *Greek Homosexuality* (Cambridge, MA: Harvard University Press, 1977), especially 185–203.

45. See Michael Pettersson, *Cults of Apollo at Sparta: The Hyakinthia, the Gymnopaidiai and the Karneia* (Stockholm: Svenska Institutet i Athen, 1992), 42–56. See also Barbara Kowalzig, "Changing Choral Worlds: Song-Dance and Society in Athens and Beyond," in *Music and the Muses: The Culture of "Mousikē" in the Classical Athenian City,* ed. Penelope Murray and Peter Wilson (Oxford: Oxford University Press, 2004), 59; and Peter Wilson, "Homeric Strings in Helenistic Athens," in ibid., 271–74.

46. See Jon Solomon, "Apollo and the Lyre," in *Apollo: Origins and Influences,* 37–46.

47. For a discussion of the association of Apollo, the lyre, and the politics of Athens, see Wilson, "Homeric Strings in Helenistic Athens," 271–306. See also Burkert, *Greek Religion,* 146.

48. Mathiesen, *Apollo's Lyre,* 37 and 60–62.

49. Pindar, Pythian 1 (ll. 1–12), in Andrew M. Miller, *Greek Lyric: An Anthology in Translation* (Indianapolis, IN: Hackett, 1996), 146.

50. My discussion of Pan owes much to Philippe Borgeaud, *The Cult of Pan in Ancient Greece,* trans. Kathleen Atlass and James Redfield (Chicago: University of Chicago Press, 1988); see especially 52–55 and 133–62. Plate 4, "Pan pursuing a goatherd" (ca. 470 B.C.E.), shows a vase painting of Pan with a fully erect penis and arms outstretched, chasing a young shepherd. Borgeaud discusses the picture on 74; see 185–87 for etymology. The Homeric Hymn to Pan (ca. 500–450 B.C.E.) includes the popular etymology from "all." See also Patricia Merivale, *Pan the Goat-God: His Myth in Modern Times* (Cambridge, MA: Harvard University Press, 1969), 9.

51. Borgeaud, *The Cult of Pan,* 80–87. See also the Homeric Hymn to Pan, in Susan C. Shelmerdine, *The Homeric Hymns* (Newburyport, MA: Focus Publishing, 1995), 153–54.

52. On Pan and Dionysus see the Homeric Hymn to Pan, l. 46, in Shelmerdine, *The Homeric Hymns,* 154. Borgeaud, *The Cult of Pan,* compares Pan's anger and punishment to Dionysian ritual *sparagmos* ("tearing apart"), 79; see also 111–12. On Pan and Orpheus see Dorothy Zayatz Baker, *Mythic Masks in Self-Reflexive Poetry: A Study of Pan and Orpheus* (Chapel Hill: University of North Carolina Press, 1986), 8–11.

53. Given the amoral unruliness of Pan, it was by a curious twist that later Christian allegories sometimes associated Pan with Christ. This came about through his nature as both god and man, his association with Orpheus, who was frequently associated with Christ, and the story of his death made famous by Plutarch. See Merivale, *Pan the Goat-God,* 12–34, and Baker, *Mythic Masks,* 11.

54. The following discussion of the Orpheus myth and cult is drawn from W. K. C. Guthrie, *Orpheus and Greek Religion* (Princeton, NJ: Princeton University Press, 1993), especially 1–62; Burkert, *Greek Religion,* 296–304; John Block Friedman, *Orpheus in the Middle Ages* (Syracuse, NY: Syracuse University Press, 2000), 1–2; and Baker, *Mythic Masks,* 3–28.

55. Apollodorus (1st or 2nd century C.E.), *Gods and Heroes of the Greeks: The Library of Apollodorus,* trans. Michael Simpson (Amherst: University of Massachusetts Press, 1976), 59.

56. See W. S. Anderson, "The Orpheus of Virgil and Ovid: *flebile nescio quid,*" in *Orpheus: The Metamorphoses of a Myth,* ed. John Warden (Toronto: University of Toronto Press, 1982), 25–50; and John F. Makowski, "Bisexual Orpheus: Pederasty and Parody in Ovid," *The Classical Journal* 92, no. 1 (1996): 25–38.

57. Ovid, *The Metamorphoses,* trans. Michael Simpson (Amherst: University of Massachusetts Press, 2001), 167.

58. For discussions of medieval condemnations of Orpheus as the instigator of homosexuality, see Bruce W. Holsinger, *Music, Body, and Desire in Medieval Culture: Hildegard of Bingen to Chaucer* (Stanford, CA: Stanford University Press, 2001), 295–343. For Christian allegories, see Friedman, *Orpheus in the Middle Ages;* and Eleanor Irwin, "The Songs of Orpheus and the New Song of Christ," in *Orpheus: The Metamorphoses of a Myth,* 51–62.

59. See Betsy Rosasco, "Albrecht Dürer's 'Death of Orpheus': Its Critical Fortunes and a New Interpretation of its Meaning," *Idea Jahrbuch der Hamburger Kunsthalle* 3 (1984): 19–41. I thank Karol Berger for calling my attention to this print and the Rosasco article.

60. In some traditions Orpheus is the son of the Thracian wine god Oreagrus. Orpheus abandons the Dionysian priesthood to become a worshiper of Apollo, thus causing the anger of the Thracian maenads. Ovid may be mixing traditions here. See Friedman, *Orpheus in the Middle Ages,* 5–6 and 214, n. 5.

61. See Ovid, *The Metamorphoses* (trans. Simpson), 182.

62. Elements of this scene stem from Orpheus's early associations with Dionysian cults. For a discussion of the humor in this scene, see Makowski, "Bisexual Orpheus," 36–38.

63. Quoted in Friedman, *Orpheus in the Middle Ages,* 9.

64. For an attempt to find Orphic traces in Sappho's poetry, see Robert Böhme, *Orpheus: Der Sänger und seine Zeit* (Munich: Frandke Verlag, 1970), 145–63.

65. Jane McIntosh Snyder writes, "Sappho is important not only because she was the

most famous woman writer in the ancient Western world but also because she remains a persistent and effective voice for the expression of a woman's desire for a woman—out of all proportion to the actual number of her surviving works." See her *Lesbian Desire in the Lyrics of Sappho* (New York: Columbia University Press, 1997), ix; also 123–59 for her discussion of Sappho's treatment by modern American women poets.

66. For a theoretical approach to the poetic fragments see Page duBois, *Sappho is Burning* (Chicago: University of Chicago Press, 1995), 31–54. Most English-language studies of Sappho take as a starting point the pioneering, though disparaging, critical study of Denys Page, *Sappho and Alcaeus: An Introduction to the Study of Ancient Lesbian Poetry* (Oxford: Clarendon Press, 1955; reprint 1975).

67. See Judith P. Hallett, "Sappho and Her Social Context: Sense and Sensuality," in *Reading Sappho: Contemporary Approaches,* ed. Ellen Greene (Berkeley: University of California Press, 1996), 125; see also Margaret Reynolds, *The Sappho Companion* (London: Chatto and Windus, 2000), 69–70.

68. For a discussion of performance in symposia see Eva Stehle, *Performance and Gender in Ancient Greece* (Princeton, NJ: Princeton University Press, 1997), 213–61. Young girls joined choirs as part of a system of education, and Sappho may have led such a choir. See Claude Calame, "Sappho's Group: An Initiation into Womanhood," in *Reading Sappho,* 113–24; Stehle, *Performance and Gender in Ancient Greece,* 263–78; and André Lardinois, "Lesbian Sappho and Sappho of Lesbos," in *From Sappho to De Sade: Moments in the History of Sexuality,* ed. Jan Bremmer (New York: Routledge, 1989), 26.

There has been much debate about how Sappho's songs were performed. André Lardinois argues for a public choral performance, perhaps with a soloist, in "Who Sang Sappho's Songs?" in *Reading Sappho,* 150–72. Stehle argues for various types of performances, from public choral to private monodic recitals, and she further argues that Sappho's more intimate poetry was as likely to be addressed to adult women companions as to *parthenoi.* See Stehle, *Performance and Gender in Ancient Greece,* 264–78.

69. For ancient and modern typologies of Sappho's songs see Lardinois, "Lesbian Sappho and Sappho of Lesbos," 16–18; Stehle, *Performance and Gender in Ancient Greece,* 275–78; and Mathiesen, *Apollo's Lyre,* 151–52.

70. See Hallett, "Sappho and Her Social Context," who argues there is no evidence for lesbian practice, and Eva Stehle, "Romantic Sensuality, Poetic Sense: A Response to Hallett on Sappho," in *Reading Sappho,* 143–49. For a discussion of the debate see Lardinois, "Lesbian Sappho and Sappho of Lesbos," 18–25; for a discussion of the theories of initiatory homosexuality on the model of Spartan pederasty see Stehle, *Performance and Gender in Ancient Greece,* 270–76.

71. See the *Testimonia* in *Greek Lyric 1: Sappho and Alcaeus,* trans. David A. Campbell (Cambridge, MA: Harvard University Press, 1982). For discussions see Dover, *Greek Homosexuality,* 174; Lardinois, "Lesbian Sappho and Sappho of Lesbos," 19–25; Hallett, "Sappho and Her Social Context"; Stehle, *Performance and Gender in Ancient Greece,* 264–66; and Reynolds, *The Sappho Companion,* 69–78.

72. Reynolds, *The Sappho Companion,* 73, 76–78; for a discussion of contextualizing Ovid see also Joan DeJean, *Fictions of Sappho: 1546–1937* (Chicago: University of Chicago Press, 1989), 17–19.

73. DuBois, *Sappho is Burning*, 163–94.

74. All Sappho texts and translations quoted from Snyder, *Lesbian Desire in the Lyrics of Sappho*, unless noted otherwise.

75. For a discussion of Terpander and Orpheus see Böhme, *Orpheus*, 112–44.

76. See Mathiesen, *Apollo's Lyre*, 250–52 (the kalathoid is pictured on p. 252, figure 40).

77. See ibid., 104.

78. See Burkert, *Greek Religion*, 152–56.

79. I have modified this translation slightly.

80. Stehle argues that this fragment presents a "mode of fostering another woman's subjectivity," as does fragment 96, both of which create "a play of intersubjectivity" and "the possibility of mutual interchange in escape from the subject-object division encoded in hegemonic culture." See her *Performance and Gender in Ancient Greece*, 302–3. Page duBois and Ellen Greene have discussed how historians of sexuality, especially Foucault, neglect Sappho's lyrics in their accounts of ancient Greek sexuality, and thus reinforce the phallocentrism. See duBois, *Sappho is Burning*, 127–45; and Ellen Greene, "Sappho, Foucault, and Women's Erotics," *Arethusa* 29 (1996): 1–14.

81. Stehle, *Performance and Gender in Ancient Greece*, 305.

82. About the connection between Aphrodite, the images of flight and fluttering in Sappho's poems, and Archaic Greek aesthetics of *poikilia* (variegation), see Snyder, *Lesbian Desire in the Lyrics of Sappho*, 10, 32, 79–80. Lyn Hatherly Wilson, *Sappho's Sweetbitter Songs: Configurations of Female and Male in Ancient Greek Lyric* (New York: Routledge, 1996), 55, notes that in fragment 22 Sappho seems to suggest that the women of her community "approbate love even more than the god of desire."

83. See Leah Rissman, *Love as War: Homeric Allusion in the Poetry of Sappho* (Königstein: Anton Hain Meisenheim, 1983), 30–53; Snyder, *Lesbian Desire in the Lyrics of Sappho*, 63–77; duBois, *Sappho is Burning*, 97–126; John J. Winkler, *The Constraints of Desire: The Anthropology of Sex and Gender in Ancient Greece* (New York: Routledge, 1990), 162–87.

84. For a discussion of *mousikē* and Muses in ancient Greek culture see Penelope Murray and Peter Wilson, "Introduction: *Mousikē*, not Music," in *Music and the Muses: The Culture of "Mousikē" in the Classical Athenian City*, ed. Penelope Murray and Peter Wilson (Oxford: Oxford University Press, 2004), 1–8; and Penelope Murray, "The Muses and Their Arts," in ibid., 365–89.

85. For a study of this opening formula see Graham Wheeler, "Sing, Muse . . . : The Introit from Homer to Apollonius," *Classical Quarterly* 52, no. 1 (2002): 33–49.

86. Hesiod, *Theogony*, trans. Norman O. Brown (New York: Macmillan, 1985), 54.

87. Eric A. Havelock, *Preface to Plato* (Cambridge, MA: Harvard University Press, 1963), 154–55.

88. See Lillian Eileen Doherty, "Sirens, Muses, and Female Narrators in the *Odyssey*," in *The Distaff Side*, 81–92.

89. Quoted and translated in Pietro Pucci, *Hesiod and the Language of Poetry* (Baltimore, MD: Johns Hopkins University Press, 1977), 9.

90. See Havelock, *Preface to Plato*, 104–5; Wheeler, "Sing, Muse," 34–35; Pucci, *Hesiod and the Language of Poetry*, 8–16; and Murray, "The Muses and Their Arts," 366–72.

91. For excellent discussions of the politics of this musical revolution and the rise of the *aulos* see Eric Csapo, "The Politics of New Music," in *Music and the Muses: The Culture of "Mousikē" in the Classical Athenian City*, ed. Penelope Murray and Peter Wilson (Oxford: Oxford University Press, 2004), 207–48; and Wilson, "Athenian Strings."

92. See Ellen Meiksins Wood and Neal Wood, *Class Ideology and Ancient Political Theory: Socrates, Plato, and Aristotle in Social Context* (New York: Oxford University Press, 1978), especially 119–208.

93. Plato, *Laws*, trans. Trevor J. Saunders, in *Complete Works*, ed. John M. Cooper (Indianapolis, IN: Hackett, 1997). All translations of *Laws* are taken from this edition.

94. Another lengthy complaint against innovations in music appears in book 2, 669b–670c. Mathiesen notes the tension between innovative musical practices and conservative philosophers and theorists throughout *Apollo's Lyre* (see especially 29 and 81). See also Csapo, "The Politics of New Music," 229–48; and Wilson, "Athenian Strings," 294–306.

95. Lawrence J. Hatab, *Myth and Philosophy: A Contest of Truths* (La Salle, IL: Open Court, 1990), 50; and Csapo, "The Politics of New Music," 229.

96. Anderson, *Music and Musicians in Ancient Greece*, 49–50.

97. See Herbert M. Schueller, *The Idea of Music: An Introduction to Musical Aesthetics in Antiquity and the Middle Ages* (Kalamazoo, MI: Medieval Institute Publications, 1988): 1–4. Plato mentions the personified Harmonia once in his dialogues, ending the discussion of the soul in *Phaedo* (95a), which will be discussed below. For a comprehensive discussion of the various meanings of *harmonia* see also Edward A. Lippman, "Hellenic Conceptions of Harmony," *Journal of the American Musicological Society* 16, no. 1 (1963): 1–35.

98. See Richard Crocker, "Pythagorean Mathematics and Music," *Journal of Aesthetics and Art Criticism* 22 (1963/64): 189–98 (Part I) and 325–35 (Part II); reprinted in Crocker, *Studies in Medieval Music Theory and the Early Sequence* (Brookfield, VT: Ashgate Publishing, 1997). See also Lippmann, "Hellenic Conceptions of Harmony," 4.

99. Plato, *Timaeus*, trans. Donald J. Zeyl, in *Complete Works*, 1239 (35a–36e) and 1246–47 (43d). The following discussion is much indebted to my correspondence with Richard Crocker. See also Jacques Handschin, "The 'Timaeus' Scale," *Musica Disciplina* 4 (1950): 3–42; Lippmann, "Hellenic Conceptions of Harmony," 18–23; Anderson, *Music and Musicians in Ancient Greece*, 50 and 145–54; Schueller, *The Idea of Music*, 17–19 and 33–34.

100. See Ernest G. McClain, *The Pythagorean Plato: Prelude to the Song Itself* (Stony Brook, NY: Nicolas Hays, 1978), 60. According to the music theory of Aristoxenus (fl. late fourth century B.C.E.), tetrachords formed the building blocks of the melodic system. These were an arrangement of four notes wherein the outer two formed a perfect fourth and were stable while the internal two notes were less stable, falling into three typical genera: diatonic ("the oldest, and most natural"), chromatic ("younger"), and enharmonic ("most difficult for the senses"). The latter two use pitches smaller than a halftone. See Mathiesen, *Apollo's Lyre*, 309–17.

101. See McClain, *The Pythagorean Plato*, 64–70.

102. Plato, *Timaeus* (trans. Zeyl), in *Complete Works*, 1250.
103. Plato, *Phaedo,* trans. G. M. A. Grube, in *Complete Works*, 82.
104. Plato, *Republic,* trans. G. M. A. Grube, rev. C. D. C. Reeve, in *Complete Works,* 1046. All translations of the *Republic* are taken from this edition unless otherwise specified.
105. For the Greek text and a discussion of this passage see Plato, *The Republic,* ed. James Adams, 2 vols. (Cambridge: Cambridge University Press, 1902), 1:159–60.
106. Wilson notes that some versions of the story have Apollo win the contest by a cunning challenge to Marsyas, namely that he play his *aulos* and sing at the same time—an impossible feat on that instrument, but entirely possible with the lyre. This ambiguous story demonstrates, on one hand, the superiority of the lyre over the *aulos,* and, on the other hand, Apollo's recourse to trickery against the appeal of the *aulos.* See "Athenian Strings," 276–77.
107. I have emended the translation based on my discussion of the passage with Charles Francis Brittain.
108. See Anderson, *Music and Musicians in Ancient Greece,* 97.
109. I have emended the translation of the first sentence.
110. I should note here Plato's detailed description of an educational system based on four choirs that correlated to four stages of life: the choir of the Muses for boys, the choir of Apollo for men under thirty, and a choir of Dionysus for those between thirty and sixty (*Laws,* 664b–672c). The last choir receives the longest and most puzzling treatment. For commentary see Seth Benardete, *Plato's "Laws": The Discovery of Being* (Chicago: University of Chicago Press, 2000), 75–87.
111. Foucault tracks Plato's concerns throughout *The Use of Pleasure.* Much of the first half of Plato's dialogue *Phaedrus* (roughly 227a–257b) concerns *erōs* and its proper control and uses between *erastēs* and *erōmenos.* The prologue to *Lysis* offers another discussion of this topic. For commentary on *Lysis* see Francisco J. Gonzalez, "How to Read a Platonic Prologue: *Lysis* 203A–207D," in *Plato as Author: The Rhetoric of Philosophy,* ed. Ann N. Michelini (Leiden: Brill, 2003), 22–36. Yet another instance in the *Symposium* will be discussed below. For full treatments of Plato's erotic dialogues see Alfred Geier, *Plato's Erotic Thought: The Tree of the Unknown* (Rochester, NY: University of Rochester Press, 2002); and James M. Rhodes, *Eros, Wisdom, and Silence: Plato's Erotic Dialogues* (Columbia: University of Missouri Press, 2003).
112. Translators note: "legendary worshipers of Cybele, who brought about their own derangement through music and dance."
113. Plato, *Symposium,* trans. Alexander Nehamas and Paul Woodruff, in *Complete Works,* 499.
114. For an excellent study of the political and social crises caused by Alcibiades, see David Gribble, *Alcibiades and Athens: A Study in Literary Presentation* (Oxford: Clarendon Press, 1999), especially his treatment by Plato and other Socratics, 214–59. About the final scene in the *Symposium,* Gribble writes, "[Alcibiades'] speech introduces a most disturbing note, making us wonder to what extent the ideal of the philosophical-erotic ascent described by Socrates can ever take place in practice" (243). See also Rhodes, *Eros, Wisdom, and Silence,* 370–410. Rhodes (410) summarizes that with Alcibiades, Plato presents "the disorder that

ruined the natural leaders of Athens," such as Alcibiades, as "tyrannical *erōs*" that yields "wrong pederasty" in contrast to Socrates' "right pederasty," which can be communicated only through poetry and philosophy.

115. See his chapter on music in *The Closing of the American Mind* (New York: Simon and Schuster, 1987), 78.
116. Ibid., 73 and 79.
117. See Rachewiltz, *De Sirenibus*, 71–73.
118. Peter Brown, *The Body and Society: Men, Women, and Sexual Renunciation in Early Christian Antiquity* (New York: Columbia University Press, 1988), 5–64; quotations from 44 and 60 respectively.
119. For a detailed discussion of this struggle for definition, see Quasten, *Music and Worship in Pagan and Christian Antiquity*, 59–120.
120. James McKinnon, *Music in Early Christian Literature* (Cambridge: Cambridge University Press, 1987), 49–50.
121. Ibid., 80.
122. For many early theologians, the motif of the *canticum novum* or "new song" became a powerful metaphor for Jesus Christ, the New Covenant, and the embodiment of Christian piety. In Psalms 33:3, 40:3, 96:1, 98:1, 144:9, and 149:1 and in Isaiah 42:10 this motif is an imperative: "O sing unto the Lord a new song." But Psalm 40:3 construes this new song as the substance of faith placed into the body by God: "And he hath put a new song in my mouth." Although this motif does not appear in the New Testament, its use in Revelation 5:9 and 14:3 connects this musically embodied faith to the redemption of the flesh through the death of Jesus Christ: "And they sung as it were a new song before the throne, and before the four beasts, and the elders: and no man could learn that song but the hundred and forty and four thousand, which were redeemed from the earth" (Rev. 14:3). For an extended excerpt of Clement's writing on pagan music and on Christ as the New Song, see Oliver Strunk, *Source Readings in Music History* (New York: W. W. Norton and Company, 1950), 59–63. See also Holsinger's discussion in *Music, Body, and Desire*, 33–36, 45–46.
123. For a history of early Christian sexual conservatism see Peter Brown, *The Body and Society*. The following discussion is indebted to his chapter on Augustine, 387–427.
124. Augustine, *Confessions*, trans. F. J. Sheed, rev. ed. (Indianapolis: Hackett, 1993). All translations from the *Confessions* are taken from this edition. I have modified slightly the translated excerpts from *Confessions* 10.33.
125. See Brown, *The Body and Society*, 406–7.
126. Augustine, *The City of God*, trans. Marcus Dods (New York: Modern Library, 1993), 465.
127. See Augustine, *Confessions*, book 8 for Augustine's agonizing prior to his conversion, which for him hinges upon his renunciation of sex and marriage. See also Fredric Jameson, "On the Sexual Production of Western Subjectivity; or, Saint Augustine as a Social Democrat," in *Gaze and Voice as Love Objects*, ed. Renata Salecl and Slavoj Žižek (Durham, NC: Duke University Press, 1996), 167–76.
128. Foucault, "Sexuality and Solitude," in *Ethics: Subjectivity and Truth*, 182–83.
129. Jameson, "On the Sexual Production of Western Subjectivity," 176–77.

130. See Richard L. Crocker, *An Introduction to Gregorian Chant* (New Haven, CT: Yale University Press, 2000), 98–99; Kenneth Levy, "Latin Chant Outside the Roman Tradition: Milanese or Ambrosian Chant," in *The New Oxford History of Music: The Early Middle Ages to 1300,* ed. Richard Crocker and David Hiley (Oxford: Oxford University Press, 1990), 83–84; and David Hiley, *Western Plainchant: A Handbook* (Oxford: Clarendon Press, 1993), 489–90. See also Ambrose's *Explanation psalmi* in McKinnon, *Music in Early Christian Literature,* 126–27.

131. The biblical source for the ideal of singing *quasi una voce* stems from the story of Shadrach, Meshach, and Abed'nego (Dan. 3:5), three Jewish officials who refused the imperial order to worship the golden image that King Nebuchadnez'zar had erected. As punishment, the three men are thrown into a "fiery furnace." The three sing praises to God as if from one mouth *(quasi ex uno ore)* and are saved. For a more detailed discussion of singing *quasi una voce* with regard to Augustine, see Peraino, "Listening to the Sirens," 441–47, especially 442. Latin quoted from *Biblia Sacra Iuxta Vulgatam Versionem,* ed. Bonifatio Fischer O.S.B., Iohanne Gribomont O.S.B., H. F. D. Sparks, and W. Theile (Stuttgart: Wüttembergische Bibelanstalt, 1969), 2:1349. I was directed to this passage by a reference in a review article by Richard Crocker, "Two Recent Editions of Aquitanian Polyphony," *Plainsong and Medieval Music* 3, no. 1 (1994): 90; see also 89–91. Quasten notes that liturgical evidence for the early ideal of unison singing in Christian worship appears in the prefaces of the Mass, which describe the angels, archangels, seraphim, and cherubim praising God with one voice (*Music and Worship in Pagan and Christian Antiquity,* 68; see also 66–72).

132. Augustine, *Exposition of the Psalms 1–32,* trans. Maria Boulding, O.S.B., vol. 15 of *The Works of Saint Augustine: A Translation for the 21st Century,* ed. John E. Rotelle (Hyde Park, NY: New City Press, 2001), 395. I have used the variant given in n. 10 on this page for the last sentence. See also 392, n. 1 for a discussion of the dating of this sermon. For the Latin, see Augustine, *Enarrationes in Psalmos,* ed. Eligius Dekkers and Johannes Fraipon, vol. 1 of *Corpus Christianorum Series Latina* 38 (Turnholti: Brepols, 1956), 1:250.

133. *The Works of Saint Augustine,* 15:396.

134. The metaphor of the body as musical instrument (especially a string instrument) in medieval religious thought is central to Holsinger's study; however, he does not discuss the doctrine of singing *quasi una voce,* nor this particular passage. For a discussion of the body as a musical instrument in Augustine, see Holsinger, *Music, Body, and Desire,* 80–81.

135. *The Works of Saint Augustine,* 15: 400–401.

136. I have modified the translation from *The Works of Saint Augustine,* 15:401. The Latin reads: "Etenim illi qui cantant, siue in messe, siue in uniea, siue in aliquo opere feruenti, cum coeperint in uerbis canticorum exultare laetitia, ueluti impleti tanta laetitia, ut eam uerbis explicare non possint" (*Enarrationes in Psalmos,* 1:254). See also Holsinger, *Music, Body, and Desire,* 76–77, for his discussion of other similar passages describing "jubilation" in Augustine's writings. Holsinger wrongly asserts that "jubilus" for Augustine "likely refers to the lengthy melisma . . . sung on the final syllable of the Alleluia" (76). There is no evidence in the writings of Augustine or any other writer for a pre-800 associa-

tion of the term with liturgical chant. The first association of *jubilus* with alleluia appears in the ninth-century writings of Amalarius of Metz (ca. 850). See James McKinnon, "Jubilus," in *The New Grove Dictionary of Music and Musicians,* 2nd ed., ed. Stanley Sadie and John Tyrrell (New York: Grove Dictionaries, 2001), 13:275–76.

137. *The Works of Saint Augustine,* 15:401.

138. For a reading of Augustine as inconsistent and disingenuous about music, see Holsinger, *Music, Body, and Desire,* 77; see also 74–78.

139. Augustine, *Confessions* (trans. Sheed), 198. I have modified this passage slightly, as discussed below.

140. Cf. McKinnon, *Music in Early Christian Literature,* 155 ("when sung with fluent voice and music that is most appropriate"); Holsinger, *Music, Body, and Desire,* 75 ("when in a fluid voice and with the most suitable measure"); and *Confessions* (trans. Sheed), 198 ("When they are sung with a clear voice and proper modulation"). I thank Charles Francis Brittain and Richard Crocker for their comments regarding this passage.

141. Augustine defines *modulatione* in book 1.2.3. See Augustine, *On Music,* trans. Robert Taliaferro, vol. 2 of *The Writings of Saint Augustine* (New York: CIMA Publishing, 1947).

142. Augustine, *Confessions* (trans. Sheed), 197–98: The Latin appears in Augustine, *Confessions,* ed. James J. O'Donnell (Oxford: Clarendon Press, 1992), 1:139: "flete mecum et pro me flete qui aliquid boni vobiscum intus agitis, unde facta procedunt. nam qui non agitis, non vos haec movent. tu autem, domine deus meus, exaudi: respice et vide et miserere et sana me, in cuius oculis mihi quaestio factus sum, et ipse est languor meus." In his commentary on the passage, O'Donnell remarks that Augustine reverses the expected position of the speaking self as questioner to the speaking self as the object of questioning in order to intimate that true answers come not from the self but from divine grace. See *Confessions,* ed. O'Donnell, 3:220.

143. Summarized from Foucault, "Technologies of the Self."

144. Marcia L. Colish, *Stoicism in Christian Latin Thought through the Sixth Century,* vol. 2 of *The Stoic Tradition from Antiquity to the Early Middle Ages* (Leiden: E. J. Brill, 1985), 207–38; see especially 212–20. See also Colish, *Medieval Foundations of the Western Intellectual Tradition, 400–1400* (New Haven, CT: Yale University Press, 1998), 28–29.

145. See Barbara Newman, *Saint Hildegard of Bingen, Symphonia: A Critical Edition of the* Symphonia armonie celestium revelationum (Ithaca, NY: Cornell University Press, 1988), 1–6. On Hildegard and monastic reform, see Jo Ann McNamara, "Forward to the Past: Hildegard of Bingen and Twelfth-century Monastic Reform," in Hildegard of Bingen, *Explanation of the Rule of Benedict,* trans. Hugh Feiss (Toronto: Peregrina, 2000), 15–16, 21–23.

146. See especially chapter 3 of Holsinger, *Music, Body, and Desire;* see also Kathryn L. Bumpass, "A Musical Reading of Hildegard's Responsory 'Spiritui Sancto,'" in *Hildegard of Bingen: A Book of Essays,* ed. Maud Burnett McInerney (New York: Garland, 1998), 155–73.

147. See R. Howard Bloch, *Medieval Misogyny and the Invention of Western Romantic Love* (Chicago: University of Chicago Press, 1991), especially 37–63, and Caro-

line Walker Bynum, *Holy Feast and Holy Fast: The Religious Significance of Food to Medieval Women* (Berkeley: University of California Press, 1987), especially 260–76.

148. Bloch, *Medieval Misogyny,* 98; see also 97–109.

149. Text and translation in Newman, *Saint Hildegard of Bingen,* 134–35. Newman offers both a literal and a poetic translation of Hildegard's lyrics. In all cases I quote from the literal translation.

150. Holsinger interprets this poem in terms of its architectural metaphors and performance practice, suggesting that "'O quam preciosa' allows the nuns of Rupertsberg to participate in Christ's own passage through the Virgin's 'secret' anatomy as they travel through the monastery" (*Music, Body, and Desire,* 104–5). Such a reading, I believe, wrongly aligns the nuns' identification with Christ rather than the Virgin.

151. This passage is from a prayer introducing three lyric pieces on the theme of nuns as brides of Christ and appears in the miscellany appended to the *Symphonia* (late 1150s). Quoted in John Stevens, "The Musical Individuality of Hildegard's Songs: A Liturgical Shadowland," in *Hildegard of Bingen: The Context of Her Thought and Art,* ed. Charles Burnet and Peter Dronke (London: Warburg Institute, 1998), 177. See also Newman, *Saint Hildegard of Bingen,* 69, item c.

152. See Stevens, "The Musical Individuality of Hildegard's Songs," 163–88; and Margot Fassler, "Composer and Dramatist: 'Melodious Singing and the Freshness of Remorse,'" in *Voice of the Living Light: Hildegard of Bingen and Her World,* ed. Barbara Newman (Berkeley: University of California Press, 1998), 149–75.

153. Hildegard wrote a few chants for the Mass, but only those genres that were still "open" to new compositions: seven sequences (considered paraliturgical), one Alleluia, and one Kyrie. See Fassler, "Composer and Dramatist," 151; for a discussion of Hildegard's use of a chant model, see 166–68.

154. Fassler, "Composer and Dramatist," notes that while male clergy were necessarily present to officiate during Mass, the nuns could sing the Divine Office by themselves (151), and that the head of the monastic community would be responsible for intoning the great responsories on major feast days (154).

155. Constant Mews, "Religious Thinker: 'A Frail Human Being' on Fiery Life," in *Voice of the Living Light,* 62. See also Mews, "Hildegard and the Schools," in *Hildegard of Bingen: The Context of Her Thought and Art,* 103.

156. Hildegard of Bingen, *Scivias,* trans. Mother Columba Hart and Jane Bishop (New York: Paulist Press, 1990), 3.13.12–13. All translations from *Scivias* are taken from this edition.

157. I have found two German sources for this image. The first is a depiction of the Annunciation in an initial from a gradual (ca. 1300, probably from the convent of Sankt Kartharinenthal, Lake Constance) that shows the dove at the left ear of the Virgin (Metropolitan Museum of Art, Purchase, Gift of J. Pierpont Morgan, by exchange, 1982); the image is available through The Art Museum Image Consortium (AMICO) Library, www.amico.org/. The second is discussed below.

158. This passage comes from a letter written in response to an initial letter from unidentified priests. Quoted in Barbara Newman, *Sister of Wisdom: Saint Hilde-*

gard's Theology of the Feminine (Berkeley: University of California Press, 1989), 175.

159. Newman, *Sister of Wisdom*, 175. Holsinger notes that Hildegard uses "wind" as a metaphor for female sexual arousal, and he finds its musical analog in her wide melodic ranges (*Music, Body, and Desire*, 114–18).

160. Metropolitan Museum of Art, The Cloisters Collection, 1993.251.1; the image is available through The Art Museum Image Consortium (AMICO) Library, www.amico.org/.

In the miniatures that accompany her visions, Hildegard sometimes appears in an annunciatory posture, receiving her visions from heavenly fiery tongues or beams of light and, notably, writing them down. This image also shares a vocabulary of motifs with depictions of Pope Gregory the Great receiving and writing down divinely inspired commentary or, since the legends of the ninth century, the sacred chant, as it was dictated to him by the Holy Spirit in the form of a dove. In one source for the Gregorian image, a depiction of the Annunciation appears below the scene of the Pope's heavenly dictation. For a discussion and illustration of the shared motifs see Lieselotte E. Saurma-Jeltsch, *Die Miniaturen im "Liber Scivias" der Hildegard von Bingen* (Wiesbaden: Dr. Ludwig Reichert Verlag, 1998), 15–18 and 25–28. For a discussion and illustrations of the legend of Pope Gregory and sacred chant, see Leo Treitler, "Homer and Gregory: The Transmission of Epic Poetry and Plainchant," *Musical Quarterly* 60, no. 3 (1974): 333–44.

161. This passage is from her famous letter to the prelates at Mainz, dated around 1178–79, explaining her theology of music in response to their punitive interdict against her nuns singing the liturgy. It is quoted in Newman, *Sister of Wisdom*, 194–95; see also Newman's discussion on these pages.

162. Barbara Newman and Rebecca L. R. Garber note that Hildegard seemed to ignore the current affective Mariology of Bernard of Clairvaux and Elisabeth von Schönau. Garber writes, "She had no visions of Mary, no images of suckling from Mary's breast, nor did she write a Marian legend. Neither did she encourage her nuns to give birth to Christ in their hearts in imitation of the Virgin. Within the *Scivias* and the Marian lyrics, Mary appears almost exclusively at the point of the Incarnation." See Rebecca L. R. Garber, "Where Is the Body? Images of Eve and Mary in the *Scivias*," in *Hildegard of Bingen: A Book of Essays*, 124. See also Newman, *Sister of Wisdom*, 159–60. Garber briefly notes that singing Hildegard's chants could be understood as a form of *imitatio Mariae* (123). For a more in-depth discussion of this idea, see Margot Fassler, "Composer and Dramatist," 159–68, especially 166–67.

163. Example 1 is my own transcription of the respond from *O quam preciosa* (Riesencodex), Wiesbaden, Hessische Landsbibliothek, Hs. 2, f. 468. Fassler, "Composer and Dramatist," argues similarly that the popular image of the Tree of Jesse functioned as a type of compositional model for Hildegard's *Scivias* songs: "the songs are musically ornate, like the fronds of the Jesse tree; they are difficult and long and could sustain a lifetime of contemplation, lifetimes of singing, as the composer intended for her nuns. They are sounding icons for study and meditation on the words and phrases of their luxuriant imagery, meant to conjure up pictures in the mind of the vibrant colors and verdure they depict, each singer/listener mentally painting as she can, each being taught and trans-

formed through the process" (161). See also her analysis of Hildegard's responsory *O tu suavissima virga,* 162–64.

164. See also Marianne Richert Pfau, "Mode and Melody Type in Hildegard von Bingen's *Symphonia,*" *Sonus* 11, no. 1 (1990): 53–71.

165. Melismatic extensions of important ultimate or penultimate words are common in the chant repertory, and by the early twelfth century there was a large repertory of "plug-in" or substitute melismas, many of which show repetition patterns such as AAB and descending sequences of note-groups. For a transcription of some plug-in melismas and a discussion see Richard H. Hoppin, *Medieval Music* (New York: Norton, 1978), 146–48.

166. Holsinger, drawing on Elizabeth Wood's idea of "Sapphonics," concludes that Hildegard's music "creates sonorous spaces of lesbian possibility in themselves and as they are performed by other Sapphonic bodies" (*Music, Body, and Desire,* 129). See also Wood, "Sapphonics," in *Queering the Pitch: The New Gay and Lesbian Musicology,* ed. Philip Brett, Elizabeth Wood, and Gary C. Thomas (New York: Routledge, 1994). Susan Schibanoff attempts to connect Hildegard's music to a specific and possibly erotic attachment to one of her nuns, Richardis of Stade. See her "Hildegard of Bingen and Richardis of Stade: The Discourse of Desire," in *Same Sex Love and Desire Among Women in the Middle Ages,* ed. Francesca Candadé Sautman and Pamela Sheingorn (New York: Palgrave, 2001), 49–83.

167. See Jocelyn Wogan-Browne, *Saints' Lives and Women's Literary Culture c. 1150–1300: Virginity and Its Authorizations* (Oxford: Oxford University Press, 2000).

168. Barbara Newman points out that by using the rhetoric of the Song of Songs, Hildegard carefully chose her terms of comparison for their symbolic significance: "in echoes and figures the description of Ecclesia evokes the divine majesty: sapphire for the throne of God (Ezek. 1:26), Bethel for Jacob's vision (Gen. 28:11–22), incense and myrrh (Song 4:6) for priesthood and the passion of Christ, and the sound of many waters (Apoc. 1:15, 14:2) for the voice of the lamb in judgment" (*Saint Hildegard of Bingen,* 311).

169. See Anna W. Astell, *The Song of Songs in the Middle Ages* (Ithaca, NY: Cornell University Press, 1990), 1–24.

170. For a transcription of this sequence see Hildegard of Bingen, *Sequences and Hymns,* ed. Christopher Page (Devon, England: Antico, 1983), 14–16.

171. See McNamara, "Forward to the Past," 23–24, for a description of Hildegard's remarkable material and political gains in her break from the monastery at Disibodenberg.

172. Julia Kristeva, *Tales of Love,* trans. Leon S. Roudiez (New York: Columbia University Press, 1987), 94–95 (emphasis in the original).

173. Ibid., 95.

174. The order of the stanzas in the manuscript tradition of this chanson is stable. See Carl Appel, *Bernart von Ventadorn, Seine Lieder* (Halle: Max Niemeyer, 1915), 85–90.

175. Occitan and adapted translation from *Anthology of Troubadour Lyric Poetry,* ed. and trans. Alan R. Press (Edinburgh: Edinburgh University Press, 1971), 66–69. I have also consulted the literal translation by Ronnie Apter, *Sugar and Salt: A*

Bilingual Edition of the Love Songs of Bernart de Ventadorn in Occitan and English (Lewiston, NY: Edwin Mellen Press, 1999), 111–13.

176. For a discussion of desire in troubadour lyrics, see Sarah Kay, "Desire and Subjectivity," in *The Troubadours: An Introduction,* ed. Simon Gaunt and Sarah Kay (Cambridge: Cambridge University Press, 1999), 212–27. For a discussion of gender and status in troubadour lyrics see her book *Subjectivity in Troubadour Poetry* (Cambridge: Cambridge University Press, 1990), 84–131.

177. See Gayle S. Rubin, "The Traffic in Women: Notes on the 'Political Economy' of Sex," in *Toward an Anthropology of Women,* ed. Rayna R. Reiter (New York: Monthly Review Press, 1975), especially 171–75.

178. Simon Gaunt, *Gender and Genre in Medieval French Literature* (Cambridge: Cambridge University Press, 1995), 146 and 147, respectively.

179. I thank Alice Colby-Hall for her translation of these *tornadas.*

180. The *vidas* of the troubadours were short biographical blurbs included in a few manuscripts, mostly fictions drawn from various songs. Arnaut's *vida,* however, has nothing to do with his songs and so has been considered truthful. The *vida* text and translation can be found in *The Poetry of Arnaut Daniel,* ed. and trans. James J. Wilhelm (New York: Garland, 1981), xiv. The miniature appears on p. x.

181. Ibid., xiii.

182. Ibid., 42 and 43.

183. For discussions of Arnaut Daniel's life, works, and influence, see the introduction in ibid., xi–xxxix; see also James J. Wilhelm, *Il Miglior Fabbro: The Cult of the Difficult in Daniel, Dante, and Pound* (Orno, ME: National Poetry Foundation, 1982).

184. Text and translation adapted from *The Poetry of Arnaut Daniel,* 6–9. I have also consulted the translation in Samuel N. Rosenberg, Margaret Switten, and Gérard Le Vot, eds., *Songs of the Troubadours and Trouvères: An Anthology of Poems and Melodies* (New York: Garland, 1998), 90–91, and Emil Levy, *Petit Dictionnaire Provençal-Français* (Heidelberg: Carl Winter, 1966). Wilhelm based his edition on the version found in troubadour manuscript A (Rome, Biblioteca Vaticana 5232), from which he also quoted Arnaut's *vida.* A facsimile is included in the appendix to *The Poetry of Arnaut Daniel.* Both musical settings survive in manuscript G (Milan, Biblioteca Ambrosiana, R 71 Superiore). A facsimile of this source appears in the musical appendix of *The Poetry of Arnaut Daniel.* The words of stanza 1 from manuscript G, used for the musical transcription, vary slightly from those in manuscript A, which will serve as base text for my analysis below. Significant changes in meaning due to such variants will be discussed.

185. For an exploration of these ideas, see Amelia E. Van Vleck, *Memory and Re-Creation in Troubadour Lyric* (Berkeley: University of California Press, 1991).

186. Other manuscripts substitute *"mon pretz"* (my value) or *"mon cors"* (my heart or my body/person) for *"mos jois"*—the former deemphasizing the sexual connotations while intensifying the parallel with the last line of the poem. The latter, with the semantic ambiguity of *cors,* possibly intensifies the sexual connotations and provides a word echo with the second line of the *tornada "Arnautz dreich cor,"* the meaning of which will be discussed.

187. See the glossary in *The Poetry of Arnaut Daniel.*

188. R. Howard Bloch, *Etymologies and Genealogies: A Literary Anthropology of the French Middle Ages* (Chicago: University of Chicago Press, 1983), 118.

189. Ibid., 113–14 and 115, respectively.

190. See Jan M. Ziolkowski, *Alan of Lille's Grammar of Sex: The Meaning of Grammar to a Twelfth-Century Intellectual* (Cambridge: Medieval Academy, 1985); Susan Schibanoff, "Sodomy's Mark: Allan of Lille, Jean de Meun, and the Medieval Theory of Authorship," in *Queering the Middle Ages,* ed. Glenn Burger and Steven F. Kruger (Minneapolis: University of Minnesota Press, 2001), 28–56. For a discussion of Allan of Lille's comparison of grammatical errors to polyphonic music see Holsinger, *Music, Body, and Desire,* 135–40. See also Allan of Lille, *The Plaint of Nature,* trans. James J. Sheridan (Toronto: Pontifical Institute of Medieval Studies, 1980).

191. Schibanoff discusses Allan's notion of *vitium* as the deviant unproductive offspring of sodomitical coupling. See "Sodomy's Mark," 30–31.

192. See Wilhelm, *Il Miglior Fabbro,* 21.

193. See William E. Burgwinkle, *Love for Sale: Materialist Readings of the Troubadour Razo Corpus* (New York: Garland, 1997), 125–34. Dante places Bertran de Born in Hell for inciting a schism between Prince Henry and his father, Henry II (*Inferno* 28:130–38).

194. See Eve Kosofsky Sedgwick, *Between Men: English Literature and Male Homosocial Desire* (New York: Columbia University Press, 1985); for a discussion of homoerotic triangles in fourteenth-century chivalric literature see Richard E. Zeikowitz, *Homoeroticism and Chivalry: Discourses of Male Same-Sex Desire in the Fourteenth Century* (New York: Palgrave Macmillan, 2003), especially 45–66. Sedgwick and Zeikowitz draw upon theories of triangulated desire in René Girard, *Deceit, Desire, and the Novel: Self and Other in Literary Structure,* trans. Yvonne Freccero (Baltimore, MD: Johns Hopkins University Press, 1972). Sedgwick's work has been widely utilized by medievalists. Some examples are: Gaunt, *Gender and Genre;* Elizabeth B. Keiser, *Courtly Desire and Medieval Homophobia: The Legitimation of Sexual Pleasure in* Cleanness *and its Contexts* (New Haven, CT: Yale University Press, 1997); Burgwinkle, *Love for Sale;* and Carolyn Dinshaw, *Getting Medieval: Sexualities and Communities, Pre- and Postmodern* (Durham, NC: Duke University Press, 1999). See also my article "Courtly Obsessions: Music and Masculine Identity in Gottfried von Strassburg's *Tristan,*" *Repercussions* 4, no. 2 (1995): 59–85.

195. Sedgwick, *Between Men,* 1–2; Zeikowitz, *Homoeroticism and Chivalry,* 1–15.

196. Orderic Vitalis, *The Ecclesiastical History,* ed. and trans. Majorie Chibnall (Oxford: Oxford University Press, 1969–80), 4:188. See also C. Stephen Jaeger, *The Origins of Courtliness: Civilizing Trends and the Formation of Courtly Ideals, 939–1210* (Philadelphia: University of Pennsylvania Press, 1985), 176–94. These criticisms frequently come from Germanic or Anglo writers who associated immoral behavior with France (and hence also Anglo-Norman courts) and Saracen-infected Spain. See Michael Goodich, *The Unmentionable Vice: Homosexuality in the Later Medieval Period* (Santa Barbara, CA: ABC-Clio, 1979), 3–10; see also John Boswell, *Christianity, Social Tolerance, and Homosexuality: Gay People in Western Europe from the Beginning of the Christian Era to the Fourteenth Century* (Chicago: University of Chicago Press, 1980), 209, n. 6.

197. This curious situation, especially the appearance of his childhood teacher Brunetto Latini in *Inferno*, has sparked much scholarship. For discussions see Joseph Pequigney, "Sodomy in Dante's *Inferno* and *Purgatorio*," *Representations* 36 (1991): 22–42; John Boswell, "Dante and the Sodomites," *Dante Studies* 112 (1994): 63–76; Bruce W. Holsinger, "Sodomy and Resurrection: The Homoerotic Subject of the *Divine Comedy*," in *Premodern Sexualities*, ed. Louise Fradenburg and Carla Freccero (New York: Routledge, 1996), 241–74; and Michael Camille, "The Pose of the Queer: Dante's Gaze, Brunetto Latini's Body," in *Queering the Middle Ages*, 57–86.

198. Text and translation from Dante Alighieri, *Purgatorio 1: Text*, trans. Charles S. Singleton (Princeton, NJ: Princeton University Press, 1973). All translations of *Purgatorio* are from this edition.

199. For medieval associations of hermaphroditism with sodomy, see Boswell, *Christianity, Social Tolerance, and Homosexuality*, 185; and Lorraine Daston and Katharine Park, "The Hermaphrodite and the Orders of Nature: Sexual Ambiguity in Early Modern France," in *Premodern Sexualities*, 121–22. See also Burgwinkle, *Love for Sale*, 26–29.

200. See Holsinger, "Sodomy and Resurrection," 245. See also Boswell, *Christianity, Social Tolerance, and Homosexuality*, 92–98 and 203–6.

201. See Holsinger, "Sodomy and Resurrection," 260–61; See also Charles S. Singleton, *Dante Alighieri, Purgatorio 2. Commentary* (Princeton, NJ: Princeton University Press, 1973), 633–66. Singleton, however, offers a sanitized reading of *"ermafrodito"* as a reference to heterosexuality "and therefore natural," citing Ovid's myth of Hermaphroditus (son of Hermes and Aphrodite), who becomes physically joined to the body of a nymph "but who retained the characteristics of both sexes" (637).

202. See Pequigney, "Sodomy in Dante's *Inferno* and *Purgatorio*," 32–33; Boswell, "Dante and the Sodomites," 72–74.

CHAPTER 2

1. See Michel Foucault, "Technologies of the Self," in *Ethics: Subjectivity and Truth*, ed. Paul Rabinow (New York: The New Press, 1994), 224 and 242.

2. For a discussion of Augustine's idiosyncratic notion of *confessio* in context see *Introduction and Text*, vol. 1 of *Confessions*, ed. James J. O'Donnell (Oxford: Clarendon Press, 1992), xvii–li; and Peter Brown, *Augustine of Hippo: A Biography* (Berkeley: University of California Press, 2000), 151–75. For an exploration of the importance of reading in Augustine see Brian Stock, *Augustine the Reader: Meditation, Self-Knowledge, and the Ethics of Interpretation* (Cambridge, MA: Harvard University Press, 1996). For a discussion of the *Confessions* in terms of asceticism see Geoffrey Galt Harpham, *The Ascetic Imperative in Culture and Criticism* (Chicago: University of Chicago Press, 1987), 91–135.

3. Jean-Jacques Rousseau, *The Confessions and Correspondence, Including the Letters to Malesherbes*, trans. Christopher Kelly, ed. Christopher Kelly, Roger D. Masters, and Peter G. Stillman, vol. 5 of *The Collected Writings of Rousseau* (Hanover, NH: University Press of New England, 1995), 5. For a discussion of Rousseau's *Confessions* in their context, see the unattributed Introduction of this volume. For

a discussion of Rousseau and Augustine see Ann Hartle, *The Modern Self in Rousseau's* Confessions: *A Reply to St. Augustine* (Notre Dame, IN: University of Notre Dame Press, 1983).

4. Rousseau, *Confessions*, 15.

5. Ibid., 318. For a pertinent discussion of music and desire in Rousseau's *Confessions*, see also Michael O'Dea, *Jean-Jacques Rousseau: Music, Illusion, and Desire* (New York: St. Martin's Press, 1995), 134–77.

6. Rousseau, *Confessions*, 324.

7. Ibid., 325.

8. See Foucault, *The History of Sexuality*, trans. Robert Hurley (New York: Vintage Books, 1980), 43, 53–73.

9. See ibid., 59–60.

10. Ibid., 65.

11. Karl Heinrich Ulrichs, *The Riddle of "Man-Manly" Love: The Pioneering Work on Male Homosexuality*, trans. Michael A. Lombardi-Nash (Buffalo, NY: Prometheus Books, 1994), 1:152.

12. Ibid., 2:384.

13. Hirschfeld claims that while only 23 percent of his sample of 500 homosexual men could not whistle at all, "most are unable to produce a particularly penetrating one." See Magnus Hirschfeld, *The Homosexuality of Men and Women*, trans. Michael A. Lombardi-Nash (Amherst: Prometheus Books, 2000), 197. See Havelock Ellis, *Psychology of Sex*, vol. 1, *Part Four: Sexual Inversion*, 3rd ed. (1915; reprint New York: Random House, 1942), 291.

14. Albert Moll, *Perversions of the Sex Instinct*, trans. Maurice Popkin (Newark, NJ: Julian Press, 1931), 72. This study was first published in German in 1891. Moll discusses the quality of Uranists' voices at 71–73.

15. See Vern L. Bullough, "Introduction," *The Riddle of "Man-Manly" Love*, 1–27.

16. Richard von Krafft-Ebing, *Psychopathia Sexualis*, 12th ed., trans. Franklin S. Klaf (1939; New York: Scarborough Books, 1978), 223.

17. Moll, *Perversions of the Sex Instinct*, 65.

18. Edward Carpenter, *The Intermediate Sex: A Study of Some Transitional Types of Men and Women* (1908; reprint London: George Allen and Unwin, 1983), 111. This study was first published in 1896.

19. Havelock Ellis and John Addington Symonds, *Sexual Inversion* (1896; reprint New York: Arno Press, 1975), 124, n. 1.

20. Ellis, *Sexual Inversion*, 295.

21. See Nicolas Slonimsky, *Lexicon of Musical Invective: Critical Assaults on Composers since Beethoven's Time* (Seattle: University of Washington Press, 1987), 205–12.

22. Havelock Ellis, *Psychology of Sex*, vol. 1, part 3, *Sexual Selection in Man*, 3rd ed. (1915; New York: Random House, 1942), 129.

23. Ellis, *Sexual Selection in Man*, 131–32.

24. Hirschfeld, *The Homosexuality of Men and Women*, 578.

25. Ibid., 580. For the German, see Magnus Hirschfeld, *Die Homosexualität des Mannes und des Weibes* (Berlin: Walter De Gruyter, 1984), 511. This study was first published in 1914.

26. See Christine Battersby, *Gender and Genius: Towards a Feminist Aesthetics* (Bloomington: Indiana University Press, 1989), especially 3, 103–12.

27. Hirschfeld, *The Homosexuality of Men and Women*, 579.

28. Ibid.

29. Mitchell Morris, "Tristan's Wounds: On Homosexual Wagnerians at the Fin de Siècle," in *Queer Episodes in Music and Modern Identity*, ed. Sophie Fuller and Lloyd Whitesell (Urbana: University of Illinois Press, 2002), 271–91.

30. I have modified Lombardi-Nash's translation from *The Homosexuality of Men and Women*, 580. I thank Art Groos for his help with the translation. The German reads: "Diese Musikdramen, die—als rein dichterische Leistung bewertet—ohne Musik den Anforderungen der poetischen Technik kaum genügen dürften, die ebensowenig reine Musik sind, diese Gefühls dramatik, die ihre Steigerung weniger durch dramatisch-logischen Aufbau, als durch Aufeinandertürmung von Ekstasen bewirkt, diese pessimistisch-märtyrerhaft-pathetische Stimmung, diese Musik, die den Text illustrierend, untermalend, gleichsam nur ein Teil des 'Gesamtkunstwerkes,' doch sein Haupterregungsmittel, streckenweise oft nur Erhöhung des Bühnenvorganges ist, dann wieder durch ein wohlbekanntes 'Leitmotiv' ab und zu die Ohren der Hörer erfreuend" (Hirschfeld, *Die Homosexualität des Mannes und des Weibes*, 511).

31. I have modified Lombardi-Nash's translation in *The Homosexuality of Men and Women*, 580. The German reads: "Es gibt Künstler, die aus Lebensüberfülle zu ihrem Berufe kommen, und solche, die es aus Feinheit, aus Überkultur werden. Zu den letzteren gehören die Homosexuellen" (Hirschfeld, *Die Homosexualität des Mannes und des Weibes*, 511).

32. Vern L. Bullough, *Science in the Bedroom: A History of Sex Research* (New York: Basic Books, 1994), 61.

33. Sigmund Freud, "The Moses of Michelangelo," in *Collected Papers*, ed. Joan Riviere (London: Hogarth Press and the Institute of Psycho-Analysis, 1957), 4:257.

34. Sigmund Freud, "Analysis of a Phobia in a Five-Year-Old Boy," in *The Standard Edition of the Complete Psychological Works of Sigmund Freud*, ed. James Strachey (London: Hogarth Press, 1955), 10:138.

35. Sigmund Freud, "Introductory Lectures on Psycho-analysis, Part II: Dreams," in *The Standard Edition of the Complete Psychological Works of Sigmund Freud* (1961), 15:108.

36. Michael A. Wallach and Carol Greenberg, "Personality Functions of Symbolic Sexual Arousal to Music," *Psychological Monographs: General and Applied* 74 (1960): 1.

37. Ibid., 16.

38. Richard Taruskin, *Defining Russia Musically* (Princeton, NJ: Princeton University Press, 1997), 251. For a study of Rousseau and the literary and cultural aspects of Romanticism, see Thomas McFarland, *Romanticism and the Heritage of Rousseau* (Oxford: Clarendon Press, 1995).

39. See Taruskin, *Defining Russia Musically*, 251–53; see also Sanna Pederson, "On the Task of the Music Historian: The Myth of the Symphony after Beethoven," *Repercussions* 2, no. 2 (1993): 5–30.

40. Taruskin, *Defining Russia Musically*, 276.

41. From the *Musical Review*, New York (February 26, 1880), quoted in Slonimsky, *Lexicon of Musical Invective*, 207; see 205–12 for more examples.

42. Eve Kosofsky Sedgwick, *Epistemology of the Closet* (Berkeley: University of California Press, 1990), 99–100.

43. Taruskin observed, "In order to turn [Chaikovsky] into a synecdoche [for a confessional composer], however, Chaikovsky himself had to be synecdochically rendered: reduced to his last three symphonies; or actually to only two of the three; or rather, as we have seen, to the subtitle of one and a letter about the other" (*Defining Russia Musically*, 263).

44. See Malcolm Hamrick Brown, "Tchaikovsky and His Music in Anglo-American Criticism, 1890s–1950s," in *Queer Episodes in Music and Modern Identity*, 138. Alexander Poznansky notes that "at the top of the 'homosexual pyramid' in Tchaikovsky's time stood the Grand Duke Sergei, son of Alexander II and brother of the reigning emperor. The Grand Duke's penchants were widely known. They were openly discussed in the salons of the capital and were the subject of various jokes." See "Tchaikovsky's Suicide: Myth and Reality," *19th-Century Music* 11 (1988): 203. See also Richard Taruskin, "Pathetic Symphonist: Chaikovsky, Russia, Sexuality and the Study of Music," *New Republic*, February 6, 1995, 26–40.

45. Taruskin, "Pathetic Symphonist," 29–32.

46. James Huneker, *Mezzotints in Modern Music: Brahms, Tschaïkowsky, Chopin, Richard Strauss, Liszt, and Wagner* (New York: Charles Scribner's Sons, 1899), 91, 92, and 98, respectively.

47. Brown, "Tchaikovsky and Anglo-American Criticism," 141.

48. To Vladimir Davidov, February 23, 1893, in Modeste Tchaikovsky, *The Life and Letters of Peter Ilich Tchaikovsky*, ed. and trans. Rosa Newmarch (New York: Dodd, Mead and Company, 1905), 702.

49. See Sedgwick, *Epistemology of the Closet*, 3–11 and 70–71.

50. Catherine Drinker Bowen and Barbara von Meck, *"Beloved Friend": The Story of Tchaikowsky and Nadejda von Meck* (New York: Random House, 1937), 81. See also Nigel Smith, "Perceptions of Homosexuality in Tchaikovsky Criticism, 1890s–1950s," *Context* 4 (Summer 1992): 5.

51. Bowen and von Meck, *"Beloved Friend,"* 444.

52. For a full discussion of this tradition of criticism see Brown, "Tchaikovsky and Anglo-American Criticism," 134–49.

53. Edward Lockspeiser, "Tchaïkovsky the Man," in *Tchaikovsky: A Symposium*, ed. Gerald Abraham (London: Lindsay Drummond, 1945), 13.

54. Ibid., 20 and 23, respectively.

55. Ibid., 23.

56. See Smith, "Perceptions of Homosexuality in Tchaikovsky Criticism," 7–8.

57. Paul C. Squires, "Peter Ilich Tschaikowsky: A Psychological Sketch," *The Psychoanalytic Review* 28, no. 4 (1941): 464.

58. Ibid., 447 and 452, respectively.

59. James A. Brussel, "The Tchaikowsky Troika," *The Psychiatric Quarterly Supplement* 36, no. 2 (1962): 313.

60. Ibid., 304. Squires, "Peter Ilich Tschaikowsky," hints at this incestuous relationship nearly twenty years earlier: "Modeste was also a homosexual. Peter and Modeste were *intimately bound together*" (452, emphasis in the original).

61. Martin Cooper, "The Symphonies," in *Tchaikovsky: A Symposium*, 45.

62. Letter to Vladimir Davidov, August 1893, quoted in Modeste Tchaikovsky, *The Life and Letters,* 714.

63. Alexander Poznansky, *Tchaikovsky's Last Days: A Documentary Study* (Oxford: Clarendon Press, 1996), 49–63.

64. Timothy L. Jackson, *Tchaikovsky: Symphony No. 6 (Pathétique)* (Cambridge: Cambridge University Press, 1999), 18.

65. See the reviews quoted in Poznansky, *Tchaikovsky's Last Days,* 56 (V. Kolomiitsov) and 59 (Nápravník).

66. See especially three studies by Alexander Poznansky: *Tchaikovsky: The Quest for the Inner Man* (New York: Schirmer Books, 1991); *Tchaikovsky's Last Days* (1996); and "Unknown Tchaikovsky: A Reconstruction of Previously Censored Letters to His Brothers (1875–1879)," in *Tchaikovsky and His World,* ed. Leslie Kearney (Princeton, NJ: Princeton University Press, 1998), 55–96.

67. Alexander Poznansky, "Tchaikovsky's Suicide," 200–201.

68. Timothy L. Jackson, "Aspects of Sexuality and Structure in the Later Symphonies of Tchaikovsky," *Music Analysis* 14, no. 1 (1995): 5.

69. See ibid., 22; and Jackson, *Tchaikovsky: Symphony No. 6,* 36–40.

70. See Jackson, *Tchaikovsky: Symphony No. 6,* 51. For a discussion of "punishment for the 'sin' of homosexuality," see 42–45; for a reading of the third movement as homoerotic amorous combat, see 45–50; and for a discussion of crucifixion motives, see 50–56. Jackson offers many examples of "Cross" motives and their transmutations, all comprised of a tetrachord of pitches that circle a single pitch or show interlocking pairs: thus E–G–F$\sharp$–A, G–F$\sharp$–A–G, D–C$\sharp$–F$\sharp$–E, and C$\sharp$–D–B–C$\sharp$ all qualify.

71. In the seven-note pick-up in m. 89 Tchaikovsky unlocks only the outer voices (first violins and cellos), leaving the two inner voices, the second violins and violas, still entangled.

72. See David Brown, *Tchaikovsky: A Biographical and Critical Study, The Final Years (1885–1893)* (New York: W. W. Norton and Company, 1991), 458. See also Henry Zajaczkowski, *Tchaikovsky's Musical Style* (Ann Arbor, MI: UMI Research Press, 1987), 108–12.

73. Jackson, *Tchaikovsky: Symphony No. 6,* 53.

74. Taruskin, *Defining Russia Musically,* 260.

75. Ibid., 294–95. See also Wye Jamison Allanbrook, *Rhythmic Gestures in Mozart:* Le Nozze di Figaro *and* Don Giovanni (Chicago: University of Chicago Press, 1983).

76. Taruskin, *Defining Russia Musically,* 299.

77. Taruskin, "The Pathetic Symphonist," 28.

78. See Elizabeth Tolbert, "The Voice of the Lament: Female Vocality and the Performative Efficacy in the Finnish-Karelian *Itkuvirsi,*" in *Embodied Voices: Representing Female Vocality in Western Culture,* 179–84; Jane Bowers, "Women's Lamenting Traditions around the World: A Survey and Some Significant Questions," *Women & Music: A Journal of Gender and Culture* 2 (1998): 125–46; James Porter, "Lament," in *The New Grove Dictionary of Music and Musicians,* 2nd ed., ed. Stanley Sadie and John Tyrrell (New York: Grove Dictionaries, 2001), 14:181–88; and T. Livanova, M. Pekelis, and T. Popova, *Istoriia Russkoi Muzyki* (Leningrad: Gos. Muz. Izd-vo, 1940), 1:24. My thanks to Dimitri Shapovalov for finding and translating this and other passages cited below.

79. Livanova, Pekelis, and Popova, *Istoriia Russkoi Muzyki*, 25.

80. Ellen Rosand, *Opera in Seventeenth-Century Venice: The Creation of a Genre* (Berkeley: University of California Press, 1993), 361.

81. See Thurston Dart, "Eye Music," in *The New Grove Dictionary of Music and Musicians*, 8:482–83. Dart cites two examples of black notation used in this manner: a 1519 song mourning the death of Maximilian, and Josquin's lament on the death of Ockeghem, *Nymphes des bois*.

82. See Elizabeth Tolbert, "The Voice of the Lament," 180, and Rosand's discussion of Claudio Monteverdi's "Lament of the Nymph" and other descending tetrachord laments in *Opera in Seventeenth-Century Venice*, 369–77.

83. For a discussion of Tchaikovsky's music in the context of psychological realism in Russian art see Leon Botstein, "Music as the Language of Psychological Realism: Tchaikovsky and Russian Art," in *Tchaikovsky and His World*, 99–144.

84. See Poznansky, *Tchaikovsky: The Quest for the Inner Man*, 131–50, and "Unknown Tchaikovsky," 61.

85. Tchaikovsky to Ladislaw Pakhulsky, June 6, 1891, quoted in Tchaikovsky, *The Life and Letters of Peter Ilich Tchaikovsky*, 616.

86. Alexander Poznansky, *Tchaikovsky Through Others' Eyes*, trans. Ralph C. Burr, Jr., and Robert Bird (Bloomington: Indiana University Press, 1999), 264. See also Poznansky, "Tchaikovsky: A Life Reconsidered," 37.

87. Donald Mitchell, ed., *Letters from a Life: The Selected Letters and Diaries of Benjamin Britten, 1923–39* (Berkeley: University of California Press, 1991), 234.

88. See Foucault, "Technologies of the Self."

89. Michel Foucault, *The Use of Pleasure*, vol. 2 of *The History of Sexuality*, trans. Robert Hurley (New York: Vintage Books, 1990), 252.

90. See Foucault, *The Use of Pleasure*, 57 and 202. Foucault describes this negotiation as an "erotics" because the regulation of behaviors was not institutionalized, as in marriage, but "was to be sought in the relation itself, in the nature of the attraction that drew them toward one another" (202).

91. See Foucault, *The Care of the Self*, vol. 3 of *The History of Sexuality*, trans. Robert Hurley (New York: Vintage Books, 1986), 190–210.

92. Throughout the following discussion references to the opera will be to the 1951 version, unless specified otherwise. For the vocal score, see Benjamin Britten, *Billy Budd, An Opera in Four Acts*, libretto by E. M. Forster and Eric Crozier, vocal score by Erwin Stein (London: Hawkes and Son, 1952).

93. The seeming transparency of Britten's music to his homosexuality is due to the pioneering critical studies by Philip Brett, beginning with his article "Britten and Grimes," published in the *Musical Times* (1977). The article is reprinted in *Benjamin Britten, Peter Grimes*, ed. Philip Brett (Cambridge: Cambridge University Press, 1983), 180–89. See also Brett's postscript to this volume, 190–96. Other relevant articles by Brett include "Salvation at Sea: *Billy Budd*," in *The Britten Companion*, ed. Christopher Palmer (Cambridge: Cambridge University Press, 1984), 133–43; "Britten's Bad Boys: Male Relations in *The Turn of the Screw*," *Repercussions* 1, no. 2 (1992): 5–25; "Britten's Dream," in *Musicology and Difference: Gender and Sexuality in Music Scholarship*, ed. Ruth Solie (Berkeley: University of California Press, 1994), 259–80; and "Eros and Orientalism in Britten's Operas," in *Queering the Pitch*, 235–56. For a recent discussion of Britten's operas in terms of their

queer aesthetics, see Lloyd Whitesell, "Britten's Dubious Trysts," *Journal of the American Musicological Society* 56, no. 3 (2003): 637–64.

94. See Humphrey Carpenter, *Benjamin Britten: A Biography* (New York: Charles Scribner's Son, 1992), especially 160–62.

95. The two infamous mutinies of 1797—the Nore and the Spithead—are briefly mentioned in the prologue, and in a discussion among Vere, the First Lieutenant, and the Sailing Master in act 2, scene 1, *after* Vere's statement about Greeks and Romans.

96. The novella, whose complete title is *Billy Budd, Sailor (An Inside Narrative)*, was left unfinished at the time of Melville's death in 1891 and published in 1924. All page numbers refer to the edition *Billy Budd and Other Stories* (New York: Penguin Books, 1986) and will be given in the text.

97. Sedgwick, *Epistemology of the Closet*, 95.

98. Melville is referring to Hawthorne's "The Artist of the Beautiful." I thank Byron Adams for calling this to my attention.

99. Joseph Bristow, *Effeminate England: Homoerotic Writings After 1885* (New York: Columbia University Press, 1995), 67. For his discussion of Forster, see 55–99.

100. On the confusion of identities in Britten's *Billy Budd* see also Whitesell, "Britten's Dubious Trysts," 674–76.

101. For a discussion of tonal symbolism in the opera see Mervyn Cooke and Philip Reed, *Benjamin Britten, Billy Budd* (Cambridge: Cambridge University Press, 1993), 87–110. See also Philip Rupprecht, *Britten's Musical Language* (Cambridge: Cambridge University Press, 2001), 75–137.

102. In an undated letter to Britten, E. M. Forster complained that Britten's setting of Claggart's monologue "O beauty, o handsomeness, goodness" was not "sufficiently important musically." He goes on to say, "I want *passion*—love constricted, perverted, poisoned, but nevertheless *flowing* down its agonizing channel; a sexual discharge gone evil." See Donald Mitchell, Philip Reed, and Mervyn Cooke, eds., *Letters from a Life: Selected Letters of Benjamin Britten, 1946–51* (Berkeley: University of California Press, 2004), 618.

103. Britten's libretto is based on W. Pollard's edition, given to him by Crozier. See Carpenter, *Benjamin Britten*, 303–4. When this book was in proofs, an article came to my attention that also reads Britten's *Abraham and Isaac*, by way of *Billy Budd*, as a sexual drama. See Allen J. Frantzen, "Tears for Abraham: The Chester Play of Abraham and Isaac and Antisacrifice in Works by Wilfred Owen, Benjamin Britten, and Derek Jarman," *Journal of Medieval and Early Modern Studies* 33 (2001): 455–61. Our arguments differ significantly in their details and conclusions.

104. Benjamin Britten, *Canticles*, London Decca Records 5698.

105. The following discussion of this canticle will refer to Benjamin Britten, *Canticle II: Abraham and Isaac, Op. 51, for Alto, Tenor, and Piano*, Text from the Chester Miracle Play (London: Boosey and Hawkes, 1953).

106. David Mills, ed., *The Chester Mystery Cycle: A New Edition with Modernised Spelling* (East Lansing, MI: Colleagues Press, 1992), 81.

107. Philip Brett, "Musicality, Essentialism, and the Closet," 11 and 17, respectively.

108. See Mervyn Cooke, *Britten: War Requiem* (Cambridge: Cambridge University Press, 1996), 67–70. See also Rupprecht, *Britten's Musical Language*, 209–15; and Whitesell, "Britten's Dubious Trysts," 646–47, 663–64.

109. Brett, "Musicality, Essentialism, and the Closet," 19.

110. From a letter addressed to Marion Harewood dated October 22, 1950. See Mitchell et al., *Letters from a Life,* 620.

111. Carpenter, *Benjamin Britten,* 304.

112. The origin of this myth, perpetuated in the popular imagination by the play and film *Amadeus,* is a forged letter. For a discussion of the myth's entrenchment in scholarship, see Neal Zaslaw, "Der neue Köchel," *Mozart Society of America Newsletter,* January 27, 1997, 4–5.

113. See Scott G. Burnham, "Beethoven, Ludwig van, § 19 (i): History of the Myth," in *The New Grove Dictionary of Music and Musicians,* 3:110–12. See also Douglas Johnson, Alan Tyson, and Robert Winter, *The Beethoven Sketchbooks: History, Reconstruction, Inventory* (Berkeley: University of California Press, 1985), 4–10.

114. Rosa Newmarch, "Tchaikovsky, Peter Ilich," in *Grove's Dictionary of Music and Musicians,* 3rd ed., ed. H. C. Colles (New York: Macmillan, 1927), 289 and 292, respectively.

115. From the London *Times,* April 28, 1924. Quoted in Slonimsky, *Lexicon of Musical Invective,* 138. For a discussion of Ravel's dandyism and sexuality see Lloyd Whitesell, "Ravel's Way," in *Queer Episodes in Music and Modern Identity,* 49–78.

116. Brett, "Musicality, Essentialism, and the Closet," 19.

117. Hans Keller, "Britten and Mozart: A Challenge in the Form of Variations on an Unfamiliar Theme," *Music and Letters* 29, no. 1 (1948): 30.

CHAPTER 3

1. Mary F. Rogers, *Barbie Culture* (London: Sage, 1999), 2–3.

2. Michel Foucault, *The Order of Things: An Archaeology of the Human Sciences,* trans. Alan Sheridan (New York: Vintage Books, 1973), 34; see also 17–44.

3. Jonathan Culler, *Ferdinand de Saussure,* rev. ed. (Ithaca, NY: Cornell University Press, 1986), 31.

4. Ibid., 63 and 93.

5. Friedrich Nietzsche, *On the Genealogy of Morals and Ecce Homo,* trans. Walter Kaufmann and R. J. Hollingdale (New York: Vintage Books, 1969), 45.

6. Judith Butler, *Bodies that Matter: On the Discursive Limits of "Sex"* (New York: Routledge, 1993), 192.

7. Michel Foucault, "The Thought of the Outside," in *Aesthetics, Method, and Epistemology,* ed. James D. Faubion (New York: The New Press, 1998), 148.

8. Judith Butler, "Imitation and Gender Insubordination," in *The Lesbian and Gay Studies Reader,* ed. Henry Abelove, Michèle Aina Barale, and David M. Halperin (New York: Routledge, 1993), 311.

9. Ibid., 313.

10. See Culler, *Ferdinand de Saussure,* 29–30.

11. Ibid., 112.

12. The following discussion of the role of music in German philosophy is indebted to Andrew Bowie, *Aesthetics and Subjectivity: From Kant to Nietzsche* (Manchester, England: Manchester University Press, 1990).

13. See ibid., 179–88.

14. Ibid., 56; see also 53–57, 182–84.

15. Peter Brooks, *The Melodramatic Imagination: Balzac, Henry James, Melodrama, and*

the Mode of Excess (New Haven, CT: Yale University Press, 1976), 13; see especially ix, 1–13.

16. Ibid., 14.

17. Radclyffe Hall, *The Well of Loneliness* (1928; New York: Pocket Books, 1974), 310.

18. For discussions of the historical problems of recognizing and representing lesbianism, see Judith C. Brown, *Immodest Acts: The Life of a Lesbian Nun in Renaissance Italy* (New York: Oxford University Press, 1986), 3–20; Teresa de Lauretis, "Sexual Indifference and Lesbian Representation," in *The Lesbian and Gay Studies Reader,* 141–58; and Patricia White, *Uninvited: Classical Hollywood Cinema and Lesbian Representability* (Bloomington: Indiana University Press, 1999).

19. The following discussion is indebted to Joan DeJean, *Fictions of Sappho, 1546–1937* (Chicago: University of Chicago Press, 1989), especially 198–299. See also Yopie Prins, *Victorian Sappho* (Princeton, NJ: Princeton University Press, 1999).

20. DeJean, *Fictions of Sappho,* 211; for the complete discussion of Weckler, see 207–11.

21. Ibid., 272–74.

22. Richard Dellamora, *Masculine Desire: The Sexual Politics of Victorian Aestheticism* (Chapel Hill: University of North Carolina Press, 1990), 75.

23. Ibid., 80.

24. The historian Johann Joachim Winckelmann wrote of this ideal beauty in his 1764 history of ancient art, and Pater elaborated on this in his essay "Winckelmann." Pater also writes of the sexual ambiguity of Leonardo da Vinci's life and work. See ibid., 130–42.

25. One should also note that the position of the two women is visually echoed by the pair of birds in the background. For a discussion of the social meaning behind drapery and clothing in Western art, see Anne Hollander, *Seeing Through Clothes* (New York: Viking Press, 1978), 1–81; see especially 71–75, where Hollander discusses the erotics of Pre-Raphaelite depictions of thick, disheveled hair as a corollary to drapery; see also Hollander, *Fabric of Vision: Dress and Drapery in Painting* (London: National Gallery Company, 2002), especially 57–77 and 139–45.

26. Algernon Charles Swinburne, "Simeon Solomon: Notes on His 'Vision of Love' and Other Studies," in *A Pilgrimage of Pleasure: Essays and Studies* (1871; Boston: Gorham Press, 1913), 58–59.

27. Ibid., 62.

28. Mel Tormé, *The Other Side of the Rainbow with Judy Garland on the Dawn Patrol* (New York: William Morrow and Company, 1970), 115–17.

29. I am quoting the back cover of an abridged version of the album, reissued by Capital Records, SM-11763

30. For a discussion of the "queer pleasures" that musicals provide for a lesbian audience, see Stacy Wolf, *A Problem Like Maria: Gender and Sexuality in the American Musical* (Ann Arbor: University of Michigan Press, 2002). Wolf offers lesbian feminist readings of the lives and roles of Mary Martin, Ethel Merman, Julie Andrews, and Barbra Streisand. She also discusses the duet between Garland and Streisand, and the subsequent entrance of Ethel Merman (173–74).

31. D. A. Miller, *Place For Us: Essay on the Broadway Musical* (Cambridge, MA: Harvard University Press, 1998), 14 and 3, respectively.

32. Ibid., 7.

33. Ibid., 24.

34. John M. Clum, *Something for the Boys: Musical Theater and Gay Culture* (New York: St. Martin's Press, 1999), 6; see also 10. Whereas Miller discusses only original cast theater productions, Clum includes the Hollywood musicals from the 1930s onward, stating that "it is particularly in the Fred Astaire–Ginger Rogers classics, that one also finds some fascinating sexual ambiguity as part of the comic sophistication" (11).

35. Gerald Mast, *Can't Help Singin': The American Musical on Stage and Screen* (Woodstock, NY: Overlook Press, 1987), 35.

36. Miller, *Place for Us*, 17.

37. See Mast, *Can't Help Singin'*, 148 and 249–50.

38. In his extensive analysis of the connection between gay men and Judy Garland, Richard Dyer remarks that Judy Garland worked "in an emotional register of great intensity which seems to bespeak equally suffering and survival, vulnerability and strength, theatricality and authenticity, passion and irony." This quality of performance was combined with the tropes of ordinariness, androgyny, and camp, which "were homologous with aspects of male gay culture." See Richard Dyer, *Heavenly Bodies: Film Stars and Society* (New York: St. Martin's Press, 1986), 155 and 156, respectively.

39. This ambivalence is best illustrated by the opposing views of two books: Andrew Sullivan, *Virtually Normal: An Argument about Homosexuality* (New York: Alfred A. Knopf, 1995), and Michael Warner, *The Trouble with Normal: Sex, Politics, and the Ethics of Queer Life* (Cambridge, MA: Harvard University Press, 2000).

40. Dyer, *Heavenly Bodies*, 167.

41. This line is from the Roger Eden song "In-between," which was written especially for Judy and was one of her most popular records. See Dyer, *Heavenly Bodies*, 170.

42. For Susan Sontag's pioneering essay, see "Notes on 'Camp,'" in *Against Interpretation and Other Essays* (New York: Dell, 1966), 275–92. The essay was first published in the *Partisan Review* (Fall 1964). Another pioneering work on camp is Esther Newton, *Mother Camp: Female Impersonators in America* (Chicago: University of Chicago Press, 1972). More recent studies appear in the following collections: David Bergman, ed., *Camp Grounds: Style and Homosexuality* (Amherst: University of Massachusetts Press, 1993); Fabio Cleto, ed., *Camp: Queer Aesthetics and the Performing Subject: A Reader* (Ann Arbor: University of Michigan Press, 1999). See also Mike Perkovich, *Nature Boys: Camp Discourse in American Literature from Whitman to Wharton* (New York: Peter Lang, 2003).

43. Apparently Judy insisted on singing this 1930 song for what was a number added to fill out the finished movie. The music for "Get Happy" was written by the same composer who wrote the music for "Over the Rainbow," Harold Arlen. See Gerald Clarke, *Get Happy: The Life of Judy Garland* (New York: Random House, 2000), 266–69.

44. Garland's daughter, Lorna Luft, describes the entourage of men, "usually gay," who surrounded and doted on Garland in her concert years in *Me and My Shadows: A Family Memoir, Living with the Legacy of Judy Garland* (New York: Pocket Books, 1998), 203–7.

45. Dyer notes that "her dancing picks up on the movements of different men at different times. In other words, she is to some degree 'one of the boys,' especially in a movement of flexing the thighs forward and heels up that is used for men in

urban ballets of the kind Jerome Robbins developed." See Dyer, *Heavenly Bodies,* 175–76.

46. Tormé, *The Other Side of the Rainbow,* 83.

47. See especially Daniel Harris, *The Rise and Fall of Gay Culture* (New York: Ballantine Books, 1997), 17–18. The independent film director John Waters has been quoted as saying "A gay man loving Judy could almost be like a black person watching a minstrel show." See Michael Joseph Gross, "The Queen Is Dead, Part One," *The Atlantic Online: The Atlantic Monthly Digital Edition* (August 2000), page 5, www.theatlantic.com/issues/2000/08/gross.html (accessed June 29, 2001). I should also note that from 1995 to 2001 many of my students either did not know who Judy Garland was or felt no affinity with her movies or biography.

48. George Chauncey, *Gay New York: Gender, Urban Culture, and the Making of the Gay Male World, 1890–1940* (New York: Basic Books, 1994), 288 and 361.

49. See Dyer, *Heavenly Bodies,* 148–50 (quote from 148).

50. See Esther Newton, *Cherry Grove, Fire Island: Sixty Years in America's First Gay and Lesbian Town* (Boston: Beacon Press, 1993).

51. See Dyer, *Heavenly Bodies,* 144, and Gross, "The Queen Is Dead," 3.

52. "Séance at the Palace," *Time,* August 18, 1967, 40.

53. Dick Michaels, "The World Is My Ashtray," *The Los Angeles Advocate,* September 1967, 2.

54. Toni Lee, "Judy: A Fragile Wisp Dies," *The Los Angeles Advocate,* September 1969, 35.

55. Donald Vining, *A Gay Diary,* 5 vols. (New York: Pepys Press, 1979–93). In his entry for November 8, 1951, he writes, "There was such a line at the Palace buying tickets for Judy Garland's personal appearance that I gave up the idea of getting Ken a ticket to that" (2:352).

56. See "The Camp Hall of Fame," in Niles Chignon, ed., *The Camp Followers' Guide!* (New York: Avon Books, 1965), 19–25 (Streisand appears on 23, and on 24 as an example of "deliberate camp"); see also "How's Your Camp I.Q.," 46 (question 43: "Are your favorite singers Barbra Streisand, Ruth Etting, the Supremes, Cilla Black, and Dionne Warwick?").

57. "The Golden Girl of the Year, Yeah! Yeah! Goes to the Movies," in *The Camp Followers' Guide!,* 53.

58. Ibid., 54.

59. Ibid., 55.

60. See, for example, Wayne Koestenbaum's association of a gay man's Judy worship in 1951 with self-sacrificing abjection and lonely vicariousness, an "out-of-body remoteness," in *The Queen's Throat: Opera, Homosexuality, and the Mystery of Desire* (New York: Poseidon Press, 1993), 33–34.

I have found one other citation of Garland as a gay icon in a publication of gay camp humor, a free-verse abecedarius by Allen Dennis called *The Gay B C Book: A Camp* (San Francisco: D. Redmond Designs, 1966). Garland is listed along with Marlene Dietrich, Barbra Streisand, and Bette Davis under the letter "x," which "stands for a quality that is pure magic." Each actress is listed with a chief attribute. Garland's attribute is being "sad but desirable"; Streisand's attribute is being "not pretty but desirable."

61. Martin Crowley, *The Boys in the Band* (New York: Farrar, Straus and Giroux, 1968), 19.

62. Tom Burke, "The New Homosexuality," *Esquire,* December 1969, 306.

63. Dyer, *Heavenly Bodies,* 150, argues that "the come-back was the defining motif of the register of feeling" that supported the affinity between Garland and gay men.

64. Martin Duberman, *Stonewall* (New York: Dutton, 1993), 190–91. See also Christopher Guly, "The Judy Connection," *The Advocate,* June 28, 1994, 49–55.

65. See Judy Garland, "How *Not* to Love a Woman," *Coronet,* February 1955, 41–44. Wolf, in *A Problem Like Maria,* mentions Garland only in passing, though Garland can be understood to share queer tomboyish qualities that Wolf attributes to Mary Martin and Ethel Merman, and the determined but self-effacing qualities that Wolf attributes to Julie Andrews and Barbra Streisand. It is possible that the melodrama conveyed by Garland's later concert career put lesbians off just as it attracted gay men.

66. I have gathered information about reactions to Melissa Etheridge and other popular lesbian personalities from a variety of sources, including personal interviews with friends, discussions with gay and lesbian students, and the writings of fans posted on the official Melissa Etheridge Information Network Web site (www.melissaetheridge.com) and other fan Web sites. Ithaca, New York, where I live, is home to a relatively large and economically diverse population of lesbians. The most popular local lesbian singer performs covers of five of Etheridge's songs, more than any other single artist. I have also drawn upon the project of my student Tracy Decker, who, in spring 2001, interviewed people at the local gay bar in Ithaca about gay icons.

67. Judy Wieder, "Our Celebrities," *The Advocate,* April 30, 2000, 43.

68. This was a pull-out section of *Rolling Stone,* December 25, 2003 / January 8, 2004.

69. In *Bodies That Matter,* 77, Judith Butler points out that Lacan denies that the phallus is "either an organ or an imaginary effect," insisting that it is a privileged signifier without specific origin. See also 72–88 for her discussion of Lacan.

70. See ibid., 61–63.

71. Ibid., 3.

72. Ibid., 73.

73. Ibid., 84.

74. Ibid.

75. Hepburn was known for playing strong, assertive women in her movies. She cross-dressed and even kissed a maid in the 1935 film *Sylvia Scarlett.*

76. This is a paraphrase of a line from the song "Killing Me Softly with His Song," written by Norman Gimbel and Charles Fox, recorded by Roberta Flack, *Killing Me Softly,* Atlantic Records, SD7271 (1973).

77. Melissa Etheridge, "I Want to Come Over," *Your Little Secret* (1995), Island Records 314-524-154-2. The lyrics and music to all of Etheridge's songs discussed in this chapter are published in the piano-vocal songbook *Melissa Etheridge: Anthology* (Milwaukee, WI: Hal Leonard, 2003).

78. Melissa Etheridge, "Bring Me Some Water," *Melissa Etheridge* (1988), Island Records 422-842-303-2; see also *Melissa Etheridge: Anthology.*

79. Melissa Etheridge with Laura Morton, *The Truth Is . . . My Life and Love in Music* (New York: Villard Books, 2001), 80.

80. Susana Darwin, personal correspondence, August 31, 2001.

81. Chris Nickson, *Melissa Etheridge: The Only One, An Unauthorized Biography* (New York: St. Martin's Griffin, 1997), 5. For Etheridge's comments, see Judy Wieder, "Melissa: Rock's Great Dyke Hope," *The Advocate*, July 26, 1994, 46.

82. Butler, *Bodies That Matter*, 68.

83. See Joke Dame, "Unveiled Voices: Sexual Difference and the Castrato," in *Queering the Pitch: The New Gay and Lesbian Musicology*, ed. Philip Brett, Elizabeth Wood, and Gary C. Thomas (New York: Routledge, 1994), especially 142–48.

84. Roland Barthes, *S/Z: An Essay*, trans. Richard Miller (New York: Hill and Wang, 1999), 110.

85. See Judy Wieder, "Melissa Etheridge: The Advocate's Person of the Year," *The Advocate*, January 23, 1998, 3, www.advocate.com/html/specials/ melissa/698_99_melissa.asp (accessed July 16, 2001).

86. Wieder, "Melissa: Rock's Great Dyke Hope," 46; for Don Henley's remark see Diane Anderson, "Melissa As You've Never Seen Her," *Girlfriends*, January–February 1996, 7; for Mark Brown's remark see his interview with Melissa Etheridge, www.melissaetheridge.com/community/interviews/mark_brown .html (accessed May 19, 2002).

87. Melissa Etheridge AOL interview, www.geocities.com/SunsetStrip/Palladium /8650/aol193.txt (accessed July 9, 2001), 6.

88. Etheridge, *The Truth Is*, 58.

89. In an interview in October 1999, Etheridge noted, "my musical sense is very middle of the road. I'm not alternative or avant garde." See Kathleen Hildenbrand, "Don't Call Me Missy (Interview with Melissa Etheridge)," *Girlfriends*, October 1999, 24.

90. See Joe Stuessy and Scotte Lipscomb, *Rock and Roll: Its History and Stylistic Development*, 3rd ed. (Upper Saddle River, NJ: Prentice Hall, 1999), 373: "This is not art-rock, jazz rock, folk rock, or any other kind of mixed rock; it is quintessential, dead-ahead rock and roll."

91. Recorded on *Born to Run*, CBS Records, CDCBS 80959.

92. *Melissa Etheridge* (1988), Island Records, 422–842–303–2. The lyrics to this song are published in Etheridge, *The Truth Is*, 76–77; copyright Almo Music Corp. / MLE Music (ASCAP); see also *Melissa Etheridge: Anthology*.

93. Elysa Gardiner, "The Singer and the Song," *Trouble Girls: The Rolling Stone Book of Women in Rock*, ed. Barbara O'Dair (New York: Random House, 1997), 368.

94. Etheridge also borrows from male rockers in her performance style. One friend (and former fan) was put off by this after seeing Etheridge perform in the late 1980s, and described Etheridge's manner as full of exaggerated motions and "gestural quotes from male rockers." While the rest of the audience (the majority lesbian) responded enthusiastically to Etheridge's male rocker posturing, this listener felt that it compromised the "honesty" she had heard in her recordings. She did not see the gestures as ironic, or as being received as ironic. After a 2003 concert, however, one audience member reported to me that she believed Etheridge was being ironic and campy with her vocabulary of male rock gestures.

95. See Elizabeth Wurtzel, "Backyard Party," *New York*, November 1989, 114–18,

quoted in Joyce Luck, *Melissa Etheridge: Our Little Secret* (Toronto: ECW Press, 1997), 89.

96. *Brave and Crazy* (1989), Island Records 91285–2. The lyrics are published in the accompanying booklet, copyright Almo Music Corp. / MLE Music (ASCAP); see also *Melissa Etheridge: Anthology*.

97. Lauren Martin, "Still Voicing Sex," *Sydney Morning Herald*, December 1, 1995, Metro 7.

98. Butler, *Bodies That Matter*, 86.

99. Joel Stein, "Melissa Etheridge," *Time*, October 25, 1999. Both the Stein and Letterman questions are quoted in Janice Dunn, "The Name of the Father and the Making of a New American Family," *Rolling Stone*, February 3, 2000, 40.

100. George Varga, "Melissa Explains It All," *San Diego Union-Tribune*, December 19, 1996, "Night and Day," 4.

101. Butler, *Bodies That Matter*, 72.

102. Etheridge, *The Truth Is*, 192.

103. Ibid., 165.

104. For example, D. Merilee Clunis and G. Dorsey, *The Lesbian Parenting Book: A Guide to Creating Families and Raising Children* (Seattle: Seal Press, 1995).

105. Etheridge, *The Truth Is*, 225.

106. Sara Miles, "Mommy Melissa," *The Advocate*, June 22, 1999, 51.

107. Stacie Stukin, "Back on Track," *The Advocate*, September 14, 1999, 60.

108. Melissa Etheridge, *Breakdown* (1999), Island Def Jam Music Group, 314–546–608–2; see also *Melissa Etheridge: Anthology*.

109. Etheridge, *The Truth Is*, 183.

110. See Bruce C. Steele, "Melissa and Tammy: A Love Story," *The Advocate*, January 20, 2004, 51–64, especially 54 for Etheridge's comments on Cypher and marriage, and 60 for Michaels's comments on her domesticity and career.

111. Associated Press, "Etheridge 'just following the rules' by marrying younger," www.houstonchronicle.com, February 23, 2004 (accessed February 26, 2004).

112. Steele, "Melissa and Tammy," 60.

113. Michael Musto, "Immaculate Connection," in *Out in Culture: Gay, Lesbian, and Queer Essays on Popular Culture*, ed. Corey K. Creekmur and Alexander Doty (Durham, NC: Duke University Press, 1995), 427.

114. Ibid., 428.

115. Ibid., 429.

116. See also Richard Smith's comments about Madonna throughout *Seduced and Abandoned: Essays on Gay Men and Popular Music* (London: Cassell, 1995), passim, and Don Shewey, "Madonna: The Saint, The Slut, The Sensation," in *The Advocate*, May 7, 1991, 44.

117. Three incidences are especially noteworthy: her sexual flirting with Sandra Bernhard on *Late Night With David Letterman* (July 2, 1988); the notorious sequence in which Madonna kisses an androgynous figure in the video for "Justify My Love" (directed by Jean-Baptiste Mondino, 1990); and her lesbian-erotic photo essay for *Rolling Stone*, June 13, 1991, 43–50.

118. *The Advocate*, June 27, 1995, 38, reported that in the October 1994 issue of the English magazine *The Face*, Madonna, hoping to tone down her image, was quoted as saying, "I have good friends who happen to be lesbians . . . and the

public assumes I'm sleeping with them. . . . I'm not a lesbian. I love men," which earned her *The Advocate*'s 1995 Sissy of the Year, an award for cowardly and insincere fakers. See also Madonna's comments about lesbian sex in her interview with Carrie Fisher, "True Confessions: The Rolling Stone Interview with Madonna," *Rolling Stone,* June 13, 1991, 40.

119. In the same song and dance number Madonna also gave a peck on the lips to Spears's chief competitor in pop stardom, Christina Aguilera. Taking a page from Madonna's own book, Spears seized the moment and made her kiss more sexual by adding a little tongue. This completely outstripped the kiss with Aguilera, who was subsequently edited out of most photographs of the moment.

120. See Alice Echols, *Daring to Be Bad: Radical Feminism in America, 1967–1975* (Minneapolis: University of Minnesota Press, 1989). For articles on third-wave feminism, see Leslie Heywood and Jennifer Drake, eds., *Third Wave Agenda: Being Feminist, Doing Feminism* (Minneapolis: University of Minnesota Press, 1997); see also the five articles on third-wave feminism in *Hypatia: A Journal of Feminist Philosophy* 12, no. 3 (1997).

121. Karlene Faith, *Madonna: Bawdy and Soul* (Toronto: University of Toronto Press, 1997), 95 and 102 (quote).

122. Ibid., 111. Faith also criticizes lesbian butch/femme roles (67): "sexually independent women, in particular, have needed the category 'lesbian' to distinguish themselves not only from the imperatives of heterosexual femininity, but also from homosexuality in all its masculinist variations. Lesbian feminists have had the prescience to challenge, via their lifestyles, butch-femme variations of the conventional hetero-homo dyad in forming their sexual identities."

123. Ibid., 5.

124. Ibid., 69; see also 59.

125. David M. Halperin, *How to Do the History of Homosexuality* (Chicago: University of Chicago Press, 2002), 118. Halperin qualifies his remark as pertaining to "the male world," but lesbians also partake of eroticizing hierarchy.

126. On *The Tonight Show with Jay Leno* on November 26, 2003, Madonna presented herself as "older and wiser," wearing a simple black dress, giving sisterly advice to Britney, talking about the joys and challenges of marriage and motherhood, and publicizing her new children's book.

127. Madonna and Guy Sigsworth, "What It Feels Like for a Girl," *Music* (2000), Maverick / Warner Brothers 9 46598–2.

128. For a discussion of Riviere, see Judith Butler, *Gender Trouble: Feminism and the Subversion of Identity* (New York: Routledge, 1990), 51.

CHAPTER 4

1. Foucault, "Technologies of the Self," in *Ethics: Subjectivity and Truth,* ed. Paul Rabinow, 223–51 (New York: The New Press, 1994), 225.

2. My discussion of the music industry draws on the following sources: Steve Chapple and Reebee Garofalo, *Rock 'n' Roll Is Here to Pay: The History and Politics of the Music Industry* (Chicago: Nelson-Hall, 1977); Simon Frith, *Sound Effects: Youth, Leisure, and the Politics of Rock 'n' Roll* (New York: Pantheon Books, 1981);

Reebee Garofalo, *Rockin' Out: Popular Music in the USA,* 2nd ed. (Upper Saddle River, NJ: Prentice Hall, 2002), 199–207.

3. The other top-selling labels were (according to 1973 sales figures) RCA, Capital-EMI, Polygram, MCA, ABC, Motown, A&M, and United Artists.

4. See R. Serge Denisoff, "Folk Music and the American Left," in *The Sounds of Social Change: Studies in Popular Culture,* ed. R. Serge Denisoff and Richard A. Peterson (Chicago: Rand McNally, 1972), 106–14.

5. For Marcuse's important analysis of systematic domination, see his *One-Dimensional Man: Studies in the Ideology of Advanced Industrial Society,* 2nd ed. (Boston: Beacon Press, 1991), which has a new introduction by Douglas Kellner. See also Kellner's "Herbert Marcuse and the Vicissitudes of Critical Theory," in *Towards a Critical Theory of Society,* ed. Douglas Kellner (New York: Routledge, 2001), 1–33.

6. Herbert Marcuse, *Counter Revolution and Revolt* (Boston: Beacon Press, 1972), 75.

7. Ibid., 49.

8. Marcuse, *One-Dimensional Man,* xlvii–xlviii. See also Kellner's introduction to the same volume, xi–xxxix.

9. See Alice Echols, *Daring to Be Bad: Radical Feminism in America, 1967–1975* (Minneapolis: University of Minnesota Press, 1989), 3–19.

10. See ibid., 210–41.

11. Radicalesbians, "The Woman Identified Woman" (1970), in *Radical Feminism,* ed. Anne Koedt, Ellen Levine, and Anita Rapone (New York: Quadrangle Books, 1973), 243. The previous quotes appear on 242 and 243, respectively.

12. See the quotes in Echols, *Daring to Be Bad,* 217–18. Echols notes that these writings "reinforced dominant cultural assumptions about women's sexuality. They spoke platitudinously about the differences between women's (and, by extension, lesbians') diffuse, romantic, and nurturing sexuality and men's aggressive, genitally oriented sexuality" (218).

13. Ibid., 243–56, 269–71. See also Rose Weitz, "From Accommodation to Rebellion: The Politicization of Lesbianism," in *Women-Identified Women,* ed. Trudy Darty and Sandee Potter (Palo Alto, CA: Mayfield, 1984), 233–48.

14. Mary Daly, *Beyond God the Father: Toward a Philosophy of Women's Liberation* (Boston: Beacon Press, 1973), 40.

15. Ibid., 98–99.

16. Ibid., 143–44.

17. Ibid., 152–53. Daly is perhaps alluding to the 1964 Simon and Garfunkel folk-rock hit "Sound of Silence."

18. Reprinted on "The CWLU Herstory Website," www.cwluherstory.com/CWLU Gallery/Liner.html (accessed September 16, 2001).

19. Susan Hiwatt, "Cock Rock," in *Twenty-minute Fandangoes and Forever Changes: A Rock Bazaar,* ed. Jonathan Eisen (New York: Random House, 1971), 141–47; quotes from 144 and 143, respectively. This piece apparently circulated as an unpublished manuscript under the name "Sabot"; Karen E. Petersen quotes extensively from a copy at the Northwestern University Library's Women's Collection. See her "An Investigation into Women-Identified Music in the United States," in *Women and Music in Cross-Cultural Perspectives,* ed. Ellen Koskoff (New York: Greenwood Press, 1987), 203–4. See also Marion Meade, "Does Rock Degrade Women?" *New York Times,* March 14, 1971, reprinted as "The Degrada-

tion of Women," in *The Sounds of Social Change: Studies in Popular Culture,* 173–77; and Arleen Pedigo, "Under My Thumb," *Off Our Backs,* March 1972, 26.

20. Reprinted on "The CWLU Herstory Website."

21. Chicago Women's Liberation Rock Band, "Developing a Revolutionary Women's Culture," *Women: A Journal of Liberation* 3, no. 2 (1972): 2.

22. In an interview Susan Abod notes, "There were lesbians in our band, but we didn't talk about it or deal with it. . . . I think we also got off the hook because Linda Shear's band 'Family of Women,' which was lesbian separatists, was playing in the Chicago area around then." See Maida Tilchen, "Lesbians and Women's Music," *Women-Identified Women,* 290. Cynthia M. Lont mistakenly describes the band as "all straight" in "Women's Music: No Longer a Private Party," in *Rockin' the Boat: Mass Music and Mass Movements,* ed. Reebee Garofalo (Boston: South End Press, 1992), 244.

23. For a study of the discrimination against women on all levels of the music industry from the 1970s to 1990s, see Mavis Bayton, *Frock Rock: Women Performing Popular Music* (Oxford: Oxford University Press, 1998).

24. Chicago Women's Liberation Rock Band, "Developing a Revolutionary Women's Culture," 3–4.

25. Ibid., 5.

26. From "Papa," words by Virginia Blaisdell and Naomi Weisstein, music traditional. Lyrics appear on "The CWLU Herstory Website," www.cwluherstory.com.

27. Lynne Shapiro, "Joy of Cooking," *Off Our Backs,* October 1971, 33.

28. Ruth Scovill, "Women's Music," in *Women's Culture: Renaissance of the Seventies,* ed. Gayle Kimball (Metuchen, NJ: Scarecrow Press, 1981), 149.

29. Simon Frith and Angela McRobbie, "Rock and Sexuality," in *On Record: Rock, Pop, and the Written Word,* ed. Simon Frith and Andrew Goodwin (New York: Pantheon Press, 1990), 374–75. This article was first published in the journal *Screen Education* 29 (1978).

30. For discussions of the complex discourse of gender in heavy metal, see Robert Walser, *Running with the Devil: Power, Gender, and Madness in Heavy Metal Music* (Hanover, NH: Wesleyan University Press, 1993); and Susan Fast, *In the Houses of the Holy: Led Zeppelin and the Power of Rock Music* (Oxford: Oxford University Press, 2001).

31. Mary S. Pollock, "The Politics of Women's Music: A Conversation With Linda Tillery and Mary Watkins," *Frontiers: A Journal of Women Studies* 10, no. 1 (1988): 18.

32. Lee Garlington, "Baby Cockroach," *Off Our Backs,* July–August 1977, 19.

33. For a study of the history and politics of African-American women's music artists, see Eileen M. Hayes, "Black Women Performers of Women-Identified Music: 'They Cut Off My Voice; I Grew Two Voices,'" Ph.D. diss., University of Washington, 1999. It should also be noted that one of the most popular and long-lived African-American women's music groups, Sweet Honey in the Rock (formed in 1973), avoided the electric guitar issue as an *a cappella* vocal group.

34. Alix Dobkin, *Adventures in Women's Music* (New York: Tomato Publications, 1979), 10. Alpert surrendered to the authorities in 1975.

35. Ibid., 11. Prior to *Lavender Jane Loves Women,* folksinger Maxine Feldman recorded the song "Angry Athis," which contains explicit lesbian lyrics, in 1969.

It was released as a 45 rpm single. In a 1974 interview, Kay Gardner places the inception of Lavender Jane on August 17, 1973, when she and Dobkin played at a gay arts, crafts, and skills festival where they hooked up with bass player Patches Attom. See Fran Moira and Anna Williams, "Lavender Jane Loves . . . ," *Off Our Backs,* April 1974, 6.

36. Fran Moira and Anna Williams indicate that the album was available in late November. See their "Lavender Jane Loves . . . ," 6.

37. All quotes in this paragraph are taken from Dobkin, *Adventures in Women's Music,* 12.

38. "Savo Vodo" is a Croatian song. I thank Jane Peppler of the ensemble Mappamundi, and Hannah Farber of the Yale Slavic Chorus for sending me a transcription of "Savo Vodo" from the chorus's archives.

39. Lee Schwing and Helaine Harris, "Building Feminist Institutions," *The Furies,* May–June 1973, 2. See also Echols, *Daring To Be Bad,* 272–73.

40. Ibid., 3.

41. Ibid.

42. The other founding members include Cyndi Gair and Kate Winter. See Judy Dlugacz, "If It Weren't for the Music: 15 Years of Olivia Records (Part 1)," *Hot Wire* 4, no. 3 (1988): 28–29.

43. Olivia Records Collective, "The Muses of Olivia: Our Own Economy, Our Own Song," interviewed by Margie Crow et al., *Off Our Backs,* August–September 1974, 3.

44. Ibid., 2.

45. Ibid., 3.

46. See Brooke L. Williams and Hannah Darby, "God, Mom, and Apple Pie: 'Feminist' Businesses as an Extension of the American Dream," *Off Our Backs,* January–February 1976, 18–20. Though she does not explicitly mention Olivia Records, Jennifer Woodul wrote a lengthy response article some months later, "From Olivia: What's This about Feminist Businesses?" *Off Our Backs,* June 1976, 24–26. She also wrote letters to Olivia Records, published in *Off Our Backs,* July–August 1976, 30. One of these letters mentions a collective response to Williams and Darby by Olivia Records published in *Plexus.* A report of a community discussion about feminist business held in Washington, D.C., by Olivia Records member Ginny Berson and two Olivia recording artists, Meg Christian and Teresa Trull, appears in Terri Poppe and Janis Kelly, "Moving Money if Not Mountains," *Off Our Backs,* December 1977, 16. See also Michele Kort, "Sisterhood Is Profitable," *Mother Jones,* July 1983, 39–44.

47. Williams and Darby, "God, Mom, and Apple Pie," 19.

48. Woodul, "From Olivia," 24.

49. Scarlet Cheng, "Kay Gardner and Urana Records," *Off Our Backs,* February 1977, 17. All passages quoted here appear on this page.

50. See Carol Edelson and Fran Pollner's interview, "Meg Christian," *Off Our Backs,* April 1973, 2–3 (this piece predates the formation of Olivia Records but mentions the precipitating conversation between Cris Williamson, Ginny Berson, and Meg Christian); and Judy Dlugacz, "If It Weren't for the Music," 28.

51. Meg Christian, *I Know You Know: A Songbook and Scrapbook of the Album* (Oakland, CA: Olivia Records, 1975), 1.

52. The first quote is from the back cover of Meg Christian, *I Know You Know* (1974), Olivia Records LF902; the second is from an advertisement in Kirsten Grimstad and Susan Rennie, eds., *The New Woman's Survival Sourcebook* (New York: Alfred A. Knopf, 1975), 178.

53. See Jennifer Woodul, "Olivia Records," in *The New Woman's Survival Sourcebook* (1975), 177. This publication is a descriptive nationwide registry of women's business, arts groups, and services.

54. *The New Woman's Survival Sourcebook* (1975), 180.

55. Sweet Honey in the Rock, an all-women African-American singing group that had been performing in the Washington, D.C., area since 1973, is not listed. This may be in part because they were not associated with the women's movement and women's music until 1977. See Bernice Johnson Reagon and Sweet Honey in the Rock, *We Who Believe in Freedom: Sweet Honey in the Rock . . . Still on the Journey* (New York: Anchor Books, 1993), 31–34.

56. Judy Collins, *Who Knows Where the Time Goes* (1968), Elektra EKS 74033.

57. Alice Cooper, *Billion Dollar Babies* (1973), Warner Brothers Records Inc. BS2685.

58. The lyrics to "Hello Hooray," by Rolf Kempf with additional words by Meg Christian, appear in Christian, *A Songbook and Scrapbook of the Album*, 3.

59. In the video documentary *The Changer: A Record of the Times* (Olivia Records OV904, 1991) Christian recounts her own ideological rigidity and particular frustrations with Cris Williamson's "out there" manner of behavior. See also the account of Meg Christian in Holly Near and Derk Richardson, *Fire in the Rain . . . Singer in the Storm* (New York: William Morrow and Company, 1990), passim.

60. Edelson and Pollner, "Meg Christian," 3. For criticisms, see Marlene Schmitz, "Christian and Earth Music," *Off Our Backs,* January 1975, 19; and C. E. et al., "Collective Concert Coverage," *Off Our Backs,* December 1976, 19. There is a hint of this criticism in the review of *I Know You Know* by Marlene Schmitz, "Product of Persistence," *Off Our Backs,* May–June 1975, 17. Here, Schmitz chooses the political "Scars" as the "superior composition" compared to the two love songs "Valentine Song" and "Morning Song." A harsher criticism of Meg Christian and Teresa Trull appears in a concert review by Wendy Stevens, "Meg and Teresa: Drop of Rain or Hurricane?" *Off Our Backs,* December 1977, 16. She writes "both Meg and Teresa's music tend to deal with no other political issue than women-loving-women. . . . Being a lesbian isn't necessarily a political statement."

61. Poppe and Kelly, "Moving Money if Not Mountains," 16.

62. Meg Christian, "Song to My Mama"; the lyrics appear in Christian, *A Songbook and Scrapbook*, 19.

63. Holly Near, *Imagine My Surprise* (1978), Redwood Records RR401.

64. Meg Christian, "Morning Song"; the lyrics appear in Christian, *A Songbook and Scrapbook*, 27.

65. Christian, *A Songbook and Scrapbook*, 29.

66. Instrumental showmanship was a trend in rock music of the mid- to late 1970s. For example, art rock and heavy metal bands such as Led Zeppelin, Cream, Yes, and Emerson, Lake & Palmer all feature extensive instrumental solos in their music.

67. Mary Pollock, "Recovery and Integrity: The Music of Meg Christian," *Frontiers: A Journal of Women's Studies* 9, no. 2 (1987): 31–32.

68. Quoted in Tilchen, "Lesbians and Women's Music," 297.
69. Marlene Schmitz, "Chicago Women's Concert II," *Off Our Backs,* November 1974, 20.
70. Patsy Lynch, "Margie Adam in Washington: A Comment," *Off Our Backs,* May 1977, 16. See also Terri Poppe, "Counter Comment," 16, which expresses even more disappointment with Adam's performance.
71. Even the feminist jazz ensemble Alive! uses a singer instead of wind instruments in order to present lyrics "with specific feminist content." See Mary S. Pollock, "Feminist Aesthetics in Jazz: An Interview with Susanne Vincenza of Alive!" *Frontiers* 8, no. 1 (1984): 61.
72. Konda Mason, "Something Moving Inside of Me," *Off Our Backs,* January 1979, 13. Efforts to integrate women's music festivals are discussed in the documentary *Radical Harmonies,* directed by Dee Mosbacher (2002). For comments about the predominance of white folk musicians in women's music recordings, see Barbara Pepe, "Women's Music," *Christopher Street,* May 1977, 41–42 and 44; and Reagon and Sweet Honey in the Rock, *We Who Believe in Freedom,* 28–33.
73. Mason, "Something Moving Inside of Me," 13.
74. Tillery's album also did not include songs with explicit themes of race. One reviewer reads some racial politics into Tillery's song "Freedom Time," with the lyric "If I could only tell you what it's like, to live this life of Triple Jeopardy." The reviewer understands the lyric as "[exposing] the network of our oppression in the larger world and in Black and women's communities." See Terri Clark, "Linda Tillery: Feminist Funk," *Off Our Backs,* November 1978, 8.
75. *The Changer: A Record of the Times;* and Dlugacz, "If It Weren't for the Music," 29–30.
76. Near and Richardson, *Fire in the Rain,* 114, 119, 142.
77. Tilchen, "Lesbians and Women's Music," 293.
78. See Kort, "Sisterhood Is Profitable," 44; Arlene Stein, "Androgyny Goes Pop: But Is It Lesbian Music?" *Out/Look,* Spring 1991, 29; and Dlugacz, "If It Weren't for the Music," 30. Kort reports that the Latin jazz group The Harp could not get a record contract with any of the women's music labels, and they had a hard time finding work outside the festivals.
79. See Kort, "Sisterhood Is Profitable," 43; Near and Richardson, *Fire in the Rain,* 137–39 and 215–16.
80. Diane Anderson, "Melissa As You've Never Seen Her," *Girlfriends,* January–February 1996, 7.
81. See Stein, "Androgyny Goes Pop," 27–33.
82. For a discussion of Phranc and Two Nice Girls, see Judith A. Peraino, "'Rip Her to Shreds': Women's Music According to a Butch-Femme Aesthetic," *Repercussions* 1, no. 1 (1992): 19–47.
83. See Mary Celeste Kearney, "The Missing Links: Riot Grrrl–Feminism–Lesbian Culture," 207–29, and Marion Leonard, "'Rebel Girl, You Are the Queen of My World': Feminism, Subculture, and Grrrl Power," 230–55, both in *Sexing the Groove: Popular Music and Gender,* ed. Sheila Whiteley (New York: Routledge, 1997); see also Andrea Juno, "Kathleen Hanna, Bikini Kill," in *Angry Women in Rock, Volume One* (New York: Juno Books, 1996), 82–103.
84. For an expression of these attitudes see Stein, "Androgyny Goes Pop"; Peraino,

"'Rip Her To Shreds'"; and Lorrie Sprecher's novel *Sister Safety Pin* (Ithaca, NY: Firebrand Books, 1994). I thank Fred Maus for providing me with this last reference.

85. Scovill, "Women's Music," 158.
86. See Gayle Kimball, "Female Composition: Interview with Kay Gardner," in *Women's Culture: The Women's Renaissance of the Seventies,* ed. Gayle Kimball (Metuchen, NJ: Scarecrow Press, 1981), 164–65; Gardner describes her own feelings when playing for an all-women audience as a "spiritual orgasm." See Moira and Williams, "Lavender Jane Loves . . . ," 7.
87. Scarlet Cheng, "Kay Gardner and Urana Records," 17.
88. See David Israel, "When Fans Wanted to Rock, the Baseball Stopped," *Chicago Tribune,* July 13, 1979, sec. 5: 1 and 3; and Richard Dozer, "Sox Promotion Ends in a Mob Scene: Tigers Ask for Forfeit of 2nd Game," sec. 5: 1; the photo essay by Edward Wagner, Jr., "Discophobia Out of Control," sec. 5: 2; and Joseph Sjostrom and Lynn Emmerman, "These Weren't Real Baseball Fans—Veeck," sec. 5: 3.
89. Frank Rose, "Discophobia: Rock & Roll Fights Back," *Village Voice,* November 12, 1979, 36.
90. Ibid.
91. Ibid., 37.
92. Nelson George, "Fatal Prognosis Wrong, Patient Alive and Well," *Billboard,* July 14, 1979, 75.
93. Arguably the first song that prefigured the classic disco sound was the "Theme from *Shaft*" (1971) by Isaac Hayes. It features the fast hi-hat subdivisions, wah-wah rhythm guitar, and orchestral instruments in an extensive introductory "break" that erupts into the verse with its pounding four-beat bass drum and spoken lyrics.
94. Radcliffe Joe, "Dearth of Superstars Dims Industry Future: Producer Rather than Artists Is Star," *Billboard,* July 14, 1979, 46.
95. Ibid.
96. Ken Emerson, "The Village People: America's Male Ideal?" *Rolling Stone,* October 5, 1978, 27.
97. Martin P. Levine, *Gay Macho: The Life and Death of the Homosexual Clone* (New York: New York University Press, 1998), 27–28.
98. See David Aiken, "Discrimination Exists in the Gay Community," *The Advocate,* March 23, 1977, 7–8; and Lenny Giteck, "How Gay Are the Ghettos?" *The Advocate,* September 6, 1979, 16.
99. See Lenny Giteck, "How Gay Are the Ghettos?" 17; and Levine, *Gay Macho,* 29.
100. Village People, *Village People* (1977), Casablanca Record and FilmWorks NBLP 7064. The connection between gay macho, camp, and the Village People has been explored by Mitchell Morris in "Disco Performance in (the) Masculine Camp: The Case of the Village People" (unpublished manuscript).
101. Stan Ellis, "The Ticket: Records," *The Advocate,* December 28, 1977, 30.
102. Guy Trebay, "How Macho Is That Doggie in the Disco?" *Village Voice,* March 27, 1978, 47.
103. Charles Herschberg, "Prophets or Profits? The Village People," *The Advocate,* April 19, 1978, 31.
104. Emerson, "The Village People," 30.

105. Andrew Kopkind, "The Dialectic of Disco: Gay Music Goes Straight," *Village Voice,* February 12, 1979, 14.

106. B. H., "The Ticket: Entertainment," *The Advocate,* December 27, 1979, 31.

107. See Stephen Holden, "The Village People Liberate Main Street," *Village Voice,* April 23, 1979, 61.

108. John Schauer, "Sylvester: A Sterling Talent Turns Gold into Platinum," *The Advocate,* January 25, 1979, 33.

109. Seymour Kleinberg, "Where Have All the Sissies Gone?" *Christopher Street,* March 1978, 6–7.

110. Walter Hughes, "In the Empire of the Beat: Discipline and Disco," in *Microphone Fiends: Youth Music and Youth Culture,* ed. Andrew Ross and Tricia Rose (New York: Routledge, 1994), 150 and 148.

111. Gregory W. Bredbeck, "Troping the Light Fantastic: Representing Disco Then and Now," *GLQ: A Journal of Lesbian and Gay Studies* 3, no. 1 (1996): 71–107. Bredbeck also draws heavily on Judith Butler's application of Althusser's scene of interpellation and the possibility of a queer reinterpretation in *Bodies That Matter: On the Discursive Limits of "Sex"* (New York: Routledge, 1993). See especially 121–40 for her discussion of the film *Paris is Burning* (1991), directed by Jennie Livingston, about drag balls in New York City's Harlem.

112. Bredbeck, "Troping the Light Fantastic," 82 and 95.

113. See ibid., 88–89.

114. Bredbrek, for example, sees "tensions of gender, race, and class" as *positive* signs of a "dynamic" between "identification and disidentification" that exposes gay identity as fragmentary, illusory, and thus uncontainable. See ibid., 100 and 102.

115. See Garofalo, *Rockin' Out,* 284–85; David P. Szatmary, *Rockin' in Time: A Social History of Rock-and-Roll,* 4th ed. (Upper Saddle River, NJ: Prentice Hall, 2000), 215–17; Michael Campbell and James Brody, *Rock and Roll: An Introduction* (New York: Schirmer Books, 1999), 325; and Ed Ward, Geoffrey Stokes, and Ken Tucker, *Rock of Ages: The Rolling Stone History of Rock and Roll* (New York: Summit Books, 1986), 532–33. John-Manuel Andriote's *Hot Stuff: A Brief History of Disco* (New York: Harper Collins, 2001) spends several pages on the Village People, but only mentions Sylvester in the appendix of "Disco Artists and Their Hits."

116. I am indebted to the many friends, colleagues, and biographers of Sylvester, especially Joshua Gamson and Tim Smyths, who participated in the conference "Sylvester: The Life and Work of a Musical Icon," organized by Carolyn Dinshaw and Jason King, which took place on October 8–9, 2004, at New York University. See also David Diebold, *Tribal Rites* (Northridge, CA: Time Warp Publishing, 1986), 27–36.

117. Sylvester's three Top 40 hits were "Dance (Disco Heat)" (September 1978), "You Make Me Feel (Mighty Real)" (February 1979), and "I (Who Have Nothing)" (May 1979). His first hit remained on the chart for ten weeks and climbed as high as number nineteen, while the other two reached only thirty-six and forty, respectively, staying on the charts for less than a month. The Village People also had three Top 40 hits; their most popular song, "Y.M.C.A.," reached number two on the charts (November 1978) and stayed in the Top 40 for twenty

weeks. Sylvester's post–disco era songs "Do Ya Wanna Funk" (1982) and "Trouble in Paradise" (1984) were moderate commercial and club successes.

118. Esther Newton, *Mother Camp: Female Impersonators in America* (Chicago: University of Chicago Press, 1972), 2.

119. Kleinberg, "Where Have All the Sissies Gone?" 7.

120. Schauer, "Sylvester," 32.

121. Newton, *Mother Camp*, xiii.

122. The song lyrics appear on the sleeve to the album *Step II* (1978), Fantasy Records F-9556.

123. The song appears on the album *Cheryl Lynn* (1978), Columbia Records / CBS Inc. CK 35486. Lynn's "Got to Be Real" was used by Jennie Livingston as the theme song for her documentary *Paris Is Burning.*

124. Butler, "Imitation and Gender Insubordination," in *The Lesbian and Gay Studies Reader,* ed. Henry Abelove, Michèle Aina Barale, and David M. Halperin (New York: Routledge, 1993), 317.

125. Butler, *Gender Trouble: Feminism and the Subversion of Identity* (New York: Routledge, 1990), 22.

126. See "real woman" and "natural woman" in *Juba to Jive: A Dictionary of African-American Slang,* ed. Clarence Major (New York: Viking Press, 1994); and in *The Cassell Dictionary of Slang,* ed. Jonathon Green (London: Cassell, 1998).

127. The Bee Gees' disco falsetto can be understood as a white stylization of the black soul falsetto. For a discussion of the use of the falsetto voice in disco, see Anne-Lise François, "Fakin' It/Makin' It: Falsetto's Bid for Transcendence in 1970s Disco," *Perspectives of New Music* 33 (1995): 443–55. François argues "for falsetto as artifice, as a vamping and performance of otherness, and, by extension, as a metaphor for alternative, fictive spaces which uncover the untruth of the real" (447). For her discussion of Sylvester, see 446–47.

128. See Schauer, "Sylvester," 32. After a similar register break on the live album *Living Proof* Sylvester shouts, "I bet you didn't know I could do that."

129. See Newton, *Mother Camp,* 48.

130. For information on Sun Ra, see John F. Szwed, *Space is the Place: The Lives and Times of Sun Ra* (New York: Pantheon Books, 1997).

131. Kopkind, "The Dialectic of Disco," 14.

132. Hughes, "In the Empire of the Beat," 152–53.

133. Robert Christgau, "Sylvester Is a Star," *The Village Voice,* June 11, 1979, 73.

134. Hughes, "In the Empire of the Beat," 154.

135. Schauer, "Sylvester," 32.

136. All the above quotes are from ibid., 33.

CHAPTER 5

1. See Michel Foucault, "Technologies of the Self," in *Ethics: Subjectivity and Truth,* ed. Paul Rabinow (New York: The New Press, 1994), 225.

2. Michel Foucault, *Discipline and Punish: The Birth of the Prison,* trans. Alan Sheridan (New York: Vintage Books, 1977), esp. 135–69.

3. Michel Foucault, *The History of Sexuality, Volume 1: An Introduction,* trans. Robert Hurley (New York: Vintage Books, 1980), 86–88, 100. See also 137–41 for his

explicit discussion of "*techniques* of power" as they pertain to the history of sexuality.

4. Ibid., 103–5.

5. Ibid., 104–5. Thomas Robert Malthus (1766–1834) was an English economist and clergyman who advocated sexual restraint in order to control the potential for a population to grow beyond its means of subsistence.

6. Bruce Rodgers, *The Queens' Vernacular: A Gay Lexicon* (San Francisco: Straight Arrow Books, 1972), 60.

7. See George Chauncey, *Gay New York: Gender, Urban Culture, and the Making of the Gay Male World, 1890–1940* (New York: Basic Books, 1994), 7–8.

8. See Michel Foucault, "Sex, Power, and the Politics of Identity," in *Ethics: Subjectivity and Truth,* ed. Paul Rabinow (New York: The New Press), 166.

9. Michel Foucault, "The Ethics of the Concern for Self as a Practice of Freedom," in *Ethics: Subjectivity and Truth,* 291–92, 297–98.

10. Foucault, *The History of Sexuality,* 35.

11. See ibid., 3, 17–19.

12. Ibid., 115.

13. For some important studies see Alan Bray, *Homosexuality in Renaissance England* (New York: Columbia University Press, 1995), 81–114; Randolph Trumbach, "The Birth of the Queen: Sodomy and the Emergence of Gender Equality in Modern Culture, 1660–1750," in *Hidden from History: Reclaiming the Gay and Lesbian Past,* ed. Martin Bauml Dauberman, Martha Vicinius, and George Chauncey, Jr. (New York: New American Library, 1989), 129–40.

14. For discussions of the various meanings and uses of "sodomy," see Alan Bray, *Homosexuality in Renaissance England,* 13–32, especially 19–26 and 75; Gregory W. Bredbeck, *Sodomy and Interpretation: Marlowe to Milton* (Ithaca, NY: Cornell University Press, 1991), 5, 18–20; Bruce R. Smith, *Homosexual Desire in Shakespeare's England: A Cultural Poetics* (Chicago: University of Chicago Press, 1991), 3, 8–11, and 52; Netta Murray Goldsmith, *The Worst of Crimes: Homosexuality and the Law in Eighteenth-Century London* (Brookfield, VT: Ashgate, 1998), 34. See also Foucault, *The History of Sexuality,* 36–40; and Ellen T. Harris, *Handel as Orpheus: Voice and Desire in the Chamber Cantatas* (Cambridge, MA: Harvard University Press, 2001), 12–18.

In 1631 Mervin Touchet, the Earl of Castlehaven, was tried and convicted on two counts of sodomy because the judge deemed that the emission of semen from intercrural masturbation was "buggery." By 1670, sodomy became legally defined as necessarily involving penetration and ejaculation between two men (see Smith). However, the transcript of Touchet's trial enjoyed wide circulation in the seventeenth century, and therefore the notion of "sodomy" in the popular imagination and usage continued to have a certain amount of discursive instability (see Bredbeck).

15. The catch was first published in John Playford, *Catch That Catch Can or the Second Part of the Musical Companion* (London, 1685); see Paul Hillier, ed., *The Catch Book* (Oxford: Oxford University Press, 1987), number 111.

16. See Bray, *Homosexuality in Renaissance England,* 81–86.

17. See Peter Holman, *Henry Purcell* (Oxford: Oxford University Press, 1994), 21–22. See also John Hawkins, *A General History of the Science and Practice of Music* (1776;

reprint New York: Dover Publications, 1963), ii, 653–54. Holman also mentions speculations that Purcell may have been Catholic, or at least a Catholic sympathizer, since his father-in-law was Catholic (20).

18. Sedgwick, *Between Men: English Literature and Male Homosocial Desire* (New York: Columbia University Press), 25; see also 1–27.

19. Hillier, *The Catch Book,* number 3.

20. See Bernard Thomas, introduction and notes to William Byrd, *The Five-Part Consort Music, Volume I: The Fantasies* (London: London Pro Musica, 1998), i.

21. Hillier, *The Catch Book,* number 57.

22. See David M. Bergeron, *King James and Letters of Homoerotic Desire* (Iowa City: University of Iowa Press, 1999); and Rictor Norton, *Mother Clap's Molly House: The Gay Subculture in England 1700–1830* (London: GMP Publishers, 1992), 15–31.

23. Sir Francis Bacon, *Essayes and Counsels, Civil and Moral: Whereunto is newly added, Table of the Colours of Good and Evil* (London: For H. R., 1664), 35–37.

24. See Norton, *Mother Clap's Molly House,* 26. The dramatist Christopher Marlowe (1564–93), who is believed to have had homosexual inclinations, was a spy for Queen Elizabeth I. Ellen Harris has revealed the spying activities of Handel. See Harris, *Handel as Orpheus,* 172–209. Cardinal Albani, the patron of the famous homosexual art historian J. J. Winckelmann and other homoerotically inclined aesthetes, was also a spy. See Lesley Lewis, *Connoisseurs and Secret Agents in Eighteenth-Century Rome* (London: Chatto and Windus, 1961).

25. London: Sold by J. Cook, 1813.

26. See Goldsmith, *The Worst of Crimes,* 3–7, and Norton, *Mother Clap's Molly House,* passim.

27. See act 3, scene 1, in "The Woman Hater," ed. George Walton Williams, in *The Dramatic Works in the Beaumont and Fletcher Canon,* vol. 1, ed. Fredson Bowers (Cambridge: Cambridge University Press, 1966), 158–235. Patricia Adams Nordstrom points out this characterization, noting that music was such an important part of Elizabethan and Jacobean stage that playwrights "used a like or dislike for music as an efficient marker for establishing character." See her notes to the recording *In the Streets and Theatres of London: Elizabethan Ballads and Theater Music,* The Musicians of Swanne Alley (1989), Virgin Classics Limited, VC 7 90789–2.

28. *Windsor-drollery: being a more exact collection of the newest songs, poems, and catches, now in use, both in city and country, then any yet extant: with additions* (London: For J. M., 1672), 6, song 9.

29. Sedgwick, *Between Men,* 49–50.

30. Hillier, *The Catch Book,* number 76.

31. *Catch that catch can, or, A new collection of catches, rounds, and canons: being three or four parts in one* (London: W. G. for John Playford and Zachariah Watkins, 1663), 114.

32. *Windsor-drollery,* song 217, 131–32.

33. I have transcribed the text from the 1663 publication *Catch that catch can,* 41. See also Hillier, *The Catch Book,* number 19, who cites a 1652 source for the catch.

34. Quoted in Trumbach, "The Birth of the Queen," 133; see also the discussion at 130–33.

35. Ruth Gilbert, "Seeing and Knowing: Science, Pornography and Early Modern Hermaphrodites," in *At the Borders of the Human: Beasts, Bodies and Natural Philosophy in the Early Modern Period*, ed. Erica Fudge, Ruth Gilbert, and Susan Wiseman (New York: St. Martin's Press, 1999), 156. See also Lorraine Daston and Katharine Park, "The Hermaphrodite and the Orders of Nature: Sexual Ambiguity in Early Modern France," in *Premodern Sexualities*, ed. Louise Fradenburg and Carla Freccero (New York: Routledge, 1996), 117–36.

36. Gilbert, "Seeing and Knowing," 153–54.

37. I have consulted *Poems by John Cleavland. With Additions, never before printed* (London: W. Shears, 1662). This publication includes two hermaphrodite poems: "Upon an Hermaphrodite," followed by "The Authors Hermaphrodite, Made after Mr. Randolph's death, yet inserted into his Poems." This second poem is a convoluted complaint about the plagiarism of his Hermaphrodite poem by a Mr. Randolph ("For, since the childe is mine, and yet the claim / Is intercepted by anothers name"). This plagiarism is likened to being cuckolded: "For since the Muses left their former nest / to found a *Nunnery* in *Randolph*'s quill / Cuckold *Parnassus* is a forked hill" (21). Gilbert mentions Cleveland's "Upon an Hermophrodite" in "Seeing and Knowing," 165.

38. *Poems by John Cleavland*, 18–20.

39. Seventeenth-century men teasing each other as cuckolds is somewhat analogous to the "your mama" taunts in African-American "signifying" traditions. See Henry Louis Gates, *The Signifying Monkey: A Theory of Afro-American Literary Criticism* (New York: Oxford University Press, 1988), especially 54–76.

40. Sedgwick, *Between Men*, 23 and 89, respectively.

41. See Gary C. Thomas, "'Was George Frideric Handel Gay?': On Closet Questions and Cultural Politics," in *Queering the Pitch: The New Gay and Lesbian Musicology*, ed. Philip Brett, Elizabeth Wood, and Gary C. Thomas (New York: Routledge, 1994), 155–203; and Ellen T. Harris, *Handel as Orpheus: Voice and Desire in the Chamber Cantatas* (Cambridge, MA: Harvard University Press, 2001). The following discussion of Handel is indebted to Harris's study.

42. Harris, *Handel as Orpheus*, 43.

43. See ibid., 25 and 42–48.

44. See ibid., 270–71.

45. Philip Mayerson, *Classical Mythology in Literature, Art, and Music* (Toronto: Xerox Corporation, 1971), 319–20. See also Jeffrey Morrison, *Winckelmann and the Notion of Aesthetic Education* (Oxford: Clarendon Press, 1996), 24; and see the entries on Daedalus in Robert Graves, *The Greek Myths*, rev. ed. (New York: Penguin Books, 1992).

46. Ovid does not explicitly recount the legend that Daedalus was responsible for constructing the wooden cow used by king Minos's wife Pasiphae to couple with Poseidon's bull. This coupling produced the hybrid offspring, the Minotaur. King Minos imprisoned Daedalus and his son in the labyrinth after finding out that the craftsman had aided his wife in coupling with the bull. As he often did, Ovid assumes the readers know these details. For an example of an almost contemporary complete transmission of the myth, see Apollodorus, *Gods and Heroes of the Greeks: The Library of Apollodorus*, trans. Michael Simpson (Amherst: University of Massachusetts Press, 1976), 139 and 220.

47. Latin and translation from Molly Myerowitz, *Ovid's Games of Love* (Detroit, MI: Wayne State University Press, 1985), 159.

48. See Ovid, *The Metamorphoses: Books 6–10*, ed. William S. Anderson (Norman, OK: University of Oklahoma Press, 1972), 8:202–11 (p. 87).

49. See the introduction by Peter Green in Ovid, *The Erotic Poems*, trans. Peter Green (New York: Viking Penguin, 1986), 44–50.

50. See Myerowitz, *Ovid's Games of Love*, 151–67. Myerowitz argues that the Daedalus and Icarus story presents a basic antithesis between art and nature. Daedalus's artistic heifer disguise for Pasiphae suggests that Daedalus is the true creator of the unnatural Minotaur, who is so dangerous that Daedalus builds a labyrinth to contain him. The labyrinth eventually serves to confine Daedalus as well; thus the inventor is himself controlled by his creations.

51. See Green's commentary in Ovid, *The Erotic Poems*, 363.

52. Italian from John H. Turner, *The Myth of Icarus in Spanish Renaissance Poetry* (London: Tamesis Books, 1976), 52; see also 52–53 for commentary. I thank Amanda Marie Smith and Carol Rosen for the translation.

53. Turner, *The Myth of Icarus*, 53.

54. Italian text from Giambattista Marino, *La galeria del cav. Distinta in pitture, & sculture* (Venice: Presso G. P. Briogonici, 1664), 307. Edward Sherburne's rendition is taken from *Poems and Translations: Amorous, Lusory, Morall, Divine* (London: W. Hunt for Thomas Dring, 1651), 122.

55. Among the passionate writings of King James to and about his various male courtiers there is one of particular interest here: a poem on the death of his beloved cousin Esmé Stuart entitled *Ane Metaphoricall Invention of a Tragedie Called Phoenix* (published in 1584). Bergeron, *King James*, argues that this poem "serves as a 'familiar letter'" that "takes us into the king's private space through allegory and gives voice to James's desire" (33; see also 53–63 and 220–29 for the text). The poem includes a shape-poem preface with a double acrostic in which the first and last letters of each line spell ESMÉ STEWART DW(U)IKE. This explicitly sets up the connection of Esmé Stuart with the figure of the phoenix in the ensuing poem in which the poet laments the loss of the phoenix, and revives her through his poetic praises.

56. S.v. "Icarus and Daedalus" in Reid, *The Oxford Guide to Classical Mythology in the Arts: 1300–1900s* (New York: Oxford University Press, 1993).

57. S. J. Freedberg, *Andrea Del Sarto: Text and Illustrations* (Cambridge, MA: Harvard University Press, 1963), 4–6.

58. Morrison, *Winckelmann and the Notion of Aesthetic Education*, 31–32.

59. Peter C. Bol, ed., *Forschungen zur Villa Albani: Katalog der antiken Bildwerke* (Berlin: Gebr. Mann Verlag, 1989), 1:405–8 and 3:125–27. Winckelmann included an engraving of the heavily restored white marble relief (then without fig leaf) in *Monumenti antichi inediti spiegati ed illustrati da Giovanni Winckelmann* (1767), vol. 2, part 2, plate 95; see also his discussion at 129–30. I have consulted the second edition (Rome: Torchj di C. Mordacchini, 1821). Georg Zoega was the first to point out the restored condition of this relief in his *Li bassirilievi antichi di Roma* (Rome: Pietro Piranesi, 1808), 1:207–9. His book included an engraving of the *rosso antico* relief (plate 44) rather than the white marble relief, and he notes Winckelmann's silence about the restoration of the white marble relief.

60. G. S. Rousseau, "The Pursuit of Homosexuality in the Eighteenth Century: 'Utterly Confused Category' and/or Rich Repository," *Eighteenth-Century Life* 9, no. 3 (1985): 155.

61. Ibid., 159–60.

62. Recent scholarship on the *Bildungsroman* has shown the genre to be fraught with incoherent narratives and depictions of an unstable subject. See, for example, Dorothea von Mücke, *Virtue and the Veil of Illusion: Generic Innovations and the Pedagogical Project in Eighteenth-Century Literature* (Stanford, CA: Stanford University Press, 1991); Marc Redfield, *Phantom Formations: Aesthetic Ideology and the Bildungsroman* (Ithaca, NY: Cornell University Press, 1996); John Blair, *Tracing Subversive Currents in Goethe's Wilhelm Meister's Apprenticeship* (Columbus, SC: Camden House, 1997). I thank Aoife Naughton for giving me a draft of her Ph.D. dissertation, "Recollecting *Bildung* Before and After the *Bildungsroman*" (Cornell University, 2002). Naughton traces the concept of *Bildung* to the reflexive verb *"sich bilden"* in Christoph Martin Wieland's writings, and further back to its roots in the medieval mystic Meister Eckhart, who described mystical self-transformation in three stages: *entbilden, einbilden,* and *umbilden.* She argues that narratives of female self-formation around 1800 recall this earlier mystical aspect of *Bildung* in their treatment of the protagonist's relationship to the aesthetics of music, and that this emphasis on music (often religious) stands as a critical response to the emphasis on visual arts in narratives of male self-transformation.

63. Catriona MacLeod, *Embodying Ambiguity: Androgyny and Aesthetics from Winckelmann to Keller* (Detroit, MI: Wayne State University Press, 1998), 25–90, especially 29–40. See also Denis M. Sweet, "The Personal, the Political, and the Aesthetic: Johann Joachim Winckelmann's German Enlightenment Life," in *The Pursuit of Sodomy: Male Homosexuality in Renaissance and Enlightenment Europe,* ed. Kent Gerard and Gert Hekma (New York: Harrington Park Press, 1989), 147–62; and Simon Richter, "Winckelmann's Progeny: Homosocial Networking in the Eighteenth Century," in *Outing Goethe and His Age,* ed. Alice A. Kuzniar (Stanford, CA: Stanford University Press, 1996), 33–46.

64. The Villa Albani was completed in 1757, and Winckelmann arrived there in 1759. See Lesley Lewis, *Connoisseurs and Secret Agents in Eighteenth-Century Rome,* 195–200.

65. All translations of this cantata are adapted from that by Avril Bardoni. The Italian and English texts appear in the accompanying booklet to Emma Kirkby and the Academy of Ancient Music, directed by Christopher Hogwood, *Handel Italian Cantatas* (1985), Decca Records, 414 473–2.

66. See Harris, *Handel as Orpheus,* 9 and 375, n. 30.

67. The eroticized relationship between father and son in Handel's cantata recalls that in Benjamin Britten's *Abraham and Isaac,* discussed in chapter 2.

68. For "fuoco" and "diletto," see Jean Toscan, *Le carnaval du langage: Le lexique érotiques des poètes de l'équivoque de Burchiello à Marino (XV ᵉ–XVII ᵉ siècles)* (Lille: Presses Universitaires de Lille, 1981), 607, 524. For "morte" and "morire" see 499; for the theme of flight and birds *(augello),* see 1159 and 1541, respectively.

69. A case in point is Giovanni Battista Guarini's *Tirsi morir volea* set by Giaches de Wert.

70. Harris, *Handel as Orpheus,* 45.

71. Ibid., 64.

72. Ibid., 65–66.

73. Ibid., 84.

74. See Lucy Robinson, "Viol, § 5: Italy from *c*1580," in *The New Grove Dictionary of Music and Musicians,* 2nd ed., ed. Stanley Sadie and John Tyrell (New York: Grove Dictionaries, 2001), 25:675.

75. Francis Bacon, *The Wisdome of the Ancients,* trans. Sir Arthur Gorges (Edinburgh: John Swintoun, 1681), 153. Niall Rudd has noted that George Sandy's 1632 allegorical commentary on his translation of the *Metamorphoses* closely paraphrases Bacon's approval of Icarus as a noble aspirer. See Niall Rudd, "Daedalus and Icarus (ii) From the Renaissance to the Present Day," in *Ovid Renewed: Ovidian Influences on Literature and Art from the Middle Ages to the Twentieth Century,* ed. Charles Martindale (Cambridge: Cambridge University Press, 1988), 38.

76. Quoted in MacLeod, *Embodying Ambiguity,* 27.

77. Ibid., 27. See also Morrison, *Winckelmann and the Notion of Aesthetic Education,* 63.

78. Quoted in MacLeod, *Embodying Ambiguity,* 38–39.

79. MacLeod notes the "uncanny doubleness that will mark the androgyne's future: monstrosity in the real world versus perfection in the aesthetic realm; overdetermination versus openness of form; instability versus peaceful harmony" (*Embodying Ambiguity,* 32). For her discussion of Daedalus and Winckelmann, see 39.

80. Quoted in MacLeod, *Embodying Ambiguity,* 27.

81. Morrison, *Winckelmann and the Notion of Aesthetic Education,* 38. See also 34–35.

82. See MacLeod, *Embodying Ambiguity,* 38–39; and Morrison, *Winckelmann and the Notion of Aesthetic Education,* 40–41.

83. See Johann Wolfgang Goethe, *Winckelmann und sein Jahrhundert in Briefen und Aufsätzen* (1805; Leipzig: Veb Seemann Verlag, 1969).

84. MacLeod, *Embodying Ambiguity,* 50; for her discussion of *Wilhelm Meisters Lehrjahre,* see 91–139, especially 102–4 and 136.

85. The record was previously held by Slim Whitman's 1957 song "Rosemarie." See Peter K. Hogan, *The Complete Guide to the Music of Queen* (London: Omnibus Press, 1994), 35.

86. In a 1977 *Rolling Stone* interview Mercury discussed his choice of the name: "It was a very strong name, very universal and very immediate; it had a lot of visual potential and was open to all sorts of interpretations. I was certainly aware of the gay connotations, but that was just one facet of it." Quoted in Jeffrey Ressner, "Freddie Mercury: 1946–1991," *Rolling Stone,* January 9, 1992, 14.

87. Peter Freestone with David Evans, *Freddie Mercury: An Intimate Memoir by the Man Who Knew Him Best* (London: Omnibus Press, 1998), 79–80, 84.

88. The lyrics appear on the album jacket of Queen, *A Night at the Opera* (1975), Elecktra 7E-1053.

89. Ken McLeod has described this opening segment as a "lament" of a "suicidal young man," and the following operatic section as an "Orpheus-like descent into the insanity of the underworld." See McLeod, "Bohemian Rhapsodies: Operatic Influences on Rock Music," *Popular Music* 20, no. 2 (2001): 192–93.

90. See ibid., 193–94.

91. Ressner, "Freddie Mercury," 14. Ressner remarks that his "arch gay-macho

stance . . . both challenged and poked fun at the decidedly homophobic hard-rock world" (13).

92. This is an actual suburb west of Chicago, near the suburb where I grew up.

93. J. Hoberman and Jonathan Rosenbaum, *Midnight Movies* (New York: Harper and Row, 1983), 3.

94. See Rebecca Bell-Metereau, *Hollywood Androgyny*, 2nd ed. (New York: Columbia University Press, 1993), 15.

95. Much has been written about this cult by film critics, cultural historians, sociologists, and even anthropologists. See especially Bell-Metereau, *Hollywood Androgyny*, 178–87; Robert E. Wood, "Don't Dream It: Performance and *The Rocky Horror Picture Show*," in *The Cult Film Experience: Beyond All Reason*, ed. J. P. Telotte (Austin: University of Texas Press, 1991), 156–66; Hoberman and Rosenbaum, *Midnight Movies*, 174–213; Bruce A. Austin, "Portrait of a Cult Film Audience: *The Rocky Horror Picture Show*," *Journal of Communication* 31, no. 2 (1981): 43–54; and Mark Siegel, "*The Rocky Horror Picture Show:* More Than a Lip Service," *Science-Fiction Studies* 7 (1980): 305–12. Early reports of the spreading New York phenomenon include Arthur Bell, "Trick or Treat at the Horror Show," *Village Voice*, September 19, 1977, 55; and Michael Segel, "'Rocky Horror': The Case of the Rampant Audience," *Rolling Stone*, April 5, 1979, 20.

96. In 1981 I often drove with a few friends to see the movie at the Biograph Theater in Chicago (listening to "Bohemian Rhapsody" on the way); by 1983 the movie was showing at the mall cineplex in my suburban hometown.

97. For discussions of the introduction of homophobic audience lines see Bell-Metereau, *Hollywood Androgyny*, 186; and Hoberman and Rosenbaum, *Midnight Movies*, 184–88.

98. Barry K. Grant makes this point in "Science Fiction Double Feature: Ideology in the Cult Film," in *The Cult Film Experience*, 128. Siegel, *"The Rocky Horror Picture Show,"* traces many of the Christian allusions; Amittai F. Aviram, "Postmodern Gay Dionysus: Dr. Frank N. Furter," *Journal of Popular Culture* 26, no. 3 (1992): 183–92, discusses the story's similarities to a variety of Greek myths and characters.

99. Aviram, "Postmodern Gay Dionysus," 189, notes this scene's parody of Genesis.

100. Majorie Garber, *Vested Interests: Cross-Dressing and Cultural Anxiety* (New York: Routledge, 1992), 111.

101. Ibid., 111; Gaylyn Studlar, "Midnight S/Excess: Cult Configurations of 'Femininity' and the Perverse," in *The Cult Film Experience*, 147–49.

102. Paul Woodruff, in the introduction to his translation of Euripides' *Bacchae*, describes Dionysus in terms strikingly similar to those used to describe Dr. Frank N. Furter quoted above: "Dionysus is a god who takes human form, a powerful male who looks soft and feminine. . . . [H]is power has both masculine and feminine aspects." See Woodruff, "Introduction," in *Bacchae by Euripedes*, trans. Paul Woodruff (Indianapolis, IN: Hackett, 1998), xl.

103. See his "Postmodern Gay Dionysus." Aviram does not treat the floor show in any substantial way.

104. At the end of Dr. Frank N. Furter's final torch song "I'm Going Home," an audience fades into the empty seats to applaud and cheer his highly melodramatic performance (perhaps a reference to Judy Garland's concerts or her singing

"Over the Rainbow"). But this audience is a phantom one that disappears soon after the song ends.

105. Siegel, "More Than a Lip Service," analyzes the whole movie according to Arnold Van Gennep's *The Rites of Passage.* Siegel writes, "Van Gennep describes the life of the individual as a series of transitions from one stage of psycho-social development to another, and from one socio-economic role to another. . . . [P]ersonal evolution [occurs] by stages Van Gennep labelled 'separation,' 'transition,' and 'incorporation'" (307). He goes on to conclude that "[Brad and Janet's] night at 'The Frankenstein Place' is, on one level, a parody of a sexual rite of passage during which they undergo several transformations, adopt ritual identities, and, after being sexually initiated, are thrust into new roles" (311).

106. The empty theater could also be understood to represent the narcissism of drag, for which the most important audience is oneself.

107. D. Keith Mano, "The Rocky Horror Cult," *National Review,* November 24, 1978, 1494.

108. Christoph Grunenberg, "Unsolved Mysteries: Gothic Tales from *Frankenstein* to the Hair-Eating Doll," in *Gothic: Transmutations of Horror in Late Twentieth Century Art* (Cambridge, MA: MIT Press; and Boston: Institute of Contemporary Art, 1997), 175.

109. For a discussion of the Living Theater as a precursor to the audience participation in *Rocky Horror,* see Hoberman and Rosenbaum, *Midnight Movies,* 192.

110. See Randall Sullivan, "A Boy's Life: Kip Kinkel and the Springfield, Oregon Shootings, Part 1," *Rolling Stone,* September 17, 1998, 81; and Peter Wilkinson with Matt Hendrickson, "Columbine, Humiliation, and Revenge: The Story of Reb and VoDka," *Rolling Stone,* June 10, 1999, 51.

111. See Jeffrey Arnett, "Heavy Metal Music and Reckless Behavior Among Adolescents," *Journal of Youth and Adolescence* 20, no. 6 (1991): 573–92; for a discussion of Manson and adolescent violence, see Robert Wright, "'I'd Sell You Suicide': Pop Music and Moral Panic in the Age of Marilyn Manson," *Popular Music* 19, no. 3 (2001): 365–85. Manson wrote an articulate response to his critics in "Columbine: Whose Fault Is It?" *Rolling Stone,* June 10, 1999, 23–24, 77. See also *Popular Music and Society* 23, no. 3 (1999), which includes a special forum on the attack on music after the Columbine shooting.

112. Manson, "Columbine," 23–24 and 77.

113. The lyrics are taken from "The Beautiful People," cowritten with Twiggy Ramirez, on *Antichrist Superstar* (1996), Nothing/Interscope, INTD 90086.

114. Foucault, "Sex, Power, and the Politics of Identity," 165–70.

115. United States Senate Committee on Governmental Affairs, *Music Violence: How Does It Affect Our Children,* 105th Congress, 1st session, November 6, 1997, 5.

116. United States Senate, *Music Violence,* 4.

117. In 1997 Seagrams, originally a Canadian liquor company, owned Universal Music Group, which included Interscope Records—the owner and distributor of Nothing Records, Manson's label. Seagrams would go on to take over Polygram records in 1999, and merge this with Universal Music Group, annihilating many smaller record companies such as A&M and Geffen.

118. United States Senate, *Music Violence,* 13.

119. Ibid., 7.

120. Ibid., 34.

121. Ibid., 40 and 41.

122. Plato, *Laws*, trans. Trevor J. Saunders, in *Complete Works*, ed. John M. Cooper (Indianapolis, IN: Hackett, 1997), 1389–90.

123. United States Senate, *Music Violence*, 3.

124. Stephen Trask, "Tear Me Down," in John Cameron Mitchell and Stephen Trask, *Hedwig and the Angry Inch* (Woodstock, NY: Overlook Press, 2000), 14.

125. Mitchell and Trask, *Hedwig and the Angry Inch*, 23.

126. Eric Weisbard, "Lost in Translation," *Village Voice*, October 13–19, 1999, www.villagevoice.com/issues/9941/sotc.php, accessed February 24, 2002.

127. Another similarity to *Rocky Horror* is the development of a cult audience, documented in "The Origins of *Hedwig and the Angry Inch*," featured on the DVD *Hedwig and the Angry Inch* (2001), New Line Cinema Home Entertainment, N5401. Audience members sometimes dress up as characters, one woman had seen the play four hundred times, and another had tattooed "Hedwig" on her arm.

128. Trask, "Tear Me Down," in *Hedwig and the Angry Inch*, 15.

129. In terms of Lacanian psychoanalytic theory, Hedwig's "angry inch" compares to the *objet a*, the impossible object of desire that is strived for but cannot be named. This imaginary object, which points to lack and void, spurs figuration and signification that is always frustrated. The "angry inch" is both indexical and empty of content, taking the measure of the thing that drives the drama without naming the thing itself.

130. Neither Mitchell nor Trask identifies himself as transsexual; *Hedwig* explores this identity for its cultural meaning rather than for its psychology. I call attention to the growing literature on transsexual and transgender perspectives and theories with regard to masculinity, though an engagement with these writings lies beyond the scope of this book. See Judith Halberstam, *Female Masculinity* (Durham, NC: Duke University Press, 1998); Jay Prosser, *Second Skin: The Body Narratives of Transsexuality* (New York: Columbia University Press, 1998); and Bernice L. Hausman, "Recent Transgender Theory," *Feminist Studies* 27, no. 2 (2001): 465–90. See also Judith Kegan Gardiner, ed., *Masculinity Studies and Feminist Theory: New Directions* (New York: Columbia University Press, 2002).

131. Plato, *Symposium*, trans. Alexander Nehamas and Paul Woodruff, in *Complete Works*, ed. John M. Cooper (Indianapolis, IN: Hackett, 1997). All translations of the *Symposium* are taken from this edition.

132. See Bruce C. Steele, "John Cameron Mitchell," *The Advocate*, August 14, 2001, 26.

133. David Bowie publicly proclaimed his bisexuality in 1972, only to retract the proclamation in the 1980s. For a concise and thoughtful history of glam rock, see Barney Hoskyns, *Glam! Bowie, Bolan and the Glitter Rock Revolution* (New York: Pocket Books, 1998). See also the movie *Velvet Goldmine* (1998, dir. Todd Haynes). Haynes's film is a fantastical exploration of the history, queerness, and disappointments of glam rock, with fictional characters that are thinly veiled, but homosexually inclined, versions of real glam rockers: Brian Slade (David Bowie), Curt Wild (Iggy Pop), and Jack Fairy (perhaps Marc Bolan). Oscar Wilde, portrayed as an alien from outer space, figures as the spiritual force of glam.

134. Stephen Trask, "Midnight Radio," in *Hedwig and the Angry Inch*, 75.

WORKS CITED

Acker, Clara. *Dionysos en transe: La voix des femmes.* Paris: L'Harmattan, 2002.

Adorno, Theodor W., with George Simpson. "On Popular Music." In *Essays on Music,* edited by Richard Leppert, translated by Susan H. Gillespie, 437–69. Berkeley: University of California Press, 2002.

Aiken, David. "Subtle or Blatant, Discrimination Exists in the Gay Community." *The Advocate,* March 23, 1977, 7–8.

Alcoff, Linda Martín. "Who's Afraid of Identity Politics?" In *Reclaiming Identity: Realist Theory and the Predicament of Postmodernism,* edited by Paula M. L. Moya and Michael R. Hames-García, 312–44. Berkeley: University of California Press, 2000.

Allan of Lille. *The Plaint of Nature.* Translated by James J. Sheridan. Toronto: Pontifical Institute of Medieval Studies, 1980.

Allanbrook, Wye Jamison. *Rhythmic Gestures in Mozart:* Le Nozze di Figaro *and* Don Giovanni. Chicago: University of Chicago Press, 1983.

Allen, Dan. "Gay Marriage Worldwide." *The Advocate,* January 22, 2002, 22.

Althusser, Louis. "Ideology and Ideological State Apparatuses (Notes towards an Investigation)." In *Essays on Ideology,* translated by Ben Brewster and Grahame Lock, 1–60. London: Verso, 1984.

Anderson, Diane. "Melissa As You've Never Seen Her." *Girlfriends,* January/February 1996, 6–9.

Anderson, W. S. "The Orpheus of Virgil and Ovid: *flebile nescio quid.*" In *Orpheus: The Metamorphoses of a Myth,* edited by John Warden, 25–50. Toronto: University of Toronto Press, 1982.

Anderson, Warren D. *Music and Musicians in Ancient Greece.* Ithaca, NY: Cornell University Press, 1994.

Androite, John-Manuel. *Hot Stuff: A Brief History of Disco.* New York: Harper Collins, 2001.

Apollodorus. *Gods and Heroes of the Greeks: The Library of Apollodorus.* Translated by Michael Simpson. Amherst: University of Massachusetts Press, 1976.

Appel, Carl. *Bernart von Ventadorn, Seine Lieder.* Halle: Max Niemeyer, 1915.

Apter, Ronnie, ed. *Sugar and Salt: A Bilingual Edition of the Love Songs of Bernart de Ventadorn in Occitan and English.* Lewiston, NY: Edwin Mellen Press, 1999.

Armstrong, Tony, Jr. "Olivia Turns Twenty." *Hot Wire,* January 1994, 24–26, 46–47, 62.

Arnaut Daniel. *The Poetry of Arnaut Daniel.* Edited and translated by James J. Wilhelm. New York: Garland, 1981.

Arnett, Jeffery. "Heavy Metal Music and Reckless Behavior Among Adolescents." *Journal of Youth and Adolescence* 20, no. 6 (1991): 573–92.

Associated Press. "Etheridge 'Just Following the Rules' by Marrying Younger." *Houston Chronicle,* February 23, 2004, www.houstonchronicle.com (accessed February 26, 2004).

Astell, Anna W. *The Song of Songs in the Middle Ages.* Ithaca, NY: Cornell University Press, 1987.

Augustine, Saint. *The City of God.* Translated by Marcus Dods. New York: The Modern Library, 1993.

———. *Confessions.* Edited by James J. O'Donnell. 3 vols. Oxford: Clarendon Press, 1992.

———. *Confessions,* rev. ed. Translated by F. J. Sheed. Indianapolis, IN: Hackett, 1993.

———. *Enarrationes in Psalmos.* Edited by Eligius Dekkers and Johannes Fraipon. 3 vols. *Corpus Christianorum Series Latina.* Turnhout: Brepols, 1956.

———. *Exposition of the Psalms 1–32.* Translated by Maria Boulding O.S.B. Edited by John E. Rotelle. Vol. 15, *The Works of Saint Augustine: A Translation for the 21st Century.* Hyde Park, NY: New City Press, 2001.

———. *On Music.* Translated by Robert Taliaferro. Vol. 2, *Writings of Saint Augustine.* New York: CIMA Publishing, 1947.

Austin, Bruce A. "Portrait of a Cult Film Audience: *The Rocky Horror Picture Show.*" *Journal of Communications* 31, no. 2 (1981): 43–54.

Aviram, Amittai F. "Postmodern Gay Dionysus: Dr. Frank N. Furter." *Journal of Popular Culture* 26, no. 3 (1992): 183–92.

B. H. "The Ticket: Entertainment." *The Advocate,* December 27, 1979, 31.

Bacon, Francis. *Essayes and Counsels, Civil and Moral: Whereunto is newly added, Table of the Colours of Good and Evil.* London: For H. R., 1664.

———. *Wisdome of the Ancients.* Translated by Sir Arthur Gorges. Edinburgh: John Swintoun, 1681.

Baker, Dorothy Zayatz. *Mythic Masks in Self-Reflexive Poetry: A Study of Pan and Orpheus.* Chapel Hill: University of North Carolina Press, 1986.

Barthes, Roland. *S/Z: An Essay.* Translated by Richard Miller. New York: Hill and Wang, 1999.

Battersby, Christine. *Gender and Genius: Towards a Feminist Aesthetics.* Bloomington: Indiana University Press, 1989.

Bayton, Mavis. *Frock Rock: Women Performing Popular Music.* Oxford: Oxford University Press, 1998.

Bell, Arthur. "Trick or Treat at the Horror Show." *Village Voice,* September 19, 1977, 55.

Bell-Metereau, Rebecca. *Hollywood Androgyny,* 2nd ed. New York: Columbia University Press, 1993.

Benardete, Seth. *Plato's "Laws": The Discovery of Being.* Chicago: University of Chicago Press, 2000.

Bergeron, David M. *King James and Letters of Homoerotic Desire.* Iowa City: University of Iowa Press, 1999.

Bergman, David, ed. *Camp Grounds: Style and Homosexuality.* Amherst: University of Massachusetts Press, 1993.

Biblia Sacra Iuxta Vulgatam Versionem. Edited by Bonifatio Fischer O.S.B., Iohanne Gribomont O.S.B., H. F. D. Sparks, and W. Theile. Stuttgart: Wüttembergische Bibelanstalt, 1969.

Blair, John. *Tracing Subversive Currents in Goethe's Wilhelm Meister's Apprenticeship.* Columbus, SC: Camden House, 1997.

Blanchot, Maurice. "The Song of the Sirens: Encountering the Imaginary." In *The Gaze of Orpheus and Other Literary Essays,* translated by Lydia Davis, edited by P. Adams Sitney, 105–13. Barrytown, NY: Station Hill, 1981.

Bloch, R. Howard. *Etymologies and Genealogies: A Literary Anthropology of the French Middle Ages.* Chicago: University of Chicago Press, 1983.

———. *Medieval Misogyny and the Invention of Western Romantic Love.* Chicago: University of Chicago Press, 1991.

Bloom, Alan. *The Closing of the American Mind.* New York: Simon and Schuster, 1987.

Böhme, Robert. *Orpheus: Der Sänger und seine Zeit.* Munich: Frandke Verlag, 1970.

Bol, Peter C., ed. *Forschungen zur Villa Albani: Katalog der antiken Bildwerke.* 5 vols. Berlin: Gebr. Mann Verlag, 1989.

Borgeaud, Philippe. *The Cult of Pan in Ancient Greece.* Translated by Kathleen Atlass and James Redfield. Chicago: University of Chicago Press, 1988.

Boswell, John. *Christianity, Social Tolerance, and Homosexuality: Gay People in Western Europe from the Beginning of the Christian Era to the Fourteenth Century.* Chicago: University of Chicago Press, 1980.

———. "Dante and the Sodomites." *Dante Studies* 112 (1994): 63–76.

Botstein, Leon. "Music as the Language of Psychological Realism: Tchaikovsky and Russian Art." In *Tchaikovsky and His World,* edited by Leslie Kearney, 99–144. Princeton, NJ: Princeton University Press, 1998.

Bowen, Catherine Drinker, and Barbara von Meck. *"Beloved Friend": The Story of Tchaikowsky and Nadejda von Meck.* New York: Random House, 1937.

Bowers, Jane. "Women's Lamenting Traditions around the World: A Survey and Some Significant Questions." *Women & Music: A Journal of Gender and Culture* 2 (1998): 125–46.

Bowie, Andrew. *Aesthetics and Subjectivity: From Kant to Nietzsche.* Manchester, England: Manchester University Press, 1990.

Branton, Michael. "Sylvester Finds Heart in San Francisco." *Rolling Stone,* April 19, 1979, 34.

Bray, Alan. *Homosexuality in Renaissance England.* New York: Columbia University Press, 1995.

Bredbeck, Gregory W. *Sodomy and Interpretation: Marlowe to Milton.* Ithaca, NY: Cornell University Press, 1991.

———. "Troping the Light Fantastic: Representing Disco Then and Now." *GLQ: A Journal of Lesbian and Gay Studies* 3, no. 1 (1996): 71–107.

Bremmer, Jan N. "Transvestite Dionysos." In *Rites of Passage in Ancient Greece: Literature, Religion, Society,* edited by Mark W. Padilla, 183–200. Lewisburg, PA: Bucknell University Press, 1999.

Brett, Philip. *Benjamin Britten, Peter Grimes.* Cambridge: Cambridge University Press, 1982.

———. "Britten's Bad Boys: Male Relations in *The Turn of the Screw.*" *Repercussions* 1, no. 2 (1992): 5–25.

———. "Britten's Dream." In *Musicology and Difference: Gender and Sexuality in Music Scholarship,* edited by Ruth Solie. Berkeley: University of California Press, 1993.

———. "Eros and Orientalism in Britten's Operas." In *Queering the Pitch: The New Gay and Lesbian Musicology,* edited by Philip Brett, Elizabeth Wood, and Gary C. Thomas, 235–56. New York: Routledge, 1994.

———. "Musicality, Essentialism, and the Closet." In *Queering the Pitch: The New Gay and Lesbian Musicology,* edited by Philip Brett, Elizabeth Wood, and Gary C. Thomas, 9–26. New York: Routledge, 1994.

———. "Salvation at Sea: *Billy Budd.*" In *The Britten Companion,* edited by Christopher Palmer, 133–43. Cambridge: Cambridge University Press, 1984.

Bristow, Joseph. *Effeminate England: Homoerotic Writings After 1885.* New York: Columbia University Press, 1995.

Britten, Benjamin. *Billy Budd, An Opera in Four Acts.* Libretto by E. M. Forster and Eric Crozier. Vocal score by Erwin Stein. London: Hawkes and Son, 1952.

———. *Canticle II: Abraham and Isaac, Op. 51, for Alto, Tenor, and Piano.* Text from the Chester Miracle Play. London: Boosey and Hawkes, 1953.

Brooks, Peter. *The Melodramatic Imagination: Balzac, Henry James, Melodrama, and the Mode of Excess.* New Haven, CT: Yale University Press, 1976.

Brown, David. *Tchaikovsky: A Biographical and Critical Study, The Final Years (1885–1893).* New York: W. W. Norton and Company, 1991.

Brown, Judith C. *Immodest Acts: The Life of a Lesbian Nun in Renaissance Italy.* New York: Oxford University Press, 1986.

Brown, Malcolm Hamrick. "Tchaikovsky and His Music in Anglo-American Criticism, 1890s–1950s." In *Queer Episodes in Music and Modern Identity,* edited by Sophie Fuller and Lloyd Whitesell, 134–49. Urbana: University of Illinois Press, 2002.

Brown, Mark. Interview with Melissa Etheridge, 2001, www.melissaetheridge.com/community/interviews/mark_brown.html (accessed May 19, 2002).

Brown, Peter. *Augustine of Hippo: A Biography.* Berkeley: University of California Press, 2000.

———. *The Body and Society: Men, Women, and Sexual Renunciation in Early Christian Antiquity.* New York: Columbia University Press, 1988.

Brussel, James A. "The Tchaikowsky Troika." *Psychiatric Quarterly Supplement* 36, no. 2 (1962): 304–22.

Buitron-Oliver, Diana, and Beth Cohen. "Between Skylla and Penelope: Female Characters of the *Odyssey* in Archaic and Classical Greek Art." In *The Distaff Side: Representing the Female in Homer's* Odyssey, edited by Beth Cohen, 29–58. Oxford: Oxford University Press, 1995.

Bullough, Vern L. *Science in the Bedroom: A History of Sex Research.* New York: Basic Books, 1994.

Bumpass, Kathryn. "A Musical Reading of Hildegard's Responsory 'Spiritui Sancto.'" In *Hildegard of Bingen: A Book of Essays,* edited by Maud Burnett McInerney, 155–73. New York: Garland, 1998.

Burgwinkle, William E. *Love for Sale: Materialist Readings of the Troubadour Razo Corpus.* New York: Garland, 1997.

Burke, Tom. "The New Homosexuality." *Esquire,* December 1969, 178–79, 304–18.

Burkert, Walter. "Apellai und Apollon." *Rheinisches Museum für Philologie* 118, no. 1 (1975): 1–21.

———. *Greek Religion.* Translated by John Raffan. Cambridge, MA: Harvard University Press, 1985.

Burnham, Scott G. "Beethoven, Ludwig van, § 19 (i): History of the Myth." In *The New Grove Dictionary of Music and Musicians,* 2nd ed., edited by Stanley Sadie and John Tyrrell, 3:110–12. New York: Grove Dictionaries, 2001.

Butler, Judith. *Bodies That Matter: On the Discursive Limits of "Sex."* New York: Routledge, 1993.

———. *Gender Trouble: Feminism and the Subversion of Identity.* New York: Routledge, 1990.

———. "Imitation and Gender Insubordination." In *The Lesbian and Gay Studies Reader,* edited by Henry Abelove, Michèle Aina Barale, and David M. Halperin, 307–20. New York: Routledge, 1993.

———. *The Psychic Life of Power: Theories in Subjection.* Stanford, CA: Stanford University Press, 1997.

Butler, Samuel. *The Authoress of the* Odyssey, *when and where she wrote, who she was, the use she made of the* Iliad, *and how the poem grew under her hands,* 2nd ed. London: Jonathan Cape, 1922.

Bynum, Caroline Walker. *Holy Feast and Holy Fast: The Religious Significance of Food to Medieval Women.* Berkeley: University of California Press, 1987.

Byrd, William. *The Five-Part Consort Music, Volume I: The Fantasies.* London: London Pro Musica, 1998.

C. E. et al. "Collective Concert Coverage." *Off Our Backs,* December 1976, 19.

Calame, Claude. "Sappho's Group: An Initiation into Womanhood." In *Reading Sappho: Contemporary Approaches,* edited by Ellen Greene, 113–24. Berkeley: University of California Press, 1996.

Camille, Michael. "The Pose of the Queer: Dante's Gaze, Brunetto Latini's Body." In *Queering the Middle Ages,* edited by Glenn Burger and Steven F. Kruger, 57–86. Minneapolis: University of Minnesota Press, 2001.

Campbell, David A., trans. *Greek Lyric I: Sappho and Alcaeus.* Cambridge, MA: Harvard University Press, 1982.

Campbell, Michael, and James Brody. *Rock and Roll: An Introduction.* New York: Schirmer Books, 1999.

Campbell, Joseph, and Bill Moyers. *The Power of Myth.* New York: Doubleday, 1988.

Carpenter, Edward. *The Intermediate Sex: A Study of Some Transitional Types of Men and Women.* 1908. Reprint, London: George Allen and Unwin, 1983.

Carpenter, Humphrey. *Benjamin Britten: A Biography.* New York: Charles Scribner's Sons, 1992.

Carpenter, Thomas H. *Dionysian Imagery in Fifth-Century Athens.* Oxford: Clarendon Press, 1997.

Carson, Ann. "The Gender of Sound." *Thamyris* 1, no. 1 (1994): 10–31.

The Cassell Dictionary of Slang. Edited by Jonathan Green. London: Cassell, 1998.

Catch that catch can, or, A new collection of catches, rounds, and canons: being three or four parts in one. London: W. G. for John Playford and Zachariah Watkins, 1663.

Chapple, Steve, and Reebee Garofalo. *Rock 'n' Roll Is Here to Pay: The History and Politics of the Music Industry.* Chicago: Nelson-Hall, 1977.

Chauncey, George. *Gay New York: Gender, Urban Culture, and the Making of the Gay Male World, 1890–1940.* New York: Basic Books, 1994.

Cheng, Scarlet. "Kay Gardner and Urana Records." *Off Our Backs,* February 1977, 17.

Chicago and New Haven Women's Liberation Rock Bands. "Mountain Moving Day." In *The New Woman's Survival Catalog,* edited by Kirsten Grimstad and Susan Rennie, 68. New York: Coward, McCann & Geoghegan, 1973.

Chicago Women's Liberation Rock Band. "Developing a Revolutionary Women's Culture." *Women: A Journal of Liberation* 3, no. 2 (1972): 2–5.

Chignon, Niles, ed. *The Camp Followers' Guide!* New York: Avon Books, 1965.

Christgau, Robert. "Sylvester Is a Star." *Village Voice,* June 11, 1979, 73.

Christian, Meg. *I Know You Know: A Songbook and Scrapbook of the Album.* Oakland, CA: Olivia Records, 1975.

Clark, Terri. "Linda Tillery: Feminist Funk." *Off Our Backs,* November 1978, 8.

Clarke, Gerald. *Get Happy: The Life of Judy Garland.* New York: Random House, 2000.

Clayton, Barbara. *A Penelopean Poetics: Reweaving the Feminine in Homer's* Odyssey. Lanham, MD: Lexington Books, 2004.

Cleto, Fabio, ed. *Camp: Queer Aesthetics and the Performing Subject: A Reader.* Ann Arbor: University of Michigan Press, 1999.

Cleveland, John. *Poems by John Cleavland. With Additions, never before Printed.* London: W. Shears, 1662.

Clum, John M. *Something for the Boys: Musical Theater and Gay Culture.* New York: St. Martin's Press, 1999.

Clunis, Merilee D., and G. Dorsey. *The Lesbian Parenting Book: A Guide to Creating Families and Raising Children.* Seattle: Seal Press, 1995.

Colish, Marcia L. *Medieval Foundations of the Western Intellectual Tradition: 400–1400.* New Haven, CT: Yale University Press, 1998.

———. *The Stoic Tradition from Antiquity to the Early Middle Ages.* Vol. 2, *Stoicism in Christian Latin Thought through the Sixth Century.* Leiden: E. J. Brill, 1985.

Cooke, Mervyn. *Britten: War Requiem.* Cambridge: Cambridge University Press, 1996.

Cooke, Mervyn, and Philip Reed. *Benjamin Britten, Billy Budd.* Cambridge: Cambridge University Press, 1993.

Cooper, Martin. "The Symphonies." In *Tchaikovsky: A Symposium,* edited by Gerald Abraham, 24–46. London: Lindsay Drummond, 1945.

Crocker, Richard. *An Introduction to Gregorian Chant.* New Haven, CT: Yale University Press, 2000.

———. "Pythagorean Mathematics and Music (Parts I and II)." *Journal of Aesthetics and Art Criticism* 22 (1963/64): 189–98, 325–35. Reprint in *Studies in Medieval Music Theory and the Early Sequence.* Brookfield, VT: Ashgate Publishing, 1997.

———. "Two Recent Editions of Aquitanian Polyphony." *Plainsong and Medieval Music* 3, no. 1 (1994): 57–101.

Crowley, Martin. *The Boys in the Band.* New York: Farrar, Straus and Giroux, 1968.

Csapo, Eric. "The Politics of New Music." In *Music and the Muses: The Culture of*

"Mousikē" in the Classical Athenian City, edited by Penelope Murray and Peter Wilson, 207–48. Oxford: Oxford University Press, 2004.

Culler, Jonathan. *Ferdinand de Saussure,* rev. ed. Ithaca, NY: Cornell University Press, 1986.

———. *The Pursuit of Signs: Semiotics, Literature, Deconstruction.* Ithaca, NY: Cornell University Press, 1981.

Cusick, Suzanne. "On a Lesbian Relationship with Music: A Serious Effort Not to Think Straight." In *Queering the Pitch: The New Gay and Lesbian Musicology,* edited by Philip Brett, Elizabeth Wood, and Gary C. Thomas, 67–83. New York: Routledge, 1994.

Daly, Mary. *Beyond God the Father: Toward a Philosophy of Women's Liberation.* Boston: Beacon Press, 1973.

Dame, Joke. "Unveiled Voices: Sexual Difference and the Castrato." In *Queering the Pitch: The New Gay and Lesbian Musicology,* edited by Philip Brett, Elizabeth Wood, and Gary C. Thomas, 137–53. New York: Routledge, 1994.

Dante Alighieri. *Purgatorio.* Translated and with a commentary by Charles S. Singleton. 2 vols. Princeton, NJ: Princeton University Press, 1973.

Darcey, L. "The Name of Circe and the Portolans of Archaic Greece." *Les études classiques* 53 (1958): 185–91.

Dart, Thurston. "Eye Music." *The New Grove Dictionary of Music and Musicians,* 2nd ed., edited by Stanley Sadie and John Tyrrell, 8:482–83. New York: Grove Dictionaries, 2001.

Datson, Lorraine, and Katharine Park. "The Hermaphrodite and the Orders of Nature: Sexual Ambiguity in Early Modern France." In *Premodern Sexualities,* edited by Louise Fradenburg and Carla Freccero, 115–36. New York: Routledge, 1996.

de Lauretis, Teresa. "Sexual Indifference and Lesbian Representation." In *The Lesbian and Gay Studies Reader,* edited by Henry Abelove, Michèle Aina Barale, and David M. Halperin, 141–58. New York: Routledge, 1993.

DeJean, Joan. *Fictions of Sappho: 1546–1937.* Chicago: University of Chicago Press, 1989.

Dellamora, Richard. *Masculine Desire: The Sexual Politics of Victorian Aestheticism.* Chapel Hill: University of North Carolina Press, 1990.

Denisoff, R. Serge. "Folk Music and the American Left." In *The Sounds of Social Change: Studies in Popular Culture,* edited by R. Serge Denisoff and Richard A. Peterson, 106–20. Chicago: Rand McNally, 1972.

Dennis, Allen. *The Gay B C Book: A Camp.* San Francisco: D. Redmond Designs, 1966.

Diebold, David. *Tribal Rites.* Northridge, CA: Time Warp Publishing, 1986.

Dinshaw, Carolyn. *Getting Medieval: Sexualities and Communities, Pre- and Postmodern.* Durham, NC: Duke University Press, 1999.

Dlugacz, Judy. "If It Weren't for the Music: 15 Years of Olivia Records (Part 1)." *Hot Wire* 4, no. 3 (1988): 28–31, 52.

Dobkin, Alix. *Adventures in Women's Music.* New York: Tomato Publications, 1979.

Doherty, Lillian Eileen. *Siren Song: Gender, Audiences, and Narrators in the* Odyssey. Ann Arbor: University of Michigan Press, 1995.

———. "Sirens, Muses, and Female Narrators in the *Odyssey.*" In *The Distaff Side: Rep-

resenting the Female in Homer's Odyssey, edited by Beth Cohen, 81–92. Oxford: Oxford University Press, 1995.

Dorat, Jean. *Mythologicum, ou interprétation allégorique de l'Odyssée X–XII et de l'hymne à Aphrodite.* Genève: Droz, 2000.

Dover, Kenneth James. *Greek Homosexuality.* Cambridge, MA: Harvard University Press, 1977.

Dozer, Richard. "Sox Promotion Ends in a Mob Scene: Tigers Ask for Forfeit of 2nd Game." *Chicago Tribune,* July 13, 1979, Sec. 5: 1.

Duberman, Martin. *Stonewall.* New York: Dutton, 1993.

duBois, Page. *Sappho is Burning.* Chicago: University of Chicago Press, 1995.

———. *Torture and Truth.* New York: Routledge, 1991.

Dunn, Janice. "The Name of the Father and the Making of a New American Family." *Rolling Stone,* February 3, 2000, 40–45.

Dyer, Richard. *Heavenly Bodies: Film Stars and Society.* New York: St. Martin's Press, 1986.

Eagleton, Terry. *Literary Theory: An Introduction.* 2nd ed. Minneapolis: University of Minnesota Press, 1996.

Echols, Alice. *Daring to Be Bad: Radical Feminism in America, 1967–1975.* Minneapolis: University of Minnesota Press, 1989.

Edelson, Carol, and Fran Pollner. "Meg Christian." *Off Our Backs,* April 1973, 2–3.

Ellis, Havelock. *Sexual Inversion.* 3rd ed. Vol. 1, part 4 of *Psychology of Sex.* 1915. Reprint, New York: Random House, 1942.

———. *Sexual Selection in Man.* 3rd ed. Vol. 1, part 3 of *Psychology of Sex.* 1915. Reprint, New York: Random House, 1942.

Ellis, Havelock, and John Addington Symonds. *Sexual Inversion.* 1896. Reprint, New York: Arno Press, 1975.

Ellis, Stan. "The Ticket: Records." *The Advocate,* December 28, 1977, 30.

Emerson, Ken. "The Village People: America's Male Ideal?" *Rolling Stone,* October 5, 1978, 26–30.

Engh, Barbara. "Adorno and the Sirens: Tele-phono-graphic Bodies." In *Embodied Voices: Representing Female Vocality in Western Culture,* edited by Leslie C. Dunn and Nancy A. Jones, 120–35. Cambridge: Cambridge University Press, 1994.

Etheridge, Melissa, with Laura Morton. *The Truth Is . . . My Life and Love in Music.* New York: Villard Books, 2001.

Evans, Arthur. *The God of Ecstasy: Sex-Roles and Musical Madness of Dionysus.* New York: St. Martin's Press, 1988.

Faith, Karlene. *Madonna: Bawdy and Soul.* Toronto: University of Toronto Press, 1997. Berkeley: University of California Press, 1998.

Fassler, Margot. "Composer and Dramatists: 'Melodious Singing and the Freshness of Remorse.'" In *Voice of the Living Light: Hildegard of Bingen and Her World,* edited by Barbara Newman, 149–75. Berkeley: University of California Press, 1988.

Fast, Susan. *Houses of the Holy: Led Zeppelin and the Power of Rock Music.* Oxford: Oxford University Press, 2001.

Fisher, Carrie. "True Confessions: The *Rolling Stone* Interview with Madonna." *Rolling Stone,* June 13, 1991, 35–40, 120.

Foucault, Michel. *The Care of the Self.* Translated by Robert Hurley. Vol. 3, *The History of Sexuality.* New York: Vintage Books, 1986.

————. *Discipline and Punish: The Birth of the Prisons*. Translated by Alan Sheridan. New York: Vintage Books, 1977.

————. "The Ethics of the Concern for Self as a Practice of Freedom." In *Ethics: Subjectivity, and Truth*, 281–301. New York: The New Press, 1997.

————. *The History of Sexuality, Volume 1: An Introduction*. Translated by Robert Hurley. New York: Vintage Books, 1980.

————. *L'herméneutique du sujet: Cours au Collège de France, 1981–1982*. Paris: Gallimard-Seuil, 2001.

————. "On the Genealogy of Ethics: An Overview of Work in Progress." In *Ethics: Subjectivity and Truth*, edited by Paul Rabinow, 253–80. New York: The New Press, 1997.

————. *The Order of Things: An Archaeology of the Human Sciences*. Translated by Alan Sheridan. New York: Vintage, 1973.

————. "Self-Writing." In *Ethics: Subjectivity and Truth*, edited by Paul Rabinow, 207–22. New York: The New Press, 1997.

————. "Sex, Power, and the Politics of Identity." In *Ethics: Subjectivity and Truth*, edited by Paul Rabinow, 163–73. New York: The New Press, 1997.

————. "Sexuality and Solitude." In *Ethics: Subjectivity and Truth*, edited by Paul Rabinow, 175–84. New York: The New Press, 1997.

————. "Technologies of the Self." In *Ethics: Subjectivity and Truth*, edited by Paul Rabinow, 223–51. New York: The New Press, 1997.

————. "The Thought of the Outside." In *Aesthetics, Method, and Epistemology*, edited by James D. Faubion, 147–69. New York: The New Press, 1998.

————. *The Use of Pleasure*. Translated by Robert Hurley. Vol. 2, *The History of Sexuality*. New York: Vintage Books, 1990.

François, Anne-Lise. "Fakin' It / Makin' It: Falsetto's Bid for Transcendence in 1970s Disco." *Perspectives of New Music* 33 (1995): 443–55.

Franklin, William. "Sounding Off on the Sound Stage: The Three Voices of the Village People." *The Advocate*, December 27, 1979, 31–33.

Frantzen, Allen J., "Tears for Abraham: The Chester Play of Abraham and Isaac and Antisacrifice in Works by Wilfred Owen, Benjamin Britten, and Derek Jarman," *Journal of Medieval and Early Modern Studies* 33 (2001): 445–76.

Freedberg, Mike. "Sylvester Gets (Too) Specific." *Village Voice*, October 15–21, 1980, 89.

Freedberg, S. J. *Andrea Del Sarto: Text and Illustrations*. Cambridge, MA: Harvard University Press, 1963.

Freestone, Peter, with David Evans. *Freddie Mercury: An Intimate Memoir by the Man Who Knew Him Best*. London: Omnibus Press, 1998.

Freud, Sigmund. "Analysis of a Phobia in a Five-Year-Old Boy." In *The Standard Edition of the Complete Psychological Works of Sigmund Freud*, edited by James Strachey, 10:3–152. London: Hogarth Press, 1955.

————. "Introductory Lectures on Psycho-analysis, Part II: Dreams." In *The Standard Edition of the Complete Psychological Works of Sigmund Freud*, edited by James Strachey, 15:83–233. London: Hogarth Press, 1961.

————. "The Moses of Michelangelo." In *Collected Papers*, edited by Joan Riviere, 4:257–87. London: Hogarth Press and the Institute of Psycho-Analysis, 1957.

Friedman, John Block. *Orpheus in the Middle Ages*. Syracuse, NY: Syracuse University Press, 2000.

Frith, Simon. *Sound Effects: Youth, Leisure, and the Politics of Rock 'n' Roll.* New York: Pantheon Books, 1981.

Frith, Simon, and Angela McRobbie. "Rock and Sexuality." In *On Record: Rock, Pop, and the Written Word,* edited by Simon Frith and Andrew Goodwin, 371–98. New York: Pantheon Press, 1990.

Fuss, Diana. *Identification Papers.* New York: Routledge, 1995.

Garber, Marjorie. *Vested Interests: Cross-Dressing and Cultural Anxiety.* New York: Routledge, 1992.

Garber, Rebecca L. R. "Where Is the Body? Images of Eve and Mary in the *Scivias.*" In *Hildegard of Bingen: A Book of Essays,* edited by Maud Burnett McInerney, 103–32. New York: Garland, 1998.

Gardiner, Elysa. "The Singer and the Song." In *Trouble Girls: The Rolling Stone Book of Women in Rock,* edited by Barbara O'Dair, 359–75. New York: Random House, 1997.

Gardiner, Judith Kegan, ed. *Masculinity Studies and Feminist Theory: New Directions.* New York: Columbia University Press, 2002.

Garland, Judy. "How *Not* to Love a Woman." *Coronet,* February 1955, 41–44.

Garlington, Lee. "Baby Cockroach." *Off Our Backs,* July–August 1977, 19.

Garofalo, Reebee. *Rock 'n' Roll Is Here to Pay: The History and Politics of the Music Industry.* Chicago: Nelson-Hall, 1977.

———. *Rockin' Out: Popular Music in the USA.* 2nd ed. Upper Saddle River, NJ: Prentice Hall, 2002.

Gates, Henry Louis. *The Signifying Monkey: A Theory of Afro-American Literary Criticism.* New York: Oxford University Press, 1988.

Gaunt, Simon. *Gender and Genre in Medieval French Literature.* Cambridge: Cambridge University Press, 1995.

Geier, Alfred. *Plato's Erotic Thought: The Tree of the Unknown.* Rochester: University of Rochester Press, 2002.

George, Nelson. "Fatal Prognosis Wrong, Patient Alive and Well." *Billboard,* July 14, 1979, 75–76.

Gibson, James E. "Celebration and Transgression: Nietzsche on Ritual." *Journal of Ritual Studies* 5, no. 2 (Summer 1991): 1–13.

Gilbert, Ruth. "Seeing and Knowing: Science, Pornography and Early Modern Hermaphrodite." In *At the Borders of the Human: Beasts, Bodies and Natural Philosophy in the Early Modern Period,* edited by Ruth Gilbert, Erica Fudge, and Susan Wiseman, 150–70. New York: St. Martin's Press, 1999.

Gilmore, Mikal. "Disco!" *Rolling Stone,* April 19, 1979, 9, 54.

Girard, René. *Deceit, Desire, and the Novel: Self and Other in Literary Structure.* Translated by Yvonne Freccero. Baltimore, MD: Johns Hopkins University Press, 1972.

Giteck, Lenny. "How Gay Are the Ghettos?" *The Advocate,* September 6, 1979, 15–18.

Goethe, Johann Wolfgang. *Wilhelm Meister's Apprenticeship.* Translated by Eric A. Blackall in cooperation with Victor Lange. Princeton, NJ: Princeton University Press, 1989.

———. *Winckelmann un sein Jahrhundert in Briefen und Aufsätzen.* 1805. Leipzig: Veb Seeman Verlag, 1969.

"The Golden Girl of the Year, Yeah, Yeah, Goes to the Movies." In *The Camp Followers' Guide!,* edited by Niles Chignon, 49–55. New York: Avon Books, 1965.

Goldsmith, Netta Murray. *The Worst of Crimes: Homosexuality and the Law in Eighteenth-Century London.* Brookfield, VT: Ashgate, 1998.

Gonzalez, Francisco J. "How to Read a Platonic Prologue: *Lysis* 203A–207D." In *Plato as Author: The Rhetoric of Philosophy*, edited by Ann N. Michelini, 22–36. Leiden: Brill, 2003.

Goodich, Michael. *The Unmentionable Vice: Homosexuality in the Later Medieval Period*. Oxford: ABC-Clio Press, 1979.

Grant, Barry K. "Science Fiction Double Feature: Ideology in the Cult Film." In *The Cult Film Experience: Beyond All Reason*, edited by J. P. Telotte, 122–37. Austin: University of Texas Press, 1991.

Graves, Robert. *The Greek Myths*, rev. ed. New York: Penguin Books, 1992.

Greene, Ellen. "Sappho, Foucault, and Women's Erotics." *Arethusa* 29 (1996): 1–14.

Grein, Paul. "Once Darlings of Gay Discos, Village People Broaden Appeal." *Billboard*, October 20, 1979, 64, 78.

———. "Village People Get Serious with New 'Macho Man' LP." *Billboard*, May 13, 1978, 54.

Gribble, David. *Alcibiades and Athens: A Study in Literary Presentation*. Oxford: Clarendon Press, 1999.

Grimstad, Kirsten, and Susan Rennie, eds. *The New Woman's Survival Sourcebook*. New York: Alfred A. Knopf, 1975.

Gross, Michael Joseph. "The Queen Is Dead, Part One." *The Atlantic Online: The Atlantic Monthly Digital Edition* (August 2000), www.theatlantic.com/issues/2000/08/gross.html (accessed June 29, 2001).

Grunenberg, Christoph. "Unsolved Mysteries: Gothic Tales from *Frankenstein* to the Hair-Eating Doll." In *Gothic: Transmutations of Horror in Late Twentieth Century Art*, edited by Christoph Grunenberg, 212–159 (reverse pagination). Cambridge, MA: MIT Press; and Boston: Institute of Contemporary Art, 1997.

Guly, Christopher. "The Judy Connection." *The Advocate*, June 28, 1994, 49–55.

Gunn, Jacky, and Jim Jenkins. *Queen, As It Began*. New York: Hyperion, 1992.

Guthrie, W. K. C. *Orpheus and Greek Religion*. Princeton, NJ: Princeton University Press, 1993.

Habermas, Jürgen. "Technology and Science as Ideology." In *Toward a Rational Society: Student Protests, Science, and Politics*, translated by Jeremy J. Shapiro. Boston: Beacon Press, 1970.

Hadleigh, Boze. *The Vinyl Closet: Gays in the Music World*. San Diego: Los Hombres Press, 1991.

Hadot, Pierre. "Reflections on the Notion of 'The Cultivation of the Self.'" In *Michel Foucault, Philosopher: Essays Translated from the French and German*, translated by Timothy J. Armstrong, 225–32. New York: Routledge, 1992.

Halberstam, Judith. *Female Masculinity*. Durham, NC: Duke University Press, 1998.

Hall, Radclyffe. *The Well of Loneliness*. 1922. New York: Pocket Books, 1974.

Hallett, Judith P. "Sappho and Her Social Context: Sense and Sensuality." In *Reading Sappho: Contemporary Approaches*, edited by Ellen Greene, 125–42. Berkeley: University of California Press, 1996.

Halperin, David M. *How to Do the History of Homosexuality*. Chicago: University of Chicago Press, 2002.

———. *One Hundred Years of Homosexuality and Other Essays on Greek Love*. New York: Routledge, 1990.

———. "Platonic *Erōs* and What Men Call Love." *Ancient Philosophy* 5 (1985): 161–204.

————. *Saint Foucault: Towards a Gay Hagiography*. New York: Oxford University Press, 1995.

Handel, George Frideric. *Tra le fiamme*. Edited by Hermann Zenck. Kassel: Bärenreiter, 1977.

Handschin, Jacques. "The 'Timaeus' Scale." *Musica Disciplina* 4 (1950): 3–42.

Harpham, Geoffrey Galt. *The Ascetic Imperative in Culture and Criticism*. Chicago: University of Chicago Press, 1987.

Harris, Daniel. *The Rise and Fall of Gay Culture*. New York: Ballantine Books, 1997.

Harris, Ellen T. *Handel as Orpheus: Voice and Desire in the Chamber Cantatas*. Cambridge, MA: Harvard University Press, 2001.

Hartle, Ann. *The Modern Self in Rousseau's* Confessions: *A Reply to St. Augustine*. Notre Dame, IN: University of Notre Dame Press, 1983.

Hatab, Lawrence J. "Apollo and Dionysus: Nietzschean Expressions of the Sacred." In *Nietzsche and the Gods*, edited by Weaver Santaniello, 45–65. Albany: State University of New York Press, 2001.

————. *Myth and Philosophy: A Contest of Truths*. La Salle, IL: Open Court, 1990.

Hausman, Bernice L. "Recent Transgender Theory." *Feminist Studies* 27, no. 2 (2001): 465–90.

Havelock, Eric A. *Preface to Plato*. Cambridge, MA: Harvard University Press, 1963.

Hawkins, John. *A General History of the Science and Practice of Music*. 1776. New York: Dover Publications, 1963.

Hayes, Eileen M. "Black Women Performers of Women-Identified Music: 'They Cut Off My Voice: I Grew Two Voices.'" Ph.D., University of Washington, 1999.

Henrichs, Albert. "'He Has a God in Him': Human and Divine in the Modern Perception of Dionysus." In *Masks of Dionysus*, edited by Thomas H. Carpenter and Christopher A. Faraone, 13–43. Ithaca, NY: Cornell University Press, 1993.

Herschberg, Charles. "The Prophets or Profits? The Village People." *The Advocate*, April 19, 1978, 31.

Hesiod. *Theogony*. Translated by Norman O. Brown. New York: Macmillan, 1985.

Heywood, Leslie, and Jennifer Drake, eds. *Third Wave Agenda: Being Feminist, Doing Feminism*. Minneapolis: University of Minnesota Press, 1997.

Hildegard of Bingen. *Scivias*. Translated by Mother Columba Hart and Jane Bishop. New York: Paulist Press, 1990.

————. *Sequences and Hymns*, edited by Christopher Page. Devon, England: Antico, 1983.

————. *Symphonia armonie celestium revelationum*. See Newman, Barbara. *Saint Hildegard of Bingen, Symphonia*.

Hildenbrand, Kathleen. "Don't Call Me Missy (Interview with Melissa Etheridge)." *Girlfriends*, October 1999, 24–27, 40.

Hiley, David. *Western Plainchant: A Handbook*. Oxford: Clarendon Press, 1993.

Hillier, Paul, ed. *The Catch Book*. Oxford: Oxford University Press, 1987.

Hirschfeld, Magnus. *Die Homosexualität des Mannes und des Weibes*. 1914. Berlin: Walter De Gruyter, 1984.

————. *The Homosexuality of Men and Women*. Translated by Michael A. Lombardi-Nash. Amherst: Prometheus Books, 2000.

Hiwatt, Susan. "Cock Rock." In *Twenty-minute Fandangoes and Forever Changes*, edited by Jonathan Eisen, 141–47. New York: Random House, 1971.

Hoberman, J., and Jonathan Rosenbaum. *Midnight Movies*. New York: Harper and Row, 1983.

Hogan, Peter K. *The Complete Guide to the Music of Queen*. London: Omnibus Press, 1994.

Holden, Stephen. "The Village People Liberate Main Street." *Village Voice*, April 23, 1979, 61.

Hollander, Anne. *Fabric of Vision: Dress and Drapery in Painting*. London: National Gallery Company, 2002.

————. *Seeing Through Clothes*. New York: Viking Press, 1978.

Holman, Peter. *Henry Purcell*. Oxford: Oxford University Press, 1994.

Holsinger, Bruce W. *Music, Body and Desire in Medieval Culture: Hildegard of Bingen to Chaucer*. Stanford, CA: Stanford University Press, 2001.

————. "Sodomy and Resurrection: The Homoerotic Subject of the *Divine Comedy*." In *Premodern Sexualities*, edited by Louise Fradenburg and Carla Freccero, 243–74. New York: Routledge, 1996.

Homer. *The Odyssey: Translation and Analysis*. Translated by R. D. Dawe. Sussex: Book Guild, 1993.

Hoppin, Richard. *Medieval Music*. New York: Norton, 1978.

Horan, Jean. "Olivia Presents . . . Meg and Cris." *Off Our Backs*, August–September 1974, 10.

Horkheimer, Max, and Theodor W. Adorno. *Dialectic of Enlightenment*. Translated by John Cumming. New York: Continuum, 1998.

Hoskyns, Barney. *Glam! Bowie, Bolan and the Glitter Rock Revolution*. New York: Pocket Books, 1998.

Hubbs, Nadine. *The Queer Composition of America's Sound: Gay Modernists, American Music, and National Identity*. Berkeley: University of California Press, 2004.

Hughes, Walter. "In the Empire of the Beat: Discipline and Disco." In *Microphone Fiends: Youth Music and Youth Culture*, edited by Andrew Ross and Tricia Rose, 147–57. New York: Routledge, 1994.

Huneker, James. *Mezzotints in Modern Music: Brahms, Tschaïkowsky, Chopin, Richard Strauss, Liszt, and Wagner*. New York: Charles Scribner's Sons, 1899.

Irwin, Eleanor. "The Songs of Orpheus and the New Song of Christ." In *Orpheus: The Metamorphoses of a Myth*, edited by John Warden, 51–62. Toronto: University of Toronto Press, 1982.

Israel, David. "When Fans Wanted to Rock, the Baseball Stopped." *Chicago Tribune*, July 13, 1979, Sec. 5: 1, 3.

Jackson, Timothy L. "Aspects of Sexuality and Structure in the Later Symphonies of Tchaikovsky." *Music Analysis* 14, no. 1 (1995): 3–25.

————. *Tchaikovsky: Symphony No. 6 (Pathétique)*. Cambridge: Cambridge University Press, 1999.

Jaeger, C. Stephen. *The Origins of Courtliness: Civilizing Trends and the Formation of Courtly Ideals, 939–1210*. Philadelphia: University of Pennsylvania Press, 1985.

Jagose, Annamarie. *Queer Theory: An Introduction*. New York: New York University Press, 1996.

Jameson, Fredric. "On the Sexual Production of Western Subjectivity; or, Saint Augustine as a Social Democrat." In *Gaze and Voice as Love Objects*, edited by Renata Salecl and Slavoj Žižek, 154–78. Durham, NC: Duke University Press, 1996.

Jameson, Michael. "The Asexuality of Dionysus." In *Masks of Dionysus,* edited by Thomas H. Carpenter and Christopher A. Faraone, 44–64. Ithaca, NY: Cornell University Press, 1993.

Joe, Radcliffe. "Dearth of Superstars Dims Industry Future: Producer Rather than Artists Is Star." *Billboard,* July 14, 1979, 46, 67, 71.

Johnson, Douglas, Alan Tyson, and Robert Winter. *The Beethoven Sketchbooks: History, Reconstruction, Inventory.* Berkeley: University of California Press, 1985.

Juba to Jive: A Dictionary of African-American Slang. Edited by Clarence Major. New York: Viking Press, 1994.

Juno, Andrea. "Kathleen Hanna, Bikini Kill." In *Angry Women in Rock, Volume One,* 82–103. New York: Juno Books, 1996.

Kay, Sarah. "Desire and Subjectivity." In *The Troubadours: An Introduction,* edited by Simon Gaunt and Sarah Kay, 212–27. Cambridge: Cambridge University Press, 1999.

———. *Subjectivity in Troubadour Poetry.* Cambridge: Cambridge University Press, 1990.

Kearney, Mary Celeste. "The Missing Links: Riot Grrrl–Feminism–Lesbian Culture." In *Sexing the Groove: Popular Music and Gender,* edited by Sheila Whitely, 207–29. New York: Routledge, 1997.

Keiser, Elizabeth B. *Courtly Desire and Medieval Homophobia: The Legitimation of Sexual Pleasure in* Cleanness *and Its Contexts.* New Haven, CT: Yale University Press, 1997.

Keller, Hans. "Britten and Mozart: A Challenge in the Form of Variations on an Unfamiliar Theme." *Music and Letters* 29, no. 1 (1948): 17–30.

Kellner, Douglas. "Herbert Marcuse and the Vicissitudes of Critical Theory." In *Towards a Critical Theory of Society,* ed. Douglas Kellner, 1–33. New York: Routledge, 2001.

Kimball, Gayle. "Female Composition: Interview with Kay Gardner." In *Women's Culture: The Women's Renaissance of the Seventies,* edited by Gayle Kimball, 163–76. Metuchen, NJ: Scarecrow Press, 1981.

Kleinberg, Seymour. "Where Have All the Sissies Gone?" *Christopher Street,* March 1978, 4–12.

Koestenbaum, Wayne. *The Queen's Throat: Opera, Homosexuality, and the Mystery of Desire.* New York: Poseidon Press, 1993.

Kopkind, Andrew. "The Dialectic of Disco: Gay Music Goes Straight." *Village Voice,* February 12, 1979, 1, 11–14, 16, 25.

Kort, Michele. "Sisterhood Is Profitable." *Mother Jones,* July 1983, 39–44.

Kowalzig, Barbara. "Changing Choral Worlds: Song-Dance and Society in Athens and Beyond." In *Music and the Muses: The Culture of "Mousikē" in the Classical Athenian City,* edited by Penelope Murray and Peter Wilson, 39–65. Oxford: Oxford University Press, 2004.

Krafft-Ebing, Richard von. *Psychopathia Sexualis.* 12th ed. Translated by Franklin S. Klaf. 1939. New York: Scarborough Books, 1978.

Kristeva, Julia. *Tales of Love.* Translated by Leon S. Roudiez. New York: Columbia University Press, 1987.

Lardinois, Andre. "Lesbian Sappho and Sappho of Lesbos." In *From Sappho to De Sade: Moments in the History of Sexuality,* edited by Jan Bremmer, 15–35. New York: Routledge, 1989.

———. "Who Sang Sappho's Songs?" In *Reading Sappho: Contemporary Approaches,* edited by Ellen Greene, 150–72. Berkeley: University of California Press, 1996.

Leap, William L. *Word's Out: Gay Men's English.* Minneapolis: University of Minnesota Press, 1996.

Lee, Toni. "Judy: A Fragile Wisp Dies." *The Los Angeles Advocate,* September 1969, 35.

Leinieks, Valdis. *The City of Dionysos: A Study of Euripedes' Bakchai.* Stuttgart: B. G. Teubner, 1996.

Leonard, Marion. "'Rebel Girl, You Are the Queen of My World': Feminism, Subculture, and Grrrl Power." In *Sexing the Groove: Popular Music and Gender,* edited by Sheila Whitely, 230–55. New York: Routledge, 1997.

Leppert, Richard. "Introduction." In *Essays on Music,* by Theodor W. Adorno, 1–82. Berkeley: University of California Press, 2002.

Letche, John. *Fifty Key Contemporary Thinkers: From Structuralism to Postmodernity.* New York: Routledge, 1994.

Levine, Martin P. *Gay Macho: The Life and Death of the Homosexual Clone.* New York: New York University Press, 1998.

Levy, Kenneth. "Latin Chant Outside the Roman Tradition: Milanese or Ambrosian Chant." In *The New Oxford History of Music: The Early Middle Ages to 1300,* edited by Richard Crocker and David Hiley, 69–110. Oxford: Oxford University Press, 1990.

Lewis, Lesley. *Connoisseurs and Secret Agents in Eighteenth-Century Rome.* London: Chatto and Windus, 1961.

Lippman, Edward A. "Hellenic Conceptions of Harmony." *Journal of the American Musicological Society* 16, no. 1 (1963): 1–35.

Livanova, T., M. Pekelis, and T. Popova. *Istoriia Russkoi Muzyki.* 2 vols. Leningrad: Gosudarstvennoe muzykal'noe izdatel'stvo, 1940.

Lockspeiser, Edward. "Tchaïkovsky the Man." In *Tchaikovsky: A Symposium,* edited by Gerald Abraham, 1–23. London: Lindsay Drummond, 1945.

Lont, Cynthia M. "Women's Music: No Longer a Private Party." In *Rockin' the Boat: Mass Music and Mass Movements,* edited by Reebee Garofalo, 241–53. Boston: South End Press, 1992.

Luck, Joyce. *Melissa Etheridge: Our Little Secret.* Toronto: ECW Press, 1997.

Luft, Lorna. *Me and My Shadow: A Family Memoir, Living with the Legacy of Judy Garland.* New York: Pocket Books, 1998.

Lynch, Patsy. "Margie Adam in Washington: A Comment." *Off Our Backs,* May 1977, 16.

MacLeod, Catriona. *Embodying Ambiguity: Androgyny and Aesthetics from Winckelmann to Keller.* Detroit, MI: Wayne State University Press, 1998.

Makowski, John F. "Bisexual Orpheus: Pederasty and Parody in Ovid." *The Classical Journal* 92, no. 1 (1996): 25–38.

Mano, D. Keith. "The Rocky Horror Cult." *National Review,* November 24, 1978, 1493–94, 1496.

Manson, Marilyn. "Columbine: Whose Fault Is It?" *Rolling Stone,* June 10, 1999, 23–24, 77.

Marcuse, Herbert. *Counter Revolution and Revolt.* Boston: Beacon Press, 1972.

———. *One-Dimensional Man: Studies in the Ideology of Advanced Industrial Society,* 2nd ed. Boston: Beacon Press, 1991.

Marino, Giambattista. *La galeria del cav. Distinta in pitture, & sculture.* Venice: Presso G. P. Briogonici, 1664.

Martin, Biddy. *Femininity Played Straight: The Significance of Being Lesbian*. New York: Routledge, 1996.

Martin, Lauren. "Still Voicing Sex." *Sydney Morning Herald*, December 1, 1995, Metro 7.

Mason, Konda. "*Something Moving* Inside of Me." *Off Our Backs*, January 1979, 13–14.

Mast, Gerald. *Can't Help Singin': The American Musical on Stage and Screen*. Woodstock, NY: Overlook Press, 1987.

Mathiesen, Thomas J. *Apollo's Lyre: Greek Music and Music Theory in Antiquity and the Middle Ages*. Lincoln: University of Nebraska Press, 1999.

Mayerson, Philip. *Classical Mythology in Literature, Art, and Music*. Toronto: Xerox Corporation, 1971.

McClain, Ernest G. *The Pythagorean Plato: Prelude to the Song Itself*. Stony Brook, NY: Nicolas Hays, 1978.

McClary, Susan. "Constructions of Subjectivity in Schubert's Music." In *Queering the Pitch: The New Gay and Lesbian Musicology*, edited by Philip Brett, Elizabeth Wood, and Gary C. Thomas, 205–33. New York: Routledge, 1994.

McFarland, Thomas. *Romanticism and the Heritage of Rousseau*. Oxford: Clarendon Press, 1995.

McKinnon, James. "Jubilus." *The New Grove Dictionary of Music and Musicians*, 2nd ed., edited by Stanley Sadie and John Tyrrell, 13:275–76. New York: Grove Dictionaries, 2001.

———. *Music in Early Christian Literature*. Cambridge: Cambridge University Press, 1987.

McLeod, Ken. "Bohemian Rhapsodies: Operatic Influences on Rock Music." *Popular Music* 20, no. 2 (2001): 189–203.

McNamara, Jo Ann. "'Forward to the Past: Hildegard of Bingen and Twelfth-century Monastic Reform." In Hildegard of Bingen, *Explanation of the Rule of Benedict*, trans. Hugh Feiss, 11–41. Toronto: Peregrina, 2000.

Meade, Marion. "The Degradation of Women." In *The Sound of Social Change: Studies in Popular Culture*, edited by R. Serge Denisoff and Richard A. Peterson, 173–77. Chicago: Rand McNally, 1972.

Melville, Herman. *Billy Budd, Sailor (An Inside Narrative)*. In *Billy Budd and Other Stories*, 287–385. New York: Penguin Books, 1986.

Merivale, Patricia. *Pan the Goat-God: His Myth in Modern Times*. Cambridge, MA: Harvard University Press, 1969.

Mews, Constant J. "Hildegard and the Schools." In *Hildegard of Bingen: The Context of Her Thought and Art*, edited by Charles Burnett and Peter Dronke, 89–110. London: Warburg Institute, 1998.

———. "Religious Thinker: 'A Frail Human Being' on Fiery Life." In *Voice of the Living Light: Hildegard of Bingen and Her World*, edited by Barbara Newman, 52–69. Berkeley: University of California Press, 1998.

Michaels, Dick. "The World Is My Ashtray." *The Los Angeles Advocate*, September 1967, 2.

Miles, Sara. "Mommy Melissa." *The Advocate*, June 22, 1999, 44–51.

Miller, Andrew M. *Greek Lyric: An Anthology in Translation*. Indianapolis, IN: Hackett, 1996.

Miller, D. A. *Place For Us: Essay on the Broadway Musical*. Cambridge, MA: Harvard University Press, 1998.

Mills, David, ed. *The Chester Mystery Cycle: A New Edition with Modernised Spelling*. East Lansing, MI: Colleagues Press, 1992.

Mitchell, Donald, ed. *Letters from a Life: The Selected Letters and Diaries of Benjamin Britten, 1923–39*. Berkeley: University of California Press, 1991.

Mitchell, Donald, Philip Reed, and Mervyn Cooke, eds. *Letters from a Life: Selected Letters of Benjamin Britten, 1946–51*. Berkeley: University of California Press, 2004.

Mitchell, John Cameron, and Stephen Trask. *Hedwig and the Angry Inch*. Woodstock, NY: Overlook Press, 2000.

Moira, Fran, and Anne Williams. "Lavender Jane Loves . . ." *Off Our Backs*, April 1974, 6–7.

Moll, Albert. *Perversions of the Sex Instinct*. Translated by Maurice Popkin. 1891. Newark, NJ: Julian Press, 1931.

Morris, Mitchell. "Disco Performance in (the) Masculine Camp: The Case of the Village People." Unpublished manuscript.

———. "Tristan's Wounds: On Homosexual Wagnerians at the Fin de Siècle." In *Queer Episodes in Music and Modern Identity*, edited by Sophie Fuller and Lloyd Whitesell, 271–91. Urbana: University of Illinois Press, 2002.

Morrison, Jeffrey. *Winckelmann and the Notion of Aesthetic Education*. Oxford: Clarendon Press, 1996.

Mücke, Dorothea von. *Virtue and the Veil of Illusion: Generic Innovations and the Pedagogical Project in Eighteenth-Century Literature*. Stanford, CA: Stanford University Press, 1991.

Murray, Penelope. "The Muses and their Arts." In *Music and the Muses: The Culture of "Mousikē" in the Classical Athenian City*, edited by Penelope Murray and Peter Wilson, 365–89. Oxford: Oxford University Press, 2004.

Murray, Penelope, and Peter Wilson. "Introduction: *Mousikē*, not Music." In *Music and the Muses: The Culture of "Mousikē" in the Classical Athenian City*, edited by Penelope Murray and Peter Wilson, 1–8. Oxford: Oxford University Press, 2004.

Musti, Domenico. *I Telchini, le Sirene: Immaginario mediterraneo e letteratura de Omero e Callimaco al romanticismo europeo*. Pisa: Istituti Editoriali e Poligrafici Internazionali, 1999.

Musto, Michael. "The Immaculate Connection." In *Out in Culture: Gay, Lesbian, and Queer Essays on Popular Culture*, edited by Corey K. Creekmur and Alexander Doty, 427–36. Durham, NC: Duke University Press, 1995.

Myerowitz, Molly. *Ovid's Games of Love*. Detroit, MI: Wayne State University, 1985.

Nagy, Gregory. "The Name of Apollo: Etymology and Essence." In *Apollo: Origins and Influences*, edited by Jon Solomon, 3–7. Tucson: University of Arizona Press, 1994.

Naughton, Aoife. "Recollecting *Bildung* Before and After the *Bildungsroman*." Ph.D. diss., Cornell University, 2002.

Near, Holly, and Derk Richardson. *Fire in the Rain . . . Singer in the Storm*. New York: William Morrow, 1990.

Nehamas, Alexander. *The Art of Living: Socratic Reflections from Plato to Foucault*. Berkeley: University of California Press, 1998.

Newman, Barbara. *Saint Hildegard of Bingen, Symphonia: A Critical Edition of the Symphonia armonie celestium revelationum*. Ithaca, NY: Cornell University Press, 1988.

———. "'Sibyl of the Rhine': Hildegard's Life and Times." In *Voice of the Living Light:*

Hildegard of Bingen and Her World, edited by Barbara Newman, 1–29. Berkeley: University of California Press, 1998.

———. *Sister of Wisdom: Saint Hildegard's Theology of the Feminine.* Berkeley: University of California Press, 1989.

Newmarch, Rosa. "Tchaikovsky, Peter Ilich." In *Grove's Dictionary of Music and Musicians,* 3rd ed., edited by H. C. Colles, 278–94. New York: Macmillan, 1927.

Newton, Esther. *Cherry Grove, Fire Island: Sixty Years in America's First Gay and Lesbian Town.* Boston: Beacon Press, 1993.

———. *Mother Camp: Female Impersonators in America.* Chicago: University of Chicago Press, 1972.

Nickson, Chris. *Melissa Etheridge: The Only One, An Unauthorized Biography.* New York: St. Martin's Griffin, 1997.

Nietzsche, Friedrich. *On the Genealogy of Morals and Ecce Homo.* Translated by Walter Kaufmann and R. J. Hollingdale. New York: Vintage Books, 1969.

Norton, Richard. *Mother Clap's Molly House: The Gay Subculture in England 1700–1830.* London: GMP Publishers, 1992.

O'Dea, Michael. *Jean-Jacques Rousseau: Music, Illusion, and Desire.* New York: St. Martin's Press, 1995.

Olivia Records Collective. "The Muses of Olivia: Our Own Economy, Our Own Song." Interviewed by Margie Crow et al. *Off Our Backs,* August–September 1974, 2–3.

Orderic Vitalis. *The Ecclesiastical History.* Translated by Majorie Chibnall. 6 vols. Oxford: Oxford University Press, 1969–80.

Otto, Walter F. *Dionysus: Myth and Cult.* Translated by Robert B. Palmer. Reprint, Dallas: Spring Publications, 1981.

Ovid. *The Erotic Poems.* Translated by Peter Green. New York: Viking Press, 1986.

———. *The Metamorphoses.* Translated by Michael Simpson. Amherst: University of Massachusetts, 2001.

———. *The Metamorphoses: Books 6–10.* Edited by William S. Anderson. Norman, OK: University of Oklahoma Press, 1972.

Page, Denys. *Sappho and Alcaeus: An Introduction to the Study of Ancient Lesbian Poetry.* 1955. Reprint, Oxford: Clarendon Press, 1975.

Partridge, Eric. *Origins: A Short Etymological Dictionary of Modern English.* 4th ed. New York: Macmillan, 1966.

Peck, Abe. "The Village People." *Rolling Stone,* April 19, 1979, 11–14.

Pederson, Sanna. "On the Task of the Music Historian: The Myth of the Symphony after Beethoven." *Repercussions* 2, no. 2 (1993): 5–30.

Pedigo, Arlene. "Under My Thumb." *Off Our Backs,* March 1972, 26.

Penchansky, Alan. "Chicago Anti-Disco Deejay Signs Ovation Record Pact." *Billboard,* August 11, 1979, 33.

Pepe, Barbara. "Women's Music." *Christopher Street,* May 1977, 41–45.

Pequigney, Joseph. "Sodomy in Dante's *Inferno* and *Purgatorio.*" *Representations* 36 (1991): 22–42.

Peraino, Judith A. "Courtly Obsessions: Music and Masculine Identity in Gottfried von Strassburg's *Tristan.*" *Repercussions* 4, no. 2 (1995): 59–85.

———. "Listening to the Sirens: Music as Queer Ethical Practice." *GLQ: A Journal of Lesbian and Gay Studies* 9, no. 4 (2003): 433–70.

————. " 'Rip Her to Shreds': Women's Music According to a Butch-Femme Aesthetic." *Repercussions* 1, no. 1 (1992): 19–47.

Perkovich, Mike. *Nature Boys: Camp Discourse in American Literature from Whitman to Wharton.* New York: Peter Lang, 2003.

Petersen, Karen E. "An Investigation into Women-Identified Music in the United States." In *Women and Music in Cross-Cultural Perspective,* edited by Ellen Koskoff, 203–12. New York: Greenwood Press, 1987.

Pettersson, Michael. *Cults of Apollo at Sparta: The Hyakinthia, the Gymnopaidiai and the Karneia.* Stockholm: Svenska Institutet i Athen, 1992.

Pfau, Marianne Richert. "Mode and Melody Type in Hildegard von Bingen's *Symphonia.*" *Sonus* 11, no. 1 (1990): 53–71.

Plato. "Laws." Translated by Trevor J. Saunders. In *Complete Works,* edited by John M. Cooper, 1318–1616. Indianapolis, IN: Hackett, 1997.

————. "Phaedo." Translated by G. M. A. Grube. In *Complete Works,* edited by John M. Cooper, 49–100. Indianapolis, IN: Hackett, 1997.

————. *The Republic.* Edited by James Adam. 2 vols. Cambridge: Cambridge University Press, 1902.

————. "Republic." Translated by G. M. A. Grube, rev. C. D. C. Reeve. In *Complete Works,* edited by John M. Cooper, 971–1223. Indianapolis, IN: Hackett, 1997.

————. "Symposium." Translated by Alexander Nehamas and Paul Woodruff. In *Complete Works,* edited by John M. Cooper, 457–505. Indianapolis, IN: Hackett, 1997.

————. "Timaeus." Translated by Donald J. Zeyl. In *Complete Works,* edited by John M. Cooper, 1224–91. Indianapolis, IN: Hackett, 1997.

Pollard, John. *Seer, Shrines, and Sirens: The Greek Religious Revolution in the Sixth Century B.C.* London: George Allen & Unwin, 1965.

Pollock, Mary S. "Feminist Aesthetics in Jazz: An Interview with Susanne Vincenza of Alive!" *Frontiers: A Journal of Women's Studies* 8, no. 1 (1984): 60–63.

————. "The Politics of Women's Music: A Conversation with Linda Tillery and Mary Watkins." *Frontiers: A Journal of Women's Studies* 10, no. 1 (1988): 14–19.

————. "Recovery and Integrity: The Music of Meg Christian." *Frontiers: A Journal of Women's Studies* 9, no. 2 (1987): 29–34.

Poppe, Terri, and Janis Kelly. "Moving Money if Not Mountains." *Off Our Backs,* December 1977, 16.

Porter, James. "Lament." In *The New Grove Dictionary of Music and Musicians,* edited by Stanley Sadie and John Tyrrell, 14:181–88. New York: Grove Dictionaries, 2001.

Poznansky, Alexander. "Tchaikovsky: A Life Reconsidered." In *Tchaikovsky and His World,* edited by Leslie Kearney, 3–54. Princeton, NJ: Princeton University Press, 1998.

————. *Tchaikovsky: The Quest for the Inner Man.* New York: Schirmer Books, 1991.

————. *Tchaikovsky Through Others' Eyes.* Translated by Ralph C. Burr, Jr., and Robert Bird. Bloomington: Indiana University Press, 1999.

————. *Tchaikovsky's Last Days: A Documentary Study.* Oxford: Clarendon Press, 1996.

————. "Tchaikovsky's Suicide: Myth and Reality." *19th-Century Music* 11 (1988): 199–220.

————. "Unknown Tchaikovsky: A Reconstruction of Previously Censored Letters to His Brothers (1875–1879)." In *Tchaikovsky and His World,* edited by Leslie Kearney, 55–96. Princeton, NJ: Princeton University Press, 1998.

Press, Alan R., ed. and trans. *Anthology of Troubadour Lyric Poetry.* Edinburgh: Edinburgh University Press, 1971.

Price, Douglas. "Sylvester." *The Advocate,* October 19, 1977, 15–17.

Price, Simon. *Religions of the Ancient Greeks.* Cambridge: Cambridge University Press, 1999.

Prins, Yopie. *Victorian Sappho.* Princeton, NJ: Princeton University Press, 1999.

Prosser, Jay. *Second Skin: The Body Narratives of Transsexuality.* New York: Columbia University Press, 1998.

Pucci, Pietro. *Hesiod and the Language of Poetry.* Baltimore, MD: Johns Hopkins University Press, 1977.

———. *Odysseus Polutropos: Intertextual Readings in the* Odyssey *and the* Iliad. Ithaca, NY: Cornell University Press, 1987.

———. "The Song of the Sirens." In *Reading the* Odyssey: *Selected Interpretive Essays,* edited by Seth L. Schein, 191–99. Princeton, NJ: Princeton University Press, 1996.

———. *The Song of the Sirens: Essays on Homer.* Lanham, MD: Rowman and Littlefield, 1998.

Quasten, Johannes. *Music and Worship in Pagan and Christian Antiquity.* Translated by Boniface Ramsey, O.P. Washington, D.C.: National Association of Pastoral Musicians, 1983.

Rachewiltz, Siegfried de. *De Sirenibus: An Inquiry into Sirens from Homer to Shakespeare.* New York: Garland, 1987.

Radical Harmonies. Directed by Dee Mosbacher. Woman Vision, 2002.

Radicalesbians. "The Woman Identified Woman." In *Radical Feminism,* edited by Anne Koedt, Ellen Levine, and Anita Rapone, 240–45. New York: Quadrangle Books, 1973.

Raphael, Jody. "Under My Thumb." *Off Our Backs,* March 1972, 26.

Reagon, Bernice Johnson, and Sweet Honey in the Rock. *We Who Believe in Freedom: Sweet Honey in the Rock . . . Still on the Journey.* New York: Anchor Books, 1993.

Redfield, Marc. *Phantom Formations: Aesthetic Ideology and the Bildungsroman.* Ithaca, NY: Cornell University Press, 1996.

Reid, Jane Davidson. *The Oxford Guide to Classical Mythology in the Arts, 1300–1900s.* 2 vols. New York: Oxford University Press, 1993.

Reinhardt, Karl. "The Adventures in the *Odyssey.*" In *Reading the* Odyssey: *Selected Interpretive Essays,* edited by Seth L. Schein, 63–132. Princeton, NJ: Princeton University Press, 1996.

Ressner, Jeffrey. "Freddie Mercury: 1946–1991." *Rolling Stone,* January 9, 1992, 13–17.

Reynolds, Margaret. *The Sappho Companion.* London: Chatto and Windus, 2000.

Rhodes, James M. *Eros, Wisdom, and Silence: Plato's Erotic Dialogues.* Columbia: University of Missouri Press, 2003.

Rich, Adrienne. "Compulsory Heterosexuality and Lesbian Existence." In *The Lesbian and Gay Studies Reader,* edited by Henry Abelove, Michèle Aina Barale, and David M. Halperin, 227–54. New York: Routledge, 1993.

Richter, Simon. "Winckelmann's Progeny: Homosocial Networking in the Eighteenth Century." In *Outing Goethe and His Age,* edited by Alice A. Kuzniar, 33–46. Stanford, CA: Stanford University Press, 1996.

Rissman, Leah. *Love as War: Homeric Allusion in the Poetry of Sappho.* Königstein: Anton Hain Meisenheim, 1983.

Robinson, Lucy. "Viol, § 5: Italy from c1580." In *The New Grove Dictionary of Music and Musicians*, 2nd ed., edited by Stanley Sadie and John Tyrrell, 25:675. London: Grove Dictionaries, 2001.

Rodgers, Bruce. *The Queens' Vernacular: A Gay Lexicon*. San Francisco: Straight Arrow Books, 1972.

Rogers, Mary F. *Barbie Culture*. London: Sage, 1999.

Rosand, Ellen. *Opera in Seventeenth-Century Venice: The Creation of a Genre*. Berkeley: University of California Press, 1993.

Rosasco, Betsy. "Albrecht Dürer's 'Death of Orpheus': Its Critical Fortunes and a New Interpretation of its Meaning." *Idea Jahrbuch der Hamburger Kunsthalle* 3 (1984): 19–41.

Rose, Frank. "Discophobia: Rock & Roll Fights Back." *Village Voice*, November 12, 1979, 36–37.

Rosenberg, Samuel N., Margaret Switten, and Gérard Le Vot, eds. *Songs of the Troubadours and Trouvères*. New York: Garland, 1998.

Rousseau, G. S. "The Pursuit of Homosexuality in the Eighteenth Century: 'Utterly Confused Category' and/or Rich Repository?" *Eighteenth-Century Life* 9, no. 3 (1985): 132–68.

Rousseau, Jean-Jacques. *The Confessions and Correspondence, Including the Letters to Malesherbes*. Translated by Christopher Kelly, edited by Christopher Kelly, Roger D. Masters, and Peter G. Stillmann. Vol. 5, *The Collected Writings of Rousseau*. Hanover, NH: University Press of New England, 1995.

Rubin, Gayle S. "Thinking Sex: Notes for a Radical Theory of the Politics of Sexuality." In *The Lesbian and Gay Studies Reader*, edited by Henry Abelove, Michèle Aina Barale, and David M. Halperin, 3–44. New York: Routledge, 1993.

———. "The Traffic in Women: Notes on the 'Political Economy' of Sex." In *Toward an Anthropology of Women*, edited by Rayna R. Reiter, 157–210. New York: Monthly Review Press, 1975.

Rudd, Niall. "Daedalus and Icarus (ii) From the Renaissance to the Present Day." In *Ovid Renewed: Ovidian Influences on Literature and Art from the Middle Ages to the Twentieth Century*, edited by Charles Martindale, 37–53. Cambridge: Cambridge University Press, 1988.

Rupprecht, Philip. *Britten's Musical Language*. Cambridge: Cambridge University Press, 2001.

Saurma-Jeltsch, Lieselotte E. *Die Miniaturen im "Liber Scivias" der Hildegard von Bingen*. Wiesbaden: Dr. Ludwig Reichert Verlag, 1998.

Schauer, John. "Sylvester: A Sterling Talent Turns Gold into Platinum." *The Advocate*, January 25, 1979, 32–33.

Schein, Seth L. "Female Representations and Interpreting the *Odyssey*." In *The Distaff Side: Representing the Female in Homer's Odyssey*, edited by Beth Cohen, 17–27. Oxford: Oxford University Press, 1995.

———. "Introduction." In *Reading the* Odyssey: *Selected Interpretive Essays*, edited by Seth L. Schein, 3–31. Princeton, NJ: Princeton University Press, 1996.

Schibanoff, Susan. "Hildegard of Bingen and Richardis of Stade: The Discourse of Desire." In *Same Sex Love and Desire Among Women in the Middle Ages*, edited by Francesca Candadé Sautman and Pamela Sheingorn, 49–83. New York: Palgrave, 2001.

———. "Sodomy's Mark: Allan of Lille, Jean de Meun, and the Medieval Theory of Authorship." In *Queering the Middle Ages,* edited by Glenn Burger and Steven F. Kruger. Minneapolis: University of Minnesota Press, 2001.

Schmitz, Marlene. "Chicago Women's Concert II." *Off Our Backs,* November 1974, 20.

———. "Christian and Earth Music." *Off Our Backs,* January 1975, 19.

———. "Product of Persistence." *Off Our Backs,* May–June 1975, 17.

Schueller, Herbert M. *The Idea of Music: An Introduction to Musical Aesthetics in Antiquity and the Middle Ages.* Kalamazoo, MI: Medieval Institute Publications, 1988.

Schwing, Lee, and Helaine Harris. "Building Feminist Institutions." *The Furies,* May–June 1973, 2–3.

Scovill, Ruth. "Women's Music." In *Women's Culture: Renaissance of the Seventies,* edited by Gayle Kimball, 148–62. Metuchen, NJ: Scarecrow Press, 1981.

"Séance at the Palace." *Time,* August 18, 1967, 40.

Sedgwick, Eve Kosofsky. *Between Men: English Literature and Male Homosocial Desire.* New York: Columbia University Press, 1985.

———. *Epistemology of the Closet.* Berkeley: University of California Press, 1990.

———. *Tendencies.* Durham, NC: Duke University Press, 1993.

Segal, Charles. "*Kleos* and its Ironies." In *Reading the* Odyssey: *Selected Interpretive Essays,* edited by Seth L. Schein, 203–21. Princeton, NJ: Princeton University Press, 1996.

Segel, Michael. " 'Rocky Horror': The Case of the Rampant Audience." *Rolling Stone,* April 5, 1979, 20.

Sergent, Bernard. *Homosexuality in Greek Myth.* Translated by Arthur Goldhammer. Boston: Beacon Press, 1986.

Shapiro, Linda. "Joy of Cooking." *Off Our Backs,* October 1971, 33.

Shelmerdine, Susan C. *The Homeric Hymns.* Translated by Susan C. Shelmerdine. Newburyport, MA: Focus, 1995.

Sherburne, Edward. *Poems and Translations: Amorous, Lusory, Morall, Divine.* London: W. Hunt for Thomas Dring, 1651.

Shewey, Don. "Madonna: The Saint, The Slut, The Sensation." *The Advocate,* May 7, 1991, 42–51.

Siegel, Mark. "*The Rocky Horror Picture Show:* More Than a Lip Service." *Science-Fiction Studies* 7 (1980): 305–12.

Sjostrom, Joseph, and Lynn Emmerman. " 'These Weren't Real Baseball Fans'— Veeck." *Chicago Tribune,* July 13, 1979, Sec. 5: 3.

Slonimsky, Nicolas. *Lexicon of Musical Invective: Critical Assaults on Composers since Beethoven's Time.* Seattle: University of Washington Press, 1987.

Smith, Bruce R. *Homosexual Desire in Shakespeare's England: A Cultural Poetics.* Chicago: University of Chicago Press, 1991.

Smith, Nigel. "Perceptions of Homosexuality in Tchaikovsky Criticism, 1890s–1950s." *Context* 4 (Summer 1992): 3–9.

Smith, Richard. *Seduced and Abandoned: Essays on Gay Men and Popular Music.* London: Cassell, 1995.

Snyder, Jane McIntosh. *Lesbian Desire in the Lyrics of Sappho.* New York: Columbia University Press, 1997.

Solomon, Jon. "Introduction." In *Apollo: Origins and Influences,* edited by Jon Solomon, ix–xii. Tucson: University of Arizona Press, 1994.

Sontag, Susan. "Notes on 'Camp.'" In *Against Interpretation,* 275–92. New York: Dell, 1966.

Sprecher, Lorrie. *Sister Safety Pin.* Ithaca, NY: Firebrand Books, 1994.

Squires, Paul C. "Peter Ilich Tschaikowsky: A Psychological Sketch." *The Psychoanalytic Review* 28, no. 4 (1941): 445–65.

Steele, Bruce C. "John Cameron Mitchell." *The Advocate,* August 14, 2001, 18–26.

———. "Melissa and Tammy: A Love Story." *The Advocate,* January 20, 2004, 51–64.

Stehle, Eva. *Performance and Gender in Ancient Greece.* Princeton, NJ: Princeton University Press, 1997.

———. "Romantic Sensuality, Poetic Sense: A Response to Hallett on Sappho." In *Reading Sappho: Contemporary Approaches,* edited by Ellen Greene, 143–49. Berkeley: University of California Press, 1996.

Stein, Arlene. "Androgyny Goes Pop, But Is It Lesbian Music?" *Out/Look,* Spring 1991, 26–33.

Stevens, John. "The Musical Individuality of Hildegard's Songs: A Liturgical Shadowland." In *Hildegard of Bingen: The Context of Her Thought and Art,* edited by Charles Burnet and Peter Dronke, 163–88. London: Warburg Institute, 1998.

Stevens, Wendy. "Meg and Teresa: Drop of Rain or Hurricane?" *Off Our Backs,* December 1977, 16.

Stock, Brian. *Augustine the Reader: Meditation, Self-Knowledge, and the Ethics of Interpretation.* Cambridge, MA: Harvard University Press, 1996.

Strunk, Oliver. *Source Readings in Music History.* New York: W. W. Norton and Company, 1950.

Studer, Wayne. *Rock on the Wild Side: Gay Male Images in Popular Music of the Rock Era.* San Francisco: Leyland Publications, 1994.

Studlar, Gaylyn. "Midnight S/Excess: Cult Configurations of 'Femininity' and the Perverse." In *The Cult Film Experience: Beyond All Reason,* edited by J. P. Telotte, 138–55. Austin: University of Texas Press, 1991.

Stuessy, Joe, and Scott Lipscomb. *Rock and Roll: Its History and Stylistic Development,* 3rd ed. Upper Saddle River, NJ: Prentice Hall, 1999.

Stukin, Stacy. "Back on Track." *The Advocate,* September 14, 1999, 60.

Sullivan, Andrew. *Virtually Normal: An Argument about Homosexuality.* New York: Alfred A. Knopf, 1995.

Sullivan, Randall. "A Boy's Life: Kip Kinkel and the Springfield, Oregon Shootings, Part 1." *Rolling Stone,* September 17, 1998, 76–85, 106.

Sweet, Denis M. "The Personal, the Political, and the Aesthetic: Johann Joachim Winckelmann's German Enlightenment Life." In *The Pursuit of Sodomy: Male Homosexuality in Renaissance and Enlightenment Europe,* edited by Kent Gerard and Gert Hekma, 147–62. New York: Harrington Park Press, 1989.

Swinburne, Algernon Charles. "Simeon Solomon: Notes on His 'Vision of Love' and Other Studies." In *A Pilgrimage of Pleasure: Essays and Studies.* 1871. Boston: Gorham Press, 1913.

Szatmary, David P. *Rockin' in Time: A Social History of Rock-and-Roll,* 4th ed. Upper Saddle River, NJ: Prentice Hall, 2000.

Szwed, John F. *Space is the Place: The Lives and Times of Sun Ra.* New York: Pantheon Books, 1997.

Taruskin, Richard. *Defining Russia Musically*. Princeton, NJ: Princeton University Press, 1997.

———. "Pathetic Symphonist: Chaikovsky, Russia, Sexuality and the Study of Music." *New Republic,* February 6, 1995, 26–40.

Tchaikovsky, Modeste. *The Life and Letters of Peter Illich Tchaikovsky*. Edited and translated by Rosa Newmarch. New York: Dodd, Mead and Company, 1905.

Thomas, Gary C. "'Was George Frideric Handel Gay?': On Closet Questions and Cultural Politics." In *Queering the Pitch: The New Gay and Lesbian Musicology,* edited by Philip Brett, Elizabeth Wood, and Gary C. Thomas, 155–201. New York: Routledge, 1994.

Tilchen, Maida. "Lesbians and Women's Music." In *Women-Identified Women,* edited by Trudy Darty and Sandee Potter, 287–303. Palo Alto, CA: Mayfield, 1984.

Tolbert, Elizabeth. "The Voice of the Lament: Female Vocality and the Performative Efficacy in the Finnish-Karelian *Itkuvirsi*." In *Embodied Voices: Representing Female Vocality in Western Culture,* edited by Leslie C. Dunn and Nancy A. Jones, 179–94. Cambridge: Cambridge University Press, 1994.

Tormé, Mel. *The Other Side of the Rainbow: With Judy Garland on the Dawn Patrol*. New York: William Morrow and Company, 1970.

Toscan, Jean. *Le carnaval du langage: Le lexique érotique des poètes de l'équivoque de Burchiello à Marino (XVe–XVIIe Siècles)*. 4 vols. Lille: Presses Universitaires de Lille, 1981.

Trebay, Guy. "How Macho Is That Doggie in the Disco?" *Village Voice,* March 27, 1978, 47–48.

Treitler, Leo. "Homer and Gregory: The Transmission of Epic Poetry and Plainchant." *Musical Quarterly* 40, no. 3 (1974): 333–72.

Trumbach, Randolph. "The Birth of the Queen: Sodomy and the Emergence of Gender Equality in Modern Culture 1660–1750." In *Hidden From History: Reclaiming the Gay and Lesbian Past,* edited by Martin Bauml Dauberman, Martha Vicinius, and George Chauncey, Jr., 129–40. New York: New American Library, 1989.

Turner, James H. *The Myth of Icarus in Spanish Renaissance Poetry*. London: Tamesis Books, 1976.

Ulrichs, Karl Heinrich. *The Riddle of "Man-Manly" Love: The Pioneering Work on Male Homosexuality*. Translated by Michael A. Lombardi-Nash. 2 vols. Buffalo, NY: Prometheus Books, 1994.

United States Senate Committee on Governmental Affairs. *Music Violence: How Does It Affect Our Children*. 105th Congress, 1st session, November 6, 1997.

Van Vleck, Amelia E. *Memory and Re-Creation in Troubadour Lyric*. Berkeley: University of California Press, 1991.

Varga, George. "Melissa Explains It All." *San Diego Union Tribune,* December 19, 1996, "Night and Day," 4–5.

Veyne, Paul. "The Final Foucault and His Ethics," translated by Catherine Porter and Arnold I. Davidson. *Critical Inquiry* 20 (Autumn 1993): 1–9.

Vining, Donald. *A Gay Diary*. 5 vols. New York: Pepys Press, 1979–93.

Wagner, Edward, Jr. "Discophobia Out of Control." *Chicago Tribune,* July 13, 1979, Sec. 5: 2.

Wallach, Michael, and Carol Greenberg. "Personality Functions of Symbolic Sexual Arousal to Music." *Psychological Monographs: General and Applied* 74 (1960): 1–18.

Walser, Robert. *Running with the Devil: Power, Gender, and Madness in Heavy Metal Music.* Hanover, NH: Wesleyan University Press, 1993.

Warner, Michael. *The Trouble with Normal: Sex, Politics, and the Ethics of Queer Life.* Cambridge, MA: Harvard University Press, 2000.

Wedner, Sabine. *Tradition und Wandel im allegorischen Verständnis des Sirenenmythos: Ein Beitrag zur Rezeptionsgeschichte Homers.* Frankfurt am Main: Peter Lang, 1994.

Weisbard, Eric. "Lost in Translation." *Village Voice,* October 13–19, 1999, www.villagevoice.com/issues/9941/sotc.php (accessed February 24, 2002).

Weitz, Rose. "From Accommodation to Rebellion: The Politicization of Lesbianism." In *Women-Identified Women,* edited by Trudy Darty and Sandee Potter, 233–48. Palo Alto, CA: Mayfield, 1984.

Wheeler, Graham. "Sing, Muse . . . : The Introit From Homer to Apollonius." *Classical Quarterly* 52, no. 1 (2002): 33–49.

White, Eric Walter. *Benjamin Britten: His Life and Operas.* Berkeley: University of California Press, 1983.

White, Patricia. *Uninvited: Classical Hollywood Cinema and Lesbian Representability.* Bloomington: Indiana University Press, 1999.

Whitesell, Lloyd. "Britten's Dubious Trysts." *Journal of the American Musicological Association,* 56, no. 3 (2003): 637–94.

———. "Ravel's Way." In *Queer Episodes in Music and Modern Identity,* edited by Lloyd Whitesell and Sophie Fuller, 40–78. Urbana: University of Illinois Press, 2002.

Wieder, Judy. "Melissa Etheridge: The Advocate's Person of the Year." *The Advocate,* January 23, 1998, 1–17, www.advocate.com/html/specials/melissa/698_99_melissa.asp (accessed July 16, 2001).

———. "Melissa: Rock's Great Dyke Hope." *The Advocate,* July 26, 1994, 45–56.

———. "Our Celebrities." *The Advocate,* April 30, 2000, 42–44.

Wild, David. *Melissa Etheridge Just Says Yes,* 1993, www.ping.be/~ping9791/kit12 .html; also www.attirentdelles.org/etheridge/articles_articles_956505651.html (accessed July 16, 2001).

Wilhelm, James J. *Il Migliore Fabbro: The Cult of the Difficult in Daniel, Dante, and Pound.* Orno, ME: National Poetry Foundation, 1982.

Wilkinson, Peter, with Matt Hendrickson. "Columbine, Humiliation, and Revenge: The Story of Reb and VoDka." *Rolling Stone,* June 10, 1999, 49–54, 140–41.

Williams, Brooke L., and Hannah Darby. "God, Mom, and Apple Pie: 'Feminist' Businesses as an Extension of the American Dream." *Off Our Backs,* January–February 1976, 18–20.

Wilson, Lyn Hatherly. *Sappho's Sweetbitter Songs: Configurations of Female and Male in Ancient Greek Lyric.* New York: Routledge, 1996.

Wilson, Peter. "Homeric Strings in Helenistic Athens." In *Music and the Muses: The Culture of "Mousikē" in the Classical Athenian City,* edited by Penelope Murray and Peter Wilson, 269–306. Oxford: Oxford University Press, 2004.

Winckelmann, Johann Joachim. *Monumenti antichi inediti spiegati ed illustrati da Giovani Winckelmann,* 2nd ed. Rome: Torchj di C. Mordacchini, 1821.

Windsor-drollery: being a more exact collection of the newest songs, poems, and catches, now in use, both in city and country, then any yet extant: with additions. London: For J. M., 1672.

Winkler, John J. *The Constraints of Desire: The Anthropology of Sex and Gender in Ancient Greece.* New York: Routledge, 1990.

Wogan-Browne, Jocelyn. *Saints' Lives and Women's Literary Culture c. 1150–1300: Virginity and Its Authorizations.* Oxford: Oxford University Press, 2000.

Wolf, Stacy. *A Problem Like Maria: Gender and Sexuality in the American Musical.* Ann Arbor: University of Michigan Press, 2002.

Wood, Elizabeth. "Sapphonics." In *Queering the Pitch: The New Gay and Lesbian Musicology,* edited by Philip Brett, Elizabeth Wood, and Gary C. Thomas, 26–77. New York: Routledge, 1994.

Wood, Ellen Meiksins, and Neal Wood. *Class Ideology and Ancient Political Theory: Socrates, Plato, and Aristotle in Social Context.* New York: Oxford University Press, 1978.

Wood, Robert E. "Don't Dream It: Performance and *The Rocky Horror Picture Show.*" In *The Cult Film Experience: Beyond All Reason,* edited by J. P. Telotte, 156–66. Austin: University of Texas Press, 1991.

Woodruff, Paul. "Introduction." In *Bacchae by Euripedes,* ix–xlii. Indianapolis, IN: Hackett, 1998.

Woodul, Jennifer. "From Olivia: What's This about Feminist Businesses?" *Off Our Backs,* June 1976, 24–26.

———. "Olivia Records." In *The New Woman's Survival Sourcebook,* edited by Susan Rennie and Kirsten Grimstad, 177–78. New York: Alfred A. Knopf, 1975.

Wright, Robert. "'I'd Sell You Suicide': Pop Music and Moral Panic in the Age of Marilyn Manson." *Popular Music* 19, no. 3 (2001): 365–85.

Zajaczkowski, Henry. *Tchaikovsky's Musical Style.* Ann Arbor, MI: UMI Research Press, 1987.

Zaslaw, Neal. "Der neue Köchel." *Mozart Society of America Newsletter,* January 27, 1997, 4–5.

Zeikowitz, Richard E. *Homoeroticism and Chivalry: Discourses of Male Same-Sex Desire in the Fourteenth Century.* New York: Columbia University Press, 2003.

Ziolkowski, Jan M. *Alan of Lille's Grammar of Sex: The Meaning of Grammar to a Twelfth-Century Intellectual.* Cambridge: Medieval Academy, 1985.

Zoega, Georg. *Li bassirilievi antichi di Roma.* 2 vols. Rome: Pietro Piranesi, 1808.

INDEX

A&M Records, 289n3, 304n117

ABC Records, 289n3

abject being, 132, 139

abjection, 126, 133–35, 137, 192, 284n60; of Tchaikovsky, 85

abject-phallic subject, 133

Abod, Susan, 290n22

active sexuality: in English Restoration tavern songs, 208; *erastēs*, 21–22, 35, 265n111; *gunaikerastria*, 26–27

Adam, Margie, 159, 171–72, 173

Adam/Eve, story of: Augustine and sexuality as punishment in, 39–40, 45; *Billy Budd* and, 95; Melissa Etheridge and, 142; *Hedwig and the Angry Inch* and, 250; hermaphroditism and, 207; Orpheus and, 25; *Rocky Horror Picture Show* as, 235, 238

Adler, Lou, 234

"administration of the self," 44, 93

Adorno, Theodor, 1–2, 5, 155

Advocate (gay magazine; *Los Angeles Advocate*), 145; on Melissa Etheridge, 136, 141; Melissa Etheridge on cover of, 131; on Judy Garland as gay icon, 126, 128; on Madonna, 287–88n118; Sylvester interview in, 184, 187; on Village People, 182–83

aesthetic faculty of homosexuals, 72, 73, 74

Aesthetic movement, 96

aesthetics, 12, 44, 83; androgyny and, 227–28, 302n79; *Bildung* and, 227–28,

301n62; Marcuse and, 155, 163; Tchaikovsky and, 79, 88–89; virgins and, 51

African-American gospel music, 189

African-American slang, 189

African-American women: disco and, 180; gay identification with, 190–91; music groups, 290n33; rock music and, 160

African-Americans: disco backlash and, 177–78; futurism and, 190; Marilyn Manson's purported impact on, 245–46; musical traditions of, 160, 172–73, 189; rock music and, 159–60; signifying traditions of, 299n39

Aguilera, Christina, 288n119

AIDS, 144, 145, 175, 185

Albani, Alessandro, 216–17, 298n24. *See also* Villa Albani

Alcoff, Linda Martín, 6, 255–56n22

Alive! (women's music jazz ensemble), 293n71

Allan of Lille, *De planctu naturae*, 63

Allanbrooke, Wye Jamison, 89

Almanac Singers, 154

Alpert, Jane, 156, 161

Althusser, Louis, 2–3, 7, 112, 185, 254n9

Amadeus (film), 281n112

Amalarius of Metz, 268n136

ambivalence: about Madonna, 144, 145; about music, 7, 11; about normalcy, 122, 143, 150, 283n39

Ambrose, Saint, 39, 40–41

identity: African-American futurism and, 190; bohemian, 230, 232; gender and, 129, 181, 187, 191, 192, 250, 251, 252; glam rock and, 247; icons and, 111; language and, 112; national, 250; Odysseus and, 14, 18; otherness and, 248, 255n20; phallus and, 251; psyche and, 6–7; of Sappho, ethnic, 27–28; sexuality and, 6, 40, 197, 198, 252; social/communal, 3, 124, 153, 176, 187, 194, 197, 255n22; songs of Hildegard of Bingen, 51–53; subjectivity vs., 6; Sylvester and, 186, 192; troubadour song and, 56, 67. *See also* gay identity; identity politics; queer identity
identity politics, 5, 8, 156, 169, 194, 197, 255–56n22
"imagined communities," 185
"Immaculate Connection" (Musto), 144–45
Incarnation, 270n162
incest, 106, 140, 277n60
Indigo Girls, 137, 174–75
individuation, music and: Augustine and, 43; Odysseus and, 18, 19; performance and, 39; Rousseau and, 70; Saint Ursula and, 52–53
insanity, 144
instrumental music, politics of, 171–73, 292n66
interiority, 16–18, 258n26
interpellation: as calling into subjectivity, 2–3, 112; gay discos and, 185; identity and, 255–56n22; ideology and, 254n9; misrecognition and, 7
Interscope Records, 304n117
intersubjectivity, 263n80
inwardness, 40, 69
Islam, as immoral, 273n196
Italy, 228, 232
Ithaca (N.Y.), lesbian community in, 285n66

Jackson, Michael, 140, 145, 193
Jackson, Timothy L., 84, 85–86
Jacobean drama, 298n27
Jagger, Mick, 37, 159–60
James, Henry, *The Turn of the Screw,* 5
James, Sylvester. *See* Sylvester
James I (king of England), 201; *Ane Metaphoricall Invention of a Tragedie Called Phoenix,* 300n55
Jameson, Frederic, 40
jazz, 78, 172, 174, 190, 293nn71,78

Jennens, Charles, 209
Jesus Christ Superstar (film), 233, 241
Jett, Joan, 137
Joe, Radcliffe, 179–80
John of Salisbury, *Metalogicon,* 63
joi (erotic fulfillment), 54, 56, 61, 62, 67, 272n186
Joplin, Janis, 160
Josquin des Pres, *Nymphes des bois,* 279n81
Joy of Cooking, 159
jubilation, 42, 43, 267–68n136

Kalypso *(Odyssey),* 16, 18–19
Keller, Hans, 109
Kelly, Gene, 122, 123, 130
Kempf, Rolf, "Hello Hooray," 168
King, Carole, "Lady," 166
kinship, 55, 140, 152
Kirke *(Odyssey),* 13, 14, 16, 18, 39
Kleinberg, Seymour, 184–85, 187, 189
Knight, Richard Payne, *A Discourse on the Worship of Priapus,* 217
Koestenbaum, Wayne, 284n60
Kopkind, Andrew, 182
Kort, Michele, 293n78
Krafft-Ebing, Richard von, 72, 73
Kristeva, Julia, 53
Kuntz, Richard, 244

LaBelle, Patti, 247, 251
labor movement, 154
Lacan, Jacques, 7, 132, 140, 285n69
lament: "eye music" and, 279n81; in opera and symphonic music, 90–91; in Queen, 302n89; in Slavic traditions, 89–90; in Tchaikovsky's sixth symphony, 84, 86, 88, 91–92; as topos, 89; *The Woman Hater's Lament,* 203
Lang, Fritz, 145
lang, k. d., 131, 175; *Ingenue,* 135
language: Butler and, 112, 129, 132; exoticism and, 148; Foucault and, 4, 111–12, 129, 258–59n28; Lacan and, 254n7; lesbians and, 132; melodrama and, 114–15; music as, 70, 107, 115; music as outside of, 113, 114, 115; in *Purgatorio,* 66; sign language, 172; sodomy and, 66; of Song of Songs, 53; subjectivity and, 3, 7, 112, 114, 140; of troubadours, 54–55, 57, 61, 63–64. *See also* sign systems
Lardinois, André, 262n68

Late Night with David Letterman (TV program), 287n117
Latini, Brunetto, 274n197
Latinos, 148, 177–78
Laurents, Arthur, 121
Lavender Jane, 160–63, 291n35; *Lavender Jane Loves Women,* 161–63, 166; "View from Gay Head," 162–63
Lawes, William, "Dainty Fine Aniseed Water Fine," 206, 207, 208
Led Zeppelin, 292n66
Leno, Jay, 288n126
Leonardo da Vinci, 117, 282n24
lesbian chic, 146, 175
lesbian culture, 161
Lesbian ethnic identity, 27
lesbian feminists, 154, 156, 163, 165, 181, 193, 194
lesbian icons, 131–33; Melissa Etheridge, 139, 142–43, 285n66; Madonna, 146–47, 287n117, 288n119; Barbra Streisand, 282n30, 285n65. *See also* gay icons
Lesbian Lifespace, 161
lesbian phallus, 116–19, 132–33, 135–43, 245; penis and, 132, 140
lesbian subjectivity, 7, 112, 132–33, 142
lesbian women's music: as business, 163–66; as communal space, 154; Melissa Etheridge and, 151; marketing of, 166–70; origins of, 161–63, 290–91n35; political influences on, 194; sexuality and, 175–76; wordless, 172. *See also* Christian, Meg; women's music
lesbianism: butch/femme roles in, 146–47, 148, 156, 174–75, 288n122; capitalism and, 165; coming out and, 197; as diffuse sensuality, 175; Melissa Etheridge and, 133–35, 142–43; feminism and, 156, 170, 194, 288n122; Judy Garland and, 110, 130, 285n65; gender inversion and, 138–39, 150; Hildegard of Bingen and, 271n166; Madonna and, 146–47, 287n117, 287–88n118, 288n119; modern musicals and, 282n30; music and, 7; politicization of, 169–70, 172, 292nn59,60; in pre-Raphaelite art, 117–19, 282n25; queer vs., 5; Sappho and, 26–28, 115, 116, 261–62n65, 262n70; separatist movement in, 155–57, 162–63; sex toys as phallus displacement, 245; as vampires, 116, 139. *See also* homo-

sexuality; identity politics; lesbian women's music; women's music
Lesbos, 26, 116
Letterman, David, 140, 287n117
Levine, Martin P., 180–81
Lewis, Juliette, 136
Lieberman, Joseph, 243–44, 246
linguisticism, 112
Liszt, Franz, *Tasso,* 90
Little Richard, 229
Living Theater, 240
Lockspeiser, Edward, 82, 85
London Spy (magazine), 202
Los Angeles, 234
"Lover I Am, A" (anon.), 202
Luft, Lorna, 283n44
Luscious Jackson, 131
Lynn, Cheryl, "Got to Be Real," 188
lyre, 21–22, 31, 41, 118–19, 265n106

"Macho Man," 180–84
MacLeod, Catriona, 227–28, 302n79
Madonna, 8, 114, 150; as antimelodramatic, 143–44; as celebrity mom, 147, 288n126; compared to Judy Garland, 144, 148–50; as cultural icon, 110–11, 148; "Don't Tell Me," 148–50; Melissa Etheridge on, 143; "Express Yourself," 145; as gay icon, 132, 143–45; gendered role-playing of, 146–47; "Justify My Love," 148, 287n117; as lesbian icon, 146–47, 287n117, 288n119; mainstream success of, 151, 287–88n118; *Music,* 149–50; "Music," 146, 148; musical influences on, 151; queer audience of, 148–50; Britney Spears as protégée of, 146; straight reaction to, 145; subjectivity and, 150; taboo image vs. mainstream music, 143–44; "What It Feels Like for a Girl," 146, 147–48
Madonna: Bawdy & Soul (Faith), 146–47
"Maiden of Late, A" (anon.), 205–6
Malthus, Thomas Robert, 297n5
Malthusian couple, 195–96
Mano, D. Keith, 239
Marcuse, Herbert, 154–55, 157, 165–66, 184
Marilyn Manson, 8, 9, 37; as androgynous, 244; *Antichrist Superstar,* 241–42, 244; anti-mainstream message of, 240–41; "The Beautiful People," 241; *Bildung* and, 241, 245–46; bullying and, 240, 243; emascu-

miracle plays, 101

"mirror stage" (Lacanian theory), 132

miscegenation, 144

misogyny: in early Christianity, 45–46; in English Restoration tavern songs, 199, 201, 202–5; gay macho and, 181, 184–86, 190, 193; in music industry, 160; Orpheus myth and, 24, 25; in rock music, 244, 251; sodomy and, 202–3, 208. *See also* "cock rock"

Mitchell, John Cameron, 246

Mitchell, Joni, 137

Moll, Albert, 71, 72

molly houses, 198, 202

Mondino, Jean-Baptiste, 148

Montaudon, Monk of, 56–57

Monterey Pop (film), 234

Morali, Jacques, 180, 182, 183–84

morality: in ancient myth, 224; in Augustine, 39; patriarchal, 157; in *Rocky Horror Picture Show*, 236; sexuality and, 93–94. *See also* ethics

Morgan, Robin, 156

Moroder, Giorgio, 188

Morris, Mitchell, 75

Morrison, Jim, 158, 240

"Moses of Michelangelo, The" (Freud), 76

Mother Camp (Newton), 187

Motown Records, 289n3

Mountain Moving Day, 157–59, 160, 167

mousikē (activity inspired by Muses), 28, 29

Mozart, Wolfgang Amadeus, 79, 89, 107, 109, 281n112

murder, 144

Murray, Anne, 247

Muses, 28–29, 35, 36, 265n110

music: anxiety/ambivalence about, 7, 11, 39; as confession/disclosure, 70, 76, 78, 79, 80–81, 82, 85; as discipline, 3–4, 8, 11–12, 30, 35, 68, 94, 106; as discursive, 195; enlightenment ideology and, 2; as excessive/hedonistic, 8, 12, 20, 22, 24; in German Romantic thought, 114, 133; hatred of, as sign of character, 202, 298n27; as illegible/ineffable, 7, 76, 77, 85, 113, 114–15, 133; impact on state, 22, 23, 29–30, 31, 34–35, 36, 37, 245–46; individuation and, 18, 19, 39, 43, 52–53, 70; as language, 70, 107, 115; masculinity/emasculation and, 229–30, 243, 245; queer identity and, 5, 7–8, 113, 197, 251–52;

questioning subjectivity/identity and, 3, 5, 12, 13, 18, 39, 43, 252; as resistance, 5, 7, 252; as self-practice, 12, 37, 49, 50, 51; sexual arousal and, 47, 78; sexual desire and, 14, 23, 29, 37; as shield, 25, 38; soul and, 32–33, 37, 38, 43, 48, 49; transgressive sexuality and, 24, 37, 242–43, 250; violence and, 240, 243–44; as weapon, 25. *See also* desire; discipline; Homeric Sirens, song of; musicality; singing

music and queer sexuality, scholarship on, 256n25

music industry: corporatization of, 153, 289n3; feminist businesses and, 174; impact of disco on, 178–79; and women's music, 163–66, 173–76, 291n46, 293n78. *See also names of record companies*

music producers, disco and, 179–80

Music Violence (U.S. Senate hearing), 36–37, 240, 243–46

musical education: "care of the self" and, 44; in Plato, 29–36; in pre-/post-Homeric poetry, 28–29. See also *Bildung*

musical instruments: body as, 267n134; early Christian prohibitions of, 37–38, 41

musical modes, ancient Greek, 33–34

musical performance, 8, 14, 28; of Margie Adam, 171–72; of chant, 40–43, 50; desire and, 11, 29; early Christian prohibitions of, 37–38; in early Christianity, 38, 39; of Melissa Etheridge, 134–35, 286n94; of Judy Garland, 129–30; of Hildegard of Bingen's chants, 47–49; of Marilyn Manson, 242–43; Plato and, 33, 34; professionalization of, 21; recordings vs., 153, 161; of Sappho's songs, 262n68; of 17th-century catches, 199–200, 201, 203, 208; of Sylvester, 198; of Tchaikovsky's *Adagio lamentoso*, 91. *See also* singing

musical techniques, 3–4

musical worship, 44

musicality, 77, 107–9; closet and, 106, 108; homosexuality and, 70–76

"Musicality, Essentialism, and the Closet" (Brett), 7

musicals, Broadway/Hollywood: gender inversion in, 283n34; homosexuality and, 76, 121–22; lesbianism and, 282n30; *Rocky Horror Picture Show* and, 235, 238–39, 303–4n104. *See also* Judy Garland, as gay icon

Text:	10/12 Baskerville
Display:	Baskerville
Compositor:	Binghamton Valley Composition
Indexer:	Kevin Millham
Music Setter:	Rolf Wulfsberg
Printer and Binder:	Thomson-Shore